P9-DVB-862

The Human Side
of Disaster

15940

HV
553
.D753
2010

The Human Side of Disaster

INFORMATION RESOURCES CENTER
ASIS INTERNATIONAL
1625 PRINCE STREET
ALEXANDRIA, VA 22314
TEL. (703) 519-6200

THOMAS E. DRABEK

CRC Press
Taylor & Francis Group
Boca Raton London New York

CRC Press is an imprint of the
Taylor & Francis Group, an **informa** business

Cover design and memorial photograph contributed by Ruth A. Drabek. *"The Spirit of Siouxland" was dedicated June 5, 1994 in memory of the 112 who perished in 1989 when Flight 232 from Denver, Colorado crashed while attempting an emergency landing at the Sioux Gateway Airport. Through heroic rescue efforts, 184 passengers survived. "The image of a man carrying a child became a symbol of our strength, compassion, and unselfish commitment." This memorial is located in Chris Larsen Park in Sioux City, Iowa.*

CRC Press
Taylor & Francis Group
6000 Broken Sound Parkway NW, Suite 300
Boca Raton, FL 33487-2742

© 2010 by Taylor and Francis Group, LLC
CRC Press is an imprint of Taylor & Francis Group, an Informa business

No claim to original U.S. Government works

Printed in the United States of America on acid-free paper
10 9 8 7 6 5 4 3 2 1

International Standard Book Number: 978-1-4398-0864-1 (Hardback)

This book contains information obtained from authentic and highly regarded sources. Reasonable efforts have been made to publish reliable data and information, but the author and publisher cannot assume responsibility for the validity of all materials or the consequences of their use. The authors and publishers have attempted to trace the copyright holders of all material reproduced in this publication and apologize to copyright holders if permission to publish in this form has not been obtained. If any copyright material has not been acknowledged please write and let us know so we may rectify in any future reprint.

Except as permitted under U.S. Copyright Law, no part of this book may be reprinted, reproduced, transmitted, or utilized in any form by any electronic, mechanical, or other means, now known or hereafter invented, including photocopying, microfilming, and recording, or in any information storage or retrieval system, without written permission from the publishers.

For permission to photocopy or use material electronically from this work, please access www.copyright. com (http://www.copyright.com/) or contact the Copyright Clearance Center, Inc. (CCC), 222 Rosewood Drive, Danvers, MA 01923, 978-750-8400. CCC is a not-for-profit organization that provides licenses and registration for a variety of users. For organizations that have been granted a photocopy license by the CCC, a separate system of payment has been arranged.

Trademark Notice: Product or corporate names may be trademarks or registered trademarks, and are used only for identification and explanation without intent to infringe.

Library of Congress Cataloging-in-Publication Data

Drabek, Thomas E., 1940-
 The human side of disaster / Thomas E. Drabek.
   p. cm.
 Includes bibliographical references and index.
 ISBN 978-1-4398-0864-1 (hardcover : alk. paper)
 1. Emergency management. 2. Disasters--Psychological aspects. I. Title.

HV551.2.D713 2010
363.34'8--dc22   2009021760

Visit the Taylor & Francis Web site at
http://www.taylorandfrancis.com

and the CRC Press Web site at
http://www.crcpress.com

To
the helpers—
employed and volunteer

CONTENTS

FOREWORD

The United States is a big, sprawling, and highly developed country. It has a varied geography with mountainous regions, plains, deserts, an extensive river system, and one of the most impressive coastlines in the world. It also has one of the largest and most ethnically and racially diverse populations. With its vast wealth, the United States has abundant technological resources and has created for its citizens advanced infrastructure systems and critical facilities, including hospitals, schools, businesses, and factories. These characteristics contribute to both the nation's vulnerability and its resilience to various types of disasters, including those resulting from natural, technological, and human agents.

Developing countries are not the only ones that face hazards and disasters. In spite of the wealth in the United States—similar to such countries as Japan and China—hazardous conditions there make it one of the countries in the world most at risk to disasters. We are reminded of this by the earthquakes that have struck California, the floods that too frequently occur throughout the nation, and the hurricanes that have recently impacted the Gulf Coast region, especially Hurricane Katrina and Hurricane Rita in 2005. But hazardous conditions alone do not create disasters. The actions people take and the decisions they make are all very important, too. For example, many families make the decision to locate their households where they will have an ocean view, but this may come with the risk of hurricane winds and storm surges, as happened in the case of the recent Gulf Coast disasters. Also, the decisions citizens and authorities make about emergency preparedness have an impact on the level of a community's vulnerability to disaster, whether the potential agent is a "natural" one, such as an earthquake, or comes in a human form, such as was the case with the September 11, 2001, terrorist attacks on New York City, Washington, D.C., and near Shanksville, Pennsylvania.

Such social and behavioral issues are part of the realm of social science disaster research, which had its beginnings as a field of study in the United States during the early twentieth century and continues to have a strong foothold in the country with each new generation of scholars. Dr. Thomas E. Drabek, the author of *The Human Side of Disaster*, has been a leading figure in the field of disaster research for well over forty years, contributing much to our understanding of how individuals, groups, organizations, and communities prepare for, respond to, and recover from disasters of all types. His distinguished career builds on the work of such pioneering sociologists as the late Charles Fritz of the National Academy of Sciences and E. L. Quarantelli and Russell Dynes, cofounders of the Disaster Research Center, as well as other leading social scientists in the disaster research field. Drabek is perhaps best known for his innovative field studies and surveys, particularly those focusing on the challenges to local emergency managers and decision makers. His research has enabled him to make major theoretical contributions to the study of the human aspects of disasters as well as to provide a knowledge base for advancing the emergency management profession and furthering more disaster resilient communities in the United States.

I am particularly honored to write this Foreword because I have known Drabek and his wife and collaborator, Ruth Ann Drabek, for more than forty years. We both were among the first graduate students selected to be a part of the staff of the Disaster Research Center (DRC) when it was established at The Ohio State University in 1963. Along with other staff members, I worked closely with Drabek on a major laboratory simulation study he designed and coordinated involving the Columbus, Ohio, Police Department. I also had the privilege of working with him on the field study he led while at the DRC on the Indianapolis Coliseum disaster, a study he refers to in this book and that was the first of many that he would conduct throughout his career. Indeed, our close ties have remained throughout our careers, including during the extended period when I served as program officer and then head of the hazard mitigation section at the National Science Foundation, where Drabek received much of his external research support for the numerous studies he conducted during his tenure at the University of Denver.

The Human Side of Disaster is a unique and much needed book. It grows out of Drabek's lifelong commitment not only to conducting basic and applied research but also to passing on vital knowledge to college students and those who are on the front lines of emergency management activities and decision making. It makes perfect sense that he would write such a book given his years teaching disaster courses at the college level and working with the Federal Emergency Management Agency's Higher Education Project to develop curricula for emergency management–related degree programs in colleges and universities throughout the country. This is also consistent with his frequent inclusion of emergency managers and policy makers on the advisory committees of his ongoing research projects so that the results would reflect their needs and interests as well as those of the scientific community.

While observations made in *The Human Side of Disaster* are well documented, the book is not written with social science disaster scholars particularly in mind. Rather, the primary audience is the thousands of college students and emergency management personnel—both paid and volunteer—who require an overview of the field that is unencumbered by overly technical language and lengthy theoretical discussions. What readers will find is a sound and highly readable discussion of insights and principles on the social and behavioral aspects of disasters that Drabek has learned from his own extensive research and from his colleagues in the field, as well as a discussion of some of the common myths that can interfere with effective decision making and action in preparing for and responding to disasters. Although the research base and examples discussed primarily reflect the U.S. experience, those interested in exploring human aspects of disaster, regardless of their locale, will find much food for thought in Drabek's compassionate statement. Following a long line of other notable books Drabek has written on the subject of disasters, this book, for an often overlooked audience, is a welcome addition to the literature in the field.

William A. Anderson, Ph.D.
National Research Council
National Academy of Sciences

PREFACE

For more than four decades, I have spoken to dozens of groups responsible for some aspect of emergency management. The message? An answer to this question: "What has been learned about human responses in disasters?"

My topics vary—family responses, adaptations by emergency organizations, reactions by individuals who just happen to be on scene. So do the issues. These range from disaster warnings and behavior during the immediate emergency to longer-term consequences. Although I mainly focus on human responses to such killers as tornadoes, floods, hurricanes, and earthquakes, there are many parallels with tragedies characterized by more obvious human culpability—airplane crashes, explosions, and hazardous chemical spills. And especially since 9/11, actions of terrorists, both actual and threatened, have become part of the mix.

For the most part, these presentations have been well received. That has meant a great deal to me. Sometimes a special treat has occurred: "You know, I was able to use a couple of your points in a commissioner's meeting. Remember? You talked to our group about three years ago. Good to see you again."

Increasingly, however, I have encountered questions that go something like this: "What I want to know is—ah, where is any of this stuff written down? I mean, I took some notes, but I'd like to go over it again after this workshop. I know I missed a lot."

Occasionally, I have distributed a short bibliography. From an academic, what would you expect?

This tactic left me uncomfortable. Why? Because after handing it out, invariably someone asks a logical question—"Will most of these be in our community bookstores?"

What can I say? "No. Most neighborhood bookstores don't carry these types of academic books. They could special order it for you. But your best bet is to e-mail the publisher." Often, I have wondered if any listeners, even those who seemed to be on the edges of their seats, ever did so. That is really where this book started. But there was another motivator.

In 1974, I first offered a course at the University of Denver titled "Community Responses to Natural Disasters." I continued teaching this course until my retirement from the university thirty years later. Never did I have the right text for that class. On several occasions during those years I actually started writing this book. But other projects developed that prevented much progress. So bits and pieces of notes and chapter outlines gathered dust and became outdated as more and more research was published. And more and more disasters brought new wrinkles to the range of human responses. Yet the dream remained.

About two and one half years after retiring from the university, I briefly returned to the classroom. Sabbatical leaves had left holes in the 2007 teaching schedule, so I accepted an invitation to offer my disaster course. Upon learning of this opportunity, I decided to prepare a rough draft of this book. When students arrived during spring 2007, I was pleased to see photocopies of my initial draft that students had purchased from our bookstore. "Cheapest textbook I ever got," I recall several saying. About midway through the term, a faculty hiring effort collapsed. I was invited to offer the course again. So the following spring (2008), I further tested the first draft of this book. It served as one of the core texts, which I supplemented with numerous research article reprints and books placed "on reserve" in our library.

Both times students responded very positively to the book draft. They provided insightful criticism for which I am grateful. As we parted, after students had received their final paper and course grade, many encouraged me to find a publisher. "This is a book that every American needs to read." And "certainly anyone interested in, or responsible for, emergency management must read this book."

Within days after the course ended, I encountered Mark Listewnik. We met following my breakout session at the annual Federal Emergency Management Agency (FEMA) Higher Education Conference in Emmitsburg, Maryland (Emergency Management Institute, National Emergency Training Center, Department of Homeland Security). Upon describing my book draft to Listewnik, he urged me to prepare a formal proposal and submit a few chapters for review purposes. A few months later, I was most pleased to sign on with the Taylor & Francis Group. I am indebted to Listewnik for his encouragement, editorial suggestions, and administrative support.

The need for a book like this was emphasized to me by the rapidly growing number of college and university faculty who currently are participating in newly created emergency management and homeland security programs. While many materials have been published by FEMA, professionally oriented groups like the International City Management Association, and several other publishing houses, their products are very different from this book. They are formal in style; this book is not. They are impersonal; this book is very personal. They are academic, meaning highly qualified and dispassionate; this book is conclusive and very passionate.

This collection of ideas reflects my classroom lectures and conference presentations, both in content and style. As in these, this book speaks actively to a "you," a student, emergency manager, first responder, disaster volunteer, city manager, county commissioner, or interested citizen. Here I have tried to tell it like it is—or, at least as I see it, after spending more than four decades conducting field research, reading extensively, writing dozens of more formal articles and books, and talking informally with hundreds of disaster victims, helpers, and researchers.

But I must add a note of caution. By my nature, I tend to be optimistic about the future. I look for the good in both people and daily occurrences, including tragedies like disasters. I know full well, however, that people really are very different. I really believe that most are rather like me. Some, however, are more greedy, deceitful, materialistic, and very self-centered. Indeed, there are a few who would not hesitate about cutting a gold tooth from the mouth of a dead disaster victim! But my experience, both in the field following dozens of disaster events and reading thousands of reports by others, suggests that *disasters make us more of what we already are.* And most people, most of the time, really are pretty good. So if there is a bias in this book, it derives from my tending to see water glasses that are one half full rather than being one half empty. Despite having said this, I firmly believe this book is a balanced interpretation of the research literature surveyed. All readers are, therefore, urged to review the Notes section for detailed documentation and what I hope are insightful elaborations. I worked very hard on these to provide additional examples, thoughts, and links to the literature. This format enabled the text to be much more readable than typical academic publications.

Throughout this effort I have been aided greatly by my wife, Ruth Ann Drabek. She has worked as my partner on numerous long-term research and writing projects. I am most appreciative of her computer skills, editorial eye, and patience. Without her assistance and encouragement this book wouldn't exist. Thanks, partner, for joining me in this venture.

Additionally, I want to thank Ruth for donating the photo that appears on the book cover. This stunning statue is located in Chris Larsen Park in Sioux City, Iowa. "The Spirit of Siouxland" was dedicated June 5, 1994, in memory of the 112 who perished in 1989 when United Flight 232 from Denver, Colorado, crashed while attempting an emergency landing at the Sioux Gateway Airport. Through heroic rescue efforts, 184 passengers survived. A man carrying a child away from danger reflects many of the core values of this community. It artfully captures the tone and focus of this book, such as strength, compassion, and unselfish commitment.

The influences of my "disaster parents"—Drs. Enrico L. Quarantelli and Russell R. Dynes—are evident throughout this book; I am forever indebted to both. Also, I want to acknowledge and thank Drs. William A. Anderson, formerly of the National Science Foundation (NSF), and B. Wayne Blanchard of FEMA. Each provided intellectual and administrative guidance that facilitated my successful completion of numerous funded projects that enriched my understanding of the human side of disaster. After several decades of service at NSF, Anderson continued to champion intellectual improvements in disaster and hazards research through his position with the National Academies of Science (NAS). I am most appreciative of the insightful and kind words he prepared for the Foreword of this book.

I also want to acknowledge the thirty-nine years of support I received as a University of Denver faculty member in the Department of Sociology and Criminology. Upon retirement, I was granted an emeritus professorship. I am grateful that the university has continued modest support of my research activities, especially through my John Evans Professorship. Of course, any errors contained within this book are fully my responsibility. All opinions, conclusions, and recommendations are mine as well and do not necessarily reflect the views of the University of Denver or any other person or institution.

Finally, I want to acknowledge and thank the staff of Taylor & Francis, especially Amy Blalock, Iris Fahrer, Mark Listewnik, Karen Schober, and Jen Spoto.

"What have you and other social science types found out?" In answering this question, I have tossed aside most cautionary remarks about research methods, be they sampling error possibilities or statistical design inadequacies. This is not to imply that such matters are unimportant. But too often methodological double-talk hides a key insight. Though I am a doubter by nature, about this I am certain: Future lives can be saved if those responsible for protecting us in times of disaster better apply these insights from the social sciences. And by "those responsible," I mean every citizen of this country.

Thomas E. Drabek

ABOUT THE AUTHOR

Thomas E. Drabek completed his graduate education at The Ohio State University Department of Sociology and Anthropology in 1965. During his last two years at OSU he was a full-time staff member of the Disaster Research Center. He is an Emeritus Professor of Sociology and Criminology at the University of Denver and was a faculty member there from 1965 to 2004 and department chair (1974–1979 and 1985–1987). Upon his retirement in 2004, he was awarded Emeritus status and continues his research on a part-time basis. In 1993, he was awarded a John Evans Professorship which continues to provide modest funding for his research. His research has examined group and organizational responses to large-scale disasters.

Professor Drabek has authored or co-authored over 100 book chapters and journal articles and 27 books including *Strategies for Coordinating Disaster Responses* (2003); *Disaster-Induced Employee Evacuation* (1999); *Disaster Evacuation Behavior: Tourists and Other Transients* (1996); *Disaster Evacuation in the Tourist Industry* (1994); *Microcomputers in Emergency Management: Implementation of Computer Technology* (1991); *Emergency Management: Principles and Practice for Local Government* (1991, co-edited with Gerard J. Hoetmer); *Emergency Management: Strategies for Maintaining Organizational Integrity* (1990); *The Professional Emergency Manager: Structures and Strategies for Success* (1987); and *Human System Responses to Disaster: An Inventory of Sociological Findings* (1986). He served as the co-editor of the *International Journal of Mass Emergencies and Disasters* (1986–1990) and was elected President of the International Sociological Association's Research Committee on Disasters (1990–1994). He prepared four Instructor Guides for the Emergency Management Institute, Federal Emergency Management Agency: *Sociology of Disaster* (1996); *The Social Dimensions of Disaster* (1996); *Emergency Management Principles and Application for Tourism, Hospitality, and Travel Management Industries* (2000, co-authored with Chuck Y. Gee); and *Social Dimensions of Disaster, 2nd Edition* (2004).

In August 2007, Dr. Drabek was the third recipient of The E.L. Quarantelli Award for Contributions to Social Science Disaster Theory by the International Research Committee on Disasters and in June 2008, he received the first Dr. B. Wayne Blanchard Award for Academic Excellence in Emergency Management Higher Education. He frequently lectures at academic and emergency management workshops and conventions throughout the United States and in other places such as Vancouver, Toronto, and Montreal, Canada; Mt. Macedon, Canberra, and Sydney, Australia; Wellington, New Zealand; Geneva, Switzerland; Messina, Italy; Bielefeld, Germany; London, England, and Bangkok, Thailand.

1

Experiences[*]

When disaster strikes, people react. Depending on the context, fear levels rise. Sometimes these exceed any experienced previously. Temporarily, however, one motivation supersedes all others: survival, of self and those nearby, especially loved ones.

During four decades of interviewing people caught in the context of disaster, I have listened to thousands describe their experiences. Each is unique. But when you listen carefully, patterns can be identified. There are elements of commonality.

What is disaster like from the human perspective? The following accounts reveal some of the commonalities documented through painstaking comparative analyses. The accounts that follow are *fictionalized.* I made them up. The contexts—the events—are real, however. The names are my invention, but the stories are representative of dozens of interviews. As such, they introduce the experience of disaster.

As I summarize various aspects of the social science research base, we will return to these stories many times throughout this book. Too often statistical details about a slice of human response—warning, evacuation, or whatever—prevent us from seeing the larger context of individual experiences. Hopefully, these stories will provide that larger context and, in so doing, will enhance your understanding of the human side of disaster.

---

* The events described in this chapter are real. The stories, actions, and names used are fictional. Any resemblance to actual names, experiences, or actions is purely coincidental.

THE TAXI

The Setting

- October 31, 1963
- Indianapolis, Indiana (Indiana State Fairgrounds Coliseum)
- Throughout the evening, it had been raining very hard. Just as the *Holiday on Ice Show* was ending (11:06 p.m.), a massive explosion killed 54 people and injured more than 400 others. Within a few days 27 of the injured died. This event remains the deadliest disaster in Indiana history.[1]

The Story

Sam Wilson glanced at his watch. "11:02," he observed. Just four minutes since his last look.

"Guess I'm getting a bit antsy. Should be about over. Damn seat has gotten hard—too hard. Knew I should have listened to her. Why does she always have to be right? Just a little hemorrhoid; it'll feel a hell of a lot better when we get out of here. When I get off this damned rock."

These thoughts were still moving inside his private person, when Sam realized he had stopped looking at the ice. Instead, he felt a slight grin, a smile really. He was focused on Tony. Wide awake and ready for more action, six-year-old Tony had insisted on staying till the end.

"Come on Grandpa. We hardly ever do anything like this. Let's make it last. We don't want to leave now."

"Yeah," Sam thought to himself. "Let's make it last. Can't disagree with that. But damn, I'd sure enjoy it more if this butt wasn't so hurt'n."

The ice was now empty. Unbeknownst to Sam the skaters were about to move out in mass. The grand finale was seconds away.

Suddenly a flash. A big flash! Not to be confused with a news photographer's camera. Then the noise. A thunderous sound. And then the screams. People from just over there across the aisle.

Sam's senses reacted to the overload. First the flash, then the roar. Then the screams. Now the smell. The smell of dust—no, concrete powder, really. And burning. Something was burning over there across the aisle.

Reflecting the instincts of grandfathers throughout the long course of human existence, Sam suspended any thoughts of personal survival or pain. Even the hurt in his butt vanished as his total being focused on Tony.

He was still there, just inches away. "Tony, you okay, kid?"

2

"Grandpa, it hurts. It hurts. What happened?"

"I don't know son. Here, let me have a look."

Sam was not prepared for the messages his eyes were transmitting. The gash looked nasty. Really nasty. Blood was now covering Tony's left hand, running down into his lap. The wound was near the top of his shoulder. His denim short-sleeved cowboy shirt was flayed open. A red-filled crevice ran nearly to his elbow.

"Oh crap! Not tonight; not tonight. Damn it! What am I gonna do?"

Before this last thought actually reached his brain for processing, Sam had acted. Without really thinking, you see, he grabbed the blue rain jacket from his lap and covered Tony's arm. This action covered the ugliness. Out of sight the scene could be processed more easily.

Holding the jacket tight against Tony's arm, Sam's brain raced. Alternatives. Alternatives. "Should we get out now? Should I wait for help?"

"Grandpa, it hurts. It's hurting worse." And now fear and pain began to take their toll. Tears no longer could be held back. With sobs that started quietly, Tony suddenly began to press for answers.

"Grandpa, what are we going to do?"

"Tony, don't you worry none. I'm here and you're going to be fine. You just got a nasty cut. The docs can fix that up in nothing flat. Nothing to worry about. You just stay calm."

As he spoke these words of comfort, Sam craned his neck. First, toward his left, up past Tony's head, which was now pressed against Sam's chest. He pulled the jacket tighter against the boy's arm.

Some still sat, just staring ahead, downward toward the blast location. Others were standing. But a few were yelling. Their shouts now penetrated Sam's awareness.

"Hey, damn it, we need some help here. My wife's bleeding. She's going to bleed to death. Has anybody got a coat or something. I need help."

"Mommy, what's happening? What's on fire? What stinks?"

These were but a few of the utterances that you might have heard if you had been sitting near Sam and Tony. Sam heard these; the others did not penetrate. His brain refused to admit them. He focused only on one thing.

"Tony, we're getting out of here. Come on. Grab me around the neck."

"Ouch. Don't pull like that! Grandpa, you're hurting me. Stop it!"

Tony's resistance came as a surprise. But Sam resisted the temptation to be abrupt. Maybe he didn't even have to resist. Maybe such actions never entered into the stream of fast-moving thoughts. Or even his reflexes. For Sam was a gentle man. A man who truly loved his grandson, his only grandson.

3

So his response to Tony paralleled his everyday dealings with him. Firm, but gentle. Directive, but soft-spoken. Nurturing, protective, trustworthy. These are the adjectives an older Tony would use years later when he spoke to those mourning Sam's death. But for now, in these moments of hurt and quick response, such qualities were reflected in Sam's actions and, most importantly to six-year-old Tony, in his voice. His tone was soft. The words flowed slowly, without a hint of impatience, panic, or uncertainty.

As he felt himself being carried up the stairs and out into the Coliseum hallways, Tony sobbed. His sobs did not prevent him from hearing the near constant comforting from Sam. "Don't worry, Tony, we're almost to the top. Just a few more steps. We'll be out of here soon. The docs will fix you up in nothing flat. You're going to be just fine."

Slowly they moved toward a sign marked "Exit," along with hundreds of others who shared their desire to get out. Some were visibly hurt. Others, like Sam, were carrying children. Some were half-carrying and half-helping other adults who also had been hit by the chunks of concrete that had flown into the audience.

The scene was one of tears, punctuated by an occasional scream. Some were still yelling for help. Most were quiet, however. Most just pressed forward. Not orderly really, but certainly not in a panic stampede either. They just pressed forward, wordlessly announcing their desire to get the hell out of this place as quickly as possible! A second explosion, much milder than the first, increased the intensity of the press.

What Tony could not know, because Sam never uttered it, was Sam's thinking. Rapid assessments of alternatives. "Should I try to find a security guy? God, they were everywhere when we came in here. Where the hell are they now?" And, as they entered the main hall, Sam saw an exit sign in the distance. The sign evoked a rush.

"Exit. Yeah, but which one? Where the hell's the car from here? That's not where we came in. Crap! I'll never find the damn car in this mess of confusion."

These were internal communications. Strictly internal! Not meant for Tony's ears. "Don't worry little guy. We're almost out of this place. You're doing fine."

Suddenly Sam spotted him. A guy in a security uniform. "Thank God. Now I'll get some help."

"Hey Mister. Hey, you over there. I've got my grandson here. He's hurt. Bleeding real bad. Where do you have the ambulances? This kid needs some stitches. Got to get him to the hospital fast."

4

"Sir, I ain't seen any ambulances. Just a lot of hurt people. I don't know what to tell you. There's just people going every direction. Maybe once you get outside you'll see them. But I ain't got no idea which way to tell you to go."

Sam felt Tony's arm tighten around his neck. "Had he heard this?" The tightening intensified. Simultaneously, the sobbing did too.

Choking back his tears, Tony's voice had a tone of desperation. A tone of growing fear.

"Grandpa, what are we going to do?"

"Tony, listen to me." The voice was firmer now. "We are going to get out of here. You're going to the hospital to get that arm fixed. The docs will have it sewed up quicker than you can imagine. Don't worry; everything's going to be fine. You just keep hanging on to my neck. We'll be outside as soon as we get over to that door."

As they exited, Sam's eyes focused. The rain had let up a bit. There in front of them was a line of taxi cabs.

"For God's sake," Sam thought to himself.

"See Tony, I told you everything would be okay. We're going to take a little taxi ride."

As they approached a cab, Sam spotted three men standing behind. All three seemed fixated on the crowd streaming out the exits.

"Hey, whose cab is this? I've got a hurt kid here. We need to get to the nearest hospital as quick as possible."

"Yes, sir. We can do that job. Let me grab that door. You just get right on in there. I'll have you to the hospital front door in nothing flat."

THE EARRING

The Setting

- June 17, 1978
- Pomona Lake, Kansas
- A tornado crossed Pomona Lake during the early evening and caused the *Showboat Whippoorwill* to capsize. As the boat turned on its side, 14 crew and theater cast members, along with 46 passengers, were tossed into the water. Of the 60 on board, 15 individuals drowned. This event remains the worst boating disaster in Kansas history.[2]

5

The Story

"It's still awfully hot. Breeze feels better. A bit cooler. Sure nice of Bobby to do this. Really was a surprise. Dinner smells wonderful. I know these guys are going to be great with the musical numbers."

Pearl Altman was lost in her thoughts. She and her boyfriend, Billy Wells, had talked more about their upcoming August wedding during the 45-minute drive from Topeka.

Pearl had been at her desk at Federal-State Insurance. Billy's call came at 9:30 that morning.

"Good morning, Federal-State. This is Pearl, how may I help you?"

"Yo, Pearl. Billy here."

"Hey, you handsome devil. What's up?"

"Well, Bobby and Louise just came by. They want us to join them for dinner tonight."

"Cool. What time?"

"How 'bout I pick you up at 4:30? Can you get away early?"

"Yeah, sure thing," Pearl replied as she fingered the heart-shaped earring that dangled from her right ear.

"What's the dress? Fancy place or what?"

"No, not fancy. But it'll be real neat. You're in for a big surprise. I know you're going to love it. It's over 100 right now, so I'm wearing shorts and a T-shirt. You ought to do the same. We're going to have a great time."

"Okay, Billy. See you at 4:30."

While the clouds looked a bit stormy, there were no indications of possible tornado activity. So the *Whippoorwill* crew had loaded the 46 passengers and backed away from shore. The intense June heat remained, but was blunted a bit as the small craft slowly made its way northward.

The tornado came from the west. Later, campers who were enjoying summer outings at Pomona State Park would advise emergency officials that they saw it coming. It came across the recently built reservoir moving in a northeasterly direction—a pattern that often defines the movement of these killer storms. It didn't make a direct hit. Undoubtedly that would have been worse. But as it neared the *Whippoorwill*, the water became increasingly turbulent.

Pearl first noticed her purse moving. Quickly she grabbed it. But in that instant she felt Billy pushing against her.

"Billy! What's happening?"

"Damned if I know. Grab that rail and hang on."

Pearl next heard Bobby, then Louise.

6

"Billy, this damned boat is going to flip! It's going over on its side."

"Bobby! Bobby, hang on to me. I'm about to go over the side. You know I can't swim. Hang on to me Bobby!"

As Pearl entered the dark water, she felt a sense of confidence. She didn't fear the water. No member of the high school swim team did. Suddenly her mind produced a photo. There she was poolside. She had finally gotten her wish after all those hours of practice. A dream had come true. She had placed among the top three in the high school regionals. There she was smiling at her parents. Smiling at her new boyfriend, Billy. That was three years ago.

Now she faced more of a challenge than she could imagine. Once in the water she was surprised. Something wasn't right. She was okay; she was swimming. Both her arms and legs followed their practiced motions. But still she went down. Down deeper into the darkness despite everything. Despite her efforts to kick harder.

What Pearl did not realize—nor did any of the other 59 disaster victims—was the boat's suction effect. As the *Whippoorwill* slowly turned on its side, completely capsizing so that only its bottom was visible atop the water, a powerful force was unleashed. Victims were pulled downward. This force temporarily neutralized their efforts to surface.

Once the boat reached its new position, the *Whippoorwill* rested. Unfortunately, when many surfaced they discovered a new horror.

"Damn, what the hell did I hit?" Billy thought to himself. Quickly outstretched arms moved his rapidly exploring hands around a large area.

"Oh, crap! I'm trapped. I must be under this damn boat."

Remembering the double decks of the *Whippoorwill*, Billy's mind raced. As his hands continued their quick exploration, his mind received a message that did not process at first.

"Hey, wait. My arm's out of the water. What the hell is going on?"

"It was like a drinking glass in the sink," Billy would explain to friends weeks later. "You see, when the boat turned over there was some air trapped in the compartments that made up the two decks. Somehow I got inside of one of those. When I got to feeling around, I was shocked to find that my arm was out of the water a little bit. So by putting my face up, hell, it was almost against the bottom of the boat; I could breathe. There was this little pocket of air there. That's what saved me. That and the diver, of course.

"Man, that guy was something," Billy would continue.

"He risked his life going under there. See, after I figured out my situation, I started pounding on the boards. I guess I was thinking I might

7

break one of them loose. I really don't even remember now what I was thinking. I was just trying to get out of there before this little bit of air was gone. The next thing I knew, although it seemed like hours at the time, this guy shows up. You know he wasn't even a fireman or anything. Just some guy who had given diving lessons out there at the park.

"I took a big breath like he told me, and down we went. See, we had to go down from where I was below the two decks that were upside down in the water. Then we just pushed off and headed up. We came out alongside the boat. He told me to hang on until someone could get me into one of the little boats. Lots of campers there had boats. They came right out to rescue people when they saw the *Whippoorwill* go down."

Usually Billy stopped there. The rest was not easy. Rarely was it shared.

Pearl's body, like a dozen others, was recovered later. This was after the *Whippoorwill* was pushed into shallow water closer to shore. Once there, cables from two wreckers were attached. Dump trucks were chained to the front of the wreckers. Slowly the *Whippoorwill* was uprighted. Professional divers from nearby Topeka continued to locate other victims' bodies.

Finally, with six victims still missing, the sheriff authorized a dragging operation. This was the following day, however, after the divers had made repeated searches throughout the area.

Billy knew in an instant!

"That's her. That's Pearl." Her limp body had been hooked by the drag boat rescuers. Pearl and four others were recovered in this way.

"As soon as I saw her I knew. The sun was hitting that earring. That little heart. I gave those to her. I remember her commenting to Louise about how much she liked them. Her folks let me keep them. That's all I've got now. Those two little earrings. But I'll never forget her. She was special.

"Kinda strange too. Bobby and Louise and I were talking about this the other night. Pearl could swim better than any of us. Yet she's the one that went. Go figure!"

THE HONEYMOON

The Setting

- September 11, 1992
- Kauai, Hawaii
- Following Hurricane Andrew's rampage through southern Florida and Louisiana, most Americans paid little attention to a storm

named Iniki. Before the attacks on the World Trade Center and the Pentagon, at least for Hawaiians, "the 9/11 disaster" referred to this hurricane. Although its toll paled next to Andrew—6 deaths versus 26; $2 billion damages versus $30 billion—Iniki's destruction had been exceeded only by Hurricane Hugo in 1989 up to that point in U.S. history. Neither the media nor most tourists paid such heed to the threat until early Friday morning, just hours after the storm raced by Waikiki Beach and other high-end Honolulu lodgings on the nearby capital island of Oahu. Later that afternoon "the Garden Island" of Kauai was hit violently.[3]

The Story

Mrs. Sally Cummings was in a deep sleep. Vaguely she heard a familiar voice, but her acute fatigue won over. Instantly she was snoring again.

"Hello. Hello! Who is this?"

"Sir, this is the front desk. Sorry to bother you, but we're notifying all of our guests. You need to be in the lobby no later than one o'clock. We are evacuating all oceanfront rooms because of a storm. I'm sure everything is going to be just fine; this is just precautionary."

"Hell no! Mister we just got to our room a few hours ago, and we're not leaving!"

With an emphasis on the "not," David slammed the phone down in disgust.

"Dumb clown," he muttered under his breath. "What the hell time is it anyway?" The question was to himself, not even spoken aloud. "No need to bother her," he thought to himself as he gazed at Sally.

Slowly his thoughts turned to the past several hours. They had arrived at the hotel just before midnight. "God, were we tired."

Their day had been a long one. Like most wedding days it was glorious, but laced with a few incidents that neither had wanted to talk about on the flight to Los Angeles. It had been nearly 4 that afternoon when they boarded the plane in Kansas City. "I wasn't sure we'd make it," David remembered. This thought evoked others—some pleasant, others less so. "Pretty. No, beautiful. God, her eyes seemed on fire when she and her Dad came down the aisle. Made my knees shake; never thought it'd be like that. And that damn Louie. Guess everyone's got an uncle who drinks too much at things like this. I could have killed the SOB when he fell into the cake. Stupid! Just real stupid."

9

David's stream of consciousness was interrupted again by a ringing. He grabbed the phone quickly and felt a sense of anger as he answered.

"Hello!"

"Yes. Sir, this is the front desk. Have you been notified of the storm?"

"Yeah, some clown called here a minute ago. I told him we weren't leaving. For crap's sake we just got here a few hours ago."

"Sir. Sir, please listen. We know you had a late arrival, but this is an emergency. We need you to report to the lobby soon. We'll be serving dinner in the ballroom tonight for our guests who have oceanside rooms. This is complimentary, of course. This storm probably will blow on by. But in the interest of guest safety, we must ask you to be prepared to leave your room within the next hour. Thank you, sir."

David hung the phone up; his anger did not subside. "Damn. Some wedding night this is turning into!"

"David? David, who was that on the phone? It wasn't Mom calling already was it?"

"No, it wasn't your Mom! It was some clown from the front desk. He says there is a storm coming, and they want everyone in an oceanview room to report downstairs. Guess they're trying to offset this room price by giving us a free dinner. What a bunch of crap!"

"David? What kind of storm? How can there be a storm already? We just got here. They didn't say anything when we checked in did they? David, did they? You wouldn't keep something like that from me, would you? I know you couldn't wait to get up here."

David took a deep breath and muttered to himself, "Married only hours and already she's pissing me off!"

And then the words jumped out of his mouth, "What kind of a remark is that, keeping something from you? Hell no, I'm not keeping anything from you. They didn't say a damn thing last night. Honest!"

"Okay. Okay. Don't shout at me."

Then after a brief pause, "Come here. Come on. I'm sorry I said that. I just felt a little scared. Remember what I told you when you first suggested this trip. Going to Hawaii sounded like fun. But I never had traveled outside of Kansas. Remember? I told you that. I mean except for the few times my family drove out to Colorado for a summer vacation. I'm not like you. This whole trip is just a little scary. And this hotel—it's just beautiful. When we got here I felt like I was in a dream. When you were checking in I just kept looking around. I remember thinking I was like Dorothy. 'Sally,' I said to myself, you sure ain't in Kansas anymore!' Come on over here, David, I need a hug."

10

David's movement came simultaneously with a ring. "Damn it, they're calling again."

"Hello! Now look!"

David's hostile words stopped quickly.

"Mrs. Wysocki? Yeah, it's me. Geeze, I never thought it'd be you.

"Yeah, I know I sounded angry. No, everything's fine here. Well, sorta, see they been calling our room about some storm. I thought it was them calling again. Sorry about that. Yeah. Yeah. She's fine. No. No problems with the flights. Actually everything worked just right. We just landed in Los Angeles and took right off for Honolulu in thirty minutes or so. And then we had a quick flight over to here. Yeah, the hotel's great. You wouldn't believe it. Here, let me pass the phone."

Long before her slender fingers touched the phone, they had begun stroking David's leg. Her eyes told him everything was going to be okay. They would survive their first married fight. Hundreds more would occur, of course, during the years ahead. But for now, the warm glow had returned.

David's fingers circled her neck and then made repeated strokes down her shoulders and back again as Sally talked to her mother.

"Yeah, Mom, it's just like David said. The hotel is beautiful. Mom, you wouldn't believe how big it is. The decorations and flowers—they just are marvelous. No, not yet. But I'll get plenty of pictures before we leave. Mom, how the heck did you hear about this storm, anyway? Oh, Dad. Yeah, I know he gets up early and always likes to check CNN and the Weather Channel. It's really on there? Yeah, we have a TV, actually two of them. One right here by the bed and another in the other room. But we were so tired after we got here; we never even turned them on."

"Okay, Mom. I'll call you tomorrow after this thing goes by. I know. I know, you don't want to interfere or anything. But I'll call you anyway 'cause you'll feel better. Okay. Bye now. We'll be fine, Mom; don't worry."

After dressing, David and Sally joined dozens of others in the main ballroom of the hotel. Iniki's fury exceeded expectations. While windows were blown out and water flowed through the lower lobby, guests talked to one another. Conversation eased the anxiety, and new acquaintances were born that otherwise never would have happened. The candlelight buffet dinner was very nice. Suddenly, everything changed. Due to structural damage, later that evening all guests were bussed to a nearby school that had been established as a shelter.

Upon entering the school, Sally pulled back.

"Good grief, David. Look at all of these people. They're packed in here. Do we have to stay here?"

11

"Don't know, sweet. Let me talk to that guy over there. He seems to be in charge."

Upon their return to Kansas, David and Sally would share their story many times. To all who wanted to listen, they could stress their initial disbelief at being told they had to leave their room. The beautiful honeymoon suite that they enjoyed much too briefly.

They would stress the friendliness of the hotel staff that pulled out all the stops to make them feel safe as Iniki pounded the area.

And what did they emphasize most? Two things were shared most frequently. First was their vow to each other during the second night in the crowded school shelter.

"Let's plan to come back here for our first anniversary," Sally had said to David as her eyes warmly searched his.

"I know this isn't fair. Not what you had planned at all. And you know, this place really is beautiful. And the people are so friendly. What do you think?"

"Done deal," David had replied.

And the other? David had said it next, in the same interchange. "And next time we'll not be sharing one working toilet with 200 other people!" And they didn't.

THE CEILING

The Setting

- January 17, 1994
- Santa Monica, California
- At 4:31 a.m. most people throughout the Los Angeles metropolitan area experienced intense shaking. Without warning, roads twisted, bridges collapsed, and thousands of buildings shifted. While the epicenter was near the city of Northridge, two massive ruptures split land and objects for miles to the north and south. Consequently, people asleep in beachfront hotels in Santa Monica, 25 miles southeast, experienced violent shaking as ceilings and walls came tumbling down around them.[4]

The Story

"Here's another one, Mom. God, look at those pictures! They're really true. But you know, if I hadn't actually seen it, I wouldn't believe it. It was just

12

awful. I was so scared, Mom. And then I was so embarrassed. Geez, I never told you this part. Not sure I should."

Valerie ran her fingers through her long, bright red hair as she spoke. Then both hands rubbed the moisture from her eyes.

"Now Valerie, you just calm down. You know what the doctor said. All this will just fade away. And you'll not need those nerve pills very long either. In a few weeks you'll be sleeping as good as ever. Your father and I are just so thankful that you and Mike got out of there without any more than cuts and bruises. And you know, you always have been a little high-strung. Guess you got that and your hair from my family. Sitting here now you look just like my mom in that picture we have of her with her four sisters. All of them had red hair. And from what Mom always said they were all a bit high-strung."

"Wow Mom, look at this one, will ya. 'Quake Opens Gates To Hell.' And look at the pictures they put on the front page. These tabloids are really something!"

Just as the word "page" left her mouth, Valeria saw her mom turn away.

"Heavens to Betsy, now who can that be? My goodness, it's past 11."

"Oh, Jeannie. Well, come on in. Valerie's here, and has she got stories."

"Sorry to barge in on you guys, but I just left the diner. Lots of folks there were still talking about the quake. Willie said he'd seen Mike. When I saw your kitchen light on, I figured you all were still up."

"Yeah," Valerie replied. "I'm waiting on Mike. I told him to pick me up here when he got done at the shop. Things kinda piled up on him while we were gone. Who'd ever think there could be so many smashed-up cars in a 'burg like Blackduck."

"Well girl, you don't know what you guys missed. Let me tell you—while you and Loverboy were out there on the beach having fun in the sun, we were having one hell of a Minnesota winter. Ain't that right, Mrs. Swenson?"

"You're right about that, Jeannie. But make no mistake. I'll take our winters any day before I'd live in a place that has earthquakes. And after hearing what Valerie and Mike went through—I mean, look at these papers she brought home. God, they're mighty lucky they got back alive."

"Val, that's why I stopped. Willie said you guys had a time of it. Mike told him some, but you know Mike. He's the quiet type. Didn't really tell any details. Except I guess your hotel was trashed."

"Yeah, you could say that. For sure, you could say that."

First a pause. Then a few eye blinks. Next a hard swallow. All this took less than a second. Then came the tears.

13

"Damn it Mom! When am I going to stop crying over this? What's wrong with me anyway? I know we're safe. I'm sitting right here. But every time I try to talk about it, I'm back in that bed. And it just starts all over again."

"Now Valerie. You know what the doctor said. The best thing for you to do is keep talking. Remember? He said every time you tell the story to someone you'll feel just a little bit better."

"Come on Jeannie. You sit down here while I make us some hot tea. And you Valerie—you've got nowhere to go until Mike gets here. So here's your chance. Go over it again."

"I'm sorry guys. This just isn't like me. I'm not some damned nut case. But this really got to me. I've never been so scared in all my life."

After a few seconds of silence, Jeannie looked at Valerie. Her smile communicated trust not mockery, friendship not sarcasm. Human bonds that are nurtured in small towns like Blackduck, Minnesota.

"Well, you gonna start, or do I have to play guessing games with ya?"

"No. Don't start asking me lots of questions. That just makes it worse. Okay. I'm okay now.

"Well see—Mike and I really did have a good time. You know that after we got married, we never really took a trip. After the wedding we went camping up north for two days before both of us had to be back to work. So this was something we'd been saving for and really planning for several months.

"You know at first it was scary. When we got on the plane in Bemidji, I just couldn't believe it. I don't think I slept an hour the night before.

"But everything was fine, and we landed in Chicago okay. Mike acted like he'd been there before—Mr. Self-Confidence, I started calling him. After him asking a few people for directions, we got to our gate, and the plane was right there. In nothing flat we were boarding. It was real smooth clear to Los Angeles, but I was still a little nervous. You know, not knowing what would happen when we actually got there. But Mike said, 'Just follow the crowd.' And when we got to the baggage place, I spotted my suitcase right away. Mike's showed up fast too. He told me we had a shuttle arranged to the hotel. Well you could have knocked me over. I mean, we just turned around and here was a guy with a little sign—*Knudson*.

"He grabbed our two suitcases and led us to his car. We were at the hotel in nothing flat. It wasn't fancy or anything, but real clean. And the people there were real friendly.

"We had arranged these tours, so all's we had to do was be in the lobby at a certain time and these buses would pull up. We went to see Mickey and SeaWorld and even to some museums during the week. The thing I liked most was seeing the sidewalk where they have all the Hollywood stars. It was really neat.

"Then we moved over to this other hotel. It was right near the Santa Monica Pier. By then I was feeling great. I remember telling Mike that night at dinner—we were in this real nice restaurant right on the beach—that this was the best time I'd ever had in my life. And you'd never guess what he said. 'Well, isn't that what a honeymoon is supposed to be?' We just laughed; I mean we'd already passed our third anniversary.

"Anyway, we were on the fifth floor. We could see the ocean and beach from our room. It was just beautiful. Then everything changed! We were both asleep. I remember waking up and my left leg hurt. When I tried to raise up, I couldn't. And I could hardly breathe. I remember grabbing Mike's arm and yelling. It was dark. Totally dark."

"'What the hell's happening? Val, you okay?'

"I don't know what I told him, but I remember his asking about my leg and why couldn't I move it. He tried to turn on the light, but it didn't work. I remember him saying, 'Just a minute, hon. Let me get my lighter.' He'd left it right on the nightstand next to the lamp. But I guess it fell off because of the shaking, 'cause I remember him grumbling, 'Where the hell did it go?'

"He must have found it on the floor next to the bed because the next thing I remember, there was a little glow in the room.

"I still remember that sight. With that little flicker of flame all's you could see was dust. Then through all the dust, I saw this big dresser. It had fallen over on our bed, and the TV was on top of my left leg. Mike jumped up and pushed it to where I could get my foot out. About that time he yelled. Hunks of the ceiling started coming down. I guess some had come down earlier, but one big chunk hit him on the head right then. Man, he started cussing. That's when I lost it. I guess I got a little hysterical; I don't know. I just remember being real scared, and I started crying.

"And now, that scene just keeps coming back to me. The light flickering and the dust and then the ceiling. It looked all jagged. Like a huge black mouth about to gobble both of us up! It's just awful.

"Mike was something though. As soon as he heard me crying, he came right back to bed. I remember him hugging me and saying that everything would be okay. I just kept crying and asking him what happened.

"He told me he was going to find out. I didn't want him to let go, but finally I got calmed down enough. So Mike went to peek out the door. But when he tried to open it, it wouldn't budge. It was really stuck. But I could see it framed in light. So I knew there were lights on in the hallway.

"I remember yelling at Mike about then. 'Come on Mike, pull on it. We've got to get out of here.'

"About then Mike said it was coming. He had gotten it open a little bit. And then I heard him yell.

"'Hey mister. How about some help. I can't get this damned door open. Could you push from out there?'

"Well, it seemed like it took forever, but suddenly the door swung open—well, halfway open.

"'Come on Val, we're getting out of here.'

"I just jumped up and headed out. My foot hurt like hell, but I didn't care. I just wanted out of that room.

"There were a few other people in the hall, and I remember someone yelling that the elevators didn't work. They kept saying, 'The stairway is down the hall on the left.' Some guy kept running down the hall telling people that. I don't think he worked for the hotel, you know, just someone like us. But he sure seemed to know what we should do.

"Well, seeing some other people and getting out of that room made me feel better. We started down the stairs. There was some light, but not much. I remember Mike saying that they must have done their emergency lighting on the cheap. It was a really nice hotel, and it pissed him off that they would cut corners on something like that. 'So much for guest safety,' I remember him saying.

"We finally got to the lobby, and people were everywhere. Mike just kinda guided me toward the front desk. There was a guy there telling people one thing and another. That's the first time I remember hearing the word 'earthquake.'

"'My God, Mike! That's what it was. We've had an earthquake. An earthquake.'

"'Yeah, Val. Guess that's it. Guess we'll remember this trip, won't we?'

"He was grinning. Standing there in the lobby just grinning. That's when it hit me. 'For crap's sake, Mike! We could have been killed. We could have died in that room. How the hell can you joke about this?' And then I started crying. I didn't want to be mad at him, but I was. I didn't want to be standing there crying, but I was.

"Mike was trying to talk to me when suddenly this guy in a hotel uniform walks up and hands Mike a cushion. A damned couch cushion.

"'We're going to have some blankets in here in a few minutes, Mister. Maybe you guys want to sit down over there on that couch. Here's this if you want it.'

"God, it was like a ton of bricks! Suddenly it hit me. All I had on was Mike's T-shirt. Since we have been married that's what I usually wear to bed. And here I am in this hotel lobby full of people, and all I have on is this T-shirt. God, I was embarrassed as hell. Mike was real good. He never got mad, never lost his head. He just said, real gently, 'Come on Val, let's sit over there.'

"Well, a few minutes later some woman started yelling that she had a cart full of blankets if anyone wanted one. After I got covered up, I remember I felt a little better. Then another woman from the hotel came by with a little cart that had coffee. I remember telling Mike that I couldn't stop shaking. I was holding this styrofoam cup with both hands, and it just wouldn't stop moving.

"Finally, they said we could go back up to our room to get our stuff. They had arranged for vans to transport all the guests to another hotel. I pulled on a pair of sweats and tried to pull on my tennis shoes, but my foot was too swollen. So Mike just said, 'Hey, this is Santa Monica. Just get your flip-flops and let's go.' Well, trying to come down all those stairs in those was no easy trick. But I did it. Of course, Mike carried our bags, so all I had to do was follow behind him.

"After we got to this other hotel, I started to calm down. Then it hit me. We were supposed to leave late that afternoon. But the TV said the airport was closed and people better check with their airline before they went to the airport. When I heard that, I lost it again. I just started crying. Fortunately, Mike talked to somebody right away. He told them that we both had to get back as soon as possible because of our jobs. God, was I ever glad when he told me that we would leave the next day. But every time one of those aftershocks hit, my mind would just go back to our room. And all that dust! And that horrible-looking ceiling. I know I'll get over it. But I'm still sleeping in sweats for awhile. I was so embarrassed to be standing there like that."

Mrs. Swenson spoke softly, but firmly as only a mother can do. "Sweetie, if that's the worst thing that happens to you in this life, you'll be damned lucky. So get over it! Hey, here comes Mike."

THE INSIGHTS

- Disaster comes in many forms reflecting different *agents* be they explosions, hurricanes, tornadoes, earthquakes, or similar such phenomena.

- When people experience disaster, they *react* both behaviorally and emotionally.
- While heightened fear levels may somewhat paralyze some, motivation to *survive* guides most victims to safe places.
- People *help* those around them who might require assistance, especially loved ones.
- Disaster experiences are *remembered*—both the good and the bad.

2

The Problem and Approach

Valerie Knudson, Sally Cummings, and the other imaginary characters in the fictional episodes that comprised Chapter 1, know "the problem." At least they "know" how their date with disaster left them feeling. They "know" the fear, the hurt, and the continuing anxiety they have about the future. They have learned the *meaning of vulnerability.* And like all other disaster victims, they are forever changed.

So despite the headlines staring at you each morning from your newspaper, or the images flowing across your computer screen or television, until you have been inside a hotel room being ripped apart by an earthquake, you can't "know" their type of experience. Think of those springtime flashes—words and pictures of tornadoes that have ripped apart sections of Wichita Falls, Texas—or maybe it was Lubbock or Ft. Worth. Maybe it was Evansville, Indiana, in, of all times, November 2005.

Think of April 2, 2006. A swarm of tornados ripped through miles of western Tennessee, parts of Missouri, southern Illinois, and other sections of the Midwest. In addition to shredding homes and businesses, these violent storms toppled railroad cars, injured dozens of people, and killed 27. Instead of a swarm, think of the one that literally wiped Greensburg, Kansas, off the map on May 4, 2007. Closer to my home is a small town just north of Denver—Windsor, Colorado. It took a bad hit about a year later, May 22, 2008. Ten months earlier our hearts had gone out to families out east when a rural community—Holly—was devastated about eight o'clock in the evening (March 29, 2007).

Contrast that destruction with the smells described by flood victims. People living near the mighty Mississippi, or those whose mountain homes sat near a small river in Colorado. Or maybe it was the Hill Country of Texas. Ever visit Bandera or Kerrville? I'll tell you about my visits to all of these places, and many others, in the pages that follow.

Think back to a time in late summer when you were watching TV or reading a newspaper. Recall the headlines from coastal areas where a hurricane ripped houses apart. Tidal surges moved entire foundations. Beautiful locations come to my mind immediately: places like Galveston (Texas), Nags Head (North Carolina), Myrtle Beach (South Carolina), to name but a few. What popped into your mind? I wonder.

Depending on where you live, hurricanes like Hugo (1989), Andrew (1992), Fran (1996), or Floyd (1999) may have been totally replaced by more recent storms like Katrina, Rita, or Wilma (2005). If not these, then maybe more recent monsters like Gustav or Ike (2008). These events taught most Americans what catastrophe looks like. Along with the remarkable media coverage of the World Trade Center collapse, responses to these five recent storms evoke intense visual images within most Americans today.

So what is "the problem," and how do you approach it? I will address both questions now, in that order. Understanding both topics will give you a better handle on the human side of disaster.

THE DANGER AROUND YOU IS INCREASING

Yes, the danger around you actually is increasing. Maybe you've noticed. Maybe you'll notice more tomorrow. Why? Is it simply because the media are reporting deaths and injuries resulting from disaster with greater frequency? They are, but make no mistake. This is not a "media-produced" fiction. More and more people are becoming disaster victims. More and more dollars are being spent to repair disaster caused damages.

But why? When we can put people into space for days, even months in some cases, why is this happening? Seems a bit odd doesn't it? New scientific knowledge ought to bring better control and wiser decisions. To some degree it has. Yet we are becoming more and more aware of why risk reduction does not lie exclusively in new gadgets, no matter how elegant. People remain people. It is to them we must turn.

Actually, our environment today is *more dangerous* because of new technologies. Now certainly, most of us are not convinced by the back-to-nature fringe. We enjoy the changed lifestyle, and added freedoms new technologies make possible. Like everything else, however, they have costs.

Did you hear that train going past? Did you realize that nearly 2 million carloads of hazardous materials travel by train every year? Of these, about 100,000 are tank cars filled with TIH, which is the acronym for "toxic inhalation hazard." Chlorine and anhydrous ammonia are examples. Although nearly all (99.996% in 2006, for example) are transported without incident, accidents do happen. But this represents less than 5% of the picture.

Trucks carry almost one-half (42.9%) of the hazardous materials that are moved about every year: "The Office of Hazardous Materials presently estimates the number of hazardous materials shipments in the United States at more than 800,000 per day."[1] Other such material is moved in pipelines (38%), shipped over water (15%), hauled on rails (4%), or transported via aircraft (.05%). These materials support new technologies but bring new risks too.

Of course, if you live near the Three Mile Island nuclear generating station you know what I'm talking about. That would be near Middletown, Pennsylvania. Nuclear power plants are simply the tip of the iceberg, however. They are but one of many new technologies that add to the environmental dangers others of our species have faced from Mother Nature over the centuries.

Yet we have lost ground on these too. Despite all efforts to make our nation safer, we really have made little headway. In part, this is because until very recently our approach reflected a "quick fix" mythology. When a flood happens, let's build a dam. If an earthquake occurs, let's design stronger buildings. Always a quick fix. What an illusion! What a myth!

Did you have any idea that the best estimate available for annual flood losses in our nation averages out at $8.8 billion?[2] This says nothing about what comes out of our pockets because of tornadoes and earthquakes or hotel fires, chemical spills, and explosions. These are only flood losses. No one knows what a total loss figure for all disasters might look like; no systematic accounting has ever been made.[3]

Why not? Well, that is a good question—one we will return to later. Maybe the reason it has never been addressed is because some people did not want it answered. Who? Why? Let's hold on that, but who comes to your mind?

Of course, these dollar figures say nothing about the misery and disruption caused to families. Have you personally ever seen the gooey mess a flood leaves? It really is something. Try talking to victims in Frankfort, Kentucky, or Lebanon, Tennessee, sometime. Better yet, walk along the Red River in North Dakota, the Guadalupe in Texas, the Pearl in Mississippi, or the Tar in North Carolina.

But no mess hurts like the death of a loved one. Folks in all of these places, like those in Florida who lost family when Hurricane Andrew ripped through community after community, met death face to face a few years back when flooding occurred. Think for a minute of the thousand-plus dead because of Hurricane Katrina. Think for a minute of the ripples. For every death, dozens of others were impacted—relatives, friends, rescuers, clergy, counselors. Well, you get the point.

When we can put a man on the moon, why do we still have some of our neighbors drowning in their beds? Did you ever see the memorial created for the 238 who drowned near Rapid City, South Dakota (1972)? Do you ever remember hearing about the 144 who died in the Big Thompson Canyon of Colorado (1976)? And as storms like Gustav and Ike (2008)—or Katrina, Rita, and Wilma (2005)—demonstrate, the list keeps growing every year.[4]

Of course, a different scene jumps out from a news photo of a tornado path. But honestly, such photos are so sterile. You really have to walk the streets of Wichita Falls, Texas (1979), Xenia, Ohio (1974), or Moore, Oklahoma (1999), to grasp what these black funnels of death leave behind. The deadly remains of the Eastbrook Mobile Home Park in Evansville, Indiana (November 6, 2005), is but another in this unending list. There, at least 17 perished while others died in nearby locations on that early Sunday morning (2:00 a.m.).

Since our historical data are not good, we really don't know if the actual number of these dancing snakes is increasing. We do know our danger level is. Why? Cheyenne, Wyoming, is a good illustration. Near, but clearly outside, "tornado alley," Cheyenne was hit hard on July 16, 1979. Many of the houses destroyed were new.

Days later, I was surveying the damage. While driving west on Dell Range Boulevard, I remember stopping at the sign announcing the anticipated opening date for the Frontier Shopping Mall. "Had this killer waited just a bit, it would have been as successful as its cousin was at the Sikes Center in Wichita Falls," I thought. I had been there in April, just weeks earlier. You see, we are building more and more onto prairie lands. Out there funnel visits used to go unnoticed.

Cheyenne was lucky in 1979. Only one human life was lost, a 14-month-old baby. This death makes an important point that few recognize. Did you realize that nearly a quarter of all new housing starts within our nation are in mobile homes? The sales figures have been rising for several years. Yet, given recent escalating prices, what are families to do? Certainly, a mobile home is better than no home at all. And thousands of American citizens continue to wander in our urban jungles without a place they can call home.

So, for many young couples and perhaps their retired grandparents whose income also is limited, mobile homes are good options. Ever drive through the coastal areas of Florida? Mobile home sales there have been booming for years, just like they have in Arizona, California, and many other sectors of the United States.

That's where the baby was when that black twister danced across the northern edge of Cheyenne. Almost anywhere, except your car, is safer than a mobile home when one of these things visits. The obliteration of the mobile home park I just mentioned in Evansville (2005) makes the point. And the damages in Florida resulting from Hurricane Wilma also illustrate this trend with another specific. Before Wilma in 2005, of course, we had 2004. Then Florida greeted Hurricanes Charley, Frances, Ivan, and finally, Jeanne. Thousands of mobile homes were ripped to shreds. Of course, hundreds of better-built dwellings were badly damaged too, but at least most were repairable.

So we have more land areas now populated where tornadoes and hurricanes have visited for centuries. A growing segment of our population lives in mobile homes, which offer minimal protection. See why things are getting worse? These are but two social trends, from among dozens, whose *cumulative consequences* remain unconnected and unnoticed by a public evermore at risk, more and more vulnerable to the extremes of nature.

Population Movement

Floodplain and coastal land encroachment has increased too. There are three different aspects of this expansion that few seem to grasp. First, the experience of Rapid City is worth remembering. What you probably don't know is that most who died there in 1972 were not in town, but up in nearby canyon areas.[5] Why? Because they lived there. So too in the Big Thompson Canyon, in my home state of Colorado. Most who died there in the 1976 flood, however, were enjoying summertime cabins.

For all kinds of reasons, mainly to escape the noise, crowdedness, and urban lifestyle, more and more people have moved out. Many have selected beautiful sites near quiet bubbly streams or along ocean coastlines. For some it's a permanent dwelling—for others, just a place to escape when work schedules, and those of children, permit.

Regardless of the use pattern, the consequence is real. The number of Americans who now live at risk from flash floods and hurricanes has increased markedly during the past three decades. Yet most sleep soundly; they remain unaware of the risk. So they dream on, oblivious to the absence of a warning system that could save their life. Rains of sufficient magnitude have occurred over the centuries; it's just that no one lived there earlier. While problems still exist, enormous progress has been made in hurricane warnings. That's why so few died when Hugo slammed into South Carolina's coast in 1989. And although the death tolls produced three years later—remember Andrew and Iniki—were much worse, the scope of damage brought by these monsters is hard to comprehend. Despite our progress in hurricane warning systems, however, Hurricane Katrina revealed a significant gap. When over a thousand people die, the grade given can't be high. Other priorities are placing growing numbers of Americans at great risk.

Climate Change

Extensive scientific evidence suggests that we are intensifying the storminess of rain showers in metro areas.[6] While the annual rainfall averages remain rather stable, the number of intense downpours is increasing. With so much concrete and asphalt around, these torrents of rain are producing new dimensions to urban flooding.

Given the multiplicity of local governments comprising metro areas, storm water management defies solution. Here the problems stem not from floodplain encroachment but from the literal creation of new flooding. This is related to factors such as increased water storage and building heat retention. So, every now and then temporary new riverbeds appear. Often, these are in the grooves cut for interstate highways. A secondary consequence has been documented too. In St. Louis, one of several study sites, a 20% increase in automobile accidents was found to be associated with this altered rain pattern.[7]

Recently, of course, many governments around the world—ours has been a conspicuous exception—have become alarmed at scientific evidence regarding global climate changes. For example, Dr. Amanda Staudt, a climate scientist with the National Wildlife Federation, put it this way: "Although no single weather event can be attributed to global warming, … the latest science paints an alarming picture about what global warming has in store for the U.S. Gulf and Atlantic Coasts: stronger hurricanes, heavier rainfall, and rising sea level."[8]

In a coauthored report she prepared for the National Research Council, Staudt summarized the knowledge base this way:

Most scientists agree that the warming in recent decades has been caused primarily by human activities that have increased the amount of greenhouse gases in the atmosphere.... In some parts of the world, global warning could bring positive effects such as longer growing seasons and milder winters.[9]

Despite potential positive effects, many have called for action, not just more research. And given statements made during his campaign, plus several high-level appointments, I fully expect President Barack Obama to implement new policies that differ greatly from those promulgated by the George W. Bush Administration.

The few aerosol cans you have used, like the carbon monoxide that has left the tailpipe of your cars during the past decade, did not create the hole in the ozone layer. It took all of us, including our neighbors down in Brazil and elsewhere who burned acres of vegetation to make way for development. Whether the climate specialists are exactly right or not really isn't the issue. If we don't monitor better, how will we ever know if the consequences of our actions are really creating the type of global warming that many scientists are predicting? If we don't monitor better, how will we ever know if actions taken are doing any good?

A few degrees in temperature may not seem like much, but surely you have encountered media coverage wherein increased numbers of monster hurricanes are expected. Whether the increase in temperature is two, three, four, or five degrees won't really matter to those whose coastal homes will be destroyed in future storms. The level of precision desired by scientists involved in technical debates is not commensurate with that needed by those of us participating in policy discussion and development. Although there is disagreement within the scientific community about the degree of temperature increase, few dispute the overall trend or the projected consequences. It is when, not if—at least, not unless significant new social policies are put into place. And frankly, that is not very likely, in any case not until thousands more die prematurely.

See the types of invisible interdependencies? Networks of social, physical, and technological trends are colliding to increase the danger level you and I live with daily. Ian Burton, Bob Kates, and Gil White documented that this is even more true in less developed nations.[10] Commonly, single events leave one-half million or more homeless. Overnight, in a single earthquake or tropical storm, hundreds of human lives are snuffed out. On October 8, 2005, it was in Kashmir. This area has been a border conflict between India and Pakistan for centuries. It was here that at least 73,000 died in just one massive quake. Millions were left homeless.

For the foreseeable future, villagers living in such nations as India, Bangladesh, or Peru also will remain at extreme risk because of tropical storms and earthquakes. While our situation is bad, there are many ways it could be much worse. Remember the Boxing Day Tsunami (December 26) of 2004 that left more than 280,000 dead in places as separated as Sri Lanka, Thailand, and India? When Cyclone Nargis pushed a wall of water 25 miles inland in southern sections of Myanmar (May 2008), officials feared death tolls reaching 100,000. Later reports indicated that more than 20,000 were known dead but that tens of thousands remained missing. More than one million were homeless. These horrible tragedies further illustrate the many forms of vulnerability.[11]

Potentials for Catastrophe

Another change is a bit more complex. Let's try an example. Recognizing the seriousness of a growing danger, emergency managers in Denver, Colorado, put a new twist on one of their training exercises several years ago. Like many communities with a flood problem, Denver's was solved partially by a massive dam built by the U.S. Army Corps of Engineers. As years have gone by, however, Cherry Creek's earlier floodplain has been too tempting. Now it contains thousands of buildings.

But all are protected by the dam, right? Yes, as long as the structure remains undisturbed. If a terrorist group of one persuasion or another detonated a bomb, or better yet a series of them, what would result? Obviously, a catastrophe. That is the point. Quite aside from the increased dangers resulting from all of the trends I have mentioned thus far, we are facing marked increases in the *potentials for catastrophe*. It is not comforting to realize that in August 2008, the National Academies of Science gave "... the U.S. Bureau of Reclamation a B– to a C for its efforts to make hundreds of dams across the American West safe from terrorist attack."[12]

We caught a glimpse of this when the levees failed in New Orleans after Katrina (2005). Recall? At first it appeared that "the Big Easy" had dodged a bullet. The storm had wobbled just enough. Of course, the slight veer to the east meant that Mississippi casinos and other structures in places like Biloxi and Gulfport would be trashed. But New Orleans would be spared once again. Then suddenly "the bowl"—recall that much of this distinctive and wonderful city sits below sea level—began to fill. And as it did, millions of Americans witnessed the horror of people trapped. Most of us were shocked at seeing bodies floating in what came to be described as "toxic soup."

But, like New Orleans, most potential catastrophes have nothing to do with actions by terrorists, who, by the way, are not going to disappear soon either. That's why emergency managers are shifting their focus. That's why the massive governmental reorganization was implemented to birth a whole new federal department—the Department of Homeland Security.[13] You see, despite actions that seem to us to border on insanity, terrorists detect such interdependencies and our vulnerability. They may seem crazy to us, but most terrorists are not dumb. They succeed in capturing media attention and thereby advertise their cause to the world.[14] Who knows when the next jet airliner will be hijacked or bombed? Do you ever remember hearing about the fate of the Pan American flight that disintegrated over Lockerbie, Scotland, in 1988? That single event left 270 dead.

Pause and recall for just a minute. Revisit the terror you saw on the faces of the thousands of office workers as they fled from the World Trade Center. Try to remember when you first learned of the earlier news from the heartland. Unfortunately, we, as American citizens, will have to endure more collective hurt like that we felt following the bombing of the Alfred P. Murrah building in Oklahoma City, Oklahoma (1995).

Of course, we all wish it would just go away. Or if that's not an option, we'd settle for success by officials working with the Department of Homeland Security, be they the Federal Bureau of Investigation (FBI), Central Intelligence Agency (CIA), Secret Service, or what have you. It would be great if they could prevent all future terrorist attacks within our borders. But while they may thwart many who seek to hurt us, it's simply unrealistic to expect them to stop all future attacks. Indeed, most experts predict a steady rise in terrorist activities for the foreseeable future.[15] See why the danger around you is increasing?

THE MANY FACES OF DISASTER

Disasters come in many forms. Most experts use the term *agent* to differentiate among disaster events. Thus, hurricanes are separated from chemical plant explosions, earthquakes, airplane crashes, train wrecks, and so on. Others use the term *hazard*. Over the years many of us have found it useful to make a distinction. E. L. (Henry) Quarantelli has emphasized that the concept of disaster is complex.[16] While a bit oversimplified by *disaster* I mean an actual event, or the threat of an event, which disrupts the normal routines of a community in a significant way. Thus, disasters bring severe danger and losses to both people and property so that the resources of a community are taxed severely.

In contrast, most of us use the term *hazard* to refer to a *class* of conditions with the potential for harm.[17] Hence, I will speak of the hurricane or tornado hazard. But I also will describe the death and injury resulting from specific events like Hurricanes Ike (2008), Katrina (2005), Iniki (1992), and Andrew (1992) or tornado disasters in Kansas, Oklahoma, or Texas.

Also, disasters (at least as I use the term) require threats or injury to people. For example, someday you could be driving in northeastern New Mexico along Highway 64 and discover the Capulin Volcano National Monument. Scientists tell us that "about 60,000 years ago ash, cinders and lava erupted and formed a classic cinder cone that stands more than 1,000 feet above the surrounding prairie."[18] But as far as we know no humans were hurt or killed by this extreme event. So while it was an extreme environmental event, it was not a disaster in the *social* sense of that term.

This "extreme environmental event" was a stark contrast to more "recent" volcanoes like the eruption of Mt. Vesuvius near Naples, Italy. Approximately 20,000 people were killed in the city of Pompeii when this eruption occurred in the year 79 AD.[19] Someday, perhaps, you'll have the opportunity to join others from around the world and tour this site. There you can ponder the faces of formerly entombed victims. Death came quickly and without warning.

Much more recent, of course, was the disastrous eruption of Mount St. Helens in 1980, which killed 60. The destructive force of such eruptions is best appreciated by a drive through the Mount St. Helens National Volcanic Monument. Here, like a trip through the Hawaii Volcanoes National Park on the big island of Hawaii, one can gain new perspective on the violence of nature. And should you ever be so lucky as to visit the island of Martinique (West Indies) in the Caribbean, you will be imprinted forever. For it was here on May 8, 1902, that 40,000 died when the City of St. Pierre was covered when Mont Pelée erupted. But such events are only one of the many faces of disaster.

Commonly, disasters are divided into three categories: *natural, technological,* and *conflict.* As indicated by the "Notes" for this chapter, others have prepared detailed historical listings of major disasters that go on for pages. Also, the relative frequencies of various types of disasters, their locations, and losses have been documented. You may find some of these helpful at some point. But without too much detail, let's skim over the surface to get a better sense of the many faces of disaster.

Natural Disasters

Starting with natural disasters, let's look at a few examples. Earthquakes are often associated in our mind's eye with California, and with good reason. The destructive 1906 quake in San Francisco is a reference point. It left 503 dead. To date, it remains the U.S. record. Of course, it pales next to dozens of more deadly events that have occurred elsewhere in places like China, Armenia, or India.[20] Within the United States, however, other record quakes include the 1964 destruction in Anchorage, Alaska (131 deaths), and three other California killers that occurred in 1971 (San Fernando, 65 deaths), 1989 (San Francisco, 67 deaths), and 1994 (Northridge, 61 deaths).[21]

Though deadly, earthquakes cost the nation millions of dollars in property losses every year. The Northridge quake alone amounted to more than $30 billion. Fortunately, it retains the record to date. Very few people realize, however, that the most violent quakes in U.S. history actually occurred in the Midwest during 1811 to 1812. The New Madrid fault crosses seven states ranging from southern Illinois and Missouri to northern Arkansas, Mississippi, and Alabama.[22] The urban communities of Memphis, Tennessee, and St. Louis, Missouri, are most at risk. More than 12 million people now reside within the areas that were most disrupted in the early 1800s ground shifts.

Nevada, Oregon, Washington, Utah, South Carolina, and even the New England states have fault lines that have collapsed within the past two centuries. They, like the New Madrid area, will do so again. When they do, the deaths, injuries, and economic losses will be huge compared with the past when the population densities were sparse. In short, the earthquake hazard, although variable, puts most areas of the United States at risk.

While this earthquake risk is formidable, flooding is the most costly hazard we face.[23] People always have settled along rivers. And like all other environmental processes, rivers are in constant flux. I still recall my amazement upon seeing cars in trees—sometimes 20 to 30 feet above from where I was standing. This was in 1979 when the Texas Hill country was ravaged.

Such extreme floods have brought record losses for years. The deadliest occurred in Johnstown, Pennsylvania, in 1889 when 2,289 died. Of course, this case illustrates a problem with our classification system. Here a dam ruptured that many thought guaranteed their safety. So some listings place this disaster into the technological category whereas others simply cross-reference it. Regardless of which list it appears on, those who died in Johnstown remain memorialized as definitions of "the problem."

Other record floods include the 1993 Mississippi valley event that left 50 dead. With losses estimated to range between $12 and $16 billion, it remains the record to date. Four years later, however, western states were hit with the "pineapple express" rains that killed 36 and netted $2 to $3 billion in property damages in California and Nevada. This occurred in January. During spring and early summer of the same year, the Midwest was hit again as waters moved south into rivers that flooded communities in Missouri, Illinois, Kentucky, Ohio, West Virginia, Tennessee, Arkansas, and Mississippi. These floodwaters were exacerbated occasionally by tornado-producing storms that combined to leave 67 dead and more than $1 billion in property losses. As I mentioned already, the continuing invasion of coastal areas has placed more and more people at risk because of annual hurricanes. Some are year-round residents, whereas others enjoy vacation homes that they own or rent. Of course, millions are just booked into a Holiday Inn or some other motel chain property.

The most deadly hurricane in our history hit Galveston, Texas, on September 8, 1900. It left more than 6,000 dead. Fortunately, since Hurricane Hazel, which left 347 dead in 1954 and Hurricane Camille (256 killed in 1969), more recent storms have been less deadly—that is, until Katrina. Her death toll of more than 1,300 left us all very disappointed in the system we really did believe was better.[24] While still unacceptable in my mind, 2008 storms like Gustav (24 killed) and Ike (67 dead) make the point. Katrina really was an exception in so many ways.

Property damages, however, are a different story. The most destructive record for many years reflected the impacts of Hurricane Andrew ($30 billion). That, of course, was pre-Katrina. Loss estimates, like the projected rebuilding costs, will be revised over the years. But the figure of $200 billion—nearly seven times the cost of Andrew—is in the ballpark. Others, however, also have cost billions, such as Hugo in 1989 ($9 billion), Fran in 1996 ($5 billion), and Floyd in 1999 ($6 billion). And during fall 2004, four hurricanes—Charley, Frances, Ivan, and Jeanne—slammed into Florida, leaving behind an estimated $50 billion in property loss. These disasters were only a warm-up, however. The 2005 hurricane season broke all prior records, with 26 named storms that included 13 hurricanes. That number actually exceeded the entire name list selected for the year! Consequently, the Greek alphabet was used so that Epsilon was used to name the four-teenth hurricane and Zeta was identified the last tropical storm of the year (December 30).

Tornadoes kill people every year in the United States, although some years are worse than others. The worst to date was in 1925, when 695 were killed in the three states of Missouri, Illinois, and Indiana. What came to be called "the Great Tri-State Tornado" also injured another 2,000 people and destroyed about 15,000 homes. But other years have been bad too. In 1974, for example, 350 died in storms that hit in 13 states. These included Alabama (72), Georgia (16), Tennessee (58), Kentucky (71), Indiana (52), and Ohio (34). Approximately 5,500 others were injured during this "Super Tornado Outbreak."

Improved warning systems, like with hurricanes, have brought the death tolls down in recent years, but many still are dying prematurely because of these horrible dancing black snakes (e.g., 1999, 41 deaths; 2000, 18 deaths; 2002, 35 deaths). Many who survived the cruel 2:00 a.m. wake-up call in Indiana (2005) reported they had no warning. Others said they had but minutes before their trailer blew apart. All told, 22 died within the swath this killer created. Apart from deaths, property damages are estimated to be in the millions of dollars every year.

Two years after the Indiana tornado, central Florida experienced an early morning outbreak that left 22 dead (February 2, 2007). Hitting areas where many elderly retirees lived, the event resurrected memories of the so-called "Kissimmee Tornado Outbreak" where in 1998, 42 people were killed. Similarly, on May 10, 2008, tornadic windstorms ripped through communities in Oklahoma and Missouri, leaving 22 dead and miles of torn-up homes and businesses.

At times, earthquakes occurring within or near an ocean will generate huge tidal waves. In 1868, for example, Hilo, Hawaii, was hit hard by waves originating from an earthquake in Peru and Chili. Following the 1964 Anchorage quake, Crescent City, California, and Valdez, Alaska, were both hit hard with tsunamis. This term—tsumani—became more a part of our language on December 26, 2004, Boxing Day on the British calendars. The damages, injuries, and enormous death toll caused by this tsunami in places like Thailand and Sri Lanka truly exposed the vulner-abilities facing major segments of the world's population. Remember: This single disaster killed at least 280,000.

As horrible as this event was, it pales in comparison to the mass epi-demics that have wiped out millions. Most deadly was the 1918 influenza epidemic that probably began in Haskell County, Kansas, early in the year.[25] Detailed studies now indicate that it spread from there throughout the nation and eventually made its way around most of the world. Military troop movements within the United States and elsewhere helped the virus move easily so that 100 million died. Hence, this single epidemic, which quickly crossed national borders and became a true pandemic, killed more people that year than the Black Death killed in a century.

Today we hear of other deadly viruses that are spread in various ways, like HIV/AIDS. Equally deadly for those who become a "host," airborne viruses pose the greatest threat. As with the 1918 virus, sometimes called "the Spanish flu," the best protection is avoidance. Hence, elaborate tracking systems have been constructed so that rapid actions can be taken to curtail the virus's movement: "The Department of Homeland Security views pandemic influenza as both the most likely and the most lethal of all threats facing the United States."[26]

Other natural disasters reflect weather changes that bring, for example, drought, fog, blizzards, avalanches, extreme heat, and hail. All of these hazards may trigger specific episodes of death and destruction, that is, disasters. Sometimes it isn't so much the natural hazard as it is just someone doing something stupid. For example, most wildfires are caused by lightning. And these are becoming more terrible as larger numbers of people build up into heavily wooded hillsides. California's wildfires illustrate this increased risk on a regular basis. For example, during November 2008, the infamous Santa Anna winds provided the final element in a dangerous mix. Hundreds were evacuated only to return to charred remains. In less than a week, nearly 64 square miles burned near Los Angeles. Within this burn area, 484 homes were destroyed. Days before these had been part of a tidy mobile home park with just over 600 units. This was but one of three blazes that burned in the L.A. area prior to Thanksgiving 2008.[27]

One of these fires was suspect, however. It turns out that some college students had thought they had extinguished a bonfire. Apparently they hadn't. This news brought a flashback to a recent drive I took through a slowly recovering area a few miles southwest of Denver. In 2002, a Forest Service employee built a fire to burn some letters related to a love gone sour. She too thought it was out when she left the area. Unfortunately, thousands had to evacuate their homes as the drought stricken forestland went ablaze. The "Hayman Fire," as it came to be known, illustrates another face of disaster reflecting a convergence of patterns—social and environmental—that define vulnerability.[28]

Technological Disasters

Like events that partially at least reflect environmental extremes, there is much diversity in disasters that have a technological origin. For example, take transportation accidents. While hundreds of Americans die in automobile crashes every year, we don't get a sense of "collective death" from them. They don't over tax the resources of most communities even if several people are killed in a single incident.

So in contrast to such "routine emergencies," we focus on accidents involving more actual or potential victims. Shipwrecks are good illustrations. When the *Titanic* sank in 1912, for example, so did 1,503 passengers and crew. Similarly, when an Egypt Air plane crashed near Nantucket Island in 1999, 217 people perished. Twenty-two years prior, 583 people perished when a KLM 747 slammed into a Pan Am 747. Both jumbo jets were on the island of Tenerife in the Canary Islands. In a heavy fog, the Pan Am plane was taxiing on the same runway as the KLM plane, which had initiated an unauthorized takeoff (March 27, 1977).

Train wrecks add another dimension. For example, in 1993, there was an incident near Mobile, Alabama, that left 47 dead. Just over 40 years earlier, 1951 to be exact, another train wreck left 84 dead near Woodbridge, New Jersey. On Friday, September 12, 2008, a commuter train collided with a freight train in San Fernando Valley, California. Officials indicated 135 people were injured; 25 others died.[29]

Sometimes technologies fail. An obvious example is the Johnstown flood previously mentioned. Dams have failed in many other locations, however. A referent case I'll detail in Chapter 10 is the Buffalo Creek flash flood. There in the mountains of West Virginia, 125 people drowned on February 26, 1972. Bridges also can fail. On August 1, 2007, the St. Anthony Falls Bridge, which links Minneapolis to St. Paul, Minnesota, did just that. Suddenly 13 people driving on I-35W were dead. Scores were injured. The Federal Highway Administration estimates that approximately one fourth of our 600,000 bridges are "structurally deficient or obsolete."[30] Large structural fires also kill. The most deadly in our history occurred in Chicago at the turn of the century. The 1903 Iroquois Theater Fire left 602 people dead. Forty-one years later, the patrons of a Boston nightclub fled when fire suddenly broke out. Nearly 500—491 to be exact—didn't make it outside, however.

Incidents involving hazardous materials form another whole class of risks we face daily.[31] Think back to Sam Wilson's story in Chapter 1. Yeah, he was the guy trying to get his grandson to a hospital in a taxi. Propane gas was discovered to be the "agent" in the Indianapolis Coliseum tragedy.

While horrible, this event pales in contrast to the 1947 fire and explosion that occurred in Texas City, Texas. During three days in April—16 to 18—a fire and subsequent explosion on a French freighter (*Grandcamp*) carrying ammonium nitrate killed at least 516 and injured more than 3,000 others.

Even more dangerous than propane or ammonium nitrate, at least potentially, are accidents at nuclear power plants. Fortunately, the 1979 incident at the Three Mile Island plant near Middletown, Pennsylvania, is our worst-case experience. No one was killed, but for several days, millions of people were on pins and needles as they awaited word about efforts to stop a possible core meltdown. This danger was brought home in 1986 when workers at the Chernobyl (Ukraine, 62 miles south of Kiev) plant could not avert damage to the core. To this day the human impacts remain controversial. One disaster writer reported that "the most conservative estimate is 10,000 cancers in the Soviet Union and 1,000 in the rest of Europe, with about half that number resulting in deaths."[32] Others have documented the costs of this accident in much broader terms, including resettlement 135,000 people whose towns will remain uninhabitable for years, agricultural losses of both existing produce and contaminated lands, and medical treatment and monitoring programs for those who fled after the explosions.[33]

Conflict Disasters

Conflict disasters also reflect much diversity. The most obvious "agent" is war. Unfortunately, for centuries now, large numbers of wars result in the killing and injuring of thousands of humans every year. Increasingly, terrorism is being used as a tactic to recruit disciples to revolutionary causes. Extremists claim that murder of the innocent is a legitimate tactic in their press for new arrangements in political, social, and geographic boundaries. Such actions, of course, are nothing new. But for us as Americans, we now find that many events are awakening us to different images of future risks.

Few alive today recall the TNT bomb that exploded near Wall Street on September 16, 1920. While the crime never was solved, Bolshevist or anarchist terrorists were believed to have been behind this act, which killed 35 and injured hundreds of others. More recently, of course, the 1993 bombing of the World Trade Center comes to mind as a precursor of the 2001 use of commercial airplanes as instruments of death. Prior to the attacks on 9/11, domestic terrorists bombed the Alfred P. Murrah Federal building in Oklahoma City, Oklahoma (1995). Foreign terrorists used small boats to move explosives close enough to the *USS Cole* while it was refueling in the Port of Aden in Yemen (October 12, 2000). Unfortunately, it looks like attacks on trains (e.g., Bombay, July 22, 2006), subways (e.g., London, July 7, 2005), hotels (e.g., Amman, Jordan, November 10, 2005), and other so-called "soft targets" (e.g., Jakarta, Indonesia, August 5, 2003) where the innocent gather—both locals and tourists—are going to be part of our "new normal" for the indefinite future.

This reality was again brought home to our television screens toward year's end in 2008. The carnage occurred at multiple locations in Mumbai, India (formerly known as Bombay). On November 26, 2008, two luxury hotels—one the famed Taj Mahal—a large restaurant, three hospitals, and a main rail station were the targets of violent terrorist attacks. Sixty hours later the last of two gunmen who had remained inside the Taj were killed. Nearly 200 were murdered in the attacks, which also left nearly 300 injured. These reflected a growing pattern of violence within India. During the past three years, 700 people have died in various terror attacks. For example, prior to the November tragedy in Mumbai, India's capital city, New Delhi, had been the scene of several explosions. In September 2008, a park and several New Delhi shopping areas were targeted. At least 21 were murdered, and another 100 were wounded. Episodes of sectarian violence between Hindus (who comprise about 80% of the population) and Muslims (14%) have occurred repeatedly since 1947 when British rule ended. At that time, the former India was split into two independent nations, Pakistan and India.

Increasingly, however, analysts warn of the potential use of weapons of mass destruction (WMD) by such groups. When one thinks of the death tolls that we could experience if biological, chemical, or nuclear devices are used by future terrorist groups, one realizes full well what I mean when I say the danger around you is increasing![34]

And I have not yet mentioned another type of conflict disaster: civil disorder. Recall hearing about the 58 deaths that occurred in April 1992? These resulted from rampages that followed the acquittal of the Los Angeles police officers charged with "excessive use of force" when they arrested Rodney King. Of course, this rampage paled compared with the series of "civil disturbances" that came to be called the "ghetto riots of the '60s." Between 1964 and 1969, at least 189 major incidents occurred in such cities as Los Angeles (Watts), Newark, and Detroit.

When societies become excessively fractured, some citizens will develop an increasing sense of disenfranchisement. Such social conditions provide political opportunity for change. Some will seek to instill a redefinition of the legitimacy of the official government. They will urge the use of violence to overthrow or otherwise change it. Tourists and other travelers discovered the ripple effects of such actions on the Tuesday before Thanksgiving Day in 2008. Antigovernment protesters shut down Bangkok's international and domestic airports. These massive protests were the largest in a series of demonstrations aimed at bringing down the elected regime.

During early November 2005, thousands of cars were torched in dozens of French communities. These actions were taken by youths who are the children of recent immigrants whose experiences with discrimination boiled over. During March 2006, hundreds of students in Paris and London protested a new law that would make it easier to sack younger employees. Unlike the earlier rampages, however, these protests were much more peaceful, but still disruptive. High levels of unemployment and other structural sources of alienation and poverty are social powder kegs that can be ignited within any society. More recently, in December 2008, Athens, Greece, experienced several days of rioting that was precipitated by police shooting a fifteen-year-old boy. His death sparked an "explosion of rage." Social cesspools of perceived injustice and inequality are another form of vulnerability that is just as real as threats from shifting land masses or violent storms.[35]

Finally, there are the lone rangers—people who murder for reasons that remain unclear. School shooters are prime examples. Of course for me, the killings in April 1999 at Columbine High School in the Denver suburb of Littleton, Colorado, come to mind first. For years afterward I taught students in my university classes who were there that fateful day. The last time I offered my course ("Community Response to Natural Disaster"; spring 2008), I learned much from a student with a different experience. His sister was enrolled at Virginia Tech. She was attending classes there the day in April 2007 that Cho Seung-Hui started his killing rampage. Unfortunately, such acts of violence are with us now and are not going to just disappear.[36]

This then is "the problem." The many faces of disaster reflect the ongoing social, economic, and political shifts that our society reflects. And, as with war, it also reflects not just what is happening here but also the shifting distribution of risk that flows from changes occurring outside our borders. Despite the complexity and diversity of potential disaster agents that define the risk levels we confront at any given instant, about one thing we can be sure: The dangers around us are increasing. This remains true even as we seek escape by watching another football or hockey game, even as we enjoy another quiet day at the beach or skiing a tranquil mountain trail.

THE APPROACH

In contrast to the individual *fictional stories* that comprised Chapter 1, I have used a different approach throughout my career. It is rooted in the empirical and comparative study of disaster behavior. This is not to say that fictional accounts have no place in improving our understanding of disaster. Scholars working within that and other traditions more reflective of the humanities can teach us much.

This is why I wrote Chapter 1. Many of my students have learned a good deal from fictional accounts and those of good investigative journalists like John Maclean. Indeed, I used Maclean's penetrating reconstruction of the response to the Storm King Mountain wildfire in my own course as a case study for several years.[37] Often, from such work we can better grasp the dynamics of human actions to improve our understanding of more quantitative reports that summarize human behavior in a very different format.

Nearly all of the information and insights contained in this book originated in the studies conducted by a new type of social scientist. We specialize in disasters. Our training varies, ranging from such disciplines as geography and economics to sociology and political science to anthropology, history, and psychology. Depending on our focus, we tend to ask slightly different types of questions. Psychologists probe into areas most economists never think about. Political scientists pose questions that contrast sharply to those explored by geographers. Despite this, we share much in common, both in methods and theory. All of us have a single aim—to better understand the nature of human behavior.

In contrast to physical scientists who study the dynamics of cloud physics or the stresses and strain patterns within the earth's crust, this community of research scholars has emerged only recently. Indeed, it was only in 1950 that the first field team was organized to study human responses across several American disasters. Directed by Charles E. Fritz, this group from the National Opinion Research Center (NORC) at the University of Chicago opened new doors through which many have entered during the last five decades.[38]

Prior to the NORC field teams, a young Episcopal priest, who had helped recover and bury some of the *Titanic* victims, narrowly missed death or injury when two ships collided near the harbor at Halifax, Nova Scotia, Canada on December 6, 1917. One of them was loaded with TNT, and the blast killed nearly 2,000 people and injured 9,000 others. About one and a half years following this massive explosion, Samuel

Henry Prince—the priest from Halifax—initiated doctoral studies at Columbia University. What better thesis topic than this catastrophe? He published what commonly is regarded as the first systematic study of the human side of disaster using the methods and theories of the social sciences.[39]

Like those who have followed Prince, these methods reflect four key principles. The first of these is *objectivity*. This does not mean that our data are value free. Data produced by social scientists are objective, but they also are biased and value laden. Where they differ from the observations offered by others, be they organizational executives, victims, or journalists, is that the biases are better explicated and controlled. We try to juxtapose the impressions of an event and the human responses to it from persons at different locations, both geographically and socially. What you see really does depend on where you sit. By integrating all of these views into a comparative portrait, more balanced and objective observations are derived.

The second principle is *typicality*. Think of a graph showing the height distribution of a college football team. Each player is more or less taller, or shorter, than all of the others. But the entire range of heights would fall within a rather narrow spectrum. None would be shorter than four feet, nor would any exceed seven feet. Indeed, if one did, he would be singled out as a real exception.

That is the point. Often, when people arrive at a disaster scene, the exception catches their eye. This especially is true for journalists who search for an angle. It will serve as a focal point for their story. Certain trained helpers, like mental health professionals, also are selective. Quite correctly, they are looking for those who are grieving the most; it is they who need help. At times, however, therapists' visions of disaster scenes reflect only their experiences with this small sector of the total population.

By focusing totally on exceptional cases, it is hard to maintain a search for the typical. Social scientists, in contrast, try to identify the range of behavior that comprises the typical response set rather than seeking only the exceptional.

There is *patterned variability*, however. That is the third principle. Think of the height distribution of the college football team again. Picture how that curve would contrast to one reflecting the basketball team. Both graphs demonstrate typicality, but they don't overlap with each other exactly. Basketball players are, on average, going to be taller than many football players. So too, when we contrast the responses to disaster by the elderly or children, we obtain pattern variations. These variations don't negate the principle of typicality. Rather, they increase our understanding of the human side of disaster. No single person is like any other, but all of us share certain behavior patterns with others, at least some others.

This brings us to the fourth principle, the concept of *generalization*. What made Prince's work so remarkable and valuable, you see, was his creative ability to use the Halifax explosion as a basis for generalizing. Every disaster, like every individual, is unique. But as human beings, there are many commonalities that we share with others of our species. Hence, knowing something about 200 disaster victims allows us to understand something about thousands of others.

Staff members of the NORC field teams examined nearly 100 events. They interviewed several hundred people to identify typical responses to these events. They also documented many areas of pattern variability. More recently, researchers associated with the Disaster Research Center at the University of Delaware, for example, are using databases of 400 and 500 different disasters from which to extract generalizations.

The downside of this principle is the specification of limitations. This is a very complex and difficult problem that researchers are working on currently.[40] What we know for sure is, that unguarded or reckless generalization across events is unacceptable. Human responses to wars or airplane bombings differ in important ways from those evoked by hurricanes, tornadoes, or earthquakes. So too, some responses differ across nation states. Mexicans do not behave exactly like Germans or Swiss in everyday life. So we shouldn't be surprised to learn that their responses differ a bit following an earthquake, for example. As more comparative research is completed during the next decade or two, we will be able to pin this matter down much better. In this way, similarities and differences among disasters reflecting different agents, cultures, and other sources of social constraint will be identified.

The bottom line? Consider all of the generalizations in this book as *guidelines*. Most will fit your community pretty well. But the exact application remains an art and probably always will. So be careful and keep a questioning mind. On the other hand, realize at the outset that everyone tends to think his or her community is unique. Our comparative database has demonstrated that the human condition reflects a lot of similarity. Mothers grieve over lost sons, and it doesn't matter what nation state they live in or what caused the death.

THE INSIGHTS

- New knowledge regarding human responses in disasters has been discovered. Unfortunately, these insights have remained locked in university libraries—gathering dust rather than being distributed or used widely.
- Due to a variety of social and technological changes, the danger level from environmental hazards is increasing. Most of these trends are not directly associated with changes in the physical dimension. Rather it is how and where we live. Disaster has many faces, and some of these reflect technological accidents while others are rooted in the despair of the disenfranchised or the ethnic and religious hatred of extremists who have little tolerance for the diversity among peoples.
- Beyond the increased frequency of destructive events—be they natural ones like tornadoes and hurricanes or human-caused crises, like toxic chemical spills—the potential for large catastrophes is increasing too. Most likely in our lifetime there will be another killer coastal hurricane, massive California earthquake, or a deadly influenza pandemic. In early 1990, we got a couple of previews—remember Hurricane Andrew and the Northridge earthquake? Then came the screeching wake-up call on the morning of September 11, 2001. Then came Katrina in fall 2005. What will the next 20 or 30 years bring?
- A new national resource, social scientists specializing in disaster research, has emerged over the past four decades. Beyond expanding our knowledge about human responses, many of these researchers assist in policy evaluation and review.
- Four key principles characterize the social science knowledge base regarding human responses to disasters: objectivity, typicality, patterned variability, and generalization.

3

Hear That Siren?

How do you warn people when they are in danger?[1] Research over the past four decades has taught us a lot. Some of this scientific knowledge has been applied in certain parts of the country, namely, coastal areas confronting hurricanes. That's the good news.

The bad news is that despite the increased need for community warning systems—because of flash floods, toxic chemical spills, tornadoes, terrorist threats, you name it—most local governments have not been convinced. So when needless death occurs, I still hear words like those spoken by a former sheriff of Larimer County, Colorado. Prior to the savage onslaught of mud-filled water that rushed down the Big Thompson Canyon in July 1976, this sheriff arrived at a campground. Later, he expressed his disappointment: "We warned them, but they wouldn't leave."

In the days following Hurricane Katrina, I was disappointed to again hear this same rhetoric. Some concluded that the inhumane evacuation experience at places like the Superdome or the New Orleans Convention Center was "earned" in a way: "Given all the warnings, how could those people be so stupid? Why didn't they leave?" Throughout this book I propose that it is the responsibility of government officials, especially those in emergency management, to design and implement warning systems that work. Blaming the victims is not an option. The lessons from the social sciences must be applied.

So this is the first lesson. Regardless of the content of the warning message, regardless of who or how the warning is conveyed, the initial human response is one of disbelief. That's right: disbelief, *not* panic. Yet researchers continue to interview local officials who delayed acting. They simply stalled for time. Precious minutes, sometimes hours, were lost because of their inaction: "Well, we didn't want to alarm people needlessly. We wanted to avoid panic."

That's the second lesson. Too often the myth of panic guides public officials. You see, they incorrectly assume that if people are warned, mass panic will occur. The result? Time is lost. And often, so are lives.

At this instant a horrifying flashback hit me. Such memories are one of the costs of listening to story after story of how people faced danger.

I am standing beside a mobile home in southeastern Colorado, near the little town of Las Animas to be exact. It is June 1965. Floodwaters spilled out of the banks of the Arkansas River. Slowly mud-filled syrup was moving east. It was projected to reach Kansas in two days. Local emergency officials were on top of things, or so they thought. A crest was expected about ten o'clock the next morning, and everyone would be ready. But during the night, intense rainfall pushed the Purgatoire into a monster. It feeds into the Arkansas there, from the south. So like a thief in the night, it hit them from behind—quite unexpectedly.

"Yeah, I heard a siren," the mobile home resident told me. "And what did I do? I rolled over and went back to sleep. Guess I figured it was just an ambulance run."

Fortunately, this young man's wife became restless upon hearing more sirens. Looking out to see what the noise was, she saw the water. It was nearly to the front door! She shook her husband.

"I looked out and told her we'd better get out while we could. I grabbed my jeans—that's all too—and ran into our baby's room. I waded. I mean, it was nearly to my waist when I got out the front door carrying her."

A happy ending. But too many experiences similar to this are not.

Three decades zipped by me very fast. Yet here I was again, another trailer park. Once again it was in Colorado, this time to the north. Ft. Collins, home of the Colorado State University Rams, is about 65 miles north of Denver. That night (June 28, 1997), five died in a trailer park that suddenly was flooded when rainwater from the west rushed through low-lying segments of the city. Once again cruiser sirens had sounded. Had it not been for heroic rescue efforts, many others would have perished.[2]

A siren in the night. Too easy to roll over. More than four decades ago, two researchers—Ray Mack and George Baker—documented that such *signals* do little more than heighten attention.[3] Alone, they do not constitute a warning. Yet where are most communities today? I suspect that Cheyenne, Wyoming, is above average, nationally speaking. Following a tornado there in 1979, the director of Laramie County/Cheyenne Civil

Defense told me that 40% of the city was out of range of his warning sirens. He had been unsuccessful with the county commissioners, who were confronting the pleas and priorities of others.

Of course, people living in Cheyenne are lucky today because of the emergency management program that was pushed forward. Following the 1979 tornado and a couple of major floods, funding for improvements in the community warning system was forthcoming. Yet these sirens will be nothing more than noise to many who will hear them someday when danger threatens. Many other places are much less well prepared. What about your town? Maybe it's one of the places where modern technologies, like a reverse 911 system, permits emergency officials to ring hundreds of home telephones within a few minutes. But maybe not. Do you know?

WHO PANICS AND WHY

But wait a minute. You're still back on panic. Can all of those news reports of people panicking be wrong? "I mean, what about those South American soccer games or hotel fires in places like Las Vegas?" Yeah, I wonder that too. Just then I had a flashback to the World Trade Center (WTC) towers on 9/11. Remember the jumpers? Certainly people panicked there, didn't they?

You can't imagine how frequently I have been challenged with that one. So before going on, let's clear the air. My point is this. When people hear a disaster warning—and I'll stand by my statement, only under very special circumstances is a siren even a warning—*they do not panic.*

If the warning is done properly, something we'll pursue in a few pages, they may sense mild anxiety. You know the feeling. Remember getting up before the class for your speech? Or if you are out of school, maybe it was the commissioners and you were submitting your budget. Or maybe you are like me and remember such feelings from childhood. Recall the first teacher who made you stand up in front of the class? Such feelings of anxiety are experienced all too often.

But mild anxiety is not panic—at least not in the sense that the term is used commonly. Right? Think of the typical movie scene: people running wildly, screaming, trampling over anything and anybody in the way. They look like cattle stampeding. While rare, that type of behavior by humans does happen. No, I didn't contradict myself. It does happen, just not very often. Soccer game stampedes are good illustrations. So are the 2001 attacks on the World Trade Center. But keep this in mind: While a

43

few did jump from locations high up within the WTC, thousands evacuated safely.

Solid evidence on victim behavior during numerous hotel, nursing home, and hospital fires has proven that most people behave quite rationally when danger threatens.[4] In 1980 there was a horrible fire at the MGM Grand Hotel in Las Vegas. It's a typical case illustration. According to the local coroner, those trapped didn't panic. Even those who died left evidence of highly rational, adaptive responses: "In a sense they had done almost the ABCs of what you should do," he has been quoted as saying.[5] Trapped in their rooms, 26 finally died because of smoke inhalation. Many had stuffed wet towels around doors trying desperately, I suppose, to keep toxic smoke out. Of course, nearly 700 were injured, and at least another 58 died who were located in stairwells, corridors, elevators, or on the casino level. Even in this most extreme form of entrapment, panic behavior was rare.

Some did panic, however. Typically, as the flames came closer a few jumped. Despite pleas from approaching rescuers, they could cope no longer. The internal push to seek escape, even if it meant probable death, no longer could be contained. And so, as we stared spellbound at the televised images of people leaping from the windows of the World Trade Center, we reinforced a myth and extend it.

Instances like this are very rare, however. And despite the tragedy of the WTC jumpers, we always need to remember the thousands who evacuated successfully. You see, for panic behavior to occur, three very special conditions have to coexist, which is almost never when disaster warnings are given. Dating back to research studies conducted during the early 1950s, Henry Quarantelli first assessed the nature and conditions of panic behavior in his master's thesis.[6] He reformulated the conditions slightly over the years, but the basic conclusion remains. The three conditions are as follows:

1. Individuals must have a perception of possible entrapment.
2. Individuals must sense powerlessness; there is nothing they can do to escape.
3. Individuals must have a feeling of social isolation or sole dependency upon themselves in the crisis.

While *aspects* of these may be present in many situations, the research literature clearly indicates the rarity of panic behavior. All three conditions have to be present, and seldom are they. Think of miners trapped hundreds of feet beneath the earth's surface in a closed shaft. Certainly this approximates these three conditions. Yet miners typically voice a continuing belief that help will come from above. Frequently it does before their oxygen is gone.[7]

Thus, they neutralize condition number three. Regardless of the objective situation, their behavior, like that of all of us, is guided by their perceptions of what they think others are doing or are going to do.

A detailed study by a researcher at the University of Cincinnati, Norris Johnson, reconfirmed these principles.[8] In 1977 there was a deadly fire at the Beverly Hills Supper Club. The club is in a suburb of Cincinnati, across the river in Southgate, Kentucky. Using transcripts of detailed interviews obtained by the local police with club patrons who were there that Memorial Day weekend, Norris exactingly reconstructed the exit routes of all survivors. First he recorded where the 165 people who died were found. Then he identified where they had been seated prior to the fire. These interviews clearly documented that the *initial* response was one of order and assistance to those needing it. While many were told to slow down, most survivors reported that there was no panic.[9]

Then Quarantelli's three conditions started to take form. The consequence? Yeah, that's right! But Norris's analysis is most instructive:

> Strong evidence that primary groups did not break down permeates the transcripts…. No evidence appears of family members abandoning each other in order to facilitate their own survival. In fact, there are instances of both family members and friends assisting others when to do so constituted a threat….[10]

You know, there is another lesson here worth pondering. It is a bit of a diversion, but the scenic loop is worth it. Behavioral studies of trapped coal miners reveal little panic behavior, in part because they neutralize condition number three. Okay. Now think for a minute about what typically is labeled citizen apathy. So often I hear it, especially at some emergency management conferences: "But they don't care about emergency management. Disaster preparedness just can't be sold." I say—excuses! Excuses for not doing your job.

I am aware of many public opinion polls. Indeed, a national survey by Peter Rossi and his colleagues[11] clearly indicated that natural hazards ranked lower in priority on the local political agenda than pornography. That is, most local political leaders were more concerned about curbing porn shows than floodwaters. Within the myriad problems facing communities, who speaks out for improved hazard management? Who is the interest group that cares?

In part, I believe that many people, like the trapped coal miners, believe that if threatened "they will warn us." You see—no one has told them the truth. No one has told them that proposed *effective* warning systems have been axed repeatedly. Of course, that's only in communities where warning systems have been proposed. Many places have not even gotten to the proposal stage.

The next time you hear someone bitching about public apathy, recall the coal miners. You see, I believe that much of the public thinks emergency managers are doing their jobs. Someone will see to it that they are warned if the need arises. Right? Boy, if they only knew. But whose job is it to tell them? Get the point?

The survey data are very clear on this point. In general, most citizens accept disaster planning as an acceptable and appropriate function of government. Just like any other public attitude, however, the question can be posed to demonstrate apathy and low priority. The public expects disaster planning to be done by local, state, and federal governments rather than left to individuals or ignored totally. But they expect a lot of other things too. So, if asked to choose between emergency management and many other public services, be it potholes, pornography, or whatever, we can expect the choice to favor what is most obvious and immediate. Disaster preparedness ranks low, but they still expect it to be done. We'll return to this point and its implications in the final chapter.

NEUTRALIZING THREAT INFORMATION

Okay. The scenic loop is over; let's get back to warning responses. So people don't panic when they get a warning; what do they do? Well, as you might suspect, that varies. We have, however, gotten a handle on important patterns in that variation. I'll get to these in just a minute, but beyond disbelief and denial there is another general response. Just as the coal miners neutralize condition number three—no help from above—so too, most people take the sting out of a warning by reinterpreting it. You would never believe how effectively they do this.

You see, most people are quite creative. And active too. So they hear a warning, and what do they do? Immediately, some will turn on a radio or TV. If regular programming is continuing, the warning may be discounted or at least reduced in urgency. Typically, their reasoning goes something like this: "I mean, if it was anything important, why would they still be showing this situation comedy?" Dozens of disaster victims I have interviewed personally gave responses just like that following floods, tornadoes, and hurricanes.

Following the 1965 flood along the South Platte River, which bisects Denver, I was told of a woman who illustrates this creative side of human responses. Now Denver is not noted for frequent floods. Did you know that for decades, outdoor water use has been restricted? We are allowed to water our lawns only every third day. And during drought years, we are limited to two days a week. Though not a desert, in Denver water is a precious and expensive resource.

I still recall my first reaction in June 1965. I was entering a Holiday Inn in Effingham, Illinois, and spotted front-page photographs with a screaming headline. We were returning to the Disaster Research Center (DRC) after vacationing in Colorado and participating in my brother's wedding. The DRC was located at The Ohio State University back then. That's where it was founded in 1963. When Henry Quarantelli relocated to the University of Delaware in 1985, he moved the DRC there and once again rejoined his longtime friend, Russ Dynes, and former student, Dennis Wenger.

"Look," I later said to my wife, Ruth Ann, "there's newspaper sensationalism. How could they have a flood like that; hell, they can't even water their grass!"

How wrong I was. We arrived in Columbus, Ohio, the next day, about 4 in the afternoon. Guess who was in the air—Denver bound—at 3:00 a.m.? One of the dozens of emergency officials I interviewed there recounted his experience. He was a police officer in Littleton, the first suburb in the Denver area that the floodwaters reached.

He had passed by house after house with his bullhorn blasting the warning: "A twenty-foot wall of water is approaching this area. You have five to fifteen minutes to evacuate. Leave for high ground immediately." Upon completing his assigned route, he noticed that one woman was still sitting in her porch swing. As he listened to updates over his radio, however, he saw some mothers herding children into cars. When he got back to the corner the third time, the woman was gone.

He listened momentarily. Exchanges over the police network confirmed the damage at the town of Castle Rock and other areas to the south. It was closing in on the metro area. It was for real: "Good thing we warned them," he was thinking. But now, here this woman was standing at the side window of his cruiser. Her line was classic; the question sincere: "What theater is this at?" Apparently, she had mistaken the disaster warning for a movie promotion!

Now that's what I mean by a creative response! An active interpretation of information to make it fit into an ongoing social situation. A movie ad? Sure! A legitimate flood warning? Come on. Not here where we hardly have enough water to keep our lawns green.

In contrast to panic behavior, the typical human response to disaster warnings is disbelief, denial, and reinterpretation to reduce or eliminate the threat potential. Even when people are convinced by various messages that a flood is coming, they often counter with defensive interpretations. They are invulnerable: "Any flooding is going to hit those other folks, not us. We're on high ground here; the water never could get way up here."

DOING IT RIGHT

"Okay. So, what can be done? How can we do it right?"

Well, the first step is to learn from Harry Williams. He too participated in the early studies—those conducted at the University of Chicago by staff of the National Opinion Research Center (NORC). Like Quarantelli's work on panic, subsequent research has validated Williams's conclusion.[12] An effective warning message must include (1) information about the threat, and (2) advice about what to do. It is not enough to try to convince people they are in danger. You must provide them with clear options about protective actions.

Realize that few will think of their house as being in a "low-lying area." Such vague boundaries easily permit neutralization. Message content must be *precise*. Even if you are a bit uncertain about what is coming, don't convey this. Remember: Every possible interpretation to foster normalcy, a rationale for doing nothing, will be forthcoming.

So the message content must be precise.

- What is threatening?
- Who is threatened? That is, what specific geographic areas are at risk?
- When is it coming?
- What protective action should be taken?

Be aware. This last element can save lives. People must be told what to do. One response emergency officials should anticipate, especially in flash floods and tornadoes, is the tendency of many people to rely on their car.

Think about it. When most of us want a loaf of bread, we jump into our car and drive six or seven blocks to get it.

Following analysis of the 144 deaths in the Big Thompson Canyon flood (July 1976), signs appeared throughout the state. Let me explain why. You see, some people finally were convinced that they might be in danger, so they tried to drive away. That proved to be a deadly error.

I still recall my helicopter survey up that canyon a few days later. Wherever the river turned, huge chunks had been taken out of Highway 34. Empty cars sat. Who can imagine the terror their occupants must have felt? Of course, at some of these breaks, others had rounded a curve and driven off into the new riverbed. They never had a chance. Inside these cars were many bodies that were recovered miles downstream.[13]

A washed-out highway is not an escape route. "Climb to Safety," the signs say. People do have to be told. Maybe seeing these signs repeatedly will save future lives. Over the years, some other nearby communities have implemented these potential lifesavers.

In April 1979, the director of the Wichita Falls Risk Management Department (Texas) told me of people who were inside shopping centers. Upon learning that a tornado was headed their way, into their cars they went. I guess they believed they could drive out of its path. Others were driving home when the warnings were issued.

Research results were conclusive: 60% of those killed and 51% of those injured were seeking escape in their cars.[14] Lying in a ditch on the roadside would have been safer. Since publication of these findings, some National Weather Service (NWS) warning messages contain appropriate advice. Would this lifesaving information be included in messages aired within your town?

Actually, reality is more complex than these last sentences imply. As our research base has grown, it turns out that running for a ditch may not be best under all tornado circumstances. Indeed, there are documented cases of people doing just that and still being killed. Example? "In 1999, a woman and a fifteen year old girl were killed near Logan, Iowa when they took shelter in a ditch, and their abandoned car and a 3-ton soybean head from a combine were blown on top of them...."[15]

When researcher John Farley looked into the knowledge base on advising people to run for a ditch, he documented many ripples. First, he discovered that at least two researchers determined that there was no evidence to support the claim that ditches were safer than automobiles. Second, as I also learned when I got to Moore, Oklahoma, after the May 3, 1999, tornado, many who were killed or injured were trying to get to their cars. They got caught outside. Third, official guidelines from the NWS are ambiguous.[16] That is, ditches and overpasses are less safe than strong buildings, but they may provide "limited protection." And finally, individual local weather offices have considerable discretion in the wording of tornado warning messages, on the theory that "it depends."[17]

After detailed review of 510 tornado warning messages (i.e., all that were issued by all NWS local offices between August 1, 2004, and July 30, 2005) and interviews with meteorologists in seven NWS offices in different parts of the country, Farley came up with two key policy recommendations:

1. Depending on their knowledge of local terrain, roadways, and the like, NWS offices should have more discretion regarding the advice they give.
2. Despite national pressure for uniformity and standardization, local NWS offices should continue to have at least as much discretion as they now have in the types of warning messages they design for specific tornado threats.[18]

So once again, reality turns out to be complex. My best advice is to take tornado warnings very seriously. Look for the best shelter available, and stay put. Unless you are certain you can improve your survival odds by driving away, look for an overpass or a ditch. Hopefully, the ditch will be deep enough to keep you safe.

Building on Williams's insights and on those I produced through study of the Denverites' responses to the 1965 flood, Dennis Mileti assessed the 1972 flash flood in Rapid City.[19] He continued refining the steps for effective warnings. Later he, Janice Hutton, and John Sorensen—along with some colleagues—examined the awesome challenges presented by earthquake prediction technology, nuclear power plants, and chemical manufacturing and storage facilities.[20]

Sharpened by Mileti's analysis of the Rapid City case, the trio underscored the importance of a critical linkage. They call it the *evaluation–dissemination subsystem*. This subsystem is composed of a collection of agencies. It fills the gap between the actual agent, say, approaching floodwaters, and you hearing a warning message over TV. For any hazard, this subsystem has seven functional components. Typically there are numerous organizations involved in each function. As you read each, try to think of an agency in your community that should be involved if a tornado threatened. Would the mix of agencies change if the threat was a flood or a group of terrorists holding an airplane and its passengers hostage?

The seven functions are as follows:

1. Detection
2. Measurement
3. Collation
4. Interpretation
5. Decision to warn
6. Message content
7. Dissemination

To do it right—to do part of the emergency management job, really—each of these seven functions must be preplanned carefully. Who will detect an approaching flood, for example? How will that information be communicated to others? Once detected, what measurement systems will be used to get adequate precision? Stream gauges? Rain gauges? Okay. But located where? Who has the technical capacity to interpret this information to know who should be warned? These principles have been validated by dozens of researchers in the decades since these early formulations.[21]

The Denver flood of 1965 first brought this home to me very dramatically. Officials throughout the metro area knew of massive destruction thirty-some miles upstream. The Douglas County Sheriff had radioed word to the Colorado State Patrol. Yet no one could interpret what the implication of this information was for the metro area. No measurements were available. Deciding which locations should be evacuated was most unclear.

Maybe the wall of water down there would just flatten out and be handled safely by the river channel. Maybe. What no one anticipated were the piles of debris that the rising water picked up as it moved into the metro area. This included mobile homes, the contents of a lumber yard, and similar such things. All of it jammed up against the bridges. As this happened, these thin, connecting arteries were ripped loose. One after another they toppled, leaving the City of Denver cut in half.

Later, it was determined that the actual path of destruction conformed almost perfectly to the 100-year flood line projected years earlier by the U.S. Army Corps of Engineers. Their maps could have been used to establish, and even disseminate, evacuation limits. In fact, a few years later when a parallel threat occurred, this was done. Under the leadership of the then director of the Denver Office of Emergency Preparedness, the multiple set of agencies got their act together. Cranes stationed on bridges removed debris as it collected. Not a single bridge was lost. But in 1965, the lack of agency coordination was astounding.

I hate to say it, but surveys completed by university research teams continue to indicate serious communication failures among the agencies— including federal, state, and local—that collectively have this responsibility.[22] It is not an easy task. Too frequently telephone lines fail when they are most needed. As a result, some, like a team from the University of Minnesota, have found public resentment. They documented negative attitudes, even anger, in most of the two dozen or so communities surveyed. Following the response to Hurricane Katrina (2005), community disappointment spilled over into many sections of the entire country. While thousands of lives were saved, the Katrina response will long be remembered as one of the worst failures in the short history of emergency management.

I, too, have walked into such hostile settings. Among the places where this was most acute for me personally was in the Hill Country of Texas. There, during August 1979, many were not warned. Or rather, they did not perceive the noises, mainly sirens on emergency vehicles, as warnings. People died there too, just like they have in hundreds of flash floods since then.

The three components described by Williams were not there. The seven functions outlined by Mileti, Hutton, and Sorensen were not performed, at least not well. And so people died. At least two dozen drowned along the Medina River and two creeks that dump into the Guadalupe— the Cypress and Verde.

Some were lucky. Someone cared. Typically, warnings that worked did not originate with employees of emergency organizations. Rather, relatives and friends got out of bed and notified those in the flood path—sometimes by telephone, other times in person. This is another lifesaver. Think it over. The results from my Denver flood survey have been validated in numerous other studies. Ron Perry and Marjorie Greene first reconfirmed this pattern following the explosive 1980 eruption of Mount St. Helens.[23] Since then the pattern has been documented in places as varied as Hawaii, Washington State, Massachusetts, and Florida.[24]

What pattern? Well, it is a pattern of unofficial warning. You see, in Denver, I found that more than one fourth (26%) of the 278 families interviewed received the first warnings from relatives, friends or neighbors. Nearly one-half were alerted by the media. Since the initial threat was detected in the middle of that June afternoon (3:00p.m.), many were enjoying radio or television entertainment. In the flash flooding of Rapid City or the Texas Hill Country, media alerts were less influential due to the late hour. Few had their TV on at three o'clock in the morning! Here the pattern of unofficial warnings was far more important. Perry and his associates have documented this pattern following several other disasters after their work on Mount St. Helens.[25]

So? What is the point? When lives are endangered shouldn't emergency officials seek to augment the warning process in any way possible? I may delay or creatively reinterpret their warning message, be it delivered in person or via TV. But what if my brother-in-law calls and asks, "When are you guys leaving?" We may just be persuaded. Even if we think he is overreacting, you know how brothers-in-laws are—that call may cause us to check further.

Not only should those in the threatened area be told what to do, but also the enormous resource citizens represent should be recognized. If circumstances permit, encourage them to contact friends or relatives who might be in the area at risk. Perhaps they didn't get the word. Maybe they reinterpreted it.

What I am stressing is this: Forget the abomination you always have heard previously—you know, that in an emergency, people should stay off the telephone. Forget it!

When a threat appears, many people will ignore this advice anyway. And it's a good thing. Some of these conversations will push people into taking actions they wouldn't have otherwise. Lives will be saved. Equally importantly, givers of such advice will be seen as being incompetent: "I wonder if those guys really know what they are doing? If I hadn't called my sister, she and her family would be dead."

You see, when Sally Cummings's mother called the hotel in Hawaii, she was reflecting a common and well-documented pattern of human behavior (recall "The Honeymoon" in Chapter 1). When your kids are on their honeymoon trip to Hawaii, you really don't want to bother them. But if there is a hurricane alert, you do want to be sure they know about it.

During disaster, the official emergency management functions in a community should not be conducted over publicly accessible telephone lines. Should public lines become overloaded, as they almost always do, that too may be a cue to some that they are at risk. Things are not okay. Typically, emergency managers need all the help they can get for people to take warning messages seriously—to push them out of bed, away from the dinner table, or whatever. To act!

BUT NOT EVERYONE RESPONDS THE SAME

No, not everyone responds the same. There are patterned differences in public responses to disaster warnings. Many have been validated across several studies. As additional research, like Mike Lindell and Ron Perry's investigation of minority group responses, is completed over the next few years, our knowledge base will be expanded.[26] We still have a lot to learn. Yet *far more is known than is being applied*. That is the tragedy.

No, it's worse than a tragedy. Many tragedies cannot be avoided. This could be. The day has arrived, however, when court actions are bringing this point home. Victims, or in some cases their families, have been awarded compensation because a jury concluded that officials did not meet their responsibilities in building an adequate warning system. Persons who occupy positions of public safety can be found guilty if they fail to apply these research insights. What kind of defense is it to state that people did not respond to your warnings? It's really the warning system that is at fault, not the victims. See the point?

Not everyone responds the same way to hearing a TV announcement about an approaching flood or tornado. What are some of these differences? Well, let's briefly review six of these.[27]

Females

Since the earliest work on civil defense warning systems, like that of Mack and Baker, which I mentioned at the beginning of this chapter, studies have demonstrated that females are more likely to believe a disaster warning message. For whatever reason, maybe male reluctance to admit danger, women are less skeptical and more willing to take adaptive action. Not all females, mind you; there is patterned variability. Some females will resist, just like men typically do. As a group, however, females respond quicker. They are easier to convince that the threat may be real. During the response to Hurricane Katrina, researchers documented that gender was the most significant and consistent quality that influenced evacuation decisions.[28]

Children

Kids too are more apt to believe disaster warnings. This is especially true of primary school-aged children. Often, they will press their parents: "But why aren't we going to leave?" While they didn't believe they really were at risk, I have talked with many parents who said they left their homes primarily because their children questioned them. The kids were scared. Their parents decided it was easier to leave than trying to convince their kids that the TV announcements were wrong. This really came home to me during interviews with employees of business firms in several communities threatened during the late 1990s.[29]

Ethnic Minorities

Hispanics, Blacks, and other minority members are less likely to respond adaptively because of skepticism. Why? Whether we like to admit it, the fact is many ethnic minorities have been treated by police and other government employees in ways they view as unfair, maybe even brutal. Also, our newest minorities, those from South American nations and locations in Southeast Asia, come from a history of police relationships rooted in fear. Even when language is not a barrier, which it often is with these groups by the way, they evidence more suspicion upon hearing official messages urging them to leave their homes.

Elderly

Not only are members of this group more skeptical, but they are also less likely to receive warning messages initially. Here is where the encouragement of citizen contact can make a critical difference. Oftentimes, however, a lot of years of experience effectively neutralize threat information. Lack of precision in warning messages feeds their experience base: "We have lived here 50 years, and it ain't gotten into our house yet. Those young guys down at City Hall are overreacting. Ain't no way it can flood here."

If warned properly elderly citizens will leave. But they take more convincing. Usually the messages received are vague enough that there are plenty of opportunities for creative reinterpretation. Often, however, they never get the warning message. Because they are less likely to be warned, they are more likely to drown. Far more elderly died in the 1972 Rapid City flood that did middle-aged or younger citizens. Unfortunately, this tragic pattern has been documented repeatedly since then.[30]

Experience

This turns out to be a double-edged sword. Some elderly survive terrible storms like Katrina or Rita. More recently (September 2008), I watched TV reporters interview some who ignored the warnings issued prior to Hurricane Ike's arrival in Galveston Island and the Houston, Texas, area. Almost all had the same story: "Next time I'll leave. I'll never go through something like this again."

But some who stayed in sturdy structures pointed to their success: "Guess we were safer here than out in those lines of traffic." In contrast, weeks earlier, Gustav's path was projected to bring it into the New Orleans area. I suspect that many residents and local officials alike had the images of Katrina well in mind. So this time most were ready to go, especially since public transportation was made available.

Yet over and over again, be it in flood-prone areas or in the Outer Banks of North Carolina, various faces of those with experience pop up for me. They have been spared time and again. "We _____s [insert a last name of your choice] never leave. This is our home, and it can handle hurricanes" (or floods, if in other parts of the country). That is the "double-edge" of the "sword" of experience.

Economics

Both one's job and socioeconomic status impact warning responses. If your job requires you to be around certain risky technologies or situations, there is a tendency to minimize the risk over time. Fishermen have been found to exhibit this pattern difference. So did loggers working around Mount St. Helens and employees at Three Mile Island and other nuclear power plants. When you are around a risky technology every day, especially if your income depends on it, you tend to neutralize the danger.

People at the bottom and the very top of the income chart also are less responsive to disaster warnings. This income pattern is confounded somewhat by ethnic group status, however, and results across studies are not totally consistent. Alternative interpretations have been offered too. Two that seem reasonable to me are as follows: (1) The poor remain more suspicious of authorities; and (2) the wealthy figure they know better. I can recall interviewing folks of both types. Some of the rich have expressed contempt: "Those clowns down at City Hall stirred this thing up just so they could look important." The view from the other side of the tracks reflected fear and distrust: "Why did they want to know who else was living here, anyway? What are they up to?"

This really hit me during the initial response to Hurricane Katrina. So after watching people wade through the toxic soup that flowed throughout much of New Orleans, I decided to write an essay to deal with some of my anger and acute disappointment. American citizens waited at the Superdome, the Convention Center, and elsewhere as officials held press conferences and publicly stated that evacuation assistance was on the way. And as thousands were plucked from rooftops and other dangerous places by skilled rescue teams in helicopters, many again asked, "Why didn't they leave?"

In my essay I tried to communicate to emergency managers the reality behind the statistical charts that many of us had generated for years. The reality of poverty is difficult for those who never have known it. So I proposed that emergency managers must realize that social factors can be just as constraining as physical dimensions. Many poor people have very narrow limits on the degrees of freedom they perceive both in their daily lives and when a disaster occurs.

> Thinking beyond the immediate is difficult at best. Often, it is so terrifying that it is far easier not to choose at all. Without hope, choice is seen as a fiction. And, for most of the poor, hope is a fleeting experience if they know it at all.[31]

A migrant family in a community near the Florida Everglades just popped into my mind. They had been warned by several officials—some they referred to as "the police"—that Hurricane Andrew was approaching and that they should leave their residence and go to a shelter. Apparently, more than one alternative for shelter was given, including a small public school and Florida Atlantic University. But they told me, my wife, and our interpreter that they didn't know how to get there. The straw through which they viewed the world simply was too limiting. So they hunkered down while the camp was ripped to shreds. Such are among the many costs of poverty.

These qualities of individuals tell only one part of the story, however. There are two other critical factors: (1) message characteristics; and (2) group context. That is, what are the characteristics of effective warning messages? And second, who are you with when you receive a warning message?

Message Characteristics

Authorities are more likely to produce adaptive behavior than any other source. This one quality, that is, message source, makes a big difference. This does not mean that a message from a police officer always will be believed fully. People still reserve the right to know what is probable. Yet more people are more likely to take the matter seriously if the message is received from legitimate authority.

What they actually do after getting a warning message is quite another matter. That is the topic we pursue in the next chapter in considerable detail. But face-to-face contact with an individual perceived to be an authority, a police officer at your door, for example, is more likely to produce a high degree of concern than any other message source.

A second quality of warning messages is content. The greater the degree of vagueness and ambiguity, the less the response. Why? Simply because there is more opportunity for creative interpretation. These interpretations are done to reduce the sense of threat, to heighten the sense of invulnerability.

In contrast to the content and source of a warning message is the matter of consistency. This is a real problem in large urban areas where numerous media organizations may be in competition. After hearing a warning on the radio, a family member may turn on the TV. Often the person obtains message variations that serve to neutralize. Any discrepancy will be used to justify inaction: "See, they really don't know what's coming."

Group Context

Groups process most warning messages. Why? Maybe you have never thought much about it, but most of us are in some type of group most of the day—if not a family or work group, then with friends, relatives, or in recreational groups. Who we are with when we receive a disaster warning makes a big difference in how we respond.

Because they talk more with relatives and more frequently answer the telephone, females are more apt to receive the warning message for the family. When they are home, children pick them up first on television. What happens next? Discussion follows. Typically, males respond by suggesting that media reports are being exaggerated. It is up to the wife and younger children to convince the husband and older males that the danger is real. They urge taking adaptive action. It is they who will propose heading for the basement in a tornado or getting out in a flood or hurricane.

So? What's the point? Maybe it's obvious—maybe not. Those responsible for community warnings should act just like marketing experts; that is, messages should be aimed at those most likely to buy. I—as an American male—may never be convinced. Since I will be in a group context that often includes my wife or children, just to shut them up I may go along with whatever emergency precaution is recommended.

This is what I mean by *using* social science knowledge to increase the effectiveness of emergency management. The time is past when officials can get away with blaming the victims. It is their job, not potential victims', to know how to use this knowledge to save lives.

Recall the sheriff's words? I mentioned them at the outset of this chapter: "We warned them, but they wouldn't leave." To him, and others trying to rationalize their own failures, I asked the obvious question: "Why didn't you use available social science knowledge to build a warning system that would have gotten them to safety?" Before he passed away, this sheriff became a vocal advocate for using social science knowledge to improve community warning systems. He recognized that the time for excuses is over.

People are people. If respected as such they will respond adaptively. But they must be warned properly. It's the responsibility of emergency managers to know how to do it correctly. Armed with that information, county commissioners and city council members can then be confronted quite forcefully. Whenever possible, I put it to them like this: "Do you want to let them drown, or shall we build a proper warning system? The choice is yours; you can pay a little now or pay a lot later."[32]

There are exceptions to the overall patterns, however. Though less frequent than evacuations stimulated by various natural disasters, hazardous materials sometimes produce "overreactions." Graniteville, South Carolina, provides a good case example.[33] Early one winter morning (January 6, 2007, 12:39 a.m.) a freight train missed a switch and crashed into a parked locomotive. Sixty tons of chlorine were released when a tank car ruptured. Nine people died after inhaling this highly toxic chemical; 550 others obtained medical help.

Initially, residents were instructed to "shelter in place." Minutes later a mandatory evacuation order was issued to all residing within a one-mile radius from the spill. Local officials reported that more than 5,000 people got out of town.[34]

The study team—Jerry Mitchell, Susan Cutter, and Andrew Edmonds—conducted two mail surveys to assess the evacuation response. Information was obtained from people who resided within the mandatory evacuation area and others who chose to evacuate even though they were not explicitly told to do so. In sharp contrast to the denial pattern I have emphasized, these survey results documented a clear overreaction. More precisely, the study team estimated "...that an additional 1,215 to 1,742 people who were not instructed to evacuate left the area."[35]

The conclusion? Accidents involving hazardous materials, especially those involving chemical or nuclear materials, are perceived as being more risky than most natural disasters. Consequently, "...evacuations in response to chemical accidents are characterized by an extreme over-response."[36] Many scholars use the term *shadow evacuations* to refer to cases like these. But, you should realize that because of the uncertainty in predicting the exact path of a large hurricane, for example, there frequently are some who decide to be extra cautious. So they leave even though the probability of harm is nonexistent or extremely low at best.

THE INSIGHTS

- Disbelief, not mass panic, is the typical initial response to disaster warnings.
- A siren—like any other noise—is not a warning; at best it may alert some, but many will ignore it.
- Panic behavior, though extremely rare, will occur if people are caught in unique situations characterized by three conditions (recall them?).
- Warning messages must include both threat information and directions for adaptive actions.
- The greater the specificity of the information given, the more likely people are to believe it.
- Warning systems are composed of seven key functions; failure on any one means that people die.
- There are variations in response: Women and children are more likely to believe, and males, elderly, poor, and ethnic minorities are less likely.
- Warnings received from individuals perceived to be authorities (e.g., a uniformed police officer at the door) are more likely to be believed than those coming from any other type of source.

- Typically, groups receive and process warning messages, not single individuals in total isolation from others.
- Warning messages should be aimed at those most likely to believe; let them convince the others.
- Don't waste your breath telling people to stay off the phone—they won't comply anyway. Instead, recognize this resource; encourage them to contact people they think might have missed the warning or who may be reluctant to believe it.
- Evacuations stimulated by chemical, nuclear, or other types of hazardous materials, often produce overresponse (i.e., higher rates of shadow evacuations).
- And most importantly, don't blame the victims! It is the responsibility of emergency managers and other public safety officials to build and implement warning systems that work.

4

It Can't Be Done

Frequently I read remarks by people who say it can't be done. They dogmatically claim that traffic accidents, mass panic, and public fears of looting preclude evacuation of cities threatened by certain types of risks. Nuclear power plant accidents seem to be a favorite whipping boy. Needless to say, their training and expertise is not in the social sciences. Yet they offer those opinions as scientific fact. The myths persist, oftentimes nurtured by false prophets.

Unfortunately, exceptional cases of failure contribute to the mythology that surrounds disaster evacuation. For example, millions of Americans caught segments of television coverage during and following Hurricane Katrina's arrival in September 2005. They watched frightened people wade through filthy floodwaters—toxic soup really! As hundreds streamed toward the Superdome, New Orleans Convention Center, or some other place of refuge, others were being plucked from rooftops by skilled helicopter rescue teams.

The fact that about 80% of the population had heeded the warnings and left before Katrina's arrival is not remembered. Rather, images of pain and despair are what stick. It is images like these from Katrina that reinforce the myth that it can't be done.

Truth be told, hundreds of American cities have been evacuated successfully. As a result, thousands of lives have been saved. These experiences don't register with everyone, however. Improved understanding of the evacuation process—indeed, just putting into application what is known already—could mold local policy developments into lifesaving weapons. Fortunately, for the United States, this is occurring in many local communities, especially in those that are hurricane prone. But too often, hurricane preparedness does not get implemented in ways that carry over to other threats, be they hazardous materials or terrorists.

THAT LADY NAMED CARLA

Despite the continuing popularity of myth to the contrary, cities can and have been evacuated successfully. That has not always been the case. Did you realize that at least 390 died when Hurricane Audrey smashed into the Gulf Coast in 1957?[1] And think of the death tolls in places like Haiti, Grenada, and other Caribbean nations.

Some survivors learned, however. So beyond picking up the pieces, a matter we'll dissect later, a few had vision. With horror, they foresaw recurrence. But they also dreamed. They started with a premise of conquering. It could be done! Their actions since are living proof to the rest of us that it can be done.

So, in 1961, when Audrey's sister—Hurricane Carla—arrived, it happened. More than 500,000 persons evacuated their homes before she got there. Equally successful, and lifesaving, have been dozens of subsequent hurricane evacuations. I still vividly recall fall 1992, when Andrew and Iniki came calling. Hundreds of lives could have been lost, but few were. While any death during a hurricane is sad, fall 2004 was further validation of my point. Recall that foursome—Charley, Frances, Ivan, and Jeanne? Once again hundreds of lives were saved despite the miles of wind-damaged and flooded homes.

And then came Katrina! Had the levees not failed, dozens still would have died because of her winds and enormous storm surge. But most deaths—like more than 1,000 in the New Orleans area—resulted from drowning. Momentarily they thought they had dodged a bullet. Once the levees gave way, "the bowl" filled rapidly. Thousands who had stayed home faced a frightening challenge. Despite all of the improvements in hurricane warning systems, Katrina stands as a haunting reminder of the work that awaits us.

But let's back up a bit. For example, the power of basic social science principles, when applied properly, first became evident to the commissioners in Pinellas County, Florida, in 1985 when Hurricane Elena threatened. The largest peacetime medical evacuation in our nation's history was coordinated effectively. Plans had been developed and exercised. While there were problems, overall these plans worked. Although 4 people died and 471 were injured, 76 of which required hospitalization, this massive evacuation saved thousands. You see, among the more than 350,000 persons who were evacuated, 211 were patients in one of three hospitals and 1,860 were residents of nineteen nursing homes.[2]

Following Elena came others, of course. For example, in 1988 prior to Hurricane Gilbert officials on Galveston Island, Texas, decided to get people out. Gilbert left Jamaica paralyzed and then unexpectedly veered sharply to the west before it crashed into the Mexican coastline just south of Corpus Christi, Texas. Although they were spared the damage from Gilbert, the city manager and his emergency management team effectively applied social science principles to get people to safer areas.

Shortly thereafter, I interviewed more than two dozen managers of tourist-oriented businesses in Galveston who remembered Gilbert well. Despite the false alarm, they unanimously supported the evacuation decision. Given the storm path projections, the lead time required to get people off Galveston Island, and the fact that further delays could have put the evacuation effort into the middle of the night, their words reflected a clear-cut consensus: "Given the information he had, it was a tough call. But he did the right thing."[3]

This same attitude prevailed three weeks after Katrina, when Rita came calling. Her target loomed just west of New Orleans. Once again Galveston was in the bull's eye. Millions elected to move inland, not just the islanders but many in Houston as well. This time, however, the system worked. Oh yes, there were problems. Long lines of traffic crept toward Dallas at a snail's pace. Some ran out of gas and discovered that filling stations had too. But the contrast to the tragedy that defined Katrina clearly demonstrated the progress made in hurricane warning systems. That progress reflected changes made during the two prior decades.

For example, one year after Gilbert (1988) came Hugo. While they were less effective than they now realize they could have been, state and local officials in northern Florida and along the South Carolina coastline told me how their microcomputers aided them in the extensive evacuations.[4] Here again, hundreds of lives were spared because this new technology was integrated with basic social science principles. Follow-up surveys that were completed after this evacuation reconfirmed what many of us had reported earlier.[5] These parallels reappeared in mid-August 1991, when 50,000 tourists fled prior to Hurricane Bob's brush past the string of islands that comprise North Carolina's Outer Banks. Since Bob, this area has been impacted by other hurricanes such as Emily (1993), Felix (1995), Fran (1996), and Floyd (1999).

In short, since the successful evacuation of numerous communities following Hurricane Carla in 1961, there have been dozens of repeats. The myth ought to die. It has been done!

That's not to say all the problems have been solved. They haven't. Katrina was evidence of that. But another of Katrina's lessons is that failure to implement social science knowledge will result in death.

A DISASTER SUBCULTURE?

The adaptive responses to Hurricane Carla led the late Harry E. Moore and his colleagues to further explore a concept that Moore had invented earlier. *Disaster subcultures* seemed to be present in Waco, San Angelo, and other tornado-threatened Texas communities.[6] Just as specialized planning has evolved to help managers deal with the mind-boggling array of problems associated with staging a Super Bowl, so too have repeated threats generated local wisdom.

Moore applied the more general notion of subcultures to penetrate aspects of these community responses. Previously, this concept had been applied by social scientists studying delinquent gangs and ethnic groups. Like the customs that guide a Polish Catholic enclave in Chicago through a wedding or funeral, so too Moore documented local customs that aided Texas families in adapting to these dancing funnels of death. These customs range from family agreements to retreat to the cellar to local emergency agency agreements regarding their respective roles. They can represent disaster planning at its best![7]

By reviewing the responses to Carla, Moore and his colleagues—Fred Bates, Marvin Layman, and Vernon Parenton—documented several new weapons that were being blended into old response traditions.[8] Most notably, of course, was the multiagency warning system that tracked Carla's path. Millions of Americans watched her progress through TV reports that took viewers from city to city along the Gulf Coast. Sound familiar?

The multiagency hurricane warning system probably is the strongest point in our nation's warning capability. It is a key element in the disaster subculture that permeates hurricane-threatened coastal areas today. Subsequent evacuations, like those prior to Hurricanes Gilbert, Hugo, and Andrew, clearly reflect the legacy of Carla, Camille, and their relatives. Prior to reading the first pages of this chapter, did you know that more than 300,000 people got out before Hurricane Elena hit Pinellas County, Florida? That was in 1985. Oh, yes. Local officials had their hands full.

But they did it. Afterward they completed a detailed review of what went right and what went wrong. Since then, they have done even better.[9] So have those in other communities who benefited from research applications stimulated by such assessments.

I have conducted a large number of interviews in hurricane-prone communities during the past twenty years in counties like Pinellas, Indian River, and Nassau, Florida, for example. In these places, capable emergency management officials reflect the modern versions of disaster subcultures. Elaborate computer-based hurricane tracking models are used routinely in their Emergency Operations Centers. Shelter locations and capacities are juxtaposed with transportation routes and population densities so that the time requirements can be displayed quickly to local elected officials. It is on their shoulders that the key decision falls.

They are aided immensely, however, by these and other electronic artifacts of this rich subculture. Computer listings are available of homes wherein handicapped persons reside. Such listings also identify other individuals who might require evacuation assistance. Of course, critical facilities like nursing homes and hospitals are highlighted too. Local elected officials quickly can be advised of historic storm paths, probability levels associated with projections offered by forecasters from the National Hurricane Center (located on the campus of Florida International University, about twelve miles west of downtown Miami, Florida). Evacuation routes also can be stored and then announced to the public. Given the relative unpredictability of hurricanes, these resources aid greatly in the decision-making process.

Equally important, however, are the newspaper supplements that arrive at the doorsteps of these Floridians each summer, right at the start of the hurricane season, and alert people to the risk and to the evacuation planning that has been completed. Obviously, subcultural elements will not eliminate hurricanes, but they certainly save lives. They are important adjustments adopted by people who want to both enjoy the beauty and unique recreational activities these coastal areas provide and to escape death when the next killer storm smashes into their community.

There are elements of the subculture, however, that neutralize adaptive responses. Ever go to a hurricane party? These are rather popular apparently; events where friends and neighbors can gather to wait out the storm. They may follow media coverage, of course, but group solidarity and mood-altering substances of various types help to neutralize their perception of threat. One fellow I interviewed on Hatteras Island in 1991, a few weeks after Hurricane Bob skipped along North Carolina's Outer

Banks, summed it up: "During times like these, most folks don't want to be alone."

Other subcultural aspects that reflect feelings of invulnerability are attitudes toward land development and protective structures like dikes and levees. Thus, in direct contrast to components of a disaster subculture that endorse and nurture preparedness actions, attitudes of invulnerability establish a mindset that promotes resistance to protective structures and increased regulation. An exaggerated sense of freedom and self-confidence and being more carefree and able to take whatever nature dishes out serve to neutralize adaptive responses that comprise the other side of these disaster subcultures.

Despite these contradictory elements, for the most part these varied customs function to increase human survivability. Even in their inconsistency, they parallel those Moore earlier identified in Waco and San Angelo.

It can be done. The development of disaster subcultures helps to ensure that it will be.

THE MYTHOLOGY OF CAR WRECKS

"But how did they cope with all the traffic accidents?" This is another myth that was exploded by the careful work of Moore and his colleagues. During their escape prior to Carla reaching land, .6% of the population either witnessed or were involved in either traffic accidents or mechanical breakdown. Although the numbers are far different, this documentation paralleled that reported earlier by Stanley Pierson.[10] Prior to a flood in California in 1955, residents left—3,500 cars in about an hour and a half. Only two roads were available. Accidents? Yeah. A total of one, and it was very minor.

Similarly, when threatened with a toxic chemical, 250,000 individuals were evacuated in Mississauga, Canada, in less than twenty-four hours. Careful analysis by Joe Scanlon and Massey Padgham revealed no traffic fatalities. Indeed, contrary to the myth, a review of sixty-four different threats precipitating the evacuation of more than one million persons documented only ten fatalities. Seven of these occurred in a single helicopter crash, however.[11]

In short, after systematically previewing all of the published literature on evacuation, Henry Quarantelli (former director of Disaster Research Center [DRC]) concluded that report after report indicates an absence of traffic accidents—a smoothness in vehicular evacuation movement.[12] Most recently, of course, responses to Hurricanes Katrina and Rita validate this conclusion. While there were problems, especially with Katrina, traffic accidents were not one of them.

Well, that's not exactly correct. Hurricane Rita, which came on the heels of Katrina, was a bit of an exception. The official death toll from direct storm impacts was seven. Unfortunately, ninety-three others died in the aftermath or during the massive evacuation out of the Houston area. In part because of the massive deaths caused by Katrina and the horrible traumatization experienced by many who required rescue, Texas officials reacted quickly as Rita approached. It was estimated that more than two million fled. That's a lot of cars!

A single—and very publicized—wreck took the lives of 23 elderly who were residents of an assisted living facility. They and twenty-one other residents and nursing staff were in a fifty-four-passenger motor coach on Interstate 45. They, like many of the other highway occupants, were en route to Dallas. The driver was alerted by someone in another vehicle that the right rear tire hub was red hot. By the time he got pulled over and out of the motor coach, a fire had started in the wheel well. He and the nursing staff, plus other people who stopped to help, immediately began evacuating the residents. Unfortunately, intense fire quickly took over before twenty-three elderly persons could be removed. A variety of new regulations regarding the transport of people with special needs, including portable oxygen containers, were created because of this event.[13]

Others died in the aftermath of Rita during accidents related to debris removal, temporary repairs, and other types of incidents. Although nearly two thirds of those who fled prior to Rita indicated they would evacuate next time a similar threat occurred, the lingering images of intense traffic congestion and the atypical, and very unfortunate, bus fire also will linger in the collective memories of many. The improved response and evacuation out of the Houston area prior to Hurricane Ike in fall 2008 validates the progress made. It also documents that the myth of car wrecks should be filed away with other misunderstandings about disaster behavior.

"RESISTERS? WE'LL ARREST THEM!"

Quarantelli's review of the evacuation literature also highlights another important point, one about which there is much confusion. I have encountered it many times through questions like this: "Sir, I can appreciate what you said about people not believing warnings. But when we evacuate an area, I mean, they have got to leave. We can't approach these things like it's a church picnic or something. They'll leave or get arrested as far as I'm concerned."

That may be a case you will confront someday, but it is a rarity. Remember what I said about warning effectiveness? The source does make a difference. The most effective warning source and communication mode is an official knocking on a door. When a police officer, sheriff's deputy, firefighter, or some other uniformed individual is standing at your door, most people will listen.

Now comes the confusion. Are officials ordering people to leave or advising them? Quarantelli's observation is germane: "DRC field observations in hurricanes, floods, and earthquakes are that sometimes law enforcement agencies will *try to convey the impression* that they might physically remove reluctant evacuees, but this is not done in actuality."[14]

Convey the impression—that is the key phrase. Relatively few local government officials have briefed their personnel on this matter adequately. Frankly, if botched badly, there is basis for legal recourse by persons removed forcibly by an overly eager deputy. Did you know that such suits have been filed?

Suggestion? I have two. First, as Quarantelli's review indicates, there frequently is a great amount of confusion among local agency heads as to whether to issue an evacuation "order" or an advisory. Despite the impression conveyed, what typically is issued is a *request* for persons to leave a designated area. Even if publicly announced as "mandatory," as it was in areas of Carteret County, North Carolina, prior to Hurricane Bob's arrival in mid-August 1991, many view such directives as applying to "them," not "us": "They were trying to clear tourists out of here, not property owners." Just prior to Katrina's landfall, Mayor Ray Nagin of New Orleans reluctantly issued a mandatory evacuation order. This was the first time in the history of this highly vulnerable community that such an order was issued. But, as I described in the last chapter, thousands did not comply. So they put not only themselves at risk but also those who tried to rescue them. And despite the mandatory order, more than 1,000 died.

Such distinctions should be reviewed carefully. It should be reflected in every community's evacuation plan. One of the many examples I have seen is a briefing paper written a while back by John Brownson (Snohomish County Department of Emergency Services, Everett, Washington). He puts it succinctly:

For political and practical reasons the use of force in evacuation in the County is not desirable for our purposes…. Such methods require the expenditure of valuable manpower whose efforts might be better used in other parts of the emergency operation.[15]

This matter was explored by members of the Select Bipartisan Committee of the U.S. House of Representatives. They were charged with investigating the preparedness for and response to Hurricane Katrina. They concluded: "The incomplete pre-landfall evacuation led to deaths, thousands of dangerous rescues, and horrible conditions for those who remained."[16]

But why did this happen? The report identified several important factors. Prior to Katrina, federal, state, and local officials had participated in an elaborate exercise. They called it "Hurricane Pam." Unfortunately, as the committee discovered, "implementation of lessons learned from Hurricane Pam was incomplete."[17]

Furthermore, they discovered that the "terms for voluntary and mandatory evacuations lack clear definitions."[18] Additionally, they concluded that "the declarations of a 'mandatory' evacuation were delayed or never made in metropolitan New Orleans."[19]

No, this does not contradict what I said before about Mayor Nagin. He did issue a mandatory evacuation order about 11:00 a.m. on August 28, 2005. This was approximately nineteen hours prior to landfall. But "Jefferson Parish—another major component of metropolitan New Orleans—never did declare a mandatory evacuation, except for the lower parts of the parish on the Gulf Coast."[20]

In his interview with staff of the Committee on Homeland Security and Governmental Affairs (U.S. Senate), the director of Homeland Security and Emergency Management for St. Bernard Parish said he did call for an evacuation. It was not actually "mandatory," however. He recalled that on some news broadcasts he was quoted as saying, "…We strongly recommend that you leave now because I don't believe I have enough body bags to cover the people that stay."[21]

So while not an official mandatory order, he was doing his best to make the reality of the threat very clear. He explained a key constraint. This is one I have encountered repeatedly in interviews with business owners and managers. And it helps to demonstrate the complexities that evacuation situations reflect—and the dollar costs.

The big decision on mandatory evacuation is monetary, the businesses themselves. When you do a mandatory evacuation, the businesses are required to close down…. It takes them roughly 8 to 12 hours to close down the refinery. Every time they close it down, it's over a million dollars to close it down and another million to bring it up.[22]

Just as we were doing the final editing on this book, I learned of John Pine's experience.[23] During one of his fall 2008 classes at Louisiana State University, a student challenged his statements about martial law. Being the brilliant professor that he is, John turned the challenge into a class research problem. One of his students tracked down an analysis completed for Congress in 2005. The report makes it clear that while ambiguity exists regarding the conditions that might be required for such declarations, most Americans expect local authorities to retain control of law enforcement. Civilian, not military, control should be maintained.

Shortly thereafter, through one of Wayne Blanchard's daily reports on the Federal Emergency Management Agency (FEMA) Higher Education Project, I learned of the November 2008 ruling by the New Hampshire Supreme Court.[24] It seems that in April 2007 the fire chief in Allenstown had declared a state of emergency because of flooding. A local police officer confronted a woman who refused to leave her home. He explained that if she refused to leave he would arrest her. She refused, so he arrested her for disobeying his order and for disorderly conduct. The local court threw out the charges against the woman. But upon appeal, the State Supreme Court ruled that although police don't have authority to remove residents from threatened homes, fire officials do. So, as of 2008, the legal rights of such "resisters" remain unclear as one moves from one locale to another. Fortunately, such cases remain rare.

In short, when we look at Americans' experience regarding evacuation, nearly always it has occurred on a voluntary basis. Of course, some people will leave even before an official evacuation request. They make things easy. Remember? The term *spontaneous evacuation* is used to refer to this behavior.[25] As you might expect, it is most pronounced where disaster subcultures are the most developed.

Once I was asked, "Okay, but what would you do if a family refused to leave? I mean, you're standing there at the door and they just tell you to your face they are staying."

Like so many questions from those on the firing line, it is a good one. To be honest, all I can say is that I'm sure my response would depend on the circumstances. The legal basis and procedural requirements for local government to forcefully remove persons from their homes are summarized nicely in Brownson's briefing paper. Certainly, if reasonable procedures are followed and documented, managers of local government agencies can resort to such actions without fear of subsequent legal sanction.

What is equally certain, however, is that employees at the bottom rungs of police and fire agencies should be advised of the limits of their authority. In an era of heightened "sue the bastard" sentiments, emergency personnel must be forewarned through careful training. My field interviews have convinced me that this is but one of several legal matters that most operational personnel rarely are briefed on adequately.

Since I first witnessed Wade Guise's (former civil defense director, Harrison County, Mississippi) response to a resistive family, I have not thought of a better approach. Guise's strategy is preserved in an informative film titled "A Lady Called Camille." Despite its age, it remains an effective teaching tool. After informing a family of Camille's projected path, Guise explains that they are advised to leave. Sensing reluctance, he displays a face of exasperation. Then he calmly asks, "Well, if you won't leave, will you please give me the names of your next of kin?"

That is a line worth remembering. Several have picked up on it over the years. Consistently they tell me it works. Tactics like this are integral aspects of the disaster subculture that exists along our Gulf Coast. They persist because they work. Hotel owners in North Carolina told me that local authorities would require locals wanting to stay home to sign "next of kin" letters: "They listen up real good when they hear this." If transported elsewhere, such subcultural wisdom could be effective.

While they agreed with many of the findings in the "majority report," two congressmen from Louisiana (Charlie Melancon, 3rd District, and William J. Jefferson, 2nd District) saw important aspects very differently.[26] For example, despite a detailed review, the report "rarely assesses *how* these problems occurred, *why* they were not corrected sooner, and *who* in particular was responsible. Instead, the report uses the passive voice to describe generic 'institutional' failures, general 'communications problems', and vague 'bureaucratic inertia.' It seldom holds anyone accountable for these failures."[27]

And regarding the issue of mandatory evacuation, these two men emphasize the positive but acknowledge failure. That is, it should be remembered that more than a million got out. It can be and was done! But people still died—lots of them. Explicit recognition of these two consequences provides important perspective:

The majority report recognizes that even under mandatory evacuations, 10% to 25% of residents will refuse to leave, and authorities cannot forcibly remove these residents from their homes. We believe emergency planners should examine additional ways to encourage all residents to evacuate in such circumstances.[28]

Maybe this book, and the work it can stimulate some readers to complete during the next decade or so, can be a step in this direction. I certainly hope so!

You see, despite the tragic situation that thousands of New Orleanians experienced, officials in Plaquemines Parish made it work. The parish president declared a mandatory evacuation on Saturday morning (August 27), and sheriff's personnel began working at intersections to more rapidly move outbound traffic. Then on Sunday, sheriff's deputies "...went door-to-door to warn people to evacuate and to identify those who needed help doing so."[29] These efforts produced a parish "evacuation rate of 97 to 98%, which helped account for the small number of fatalities there—only three."[30]

In late August 2008, Gulf Coast residents learned that Hurricane Gustav was headed their way. In fact, as news of this hurricane flooded the airwaves, mourners were laying to rest eighty-five Katrina victims whose bodies never had been claimed. That was on Friday, August 29, 2008—exactly three years after the levees had been breached.[31]

And this time Mayor Nagin did not wait. By Sunday, August 31, 2008, a mandatory evacuation order had been implemented successfully, and thousands of disabled and poor were assisted in evacuating by bus, train, and air. An estimated 1.9 million fled, making this the largest evacuation in Louisiana's history.[32] Even though two dozen died in that storm, the successful evacuation proved again that "it can be done."

After Gustav came Ike—a little over a week later. This time, however, Galveston Island, Texas, was in the bull's-eye. And for the first time in my memory, National Weather Service officials pulled out all the stops. In contrast to prior types of warning messages, Ike's alarm was reminiscent of Guise's tone of urgency: "Persons not heeding evacuation orders in single-family one-or two-story homes will face certain death." Can't get much clearer than that! To nearly a million—especially those on Galveston Island and the greater Houston area—it was. They left.

Yet, days later, when officials continued rescue efforts, "brave"—or maybe "stupid"—survivors tried to explain to reporters why they stayed. The reasons varied, of course, but once again the power of inertia and denial were documented.[33]

CONFIRMATION: A LIKELY ACTION

If a warning message evokes any response at all, people commonly try to confirm the information in some manner. This can be done in more ways than you could believe. Through our detailed interviews following the 1965 flood in Denver, I discovered and first documented that most behavioral responses could be classified into one of four categories. These have been validated by much subsequent research.[34]

Appeal to Authority

Typically, only a small percentage of people telephone emergency service agencies. This may be enough to tie up every available line, however. In the Denver study, 9% percent said they tried such calls. Nearly one in five got only the buzz of a busy signal.

Hence, a myth commonly believed by emergency communications personnel is reinforced by their experience. Many continue to think that they have far-reaching public contact through personal telephone conversations. It sure depends on how you view it, doesn't it?

A majority of people will turn on a radio or television, if circumstances permit. This is a type of indirect appeal to authorities. It reaches more but is believed less.

In short, only a very small percentage of people actually try to confirm disaster warnings by directly contacting any type of authority. Furthermore, many who try receive only the buzz of a busy signal. Of course, since this study was done in 1966, the technology of the Internet has changed how many communicate, including review of breaking news stories. So an increasing but still relatively small percentage of people will appeal to authorities indirectly by going directly to websites supported by the National Weather Service, National Hurricane Center, their local government, or others. For example, following Hurricane Floyd (1999), Kirstin Dow and Susan Cutter documented that 30% of those surveyed indicated use of the Internet to obtain storm-related information. But only one in ten (11%) would comment on the type of information they obtained. Obviously, as our culture integrates this technology more fully these usage rates will continue to increase.[35]

Appeal to Peer

This may seem strange. The data are very clear, however. If people telephone anyone to confirm a disaster warning, most likely it will be a relative or friend. Of course, they may consult neighbors too. Often this is done by just going next door, rather than phoning.

This is a specific example of a more general principle with profound implications. In disaster, people do not abandon their traditional values or habit patterns; rather, there is continuity. See the point?

Observational Confirmation

Some flood evacuees I interviewed in Denver said that they didn't telephone or talk to anyone. Rather, they watched out their front window. Maybe they did this routinely, in contrast to others who were used to running over to their neighbor's house.

When they saw neighbor families loading up their cars, this told them that they too had better get out. In some cases, they watched a police officer going from house to house: "When I saw him warn all of those other people, I figured it must be true."

Latent Confirmation

This refers to unintentional actions that act to confirm warning messages. Most common is receiving a telephone call from a relative or friend. A family might be standing in their living room talking the situation over and then receive a telephone call. There may not be any new factual information given about the threat. But the fact that they called was taken as a cue that the situation might be serious: "Maybe we better leave; it just might be more dangerous than we thought." Remember how Sally and David reacted when her mother called them in Kauai? They were the fictional couple who had left Kansas to enjoy their honeymoon when Hurricane Iniki came calling (Chapter 1).

These processes reflect what families actually do, not myths as to what someone thinks they ought to do. They form the backdrop for understanding the next step, that is, evacuation behavior itself.

FAMILIES ARE THE UNITS

Moore's research on Hurricane Carla underscored another critical principle. When individuals evacuated, they left as family units. I found this repeated in the 1965 response to the Denver flood. Here, about three-fourths of the families left together. This was a lower proportion than what the Carla study found. But remember, in the Denver case, immediate action was required. Recall the types of messages I described in the last chapter? Police were advising families they had from five to twenty minutes to leave the area. Carla evacuees began receiving warnings four days before she reached land. Thus, the perception of the threat affects the behavior pattern: "How much time do we have to decide?"

There was another aspect of the time dimension in the Denver case that is crucial. Think about a typical family at 4:00 p.m. on a summer afternoon. Many family members were not at home. Children were out playing; many spouses were not yet home from work. Of the families that were physically together when the warning message was received, the proportion that left together as a family unit jumped up to 92%

What about those families that were physically separated, that is, those with members scattered—children playing, spouses at work? While our sample of these was not too large, John Stephenson and I were able to ascertain a very important response pattern.[36] Recall the theme of group context in the last chapter. Your response to a warning message will vary depending upon the group you are with at the time. If your family is scattered, the initial reaction is to delay until all members can be called home.

In a study of four communities in Washington State—Sumner, Valley, Fillmore, and Snoqualmie—Ron Perry, with his colleagues Mike Lindell and Marjorie Greene, took this observation one step further[37] and added a key insight we failed to detect. They found a large number of families who were not united when they left home prior to floodwaters reaching them. Perry and his team noted that this seemed to run counter both to our research and that of the WWII bombing studies done in England.[38]

They found an explanation, however. Prior to leaving, the missing members were contacted and places to meet were established.[39] Thus, the insight is that should families be physically separated, they will delay evacuation. If missing members can be contacted so that arrangements to meet elsewhere can be established, the constraint is removed. This social barrier can be as real in its consequences as any physical one could be.

As Hurricane Katrina approached the Gulf Coast, millions of residents learned of the danger it represented several days before landfall was anticipated. So the warning context was very different from the flooding events in either Denver or Washington State. Here again, there was a wrinkle in the response pattern. This was documented by a research team who dug deep into a database created by the Gallup Organization, which collaborated with the American Red Cross.[40] They determined that sizeable proportions of these evacuated families left as units—over a third—but almost as many made the decision to separate, with one or more members remaining behind.

So who stayed? The data pattern was remarkably consistent, although there were other subplots. Roughly 15% decided to stay together and ride out the storm. A near equal number stayed but split the family unit up with some seeking refuge in one location and others going elsewhere. But for those who made a decision not to "evacuate in unison," the key predictors were (1) gender, (2) employment status, (3) income, (4) ethnicity, and (5) religion.

So specifically, who stayed behind as Katrina approached? The portrait from this analysis is clear, at least for a significant proportion of the nonevacuees whose family split up. They were African American men with low-paying jobs and strong religious faith.[41]

This key insight reflects the essence of what this book is all about. Too often our explanations of why people do things or don't do them fail to take into account these types of social constraints. Like invisible walls, they guide and shape the choices people make. When they make choices to behave in ways contrary to what we desire, too frequently our reaction is to label them as dumb, deviant, or worse. Remember the lesson from Hurricane Katrina: Don't blame the victim. While labels like *dumb* or *foolish* may ease our anger, it accomplishes little else. Ever yell at a hammer?

By the way, limited data also indicate that these confirmation patterns will be found in many places with cultures similar to the United States. For example, David King surveyed more than 700 households in Townsville and Cairns shortly after a tsunami warning was issued on April 2, 2007.[42] These two coastal communities are in the upper northeastern edge of Australia within the state of Queensland. Both are popular tourist destinations for those wishing to get a firsthand look at the Great Barrier Reef.

King's results indicated that most people had become aware of the warnings, although there were differences between the two communities (Townsville, 73%; Cairns, 79%).[43] And just like the Denverites I have noted, the most common follow-up response was confirmation. Of course, most (70%) just ignored the warnings and didn't seek any further information. Intercommunity differences did occur, however. Over one third (38%) of those surveyed in Cairns said that they did seek further information, whereas only 22% in Townsville did so.

Nevertheless, the event triggered some in Cairns to evacuate inland. Their departure "...created the gridlock on the roads during the tsunami warning period."[44] Hence, local officials learned "...that Cairns would have significant problems coping with a mass evacuation—whether from a tsunami threat or storm surge."[45]

Now we're ready to penetrate the actual social pathways that get families out of their homes when danger threatens. You may find some surprises. I know I did. Before going on, however, let's be sure the key principles are in hand.

THE INSIGHTS

- Public evacuation of cities, including large ones, can be done; it has been done.
- Varied in content and reflecting the most recurring type of hazard, many American communities evidence disaster subcultures. That is, residents have developed specialized customs that promote highly adaptive disaster responses.
- Community evacuations have been done voluntarily. Mass arrests, or other forms of legal force, are not used. Although advisories frequently contain terms like *mandatory* and *state of emergency*, noncompliers rarely are arrested or prosecuted.
- Upon receiving warning messages, if they do anything, individuals first seek confirmation. This is done in numerous ways. Although the most common action is to monitor the media, many contact a relative, friend, or neighbor.
- The percentage of residents who will seek warning message confirmation by telephoning police, fire, or other emergency agency is relatively low—typically, less than 10%. This volume may overload telephone lines and thereby create the illusion that large proportions of the public are receiving confirmation direct from emergency officials.
- When people evacuate their residences, most depart as family units. Those not physically together at the time a warning is issued will try to have all members accounted for before leaving.

5

Shall We Leave?

Have you ever experienced it? There you are. The TV is blaring. It's clear that your house is in the threatened area. The possibility that the flood may hit has become more real now that you have seen the last few minutes of TV coverage. Maybe your sister just called. But should you leave? If you do, where are you going to go? Are you certain the house will be safe from looters? What should you take with you? So many questions keep racing through your head. Most importantly, how much longer can you stall?

If you have never found yourself in this situation, be grateful. It isn't pleasant.

This is the human side of fleeing from danger. Community evacuation is a complex process. When done with some degree of organization, it does save lives. Yet knowledge about *the behavioral process* by which large-scale evacuations occur has not reached many of the emergency managers and local elected officials on whose shoulders the responsibility lies. Let's see how it really happens.

PATHWAYS TO EVACUATION

Like warning message confirmation behavior, it turns out that there are many social routes by which families come to leave their homes in times of danger. My research on the 1965 Denver flood uncovered four different pathways. Others have documented their presence in subsequent disasters. As I am writing this, my mind flashes back to their discovery. The story has several important lessons.

Evacuation by Default

Initially, I reviewed several interview schedules. These had been used by persons who previously had studied aspects of public response to warnings. Recall Harry Moore's study of Hurricane Carla? The interview schedule he and his associates used was most helpful.[1] By using it and other schedules I obtained, I was determined to discover the key piece of information that had convinced these Denverites they were in danger. What was the key element in a warning message that persuaded them to leave?

After pretesting the schedule with a few families myself, I asked three students whom I had trained to proceed with the interviewing. Things went okay for a week or so. Each of them reported some difficulties, however. A few families had trouble with the wording of some of the questions: "a simple matter of vocabulary," I recall thinking at the time. But as we tried to reword the questions on evacuation, it became clear that they had encountered stories that didn't fit the neat, logical ordering the schedule reflected.

Shortly thereafter, I was conducting an interview myself. I asked, "Did you evacuate your home?" The reply was, "No." I already had asked more than sixty other questions by this time and knew they had left. So I was puzzled. Fortunately, I finally gave them a chance to talk and explain what had happened.

Briefly, their story went like this. A police officer had warned them, but they really didn't believe their house was in danger. Largely out of curiosity, they got into their car and drove to the river. Since there was nothing unusual there, they decided to drive upstream. As they drove, news flashes began to make them think that there was a chance their house might be hit. So they turned around and headed home. Before getting there, however, they were stopped at a police blockage. The neighborhood was now vacated, and no entry was permitted until the flood crest passed.

They actually *evacuated by default*. It happens in many different ways. Their story was but one of many we turned up in other interviews. But that interview was how I first discovered this process. It opened the door. The total inadequacy of my original line of questioning became apparent. Previous research did not reflect the perceptual reality these people were experiencing.

Evacuation by Invitation

After beginning to *listen* to these families, another route was discovered that turned out to have far more significant implications. Remember my comments about confirmation behavior? Most people don't telephone the police or fire department; they call their brother or, maybe if available, their sister, mother, uncle, or grandfather.

Often, a relative or friend will call them. Remember the notion of latent confirmation? Okay. So what's the point? Well, really there are two messages. First, forget about the nonsense you have heard for years. You know, "Stay off the telephone; the lines are needed for emergency workers." Forget it. Don't waste your breath. People will not listen to that type of advice. They didn't listen in 1965 and in today's world of cell phones—what a joke! Seems like some people can't drive anymore without talking on the phone. Frankly, it's a good thing they won't listen to officials telling them to stay off the phone.

You see, the second insight here is that in these conversations, which certainly serve to reduce anxiety, *invitations are offered*. Invitations? Yes, that's right. A typical interchange might go like this:

Well, what are you guys going to do?

We're trying to decide that right now. I want to leave, but Bob's sure our house is safe. We sit up pretty high on the hill, you know.

Yeah, but this thing sounds really bad. Those shots on TV are hard to believe. I mean, he's probably right; your house is up there a ways. But I don't know.

Well, we don't know either. Guess we'll just sit tight for awhile. We'll keep our TV going. If we have to leave, I'm sure we'll have plenty of time. We can always just drive up the hill a ways.

Look. I've got a roast in the oven. Why don't you come on over here? We can watch this thing on TV over here. If it turns out not to be as bad as they're saying, you can go back home. No sense sitting there wondering. You can't start cooking dinner. Why don't you come on over?

So, along comes this sociology student with an interview schedule designed to elicit that elemental piece of information that finally convinced this family that they were in danger. See the point? Fortunately, we listened. In doing so we discovered that social reality was far more complex than we imagined. Many families left their homes because they received an invitation, not because all members, especially the husband, actually perceived a serious threat.

These invitations come from relatives most often; close friends issue them too. At times there are important changes. For example, several victim families in Denver commented on the fright and concern of elderly relatives. A typical case went like this:

> Well, see, her mother called. I told all of them that we really were not in danger. I'll bet it wasn't ten minutes later that her mom called back. Then, as we were getting a little more information, I'll be damned if she didn't call back again!
>
> So, I could see that I wasn't going to have any peace and quiet until this thing was over. So I told her, finally, "Okay, damn it! We'll all go over to your mother's house. But the first thing I'm going to do is turn off her TV."
>
> Well, we got over there, and then could see from the TV reports that this thing was serious. Real serious. But honestly, when we left I really didn't think we were in any danger.

And here we were trying to discover the single piece of information about the flood severity that convinced people like this to leave their home. Social reality is much more complex than what we had envisioned when we constructed the interview schedule.

Years later, in the four Washington State communities they studied, Ron Perry, Mike Lindell, and Marjorie Greene confirmed this process. More than one fifth of the families they interviewed reported receiving invitations.[2] And when Perry and Greene surveyed families threatened by flooding after the eruption of Mount St. Helens, they again emphasized this invitational process.[3] As before, they extended our understanding of it by examining social characteristics of the event. You see, one of the ways we are trying to sort out the patterned variability in human responses is to classify events according to certain key social characteristics, like the length of the warning period: "...This process (i.e., evacuation by invitation) apparently operated in Toutle/Silverlake where 24.4 percent of the evacuees report that they were first contacted by someone at their destination. This finding supports Drabek's contention...."[4]

The evacuations after Mount St. Helens erupted were the first to confirm what I had discovered in Denver after the 1965 flood. But the team also documented an important difference: The invitational process may be greater when community preparedness has been supported. So when circumstances and effective local warning systems are in place, advanced warnings precipitate larger numbers of invitations. Once received, many will accept.

People do get invitations. People do use their telephones. Lives get saved in the process.

Evacuation by Compromise

Recall the differential reactions to warning messages I discussed previously. Females do tend to be easier to convince than males. Yet if the family is going to remain as a unit, someone has to give in. As Moore and his colleagues put it, "…Families move as units and remain together, even at the cost of overriding dissenting opinions."[5] Evacuation by compromise reflects the last part of their statement. Cross pressures emerge because of different responses to disaster warning messages.

As I emphasized in Chapter 3, females tend to take warnings more seriously, especially if they have children at home. Some I interviewed told me that they repeatedly told their husband they should leave, to which he would respond, "No way. This thing's not that big a deal." So the tension levels increased. Calls from relatives and friends made matters only worse. But finally they left even though many of the men I have talked to have consistently said they were certain the family was not at risk.

"Well, why then did you leave? What piece of warning information finally got through to you?"

"Look. I told you. I was never convinced by anything she said, what we heard on TV, or by anything else. I just gave in to cut the crap."

So, like in everyday life, compromises get made to keep peace in the family. When did you last give in? Compromises occur in families all the time. Disaster situations are no different.

Maybe he really was convinced and, as a male, felt he couldn't admit it. That remains a possibility, but I have my doubts. The point is akin to television ads aimed at kids. Ten-year-olds are not going to walk into Wal-Mart and buy dolls, DVD players, or cell phones. They will convince their parents to do so. So too, it is within many families. Think about some of the things you have done during the past month just to "keep the peace."

Three decades after the Denver flood, I again encountered stories of conflict.[6] In 1999, I was interviewing people who were at work when disaster threatened in places like Reno, Nevada, and Modesto, California, after extensive flooding. Prior to these interviews I had spent time in North and South Carolina listening to victims of Hurricane Fran. In total, I visited 12 different communities and documented the role of conflict within work groups and families during evacuations.

When I focused on this issue, it turned out to be more frequent and important than I had realized. First, nearly all (93%) reported "extensive" or "some" discussion of the initial warning information among coworkers, either on site or by telephone if they were not at work when they first got the word. As you might expect, this varied by the length of the forewarning period. Those threatened by a hurricane had a longer period of time to engage in such conversations than did those caught up in a flash flood. Regardless of the time involved, most of these discussions reflected some degree of conflict since different people perceived the threats differently.

Of course, for employees, most conflict within the work group was resolved by the hierarchy. Even though they might have disagreed with their boss's assessment, most did as they were told. Consequently, many remained at or reported to work even though they had serious doubts. They described discussions revolving around such matters as the safety of the workplace, when best to leave, and where to go.

More importantly for many, however, were tensions that emerged between these workplace decisions and family desires. About one in five told me that these tensions were serious. Usually family members wanted to evacuate to another location but were reluctant to go without the person being required to stay at work. These family–work conflicts occurred more frequently when the warning period was longer.

In my mind's eye I can still picture many—mostly females—who told me of their anger. Their children were calling work wanting to know when they would be home so they could leave to go to Grandma's. Trying to keep the peace gets very complicated when family priorities are in conflict with bureaucratic systems. All sorts of compromises were described to me, including a few who just said to an uncaring boss, "Take this job and shove it!"

Evacuation by Decision

Lest I imply that no families make decisions (i.e., conscious and deliberate choices to evacuate), let me clarify. Some families do. Upon receiving a warning, they proceed to confirm it in some manner. Slowly, they reach a collective decision: "Okay, get the kids, and we'll go over to Mother's for a while. She ought to be home by now."

The other three pathways get people to safety too, however. By recognizing their presence and understanding how they operate, emergency managers can use them. Such insights, if used creatively, can save lives.[7]

WHERE DO THEY GO?

We have families leaving their homes. The next problem must be traffic jams around schools, churches, and other designated shelters, right? No! That too is another myth. Yet too often this false imagery prevails.

This myth is found most commonly among agency directors who may not have had a flood, tornado, or hurricane strike their community recently. After reviewing numerous studies, Henry Quarantelli summarized the myth and its consequence this way:

> Groups without experience and knowledge of disasters typically will overestimate the number of evacuees who will need housing; not realizing *most people seek refuge with friends and relatives*; even worse, they may not be aware that other agencies such as the Red Cross have certain formal responsibilities for emergency sheltering....[8]

We'll pursue this last point later because interagency coordination, or rather the lack of it, is a very important issue. Right now, let's stay on target. Typically, the need for public sheltering is overestimated. In recent years, however, because of numerous lectures by Quarantelli, Russ Dynes, and others, the message has gotten out to representatives of many agencies. Also, knowledgeable national leaders like Roy Popkin, formerly with the American Red Cross, built this insight into their organizational instruction.[9]

So inexperienced managers and local officials do overestimate the need for public shelters. How many people require such a resource? Also, where do the other families go? These are the right questions, so let's look at some specifics.

The Hurricane Carla study was one of the earliest to document this behavior pattern. It revealed that more than one-half (56%) of the evacuees stayed in homes of relatives or friends. Some went to motels or other such places, leaving just under one-fourth (23%) turning to public shelters.[10] In more localized events, like the Denver flood, these figures changed dramatically. There, only a tiny fraction (3.5%) stayed in any type of public shelter.

These patterned variations were clarified nicely through Perry et al.'s four-community study in Washington State:

> ...The use of public shelter increases when community preparedness is high, when the entire community must be evacuated, and when the evacuees anticipate that the necessary period of absence will be long. Even under these conditions, however, public shelters seem to attract only about one-fourth of the evacuees....[11]

What about other types of disasters? The previously listed qualities point to some of the key indicators: length of forewarning, anticipated length of departure, and level of community preparedness. Statistics cited by Quarantelli[12] spell out the percentages using public shelters in such disasters as these:

1. Wilkes-Barre, Pennsylvania: flood, 3.3%
2. Xenia, Ohio: tornado, 1.8%
3. Mississauga, Canada: hazardous chemical, 2% (or less)
4. Managua, Nicaragua: earthquake, 6%

Other events studied produced parallel figures. After Mount St. Helens' eruption, just over 6% of the evacuees from the threatened areas around Toutle and Silverlake arrived at public shelters. Perry et al.'s study of four flood-threatened communities also substantiated this overall pattern and added important insight into its variation. In two communities, Sumner and Snoqualmie, the proportion seeking public shelters was similar (3.4% and 2.5%, respectively) to the Denver rate of 3.5%. But in both Fillmore and Valley the rates were much higher (26.4% and 29.0%, respectively).[13]

Why? Well, in Fillmore the warning messages issued told of the locations of public shelters and advised people to go there. In Valley, the entire town was evacuated, so the amount of housing available to the Denverites, for example, was not present. Reflecting a high level of preparedness, local officials assured the public that shelters had been set up and advised them of their locations. Furthermore, some victims had to be away from home for extended periods of time. In a few cases this was nearly a week or more.[14] Location wise, the public shelters were closer to their flooded homes than any other housing. So rather than stay with friends or relatives and have to drive farther during clean-up, many opted to stay in public shelters—hence, the higher rates.

When the nuclear power plant incident occurred at Three Mile Island (TMI) in 1979, the evacuees responded similarly to the people who were seeking safety from the toxic chemicals that became airborne following a train derailment in Mississauga, Ontario, Canada, in 1979. That is, once they reached a public shelter, such as a sports arena in the TMI case, they quickly began making arrangements with friends and relatives. Hence, even among those arriving at public shelters, other alternatives will be sought once they sense they will not be able to return home that day.[15]

Other social characteristics add ripples to the general pattern. For example, as you might expect, farmers and other rural residents are less likely to appear at the door of a public shelter; this is in contrast to city dwellers. Why? In part, it's their location. There are lots of neighbors between their home and a designated public shelter, like a school. But more importantly, as those of us who live in mountain villages, even part time, know very well, neighbors still help neighbors. Or more correctly, "real neighbors" still exist in rural areas of our nation.

Among city dwellers, more of those arriving will be poorer. As in everyday life, their social resources and perceptions of options are narrow. Thus, events striking an area that houses lower-income city dwellers will constitute the largest public sheltering need. But even among these families with more limited resources, most will take refuge elsewhere. Still, when you have a large percentage of poor, like in New Orleans, the sheer numbers within an urban area can be overwhelming. Probably the best example of this reality was the badly botched evacuation of New Orleans prior to Hurricane Katrina.

Another interesting ripple in this pattern was documented after the 9/11 attacks. Several thousand people in Lower Manhattan—commuters, tourists, residents—boarded watercraft of all sorts to get out of the area. Here again was an important improvisation. Those types of emergent adaptations will be documented again and again throughout this book:

> Even before the towers collapsed, some ferries turned around with their passengers, while others returned to pick up their regular clientele.... Some vessels asked and waited for permission from the Coast Guard, but others acted on their own.[16]

Think back now to my story about the honeymoon in Chapter 1. Remember the experiences of the newlyweds, David and Sally Cummings, in Kauai? Undoubtedly, others from their home state of Kansas also were victimized by Hurricane Iniki. But most, if not all of them, were encouraged to evacuate by hotel or condo staff members. When I interviewed 150 such people afterward, I discovered that most went to a public shelter.[17] Why? Well, think about it. First, they were on an island, so driving to a nearby relative's home was not an option. They didn't have any relatives or friends living on Kauai. Second, although a few tried to book into another hotel or condo unit that was not directly on the beach, these were already filled. Very few even tried to check any out since they were unfamiliar with this location. Furthermore, hotel staff gave them directions to nearby schools that served as shelters. So tourists, business travelers, and others who encounter disaster when they are away from home, represent another important wrinkle to the modal evacuation patterns.

Finally, the TMI episode illustrates another important pattern variation. Recall that in the last chapter I stressed that when families leave their homes, they generally do so as complete units. TMI presented a slight twist to this axiom. Again, the puzzle reflects the importance of our recognition of social barriers that constrain human behavior. Families who resided within six miles of the plant nearly always left together. If they lived further away, that is, beyond fifteen miles, more of them left some members at home.[18]

Why was this? Interviews revealed the interpretations. You see, the threat of radiation exposure was perceived as being especially critical to pregnant women and young children. So although more than two thirds of the families who left their homes went as complete units, some decided that only those who were perceived as being at risk should leave. The farther they were from the plant, the more this patterned variability characterized their response.

Let's think about three other variations that are important in all disasters. In large and complex evacuations like those we saw prior to Katrina in 2005 and more recently prior to Gustav and Ike in 2008, sheltering for special needs victims is a critical matter. All too often, departure is delayed or avoided because those at risk are worried about their caregiver responsibilities. Think about three types of evacuees: (1) infant children; (2) sick or elderly (e.g., homebound on oxygen); and (3) pets. Many people I have interviewed over the years have described their reluctance to leave because of their devotion to such highly vulnerable populations.[19] During the evacuations both prior to and after Katrina, this lesson was hammered home.

Fortunately, during the evacuations prior to both Gustav and Ike, these lessons were implemented rather well. The contrast to Katrina was encouraging to witness. In part, these responses reflected 2006 legislation that provided resources for pets in situations like these. And emergency officials pulled out all the stops to assist elderly and those with medical disabilities in fleeing.

In these instances, however, as with Katrina, escaping to public shelters meant dislocation. That is, shelters were located miles away and in some cases in other states. But the systems worked well in contrast to Katrina.

Pets and people with special medical needs were sheltered better, but shelters to which some children were taken were less prepared.[20] For example, prior to Ike, officials in San Antonio were advised they would need to care for more than 5,000 evacuees plus 642 pets. About 10% (561) of the evacuees would have special medical needs. But they had no information about the number or ages of children that might arrive. So improvisations were made on the spot. Advance information could have allowed for better arrangements and essentials like cribs, diapers, and other baby-related needs.

It's hard to believe that three years after the lessons of Katrina, the National Commission on Children and Disaster, which had been created in December 2007, had not met prior to fall 2008. That's when Gustav and Ike arrived. The ten-member commission did meet in mid-October 2008. And the chair, Mark Shriver, vice president and managing director of Save the Children's U.S. Programs, indicated that he wanted the group to bring specific proposals to lawmakers within the next six to eight months. Hopefully these will be forthcoming before too many more large-scale evacuations occur. Stay tuned!

"WE WANNA GO HOME"

These studies fail to communicate the volatility in temporary relocations. Until victims can return home, their lives are unsettled. The internal pressure to return home is intense. Too often, it seems to me, emergency officials fail to appreciate this. To fully understand the importance and implications of this pressure, we have to go back to the very beginning of the evacuation process. For example, recall the story of the family who drove to the river to see if they might be in danger. Initially, they doubted the credibility of the warning messages. Later, because of hearing media reports over their car radio, they changed their minds. So, back home they drove. Police blockades stopped them before they got there. They were delayed only momentarily, however. Remember, people are creative and resourceful. Generally, they are law abiding too. What would you tell your eight-year-old? "But Dad, Belle's still at home. We can't leave her there."

Nearly one-third of the families we interviewed after the Denver flood indicated that they returned home after their initial departure. There were many reasons for doing so. These varied with the family, but what didn't fluctuate was the pattern of choice. When confronted with a conflict between a legal authority and a *perceived need* to return home, many broke the law. Police blockades could, and were, infiltrated.

This behavior pattern does not reflect hostility or latent criminal instincts. Rather, it reveals the true values held by most Americans. Home and family remain central, despite media images to the contrary. My plea is that emergency officials incorporate this awareness into their planning.

Don't ridicule family members who value their homes—and maybe pets who got left behind. Rather, anticipate this behavior pattern. Indeed, be grateful it is there. It provides much strength, a crucial basis of resiliency.

Years later I tried to pin this matter down more carefully. In my study of tourists and others who were away from home when disaster hit, I dug deeper.[21] My questioning documented that just over one third (37%) went to more than one evacuation site. Unfortunately, I didn't ask how long they stayed at the second location, nor did I ask if they went anywhere else prior to returning home. So in my next study—the one focused on workplace evacuations—I asked more questions. I also specified that to count as a multiple evacuation location, they had to stay there at least one night.[22]

I interviewed 429 employees who worked for 118 different companies. I selected seven disaster events that occurred during the late 1990s, such as floods in Reno and in Yuba and Sutter Counties in California and also Hurricane Fran, which impacted coastal areas of North and South Carolina. My interviews documented that more than one in ten (12%) of these employees experienced multiple evacuations. Of these, about one-quarter (27%) stayed overnight at a second location after spending at least one night at the place they went to first. But others moved on afterward to a third (62%), fourth (9%), or even a fifth (2%) location before they finally got home. I can't imagine what the pathways might look like for many of the victims of Hurricane Katrina. Many may never return to their original home locations. And with every move there is pain and uncertainty. Maintaining hope is difficult under such conditions.[23]

In complex disasters like Hurricane Katrina, and more recently Gustav and Ike, urges to return home frequently create conflict with local authorities, who are focused on public safety. Downed electric wires and loss of basic services like water, gas, and power render many areas uninhabitable for days, sometimes weeks. Such realities do not compute well for the displaced, however.

Evacuees want to return home as quickly as possible. This is true for most even if media coverage has indicated that their homes were totally destroyed. Such motivations are complex and multifaceted. I recall numerous interviews among business owners, for example, from my studies of tourist behavior. They described their frustration, which boiled over into anger for some, when they sat in long lines of traffic awaiting access to damaged areas.

As I reviewed media reports after Ike's destruction on Galveston Island, I had flashbacks to some of these interviews. Six days after Ike made landfall, city officials announced that people could "...briefly return under a new 'look and leave' plan."[24] For some, this triggered a false conclusion that "we can go home." Hours after the announcement, local officials halted the policy. Unfortunately, the lines of traffic continued to increase, as did victim frustration.

Then media reports indicated that some might be barred from ever rebuilding. Furthermore, "...if these homeowners do lose their beachfront property, they may get nothing in compensation from the state."[25] Final decisions for such matters may be months, perhaps more than a year, away. Such are the costs of being caught in clashes between building in hazardous areas and the governmental responsibility for public safety and protection, both short term and beyond.

Public policy should be formulated to *facilitate* the evacuation of "families," in the broadest sense of that term. It should not become a barrier. It should recognize that when necessary, threatened families have the capacity to complete end runs. The limits of police powers are very real. Times of disaster reveal the glue that bonds the social fabric, the essences of cohesion and stability in human life.

EVACUATION FACILITATORS

Okay. So you can accept the idea that families will resent being kept from their homes, even in the face of danger. How might an awareness of these behavior patterns help individuals involved in emergency management do their job better?

Frankly, I can't make the cake for them. I can tell you, however, that if they leave it in a hot oven all day it's going to get burned. Exact recipes for matters of this type have to be tailored to specifics. Officials have to consider for example the event, the community, and available resources. Taking these insights and fitting them into the local situation is their job. That's the essence of professional behavior.

Let me mention a specific that might illustrate the point. In a way, it is a relatively minor detail, but like road signs in flood-prone areas that alert drivers not to enter, the example may help to make the point. Since the Big Thompson Canyon flood in 1976, many places also have implemented "Climb to Safety" signs. As drivers whiz by these, they reinforce the lesson that could have saved lives that fateful summer evening: if only people would have gotten out of their cars.

I had published a set of research findings on tourist behavior during such events as Hurricanes Andrew and Iniki in 1992 and the Northridge, California earthquake on January 17, 1994.[26] The director of our local emergency management office had served as a member of the Advisory Committee for this project. He had made his staff aware of the conclusions, and that triggered a lightbulb.

I was invited to address the administrative and security staff at our airport. If you have not yet been there, Denver International Airport (DIA) is a huge complex. It is among the busiest in the nation. My talk was followed by a question-and-answer session wherein various cultural differences surfaced. As you might expect, security types figured they would control all visitors. Those with various shops didn't want disasters discussed at all for fear of alarming people.

As the discussion ensued, the issue of turnover surfaced. Obviously, many people travel through this airport regularly, but most just show up to catch a flight. So trying to train them or even the employees within the various businesses did not seem to be cost effective. Yet here this huge complex sits with its beautiful fabric roof that reminds one of tepees on the plains. It is beautiful to look at as you approach by air, car, or taxi, but it's not the best place to be during a tornado!

Weeks later I received a call from the emergency manager who ran the airport workshop. I had drawn a parallel to the canyon signs and asked where I would be safest if a tornado hit the airport. It turns out that when you next visit DIA, you will notice a new sign near the restroom: Tornado Shelter. For me it's a source of satisfaction to have seen a wise application and a smart professional who guided others to give employees a subtle reminder. The sign is a simple and inexpensive action, but it is one that may save lives someday. Have you seen any in other airports? There are several additional applications that I urge you to consider, however. As you ponder the behavior patterns documented in this chapter, I urge you to try to identify additional applications to agency policy. The better the fit between operating policies and these behavior patterns, the smoother future evacuations will go. Such agency policies can then begin to guide family responses gently pressing them into side channels away from danger. When they perceive policies as trying to shove them upstream, they will resist. They must resist. And they can be amazingly creative in their resistance.

Encourage Family Planning for an Evacuation

One of the more successful efforts along these lines was documented by Perry and Greene.[27] No, not in the flood-threatened communities I discussed earlier—this time the threat was far more awesome. Remember hearing about the 1980 eruption of Mount St. Helens?

These two researchers learned that the Cowlitz County Sheriff's office had distributed a pamphlet throughout the potentially threatened area. If the volcano erupts, families were told, these will be our warning procedures. This pamphlet was distributed in individual mailboxes rather than a mass mailing or media broadcast. Families were urged to consider ahead of time the escape routes they would use and where they would go. All family members should know of this location in case the evacuation began while some were not home.

Not only did this technique make for a smoother evacuation, but when the actual warnings came the residents responded with a much greater propensity to believe. Sure, they all went through the confirmation efforts I described. And many (24.4%) received invitations too. This public education program worked exceedingly well, however. Of course, the eruption came within a reasonable time after this pamphlet had been distributed. After scientists predicted that a large eruption was likely—local authorities were advised at the end of March, just prior to the May 18 catastrophe—subsequent media coverage stimulated continuing public sensitivity. This somewhat parallels tornado and hurricane seasons.[28] So too, much flooding is seasonal. The time to strike is when public awareness is at its highest.

Media Consistency

During the warning period, people will check out the media. Dial flipping is common and many times is a source of misinformation. During many of the hurricane evacuation studies and those caused by floods and chemical disasters, overlapping radio listening areas result in public confusion.

At times this can be dramatic. For example, years ago when I was in Cheyenne, Wyoming, after the 1979 tornado I discovered that the local National Weather Service office did relay warning information to the local TV stations via cable. At that time, however, most TV sets were tuned to stations in Denver, as they were most of the time. In the Colorado mountain community Lake City where we're living while I'm writing this book, we receive TV channels via satellite. Hence, we get news from three Denver stations, which are well over 250 miles away. But we also enjoy CNN, the Weather Channel, and dozens of others. Sitting here in this remote area where the nearest town is nearly sixty miles away adds a special context to the Denver traffic reports.

Which media will citizens be attuned to at different times of the day? Simply having a message over one local station will not reach most. Again, you have to look at the situation behaviorally, through their eyes. When you do that, public responses begin to make a lot more sense; the bases for their rationality must be your planning base.

Forceful, but Not Mandatory

In Chapter 4, I described John Brownson's approach. He emphasized that legally mandated evacuations rarely, if ever, occur. Hopefully, some of the insights I have provided in this chapter help you to see why this is so. Using the threat of arrest, like any other kind of stick, has serious limitations. A spoonful of sugar does help the medicine go down.

But remember Wade Guise? If you have forgotten, you may want to go back to the last chapter. He was the director in Harrison County, Mississippi, who was featured in the film, "A Lady Called Camille." His line was, "May I have the names of your next of kin?" Doesn't that send a chill right down your spine? Even the most macho male would have a hard time looking his five-year-old in the eye and telling him that they were not going to leave after a visit from Guise.

I first encountered use of *next of kin* forms after Hurricane Bob raced past North Carolina's Outer Banks. Officials in Carteret and Dare counties used these effectively to encourage people to leave. Up north, where Guise's wisdom had not penetrated the heads of police or firefighters, people were threatened with arrest. Their actions left a bad taste with many I interviewed along the southern coast in Maine in 1991.

Allay Looting Fears

Here is another myth. During an evacuation, and afterward, looting does not occur. Oh, I know, media reports suggest that it does. In a very few disasters, like the 1979 Wichita Falls, Texas, tornado, there are episodes, or during the response to Hurricane Katrina. I watched people coming out of stores in New Orleans with several shoeboxes or slacks. In general, however, as I detail later, looting rarely happens in times of disaster. Our image of it, however, is highly exaggerated! My point is that the public doesn't know this. They, like you maybe, believe a myth. They will act in accordance with their belief, however. Thus, a fear of looting will detain some. The myth acts as a constraint. When combined with others, it causes delay or total refusal to leave.

Perry et al., for example, found that nearly one-half of those they interviewed in the four Washington State communities expressed concern about looters.[29] Although relatively few did not evacuate solely because of this, it remains a neutralizer. It is a fairly weak constraint for most; but it can be much stronger for more paranoid types.

What can you do? I doubt that you would be very effective going on TV and announcing that social science researchers have documented that looting is near nonexistent in disaster settings. Agreed? I suggest that you consider two things. Both of these ideas are recommended formally in Perry et al.'s report.[30] First, communicate loudly and clearly that security will be tight. If the National Guard is not going to be involved, the public, in all honesty, can be told that they are available if needed, so emphasize security. In this sense, every disaster plan must contain procedures for dealing with looting. While minimal, some instances will occur. Don't overallocate resources to this, however. It is an impression you are trying to create. The problem is not looters per se but rather public fear of them.

Second, and this could be far more beneficial than you might imagine, why not announce that local agency personnel have been buttressed with a citizens' patrol? Not everyone would agree with this idea, but I truly believe it is the direction in which we should push emergency management in the future. The goal is broader community participation built on the ideas of trust and respect for the average community citizen.

I saw a well-organized dike patrol system, one involving more than 1,400 local volunteers, in East Grand Forks, Minnesota. The local emergency manager welded this group of citizens into one of the most effective weapons I have seen. They were aided by CB radios: "The flood breakers" my colleagues and I called them in a short book describing their actions and those of their neighbors—northward and across the Red River into North Dakota.[31]

Perry et al. indicated that more than three-fourths of the evacuees they interviewed expressed willingness to participate in some capacity in such a venture.[32] They were willing, that is, *if* such a program were organized in their community.

I come back to this point later, because I believe it reveals one of the biggest mistakes made by emergency managers. You see, we average citizens really are a lot more resourceful and willing than many seem to realize, especially in times of disaster.

Facilitate Transportation

Go back to images: long lines of cars, numerous traffic accidents. You now know that a large number of traffic accidents probably will not occur during most community evacuations. But most people still don't believe it.

But what about traffic? Actually, since most families will try to leave in a private vehicle, traffic can't be avoided, but its flow can be enhanced. While the systems still require a lot of work, the concept of *contraflow* is being implemented more rapidly than ever before in our history. Thus, following the horrific scenes televised during Hurricane Katrina, thousands moved in long lines of traffic prior to Rita's arrival weeks later. Contraflow, by the way, refers to temporarily converting all major highway traffic in a one-way direction. Rapid implementation can greatly improve the traffic flow.

But much more is needed. For example, some will run out of gas. Even filling stations can run dry. So both possibilities have to be included in emergency plans, if *facilitation* is the goal. And yes, in urban areas especially, some will not have cars. The higher the percentage of elderly and poor within the community, the more this will be true. Lindell and Perry emphasized this *prior* to Hurricane Katrina. Most people like this get "… transportation to work, shopping, and other daily activities by receiving rides with friends, relatives, neighbors, and co-workers … also will be those who have personal mobility limitations that will prevent them from walking to bus pick-up locations, so they will need to be picked up at their homes."[33] Failure to implement these types of transportation facilitators was a key lesson from the response to Hurricane Katrina. Fortunately, we saw it implemented more successfully during fall 2008 prior to Hurricanes Gustav and Ike.

Establish Family Message Centers

Recall the insight Perry et al. added to our earlier study of the families in Denver that were physically separated when the flood warnings were issued? We saw delay. Families do leave as units, but Perry et al. picked up on an essential insight we missed: People will delay under these circumstances until all members are accounted for.

Hence, these researchers recommend—and I certainly would concur—that officials make media announcements of a Family Message Center. This will encourage evacuation, because it conveys, quite apart from information about the threat itself, that the situation is serious. If a large area is to be evacuated, such as is common with much flooding, for example, I think several of these should be located along the river path. This would be more efficient than a single location.

Here again is another opportunity for citizen involvement. If preplanned, just like the neighborhood patrol concept, a very small number of paid personnel can be expanded into a powerful weapon almost instantly. You see, you don't need elaborate training sessions and frequent committee meetings to use volunteers in this way. The threat appears; you move. After recruiting some initial volunteers, you put them to work instantly. People really can pull it off. It gives them something to do during a time of danger, probably the best anxiety-reducing device there is. More importantly, afterward they are going to have a more positive view toward emergency management. See the constituency-building dimension?

Shall we leave? That is a question hundreds of American families are going to have to answer during the next year. The reason may stem from a derailed train carrying chlorine or phosgene, an unusual rain storm, maybe an earthquake. Let's hope they answer correctly.

AN ASIDE: CRISIS RELOCATION PLANNING AND HOMELAND SECURITY ADVISORY SYSTEM

It is not the purpose of this book to critique federal emergency management or homeland security policies.[34] Such matters are very complex and are far beyond what I have accomplished here. But following my lectures, either in formal question-and-answer sessions or informally in hallways, my views have been solicited. While the topics have varied over the years, two frequently came up especially after I had laid out some of these conclusions about warning responses and evacuation behavior. Both topics have challenged the credibility and legitimacy of many local emergency management programs. Even though local governments did not promulgate either, officials still had to defend them to their constituents.[35]

So what does all this research have to say about crisis relocation planning (CRP) and the homeland security advisory system (HSAS)? You never may have heard of CRP depending on your age. It became most controversial during the mid-1980s. The HSAS, however, was implemented shortly after 9/11—you know, the color codes that used to move across the bottom of your TV screen when you were watching a cable news channel. Presumably, these let you know the probability of a terrorist attack within the near future. I'm not an expert on either matter, but I would be remiss if I didn't offer some comment. So let's go back in time a bit, and then we'll examine the HSAS.

Crisis Relocation Planning

Should you visit the Tampa, Florida, area someday, I recommend a side trip to St. Petersburg to the Cuban Missile Crisis permanent exhibit at the Florida International Museum. There you can easily get the details. Study the photos of President John F. Kennedy as he and his brother Robert pondered options during fall 1962. Consider the information flows, the public denials of weapons being transported from the former Soviet Union, and try to role-play yourself into the decision team.

Clearly, there were missile sites in Cuba. Now, in October 1962, another ship was bringing more despite continuing denials. What is a president to do? Fortunately, at the last minute, the Russian ship turned back and headed home. Our military was prepared to take it out on the president's order, but in the last minutes of the escalating confrontation, Russian leaders called it quits.

Afterward, President Kennedy asked, "What could have happened? Could destruction or capture of that ship have triggered a nuclear attack?" Kennedy was advised that plans were in place for his protection if such a nightmare were to occur. Even in the event of an all-out nuclear attack, the U.S. government would continue given existing protective shelters. "But what about the public?" The answer was not comforting since the civil defense programs initiated during the Korean conflict and WWII had been truncated. The days of the "fallout shelter craze" were history. But the reality of hundreds of missiles loaded and aimed at our cities remained a threat.

So what kind of protection made sense? Federal planners came up with a strategy. Gradually word of a new policy filtered downward through the intergovernmental system that comprises emergency management. But President Lyndon Johnson's focus was on domestic wars, not threats from Russia. The war on poverty became one of his prime priorities, as did civil rights. But the fighting in Vietnam required more and more American troops. And calls for a withdrawal became intense. Eventually President Richard Nixon oversaw the withdrawal from Vietnam as a divided nation sought time to heal. CRP remained a concept with minimal implementation.

CRP reflected certain assumptions. For example, it was assumed that the Soviet Union leadership would not authorize an attack on the United States until they had moved significant portions of their population into rural areas. Thus, escalating international tensions, along with such population movement, might require a response that could keep matters in check.

By having an increased capacity to temporarily relocate city dwellers into rural areas, it was argued that the effectiveness of nuclear attack would be reduced. If viewed as less effective, any enemy would be less likely to initiate an attack, especially knowing that its own cities would be destroyed immediately. Though oversimplified, that is the essence of the Mutually Assured Destruction (MAD) doctrine that prevailed during those years of the cold war and an ever increasingly expensive arms race. MAD required a plan for population protection, at least in the eyes of some.

When President Jimmy Carter looked at the myriad federal agencies claiming pieces of the disaster preparedness and relief pie, he accepted the conclusions of a key report issued by the National Governor's Association.[36] So he issued an Executive Order, and the Federal Emergency Management Agency (FEMA) was born in July 1979.[37] This single agency was destined to become the lead federal disaster agency for all hazards including potential military threats to the homeland. Toward the end of his term, Carter decided the time had come to increase the use of federal expertise and dollars so that Comprehensive Emergency Management (CEM) could become a reality, not just a vision. This meant that emergency managers would design programs *comprehensively* so as to include the full life cycle of a disaster, that is, from response and recovery to preparedness and mitigation. It also meant that disasters of all types would be included, regardless of the "agent." Hence, floods, hurricanes, and other natural disasters would be planned for as would both technological and conflict based events, including war.

On taking office, President Ronald Reagan elevated the priority on the implementation of CEM through an Integrated Emergency Management System (IEMS). Soon thereafter CRP became a matter of increased controversy in many American communities.

I still recall attending a national conference in Portland, Oregon, where demonstrators carried signs calling for peace, not attack preparedness.

Some local emergency managers now faced stiff questioning. Were they willing to challenge FEMA? You see, for many in large cities especially, federal dollars comprised an important part of the local agency budget. Shared governance required that they begin CRP implementation if the money was to be forthcoming.

Others saw this strategy as flawed. Carl Sagan and others argued that policy makers had been ill-advised.[38] Nuclear attack could bring nuclear winter. The entire planet, not just two nation-states, could be in jeopardy. It was during the height of this controversy—mid- to late 1980s—that I most frequently was asked, "Will CRP work?" Always I responded within the limits of the knowledge base,[39] so I had to admit that I didn't know—but then neither did anyone else, in my opinion. Yet unlike those who projected mass panic and hysteria if orders to evacuate ever were given, I maintained a view that emphasized family loyalty, resilience, and reasoned choice. I firmly believed that agency personnel could and would participate in CRP exercises, all the while aware of the snickers promoted by late-night comedians.

So would most people evacuate from urban areas if federal officials ordered them to do so? The answer is we really don't know. But given the factors that we know impact evacuation compliance prior to hurricanes and other events, my opinion is that it would take a lot of convincing. Perceived credibility of source and a lot of other factors would go into the prediction equations.

As one who has studied disasters even longer than me, I believe that Quarantelli's cautions are well taken. He was asked if one could predict how people might react in a military attack involving nuclear bombs based on natural disaster research. His response is worth remembering:

> ...Fundamentally, we thought that a nuclear attack was qualitatively different from any other situation. Therefore, we could not say to what degree the response to a nuclear attack or a hurricane would be similar.[40]

The basic principles of warning response and evacuation behavior summarized in this book seemed to me to be applicable to most military-based threats. Potential nuclear attacks, however, represent conditions of high uncertainty—very high uncertainty, in my opinion.[41] But given the enormous gaps within emergency management programs focused on *more probable events* (i.e., hurricanes, tornadoes, floods, and earthquakes), I concluded that the money would better be spent there. Some federal-level planning for the nuclear war case should be continued, but it should be limited. Improvisation and adaptability by those at the local level could be counted on if the unthinkable ever occurred.[42] Fortunately, the breakup of the Soviet Union and the leadership of President Bill Clinton's FEMA director, James Lee Witt, took CRP out of the public agenda.

Homeland Security Advisory System

Then came 9/11. Unlike a massive attack from a single nation-state, the tactics of terrorists require different approaches.[43] And as we learn of civilians being snatched and sometimes beheaded, our anger may parallel what we felt after the 9/11 attacks. Clearly, as numerous "Paul Reveres" told us prior to that, the American homeland is not secure.[44] Efforts should be focused on reducing the proliferation of nuclear weapons still housed within the countries that once comprised the Soviet Union. And our national capacity must be enhanced to detect and respond quickly to chemically and biologically based threats. Unfortunately, the possible use of such weapons of mass destruction will remain a threat for the foreseeable future.[45] So too, however, will the threat of a future pandemic, be it caused by bird flu or whatever as I noted in Chapter 2.

The 9/11 attacks, however, clearly exposed the vulnerability of our "open" society. After some initial delays, President George W. Bush proposed a reorganization that made Carter's FEMA initiative look minuscule. The creation of the Department of Homeland Security was the largest governmental reorganization in our history.[46] Although FEMA was moved into this new department and permitted some continuity in mission and autonomy in operation, other segments were repackaged in hopes that port, airport, and border security would improve. Following the 2005 Gulf Coast hurricanes (i.e., Katrina, Rita, and Wilma), however, the future role and mission of FEMA was "questioned" as new "visions" of national preparedness were debated.

While new intelligence initiatives might thwart future terrorist actions, however, citizens would be apprised of changing risk assessments through the newly created Homeland Security Advisory System (HSAS), which announces threat levels via a color-coded scale with green signaling a "low threat level," yellow indicating an "elevated" condition, and red standing for "severe" (blue = "guarded" and orange = "high").

But what does the research presented in this chapter, as well as additional volumes not summarized here, tell us about such a system? While the situation may change, especially if our homeland ever begins to approximate the conflict levels currently existing in Israel or Iraq, the HSAS *does not* reflect the fundamental principles I have documented thus far. For example, effective warnings require specificity, precision, and information about what to do. When levels have been changed, the public remains uninformed about all of these qualities.

Future research may produce different results, but the early assessments support my conclusion. For example, Ann Marie Major and Erwin Atwood analyzed a nationally representative sample of 1,023 U.S. adults regarding the sources they used to obtain information about terrorism and their assessment of the usefulness of the HSAS.[47] Like the other disasters I have discussed already, they documented the importance of the news media that people *use routinely*. About one-half (48.8%) rated the advisory system as "useful," whereas a near equal portion (47.0%) indicated that it was "not useful."[48]

Even more penetrating and critical, however, is Ben Aguirre's assessment, wherein he too specified the characteristics of effective warning systems and found HSAS lacking.[49] His overall conclusion is one with which I concur:

> The current Homeland Security Advisory System does not draw from years of social science study and does not benefit the nation. It is not a warning system. At best, HSAS is a mitigation and anticipatory public relations tool.[50]

Some argue that HSAS is akin to having a "Climb to High Ground" warning sign in a mountain canyon. Such flash flood warning instructions do remind people of the risk and repeatedly tell them what to do every time they notice one. As such, HSAS may be a reminder of the continuing threat of terrorism. But to date, at least, the benefits of that sensitization payoff may be offset by the loss of credibility and public support. Obviously it is a matter that will remain controversial for the foreseeable future.

THE INSIGHTS

- Family evacuation is a complex social process composed of several alternative behavioral routes (i.e., invitation, compromise, default, decision).
- Most evacuees take refuge in the homes of relatives or friends.
- Depending on several specific factors that are known (e.g., is the entire town evacuated), varying proportions of families, typically

ranging between 2 percent and 6 percent, will go to public shelters. Commonly, this number is overestimated by local authorities.

- Community evacuation can be facilitated by implementing many incentives, including the following: (1) encouragement of family planning for evacuation; (2) seeking media consistency; (3) forceful but not mandatory evacuation policies; (4) allaying public fears of looting; (5) facilitating transportation; and (6) establishing Family Message Centers.

- Attack-related population protection planning has occurred, but exactly what its future form will be remains highly uncertain. So too is the degree of consistency between family responses documented to date and those that might be evoked by warnings of enemy attack. Yet no more relevant base of information exists, for either planners or family members. Without denying the uncertainties, let's recognize that these behavioral principles are the best guides we have for this exceedingly important, albeit controversial, task.

6

Why Me?

Let's return momentarily to the first story in Chapter 1. There we learned of Sam Wilson's experiences following the explosion that rocked the audience toward the end of the *Holiday on Ice* show. Remember? If not, you may want to return briefly to set the mood. Try to project yourself. In your mind's eye picture yourself as a father—just a little younger than Sam, who was a grandfather. Can you play the role?[1]

The time is 11:08 p.m. Just moments ago you were enjoying the magical beauty of colorful, costumed skaters. Now, your eyes see only red. Your three-year-old daughter is bleeding profusely. Your wife's dress—purchased just days ago—is one big smear. The four-inch slit in your daughter's left leg still drips from around the handkerchief you tied seconds ago. You are trying to calm both of them.

People around you are moving. Without realizing what is happening, you too start to walk up the coliseum stairway. Despite your daughter's pain, she only sobs—and nestles closer to your chest. Turning right, aware of the hundreds who are crowding around you, you see the outer doors.

Your thoughts? Most likely a jumble, racing fast. The adrenalin is flowing. "Where the hell are the police? Maybe we ought to just take her to the hospital ourselves. Let's see now, where did we park? It was pouring rain earlier. Oh, God, that parking lot is going to be a madhouse. Why did this have to happen tonight?"

Out the door now. Your wife has followed despite her new heels, which made for a snail's pace when you went in a couple of hours ago. Suddenly, you spot a taxi. "God, there's a whole line of them. To hell with the car."

The decision is made. You turn to your wife. She nods and tries hard to smile. The dampness of her eyes clearly reveals how hard she is fighting to hold back the tears. She will keep them inside so as not to scare the child. Later they can flow freely, but not now. Not when her outward appearance of calmness is needed. And the same goes for you too.

Now you shout at the taxi driver. "Get us out of here, will ya? This kid's hurt. Get us to the nearest hospital."

Not a pretty scene. But disasters aren't. There is pain. There is hurt. There is death. And when any of us happens to be in the wrong place at the wrong time, it's only normal to ask, "Why me?"

This story, like the one in Chapter 1, was invented. I made it up just now. The event was real, however. Though the tale is a product of my imagination, I believe that it closely parallels the story of many who happened to have been at the Indianapolis Coliseum on Halloween night 1963. Though fictitious, these words are representative of the types of thoughts many find racing inside their skulls when disaster strikes. Today, using interviews obtained from literally thousands of victims, social scientists have a fix on both probable thoughts and likely behavior. It may or may not parallel the image that would have emerged in your mind if I had asked. Maybe you have been lucky—so far!

While not pleasant to think about, victim responses are an essential behavioral component of emergency management. Equally essential is our understanding of them. This knowledge must be rooted in scientific fact, not mythology.

VICTIM RESPONSES

Let's start by listening to a few who tried to reconstruct their experience. On the night of June 8, 1966, these thoughts and actions occurred in Topeka, Kansas. That night one of the most destructive tornadoes in America's history ripped diagonally across the town. These words are but a few of those contained in an insightful book by Jim Taylor and two colleagues, Lou Zurcher and Bill Key, who have since died.[2] They were staff members at the world-famous Menninger Foundation. They and the foundation were just outside the tornado's path:

Daze: It was a strange, a real strange feeling. A real unhealthy calm. People just wandered up and down, kind of like nobody knew what happened and nobody knew what to do. They didn't talk about the tornado; they didn't talk about their house. They all needed to go somewhere but they did not know where to go.[3]

This behavior comes later. First, are two other types of responses:

Rescue: All this debris had fallen down the stairwell into the basement and we couldn't get out. The men there of course tried to push out from underneath and they couldn't. People started to get more panicky then. We looked up at the ceiling and saw that it was caving in; plaster had fallen in, and it looked as if there were sheets up there with water in them. We could smell gas, maybe from the gas main from the apartment. And the water was pouring out of the burst pipes, and I thought, "Oh my God, if we can't get out we'll get drowned." But no one got really hysterical….[4]

This girl, and others who had sought refuge in the basement, were found. The debris that trapped them was removed, and they were pulled to safety. Now they had to deal with the messages their eyes were sending inside. Being trapped temporarily, they now responded as others had earlier:

Disbelief: After we came out I had a feeling of disbelief, like a bad dream. I was saying to myself, like, "Oh, this just can't be." It happens too quick for you to comprehend at the moment. It just seems as if you were maybe looking at a picture.[5]

Years later when I talked with victims and emergency officials following other tornado disasters, these responses were validated, for example, in Wichita Falls, Texas in 1979. And twenty years later, it was Wichita, Kansas, and Moore, Oklahoma, and the list goes on. But always the response patterns are remarkably similar.[6]

THE DISASTER SYNDROME: ANOTHER MYTH EXPLODED

Decades ago, Anthony Wallace listened to other tornado victims.[7] He too was impressed with their responses. And he invented a label: *the disaster syndrome.* He suggested that disaster victims traverse a series of stages, trying to cope with their internal upheaval. These are the invisible psychological pains, in contrast to those that are more readily treatable.

Wallace described the sequential progress of these four stages like this:

109

1. Appearance of being dazed, stunned, apathetic, passive, immobile, or aimlessly puttering around.
2. Extreme suggestibility, altruism, gratitude for help, personal loss minimized, concern for family and community.
3. Euphoric identification with the damaged community, enthusiastic participation in repair and rehabilitation.
4. Fading of euphoria and return to "normal" ambivalent attitudes.

Today, we know that Wallace was wrong—at least in part. People simply are much more varied than is depicted by his so-called disaster syndrome characterization. He was the first to provide documentation, albeit crude, of a process—a sequence really—that we have since come to understand much better.

These four steps may require two to four weeks, depending on the scope of the disaster, the nature of the recovery response, and the individual. We'll dissect stages three and four in the next chapter. But for now let's focus on the first two and add some precision.

Circumstances vary, and so do victims. A few will be paralyzed momentarily if the sensory shock is extreme and fear provoking. Others, especially those with disaster-related training, will seek safety—first for self, then for others who might be near. Reactions to stress that state when our senses are overloaded or excessively deprived do vary.[8] But rarely, and then with only a tiny fraction of the population, do we see the zombie-like behavior that Wallace's characterization emphasized.

There is disbelief. Daze too. Generally these are short-lived responses, however. For most, people's memory of the initial adjustment is a sharp contrast to Wallace's caricature. Let's return to Topeka, Kansas, for two additional response patterns. First, the words of a therapist:

> Stoic Calm: He is an extremely intelligent professional man, extremely methodological in his thinking. Isolation and reaction formation are very much a part of his character. No great emotionalism, almost at any time. When he heard on the radio the tornado was coming he went around the house methodically. He opened the doors and windows. This is typical; he's too self-controlled for his own good.[9]

This may be an extreme case. It illustrates, however, the variability in response to stress. In contrast to a dazed reaction, some will evidence extreme control. It is as if they refuse to accept any disruption of their routine. Regardless of the severity of the threat, they must remain in control. They react with little evidence of fear or any other outward sign of emotion.

But then, that's how they respond to everything else: always in control, always methodical, rational at all costs, tears rarely wetting their cheeks.

More frequent, I suspect, is the polar opposite—a hyper response:

> Hyperactivity: As soon as I got to safety I became very hyper, and I talked a lot. I was a little shaky, and a little sick to my stomach, but really all right. It's just that I felt I wasn't quite with it. Shook up, I guess, would be a better way to describe it.[10]

Okay, so what is it like seconds after a massive explosion or down in a cellar after a funnel of death has danced by? It depends, but in general, despite great variability regarding what is being felt inside, Americans react.[11] They don't go bonkers. They don't become hysterical. They don't become zombies. In an extremely horrifying situation, a few might crack. But the overwhelming majority will reach inside and cope, behaving in a manner reflective of—of what? I know of only one word—heroes.

Sure, their dinner may come up. And for most, there will be a momentary halt; daze and disbelief are part of the stress response sequence. Restructuring must occur. But for most, their minds adapt rapidly, and they react quickly. If the threat is approaching, they withdraw. For those needing medical attention, they will do the best they can—maybe remembering, with regret, their refusal to attend a first aid course. If a taxi cab is available, they may grab it. After all, who can remember where they parked most of the time, anyway?

The first major terrorist attacks on our nation's soil left nearly 3,000 dead when four airplanes crashed into the World Trade Center (WTC) towers, the Pentagon, and that field near Shanksville, Pennsylvania. These deaths will not be forgotten. But we also should not forget that most got out. That's right: Despite the total collapse of the towers shortly after the aircraft struck, "approximately 87% of the estimated 17,400 occupants of the towers, and 99% of those located below the impact floors, evacuated successfully."[12]

Despite uncertainty about what happened or why, "The median time to initiate evacuation was 3 minutes for occupants from the ground floor to floor 76, and 5 minutes for occupants near the impact region (floors 77 through 91)." This was in WTC Tower 1. In WTC Tower 2, we had validation of the "spontaneous evacuation" pattern I described in Chapter 5: "Over 90% of the occupants had started to self-evacuate before the second aircraft struck, and three-quarters of those from above the 78th floor had descended below the impact region prior to the second attack."[13] And this was despite a 9:00 a.m. announcement that instructed them to return to

111

their workspaces. This is another case illustration of both the strong will to survive and the capacity for rational behavior among disaster victims.

HEROES: THEY ARE FOR REAL

When I used the word *hero*, I meant it, for if there is anything that comes through in the literature on disaster responses, it is the frequency of heroic behavior. Occasionally—but not very often really—one will pop up in the press and be recognized formally. I still recall the Congressional Budget Office employee who joined Mrs. Reagan for the 1982 State of the Union Speech. Days before, he just happened to be near the 14th Street Bridge in our nation's capital. There he watched a young flight attendant struggle. She seemed unable to grab the rescue ring dangling from a Capital Park Police helicopter. The icy waters of the Potomac had sucked her strength; her will to survive was winding down.

He wasn't paid to face danger, unlike personnel in emergency organizations who do risk their own safety pulling persons from burning buildings. That's heroic too, in my book. But here—like so many others I have had the personal privilege of meeting—was this young man, no one special really, no different from whom you discover at every disaster scene.

Media coverage of that tragic 737 crash (January 13, 1982) captured actions of another hero. Unlike this young man, however, he not only risked his life—he gave it. Sure, he could have gone ahead of the others around him who were thrashing frantically in the icy river. Instead, as the cold penetrated deeper, he looked around and called to others. He aided several as they reached out to the thin cord dangling from the helicopter. It was their gift. Through it they would live to see another day. Finally, only he was left. Before the chopper returned, the icy waters covered him over.[14]

On Saturday night, December 20, 2008, my mind flashed back to images of this plane sitting in the icy waters of the Potomac. Why? Because it was cold and I was learning of a plane crash at our local airport in Denver. As Continental Flight 1404 moved down the runway, something went wrong. Suddenly the plane veered off the runway and skidded to a stop in a forty-foot ravine.

But mass panic did not set in. Flight attendants and crew members quickly assisted the 110 passengers. All evacuated the craft safely only seconds before fire engulfed one entire side of the plane. Although thirty-eight were injured, the others bravely confronted the twenty-four-degree cold. Firefighters were on the scene immediately and quickly extinguished the blaze. Other helpers arrived soon after.

Passengers interviewed during the next several hours and days afterward used different words to express a common theme: "There were lots of heroes here that night." And while five of the injured remained hospitalized for a few days, there were no deaths. Had mass panic set in, had "heroes" not risen to the task, many could have been consumed in the plane's fire.[15]

Then a few weeks later my flashbacks matched the TV images even more closely. In mid-afternoon on Thursday, January 15, 2009, the serenity of our mountain cabin was interrupted with a news alert. An airbus A-320, US Airways Flight 1549, was floating in the icy waters on the Hudson River just north of 42nd Street in Manhattan. In all, 150 passengers and a 5-person flight crew remained calm after a remarkable emergency landing. Quick responses by people on numerous water taxis, ferry boats, and then numerous official first-responder crafts permitted everyone to escape what could have been certain death. While some suffered from hypothermia and certainly some from emotional stress, interviewees reported a consistent portrait of calmness and purpose—the key ingredients for survival. This event was a sharp contrast to the crash twenty-seven years earlier when seventy-eight died in the frozen waters of the Potomac (only five survived).[16]

These examples make the point. They parallel countless others. As I write this now, I remember Lake Pomona and the night the *Whippoorwill* capsized. There I had the honor of spending five hours or so with another hero—a man who also risked his life and prolonged that of others. His story, plus those of others I talked to there, was the basis for the second case study in Chapter 1. Remember the death of Pearl Altman?

The diver's story is but another instance of dozens that permeate the research literature. This man's experience is typical of hundreds of others. Their accounts document the reactions of human beings who discover a hidden reservoir of courage when they happen to be in the wrong place at the wrong time.

By my memory, his interview went something like this. I'm ad-libbing here and inventing the dialogue. Because I've interviewed a goodly number of other heroes—and because three decades have passed—I may have inadvertently interjected a few details from another case, distorted the timeline a bit, or otherwise altered his story. But to the best of my recollection, what he told me went about like this.

He owned a marina. For several years he had given diving instructions at Lake Pomona—a reservoir that sits in eastern Kansas, about thirty miles south of Topeka. When he learned of the *Whippoorwill*'s fate, he rushed to the craft in his pontoon boat. He pulled numerous survivors from the water, which still remained highly turbulent. Remember? A tornado had just passed over the lake.

Many victims were clinging to the *Whippoorwill*. Now capsized, its bottom side resembled a large raft. Upon assisting a dozen or so to board his boat, he yelled to others who were fighting hard to stay afloat.

"Hang on to the *Whippoorwill*! I'll be back."

As he departed, several yelled out. "There are people trapped under here! We can hear them pounding."

The journey to shore was discomforting. "'No man's land.' Why did it have to happen there? Who the hell is the sheriff going to get to dive under there?"

These thoughts were interrupted by a chill. You know the sensation: that intense tingle down your spine that reminds you of your worst childhood nightmares; the stuff of Stephen King, Freddy Kruger, and Chuckie.

Countless times he had emphasized to his young eager beaver divers that this area of the reservoir was off limits. It was filled with trees and other vegetation that continued to remain beneath the water that had arrived only a few years earlier when the reservoir was established—a real no-man's land for any diver who could easily become entangled.

Reflecting the mental hyperactivity experienced by most disaster helpers, his thoughts raced rapidly. They jumped from topic to topic with lightning speed. As options emerged and were discarded quickly, one came back again and again. "Christ! Maybe I should dive. No, that would be foolish. It's too risky. Besides, it's not my job."

Relief was not to be. The plight of those trapped was too overpowering. "I wonder who the sheriff will get. I'll bet his office will get a hold of those guys in Topeka. They ought to be able to handle it. They're good."

Then another chill, followed by another. "I wonder if they have been called out yet? I wonder if the sheriff even knows those people are trapped under there. God! I wonder how much time they get. How much air could be under that boat. What a mess, what a way to...."

His mind refused to ponder the obvious. "Damn it. Somebody's got to do something." Another chill. This one was even more intense.

Suddenly there was relief. Calmness. A sense of serenity. Had we been there, we might have seen a slight smile. Facial muscles do relax when problems finally are solved. Closure.

"Hell, I can't dive. My tanks are empty. Somebody else is going to have to go under."

The emotional relief was short-lived. As his boat approached the marina, another chill hit. His mind reached back to the recent past. Days earlier, he now recalled, he had directed his teenage son to have the tanks filled. Other times, of course, comparable requests had been ignored or delayed. Such sagas are known well by any parent.

Suddenly his mental gymnastics were interrupted. His eyes focused on the small crowd gathered at the marina. As those rescued arrived, the noise level intensified. Everyone was talking. Victims were telling of their ordeal. Others were asking questions. Had we been there, this is what we might have heard.

"Where is the sheriff?" the diver asked.

"He's on his way. Should be here any minute."

"There's people trapped under the *Whippoorwill*! Somebody's got to get to them."

"Yeah, we know. Those people over there came in on one of the little boats. We've called the Sheriff's Office and told them."

"I guess he can call out that team from Topeka. But they better get here quick. Those people can't stay under there very long. Once the air's gone."

His voice trailed off; the thought did not require expression.

"Hey, what about you? You know this reservoir better than anyone else."

The diver's head turned toward the questioner. As their eyes met, his response rushed out. The fear inside would not be put to rest.

"Me? No, I can't. My tanks are empty. Ran out last week. Just didn't get around to filling them. Hell of a time to be out of air."

Suddenly he spotted him. Coming toward the dock, just reaching the rear of the crowd was a familiar face. It looked different than normal. The smile was intense, beaming really. He had remembered. He had done it. His dad was going to be proud.

As he entered the crowd, he yelled out. "Let me through! I've got to get up there. Let me through."

His eyes caught his father's. "Dad! Dad, over here. Dad, I remembered." What's a father to do?

Several people got a time extension of their life because this man—this hero—did what he had to do. He took the tanks, put his fears aside, and dove under the capsized *Whippoorwill*. His actions comprise another dimension of the human side of disaster.

Not everyone, of course, will so respond. For one reason or another—skill, courage, but most of all, circumstance—few are called. But after going from one disaster to another, I can't stress this quality enough. The myth of human frailty must not persist.

HELPERS: HOW MANY ARE THERE?

At about this point in some of my lectures, I have noticed some nervous looks. If acute, I have on occasion singled out the workshop attendee: "Your face tells me that you may disagree. Do you think I am overemphasizing the contributions of these heroes?"

"Well, yes I do. I'm bothered by all this for several reasons. I mean, the stories are dramatic and all—they're good. I don't want to put down any of the people you've mentioned. I mean, they risked their lives and all.

"But what bothers me is this. In the first place, you seem to be overstating the case. Are there really these types of heroes at every disaster? I mean, how prevalent is this type of thing anyway? Are you sure you haven't been sucked in by the press? And second, you seem to be condoning this. From my view, what we need is for people to stay away from disaster areas, not try to get in there and play hero."

These points are well taken. But they reflect a whole series of myths that reflect a lack of understanding. Lack of knowledge encourages subsequent planning rooted in false premises. The consequence? Plans that fail.

For an example, recall my opening illustrations. These fictional creations are based on actual interviews in several disasters and rooted in a real event. They speak to a couple of points. Was the behavior of this grandparent, Sam Wilson, abnormal? Not really. Indeed, we have ample evidence now from numerous studies of search and rescue actions and emergency medical responses to document a key fact. This was a typical response.

Following the 1979 tornado in Cheyenne, Wyoming, for example, I discovered that not a single victim was taken to any hospital by an ambulance. Several studies have now documented this pattern. Most victims arrive at medical treatment facilities through unofficial means. They come in a cab or neighbor's car, not an ambulance or fire rescue truck.

The message is this. Too often I've seen elaborate plans for patient dispersal so that no one hospital gets overloaded. Can you imagine a grandparent like the one I described telling the taxi cab driver something like this? "Take us to the hospital that the emergency management plan calls for." Of course not. Unless the most unusual circumstances prevail—say, a plane crash at an airport, after the pilot has notified the air control tower of potential trouble—few disaster victims are transported to medical treatment facilities in official emergency vehicles. Typically, before adequate resources can be mobilized, most victims are gone.

In the Indianapolis case, after some delay, a semblance of a patient dispersal was established; ambulance drivers were directed to go to certain hospitals. Yet a serious imbalance in patient dispersal occurred. The hospital best equipped to take emergency cases received only twenty-seven, whereas others with less capabilities were severely overloaded.

Why? My example illustrates the general principle. It is not that taxi cabs always are used. In this case many just happened to be present because the show was due to end momentarily. The specifics will vary. What doesn't vary, however, is the principle: People react! People improvise! People don't wait around for authorities to tell them what to do. They are resourceful. They will improvise unexpected means to get victims out of danger and to treatment facilities.

Okay, so should we just ignore disasters? Heroes will be there, so why even make plans? No, that doesn't follow. My point is that emergency managers must begin the planning process with this realization. Sure, mechanisms for control and coordination of patient dispersal should be built into any plan. But you must realize that many victims—maybe all— will arrive at treatment centers through improvised means. Personnel there must be prepared to deal with this. That's what the emergency plan must take into account.[17]

Too often, what is overlooked is the localized nature of most disasters. Even for most of the big ones, this remains true. The 1979 tornado in Wichita Falls, Texas, illustrates this very well. The community had a population of about 96,000. The killer tornado of April 10, 1979, destroyed 3,000 houses and nearly 1,300 apartment units. Another 1,000 houses experienced major damage. More than 950 persons required hospital treatment. Another forty-five did not celebrate Easter Sunday—not that Sunday or any thereafter.

When we interviewed victims regarding their actions during the first few hours afterward, we discovered that nearly three-fifths (59%) immediately began helping. First, they turned to household members. Then immediately, neighbors' homes—or rather the debris piles left by this savage monster—were searched. When we projected the response pattern within our sample to the entire victim population, we concluded that something like 10,000 individuals were participating in these search and rescue efforts.[18]

This really is a conservative estimate, too. Why? Well, it doesn't say a thing about persons outside the tornado path who may have rushed there looking for a friend or relative. We know that this type of convergence behavior is another response that always occurs.[19]

Even if they might be endangered—say, radioactive contamination or toxic chemicals are present—a goodly percentage of people nearby will still rush to the scene. In part, they are curious. Studies of such actions also indicate that many are motivated primarily because they want to help. Upon arriving, they frequently stand around looking for something to do. Recall the hero in the Washington, D.C., jet airliner crash? He was one in a crowd who stood on the banks of the Potomac—just watching. But a human life continued because he was there, because he reacted.

His behavior paralleled actions documented in disasters long ago. For example, David McCullough's detailed history of the 1889 Johnstown flood remains one of the best case examples ever written. Shortly after the dam above Johnstown gave way, many were trapped on a train:

> ...Most of the male passengers on board the train were out on the river-banks doing everything possible to help. They got hold of long poles and big limbs and held them out over the current as far as they could, hoping maybe the people going by could reach them. They threw ropes, and at one point, one of them actually stripped off his coat and jumped into the water to save a mother and her small child.[20]

Russ Dynes and Henry Quarantelli have pushed this point much further.[21] First, they point out the capability. Most are not injured or killed in most disasters. I saw this very dramatically following the Wichita Falls tornado in 1979. Around 1,000 received medical treatment. But that still left 95,000 within the area who were uninjured. So despite this exceptional demand, the casualty rate was about 1%. If the number injured was tripled—3,000 total—what happens to the rate? It becomes 3%. The point is then to recognize the number of potential helpers, quite independent of emergency organization personnel.

The estimates I made for Wichita Falls were not atypical. In their review of earlier studies, Dynes and Quarantelli point out several parallels. In one of the earliest studies, it was determined that 27% of all adults (about 40% of all males) in the immediate tornado area participated in rescue efforts. This was in White County, Arkansas in 1952.

People are present, and even if they have minor injuries, they will try to help others in need. Sometimes this means pulling people from cellars now covered with debris. Other times it means transporting them to treatment facilities. Americans simply are not going to wait around until emergency organizational personnel get their act together.

Following the 1974 Xenia, Ohio, tornado, researchers discovered that more than one-fourth (26%) of all adults in a nearby community engaged in some form of aid or offered to help. This community became the medical headquarters for the impacted area. Of course, most just helped in whatever way they could, but 6% put specialized skills, like nursing, to work.

Paul O'Brien and Dennis Mileti further documented these patterns of helping behavior following the Loma Prieta earthquake (San Francisco and Santa Cruz areas of California, October 17, 1989).[22] Their carefully selected samples indicated that 60% of the people residing in the San Francisco area engaged in some form of helping behavior after the earthquake. In Santa Cruz the rate was even higher (70%). When these rates were projected on the community populations, we can estimate that there were about 434,375 helpers in the San Francisco region and 34,798 in Santa Cruz.

The massive search and rescue efforts made after Hurricane Katrina bring perspective. The Committee on Homeland Security and Governmental Affairs of the U.S. Senate documented important details. And the magnificent job done by Coast Guard personnel should be remembered and emphasized; they rescued more than 33,000 victims. Also, Department of Defense (DoD) and Federal Emergency Management Association (FEMA) personnel should be noted, although their number of rescues were far outnumbered by the Coast Guard (DoD, 2,911; FEMA, 6,000).[23]

But here again, the quick responses by ordinary citizens also were highlighted. There were problems, however. These reflected such issues as volunteers arriving to participate but lacking the necessary equipment to be self-sufficient (e.g., food, water). This alone kept many—on one day, nearly one-half—of the willing from being used effectively. Others showed up with boats that were too large. Areas of New Orleans, for example, could not accommodate them.[24]

In spite of these and other difficulties, the Senate report provides dozens of examples of helping behaviors enacted by unofficial volunteers. Their lack of organization frustrated many who thought they should be "in charge." Yet they came and when necessary improvised ways to "get the job done."

A good example is the emergency management technician from a nearby town who was joined by several firefighters and police officers. Seeing a sixteen-year-old girl who had been pulled from her rooftop and then actually delivered her baby in a boat, he saw the acute need, so he improvised.[25] This unofficial group hot-wired boats and rescued 350 people from rooftops before day's end. I'm certain that those rescued were grateful and couldn't care one whit whether these men were working within an "official command structure."

Is such helping behavior unique to natural disasters like hurricanes, earthquakes, or tornadoes? For example, could we expect it following terrorist attacks? Obviously, as I noted previously, those fleeing from the World Trade Towers after the 9/11 attacks, like those in the Pentagon, clearly helped and were helped by others. Following the bombings in the London subway on July 7, 2005, Joe Scanlon noted that this response reflected the same pattern; that is, people nearby, not emergency personnel, were the first helpers.[26] And Scanlon documented his conclusion with plenty of examples. He detailed the actions of one female passenger who was riding in the same car as the bombers. She suffered minor cuts and bruises, including head injuries and burns. One shoe was covered in blood, the other missing. Did she become a zombie after the explosion? Scanlon's summary makes my case:

> Before leaving the car to walk barefoot out of the Underground, she noticed a man sitting across from her with severe leg injuries. "His legs had been ripped apart. I took off my jacket and pressed it onto his legs to try and stem the blood flow."[27]

So should emergency managers just turn over disaster areas to volunteers? Of course not. But as stressed earlier, my point is that the planning process must begin with a correct understanding of the behavioral responses in such settings. People will react. And frankly, many lives are saved because they do. Such volunteers are a key resource and should be viewed as such. Also, any efforts, like those of a junior high school science teacher I encountered in a small mountain town in Colorado, to integrate first aid skills within regular classroom instruction will increase the quality of this resource. Certainly, attempts to enroll more citizens in various levels of first aid classes should not be discouraged. Rather, additional ways to implant such lifesaving knowledge should be pursued. Too many of us just will never get around to setting aside the time. In short, every opportunity to *integrate* aspects of emergency management *within community routines* should be pursued. This perspective offers a different view of emergency management from that held by many. It broadens emergency management into a community function that goes far beyond the limited resources represented by relatively small numbers of emergency agency personnel.

Now let's get to the final aspect of the question posed previously. Officials should try to keep people away from disaster scenes. Media personnel can be a big help here. But during the first few hours, except, as I said before, in locations where unusual circumstances prevail, total security simply will be impossible. In the Indianapolis explosion, the Coliseum was located within the Indiana State Fairgrounds, which was fenced. While delayed, security was made much easier than is typically the case following disasters that are more widespread—tornadoes, floods, or earthquakes.

People are people. Just as we saw regarding the infiltration of police blockades during community evacuations—remember, the dog was still home—so too they will try to converge on a tornado-damaged neighborhood. This could be the event of a lifetime, surely not one to be missed. I stressed the need for a Family Message Center when I discussed evacuation. After any disaster, this need is acute. Some people could be put to work in such tasks immediately.

"WHERE IS MY DAUGHTER?"

Listen to the voice of one who has been there: the Topeka police chief, as quoted by Taylor, Zurcher, and Key:

> It is difficult to hold back anyone who is searching for his daughter. I don't think they've ever passed laws that say what you can do with human behavior in the time of disaster.[28]

Pondering this statement momentarily brings numerous fragments of interviews back to me. I recall still the horror I felt when I listened to call after call from the tape-recordings made of telephones in the Indianapolis Police Department that Halloween night when the explosion ended the ice show at the Coliseum.

Horror? Yeah, horror! Family member after family member was trying to locate those who had gone for a night of fun. Tight security—remember, it was within the fenced fairgrounds—precluded their personal search. Many, of course, went there only to be turned away. Others, after repeatedly getting busy signals at hospital after hospital, drove from one to another. Others just sat, glued to their television—hoping, maybe with dampened eyes.

Eventually, an elaborate welfare inquiry system was established. Through the coordination efforts of the local Red Cross chapter, hundreds of questions were answered. Too often the scope of such tasks is grossly underestimated, as is its importance.

Yet nearly two decades later, I encountered husbands who were stopped near debris piles. Security had been established after a tornado. Down the road a block or two, they could see a heap of debris that had been their home three hours earlier. Where had their family been taken? "Are you certain they still aren't in the basement? Couldn't one of you come with me just to be sure? I can't locate them anywhere. Yeah, damn it I have telephoned. I went to six different places where I thought they might have gone."

You see, despite media stories highlighting neglect and callous behavior when people require help, disaster scenes are different. Facing a multiblock path of flood-damaged homes or a tornado-ripped shopping center is just not the same experience as seeing a single individual about to be a robbery victim. Tales of a female screaming for help while passersby ignore her remain newsworthy because they are rare. Let's hope they remain that way. In times of disaster, people—ordinary folks—rush to help. Heroes are born!

But there are signs that bother me. Certain constraints—both social and legal—may be blunting this reservoir of national capability. In my judgment, no one interested in emergency management can afford to ignore the danger these social forces represent.

BUT THERE ARE CONSTRAINTS

Up to this point I have stressed the presence of helping behaviors as an integral dimension of disaster responses. They are there. If anticipated and coordinated with the actions of emergency organization personnel, the response capability of every American community can be nurtured—as I believe it should be—or it can gradually rot. Improved understanding of social processes that facilitate, and those undermining, volunteer actions is a matter that the research community has neglected for the most part.[29] Yet a bit of research has been completed that provides some guidelines for action.

The Age of Litigation

First is the matter of legal fright. I encountered this for the first time in 1978. Upon interviewing several who rushed to the capsized *Whippoorwill* showboat, I uncovered a theme that reappeared in subsequent cities.[30] Rescue actions had been taken; lives had been spared. Not one of those interviewed had doubts or misgivings about what they had done. If confronted with the same situation tomorrow, I have every reason to believe they would again rise to the occasion.

Yet they volunteered messages I didn't anticipate. Never had I seen it in the disaster literature. Discussion with longtime disaster researchers like Henry Quarantelli and Charlie Fritz validated my conclusion that this was something new. It is a product of the times, a period some have labeled "the age of litigation."

What they volunteered in these interviews was a concern that they might be subject to a lawsuit. While all indicated total commitment to their actions, they revealed that this fear had entered their minds afterwards. Let me stress that these expressions were not responses to direct questioning about the legality of what they had done. In response to my questions, they described their responses and offered suggestions to others who might someday confront similar situations. This element of legal fright was then mentioned, sort of in passing. They volunteered it; I didn't ask.

In subsequent field studies we queried samples of emergency personnel. I'm not referring to citizens who had acted as rescuers; rather, I mean paid employees with disaster planning or operational responsibilities. Since this was not our research focus, we could explore the matter only superficially. These interviews indicated that their understanding of legal matters was rather poor. Local emergency personnel often didn't even know whether their state had a Good Samaritan law or who might be protected by it. Equally importantly, many didn't seem to grasp the legal process. So, for example, I was told by one local agency representative something to the effect of, "Oh, yeah, we have that here. It prevents anyone who helps somebody in need from being sued." That simply is wrong. And if this person tells that to others who then read a newspaper accounting of a subsequent suit, they can't help but be confused. My point is that emergency managers need to give this matter a hard look. Actions should be taken before this potential barrier to volunteer help becomes stronger.

Amanda Ripley explored this matter in her excellent investigation of survival behavior. As she put it, "Like fear of panic, the fear of litigation is a silent partner in emergency management."[31] Such fears have resulted in numerous bad policy decisions ranging from delays in evacuation advisories to suspension of driver's education programs: "Schools teach typing, but they no longer do anything to protect your children from the most likely cause of their accidental deaths."[32]

What ought to be done? First, every person involved formally in some aspect of emergency management should be familiar with the statutes and legal processes existent in their state. If asked whether their state has a Good Samaritan law, they should not be vague. Become informed!

Second, my review of several of the legislative acts that mandate such protections indicates gross inconsistency and many voids. Perhaps reflecting those special interests instrumental in lobbying for passage, identification of who is covered varies widely from state to state. Sometimes nurses or paramedics are included, other times not. The legal protection afforded a citizen with no formal medical training often is unclear. So, the second type of action needed is legal reform.

Finally, once these steps are taken—even before, really—efforts at public education must take place. Obviously, that is a big job. Unless those committed to emergency management make greater effort, I fear that the willingness to respond may be eroded. That would be a loss no one can afford. A nation of onlookers is not consistent with my image of America.

Expanding Poverty

Despite my emphasis on helping behaviors, the image must be fine-tuned. There are many who don't participate, or, more accurately, the scope, intensity, and frequency of their participation are less. This is true from both sides—that is, giving and receiving. There are clear patterns of neglect within American communities after disaster, just as there are on a daily basis.

That is what we saw following the flooding brought on by Hurricane Katrina. As a community, like many other urban areas of the United States, New Orleans was populated partially by people of very limited means. And many were elderly, poor, and black. Minority status with the accompanying life experiences of discrimination, like poverty and limited mobility that often accompanies age, were important social factors. Collectively, these three conditions may have reduced the volume of helping behavior. This was further exacerbated by the circumstances of the sudden flooding that occurred when sections of the levee system failed.

If the gap between the rich and poor continues to increase, more and more Americans will experience the harsh reality of poverty. Given the demographics of our post-World War II population curve, increased numbers of these poor will be elderly. Unless new social policies are enacted to reverse these trend lines, the emergent post-disaster helping behaviors

I have emphasized will decline. Aside from a societal goal reflecting values of justice and compassion, reduction of poverty has become an issue of national security. Citizens existing within conditions of urban squalor will not respond to disaster much differently from how they respond to their everyday problems of life. Diminished participation in postdisaster helping is a consequence that we should not tolerate. Expanded poverty levels are not the America I want to see. Do you?

Bureaucratic Mindsets

Without devoting too much more space to this issue, let's consider one other critical constraint: the attitudes of emergency managers. What I mean by this are qualities I have detected. These reflect management styles that are authoritarian, top-down, and exclusive rather than inclusive. Since the 9/11 attacks and escalating fears of future episodes that may be even more deadly, such views have become more widespread. At times it seems like we are returning to the autocratic mindset that defined many civil defense directors during the 1950s. In my view, however, this trend will prove counterproductive if continued. One can be a professional yet share my conclusion that volunteers must be nurtured. Volunteer actions must be encouraged.

In his comparisons of the London subway bombings and the 2004 Indian Ocean tsunami disaster, Scanlon emphasized this same theme. He argued that too many emergency workers really believe they will be in control. He was amazed at how the tsunami response paralleled what happened about twenty-eight months later in the London subway. He had been in "the tube" about seventy-two hours before the bombs exploded, so his interest in this event went beyond the typical motivations of disaster researchers! The helping behaviors of victims able to do so—like others who happen to be in near proximity—was emphasized. So too was the bureaucratic mindset of officials that search and rescue and emergency transport was their turf.[33]

Too often, however, I have been told by some emergency managers that response effectiveness requires more trained staff, more hardware, more discipline. So when I mention, for example, that perhaps their communication needs could have been partially met by requesting assistance from HAM radio organizations or CB clubs, I get told something like, "Oh, those guys. They're more trouble than they're worth. I tried to get them involved years ago. Oh sure, they were real eager beavers for a few weeks, but they quit coming to our monthly meetings after a while so I finally gave up trying to get them here. I mean, if they aren't willing to even come to our monthly meetings, how in the hell could I depend on them in a disaster?"

Attitudes like this are widespread. They can surface among officials at all levels of the inter-governmental system. Not too long ago I read a news report that summarized reactions to a FEMA-based initiative whereby "official" potential rescuers would be given a special identification card. This way, even off-duty fire and police personnel who arrived at the scene of a disaster could be granted quick access. And the others could be kept away—at least that is the theory.[34]

Apparently, executives with such groups as the National Demolition Association really like the idea and are trying to implement it in California. The executive director said, "If California goes ahead and does that, it will flow across the country. This is a really smart idea by someone in the Bush administration to be able to control access to the site and frankly, make sure there are no untrained people."[35]

Such attitudes reflect a philosophy that permeates too much of the emergency management sector today. It is a philosophy paralleling the drift in many other facets of American society. It reflects an oversubscription to the principles of bureaucratic management. These have worked well within business firms, although even there we are learning of the costs and grave limitations.[36] But emergency management in a relatively decentralized society like America requires an alternative theory. The outlines of such a theory are just now beginning to be crystallized by a few scholars—a matter I explore in the final chapter of this book.

Yet more needs to be said about the role of volunteers in disaster responses. So we'll pursue this matter in the next chapter. Let's be clear though about the insights we have just reviewed.

THE INSIGHTS

- Victims at disaster scenes react immediately. They don't wait around for emergency officials to arrive and direct them.
- Following a brief restructuring period—a type of disbelief or denial response, which is momentary for most—a majority of victims begin rescuing and helping any who might be around them.

- Unlike the uniformity depicted in Wallace's disaster syndrome, victim responses vary. Some may experience daze for a brief period, but hyperactivity and a stoic calm are more common.
- Heroic behavior will be forthcoming, although most such actions will be known only to very limited numbers of victims—those who were helped.
- Most people injured, except when unusual circumstances prevent volunteer helpers from getting to the scene, will be transported to medical treatment facilities by unofficial means.
- Convergence behavior, that is, people rushing to a disaster impacted area, is widespread. Even if they may be at risk, many people will try to converge at a disaster scene.
- Many who arrive at disaster scenes could be integrated into more coordinated volunteer teams if officials viewed them as a resource rather than a problem source.
- Field interviews have revealed legal concerns among some who have helped at disaster scenes. This, like negative attitudes exhibited by some local emergency managers, may deter future helping actions.
- Expanding poverty is a serious societal illness that must be addressed. Failure to do so will have the undesired consequence of dampening the rate and intensity of postdisaster helping behavior.
- A new theory of emergency management is required. It cannot be rooted in notions commonly found within highly centralized bureaucracies.

7

Volunteers? You Bet!

People caught at a disaster scene are going to help. A lot of people who are nearby will too. This is one facet of a much larger category of volunteerism. Although you can anticipate these responses, they are difficult to mold and channel simply because they happen so suddenly.

Sometimes, however, more time is available. Even so, too many officials turn inward. They fail to reach out and mobilize one of the best resources they can get: the average citizen. It can be done, however. Sometimes it is. One of the best examples I have ever seen emerged along the banks of the Red River of the North. Ever been to East Grand Forks, Minnesota?

THE FLOOD BREAKERS

The Red River of the North flows near the homes and businesses that border the states of Minnesota and North Dakota. Grand Forks sits on the west side, and, as the name implies, East Grand Forks sits on the east side. My first visit to this area occurred in 1978, one of the many times this river has caused pain for local residents.[1] There I encountered a splendid illustration of how large numbers of volunteers can be integrated into an effective emergency management weapon. Let me stress at the outset, however, that they had not attended numerous meetings months prior. Indeed, to have encouraged them to do so would have been an error. It is one commonly made.

There are many forms of volunteering. Only a very small segment of the population desires the ongoing continuity of a formally organized group. We have other interests and other ways to spend our time. But when the chips are down, we can be counted on—that is, if we're invited and, most importantly, if we are given tasks that make us feel needed.

Flashing back to me now is a conference room in the administrative building of the Area Vocational Institute.[2] It is April 1978. Seated around the table are a couple of dozen persons who had directed various aspects of the highly successful dike-monitoring effort.

As each described his or her respective actions, I was impressed with three different things. First, most units were composed strictly of volunteers. Second, the task assignments had been preplanned by the director of Civil Defense for East Grand Forks. For the most part, however, the actual people to fit into his overall structure had not participated in numerous training sessions but rather were assigned jobs they could carry out using skills and equipment they had. Thus, lengthy training really wasn't necessary. Third, and finally, much of this multiorganizational network was held together—coordinated, really—through the use of CB radios. This resource is available readily in most American communities. Remember, there was communication before cell phones! In today's world of texting, instant messaging, and the like, this response might have emerged quite differently.

The precise structure of the organization that emerged in April 1978, however, did not become clear to these volunteer leaders until I started diagramming their linkages on the chalkboard that day. Each had realized segments of the response, but none had seen the whole. As each person added bits and pieces, my diagram began to take shape. Gradually, a rather complex network emerged. Finally, I ended up with a drawing that looked like a giant spider web. Dike walkers were linked to the Flood Control Center, which in turn was linked to the Red Cross, city shops, fire and police officials, and numerous others. All of these links were CB radio conduits.

For twenty-four days, twenty-four hour shifts of volunteer dike walkers were coordinated. As weak spots along the several miles of dikes were detected, engineering personnel were informed. When repairs were required, a decision best made by the engineers, school busses transported high school students to the locations where sandbags had been delivered earlier. National Guard troops assisted also. The complexity of the whole operation was best captured in my diagram.[3] The picture truly amazed all of us in the room that day.

An emergent structure? Yes, it came into being solely in response to the flood threat. A coordinated response? You bet! A voluntary effort? Not totally, but for the most part. And unlike ponderous bureaucratic structures struggling to survive despite changed conditions that may make their continuity unnecessary, this organization drifted away for the most part. Only those within its core continue to meet. But when needed again, it has been reborn.[4]

For repetitive tasks, which exhibit stability and require exactness, bureaucratic managerial principles are effective tools. They have limited applicability in the irregular, nonpredictable challenges most disasters create, however. Make no mistake here. Disciplined and continuing volunteer groups can be nurtured and integrated within the ongoing bureaucratized community organizations responsible for the daily, and rather routinized, everyday emergencies. Thus, in contrast to that type of emergent organization just described in East Grand Forks, directly across the Red River a different pattern occurred. In Grand Forks, North Dakota, a Civil Defense director and a police chief absorbed numerous volunteers. They augmented the capability of the emergency response system.

Unfortunately, the Red River of the North was not done flooding. Like other rivers, it never will be actually. But nineteen years after my first visit to the Grand Forks area, winter snows really piled up. And when melt time came, there just was too much water. Soils reached their capacity to absorb. As the river rose, more and more water moved. Dikes that had held prior flows back from built structures on both sides of the river finally gave way. April 18, 1997, was a bad day in both riverside communities. When fires broke out in the downtown area of Grand Forks, destroying the home of the local newspaper and many other buildings, the disaster took on a new life. Despite losses of $2 billion, not a single life was lost.[5]

I believe that far greater responsibilities could be assumed by volunteer units, both in disaster responses and, frankly, in daily emergencies. Among the best examples of this I have seen are represented by the hundreds of volunteer search and rescue (SAR) teams scattered across the United States. Their assortment is remarkably varied, as are the skills and competencies they represent. Some are divers. The Osage County sheriff saw them in action the night of the *Whippoorwill* tragedy. For after several survivors were pulled out by the hero I described in the last chapter, these divers began the traumatic task of body recovery. Remember the fate of Pearl Altman, my fictional character in Chapter 1—the woman with the earrings?

Other volunteers love dogs. I first saw them at work after a tornado had ripped through Wichita Falls, Texas, in 1979.[6] Think of television footage you have seen in more recent years following earthquakes, tornadoes, or explosions. The unique contributions these rescue animals can make are recognized more widely every year. Following Hurricane Katrina, for example, numerous SAR dog teams assisted. Now through state-to-state agreements, formally referred to as the Emergency Management Assistance Compact (EMAC), the procedures to transport such teams have been streamlined. For example, a six-member team from Virginia responded to a request for twenty dog teams from Louisiana officials. A twenty-block square area in the badly flooded Ninth Ward neighborhood required the special help these teams could provide. The Virginia team was on site from October 10 to 15, 2005. Numerous others assisted throughout the hurricane-ravaged Gulf Coast area. Six months after Hurricane Katrina's landfall, SAR dog teams were still leading handlers to dead bodies within debris piles in sections of New Orleans.[7]

Other rescue personnel risk their personal safety when they search an avalanche-created snow field, rappel 200 feet down a rock face, or crawl deep within a black cavern. The environs vary widely; the skill and commitment to helping others are the constants. Most Americans frequently read of small aircraft crashes. Few realize the important contributions made by Civil Air Patrol (CAP) members. They too are volunteers. Minimal amounts of public funds are expanded immensely by CAP units and the many other varieties of disaster volunteers.

If the full costs of all search missions—be they due to boat, airplane, or snowmobile failures; be they cross-country skiers, hunters, or picnickers—were ever aggregated nationally, the American public would be in for quite a shock. But because of volunteers, these costs are but a tiny fraction of what they would be if we resorted to specialized bureaucracies to meet these challenges. This set of challenges, by the way, is going to increase in the decades ahead. The lifestyle changes are already in process. Have you seen annual sales figures on snowmobiles or cross-country ski equipment? Hang gliding is here to stay; small private aircraft use is going to increase just as dramatically as small boat use.

As the need for emergency responses increases, the budget pressures on local organizations will become exacerbated. Many county sheriffs are sensing this now, especially in the Western states wherein many of the newer recreational toys are enjoyed the most. In my view, this future challenge can best be met by nurturing volunteer organizations using the proven model of the CAP. Today, more than ever before, capable persons are searching for challenges that too often are lacking within the bureaucratic death traps from which their income is derived. Involvement in one of these volunteer organizations can provide an important source of personal renewal.

ARE VOLUNTEERS LIKE YACHTS?

Volunteer groups require nurturing. The volunteer spirit cannot be taken for granted. As with the CAP and Red Cross, small amounts of public funds can transform a hobby group into a rich community resource. Erma Bombeck, who always seemed to capture the essence of things, once said that volunteers and yachts reflect "an era that is disappearing from the American scene.... More and more of them equate their worth in terms of dollars and cents. They are the only human beings on the face of this earth who reflect this Nation's compassion, unselfish caring, patience, and just plain loving one another."[8]

This is quite a statement—one that reflects my concerns too. What social forces are operating? It is not just the popularity of "sue the bastard;" rather, we are experiencing a whole range of social trends that are neutralizing the volunteer spirit. For some, it is the myth of the dollar, for others, a myth of professionalism. "Volunteer work was fine for a while, but I want a professional degree now so I can get a job and really help people." You can't imagine how often I have heard such statements. After two or three years of working as a professional, a new reality is expressed. "Boy, was I ever wrong. There are days I think I was doing more good when I was a volunteer."

There is a unique contribution made to one's sense of self upon receiving a paycheck. As gender roles continue to change in our society, however, males will no longer have the upper hand on the marketplace. As more females are free from past constraints that precluded commitment to both family and career, the composition of volunteer organizations will change—if not in gender ratios then in the death rates of such groups. Organizational stability always is problematic, especially in times of rapid social change.

Yet having a full-time job does not preclude participation in a volunteer organization. It never has. The present transformation, wherein American females are facing greater freedom of choice than ever before, does not mean the death of the volunteer spirit. It does mean, however, that such organizations must adapt, both in expectations for members and in incentives for belonging.

Remember my warning in the last chapter about the negative consequences of expanding poverty? Here is another one. Today, many are working two jobs just to make ends meet, some even three. As more and more citizens are employed in lower-paying jobs, interest in volunteering declines. When there just isn't enough money to pay the bills each month, hope begins to fade. And the perceived limits of choice close tighter and tighter. Poverty curtails hope in the future and the sense of power to make things better. Such mindsets do not nurture or birth volunteering activity.

Years ago I learned of several incentives being used in California through a statement by a former president of the National Association for Search and Rescue (NASAR).[9] For example, local governments could register volunteers as "Civil Defense Workers." This allowed coverage under worker's compensation insurance during training and actual SAR missions at no cost to the individual, their local agency, or local government. Similarly, in exchange for instructional time donated in several search and rescue courses, food and travel costs were subsidized.

These and other forms of incentives that have been introduced more recently have rich payoff. They are a logical alternative to further bureaucratization. They provide an approach that encourages participation in the society, not further withdrawal into spectator or consumer roles. Not that there is anything wrong with either, but the lives of many could be so enriched if they found a niche in which to spend a few hours of their week. This is another reason the expansion of poverty must be reversed.

THE UTOPIAN MOOD

Most of us have many social linkages. For some, these carry us into various voluntary organizations, be they a church, CB radio club, or Red Cross chapter. I have stressed my belief that emergency managers should do everything possible to nurture such units and seek to attack threats to their survival. But there is another whole dimension to this notion of *the volunteer*. Usually it isn't put into this context, yet it is an aspect of equal importance.

When you talk with disaster victims about their experience beyond the immediate emergency period, one theme hits hardest. Most are awed by the mood or climate of their community. This has come to be called the *utopian mood*. It is reflected in the second phase of Anthony Wallace's disaster syndrome. Recall the four stages I introduced in the last chapter? Wallace suggested that after their initial shock, which for most is very short-lived, many victims feel intense gratitude for the help they received that minimized their personal loss. Many express concern for family and community.[10]

Here Wallace was far more on target. But again there is variation. Not all victims express this equally, because not all have equal reason to do so. Some are helped more than others, regardless of damage incurred.

Typically, however, there is an immediate, massive outpouring of help. And some persons who have little interest in a volunteer organization react in accordance with their daily mode of social participation. Their commitment—both in time and emotion—lies with their family, often one reaching across several households and frequently two or three generations. For the very lucky, it may even be four or five generations.

So, in a time of disaster, they volunteer. No, they don't rush to the headquarters of a CB club; rather, they open their home to relatives or friends needing help. Remember the importance I placed on this when I discussed evacuation? Except for a small percentage, people don't go to public shelters. Rather, they go to homes of relatives or friends. Typically, they are invited. They don't arrive there after having begged or even asked. They go because someone else cared. Someone else extended an invitation.

This form of volunteering ought to be encouraged. Emergency managers ought to be far more aggressive than they have been in seeking incentives to encourage such actions. Among the many transformations we are experiencing as a nation is a dampening of such social networks. The social processes are complex and varied. Disasters, like other special occasions—funerals and births—rekindle family ties. Even weak ties are energized. Kin linkages are ignited and become pathways for all kinds of assistance, both physical and emotional.

Most disaster victims express a sense of being overwhelmed at the type and range of help they receive from relatives and friends. Typically, after a tornado or flood, about 55% will receive such assistance, but this still leaves 45% who don't.[11]

We now know the characteristics of those most subject to this *pattern of neglect*. They are disproportionately the elderly, the poor, and ethnic minorities.[12] There is a parallel here. It is not unexpected. You see, when we survey disaster volunteers, some of the same characteristics turn out to be important. Russ Dynes and Henry Quarantelli analyzed those volunteering to temporarily help in various community agencies following the extensive flooding in Wilkes-Barre, Pennsylvania, that Hurricane Agnes (1972) produced. What characteristics did they reflect? ":...Primarily families with children. They were likely to be young and male. Most of them had full-time jobs, primarily at high skill levels—professional and managerial. They tended to work for large organizations as opposed to being self-employed or working in small organizations."[13] When disaster strikes, large segments of most communities will experience a rare outpouring of help—the Utopian mood. In Chapter 6, I highlighted several examples. Recall that following the 1979 tornado in Wichita Falls, Texas, my research team documented that nearly three-fifths (59%) of all noninjured victims interviewed helped someone nearby within minutes.[14] Similarly, after the Loma Prieta, California, earthquake (1989) left people scrambling, Paul O'Brien and Dennis Mileti documented that 60% of the noninjured in the San Francisco area provided assistance of some form. In the Santa Cruz area, the proportion jumped to 70% .[15] And typically, those helping at the scene reflect the qualities noted by Dynes and Quarantelli; that is, they are younger males who have more years of schooling. Then later, the volunteer core changes gender and becomes more female based.

During the first few hours after the Loma Prieta earthquake, for example, many Santa Cruz residents provided food and water to survivors (35%).[16] Even more (44%) reported that they removed debris or otherwise helped clean up. A small percentage (5%) said they actually performed various types of search and rescue actions. But remember, just like in our Wichita Falls tornado study, where we estimated that 10,000 residents did so, for Santa Cruz the figure would be 34,798 people (1990 population, 49,711). Similarly, the estimated number of volunteer helpers in the San Francisco area was 434,375! That's a lot of help!

Of course, many feared returning home or simply could not, given the damage done. So nearly one-fifth of the interviewees said they provided shelter to people needing it (18%). I suspect that many times they also provided emotional comfort, which is among the best forms of counseling (17%). Also reported by the Santa Cruz interviewees were such forms of helping as putting out fires (7%), evacuation assistance (4%), medical assistance (4%), and directing traffic (2%).

More recently, I saw this outpouring of help when a tornado hit the town of Windsor, which is near my home in Denver. By circumstance, May 22, 2008, was the Weld County Sheriff's Office seventeenth annual golf tournament. So, as Deputy Shane Scofield reported to our state sheriff's magazine,[17] more than 100 law enforcement personnel were focused on a day of fun. Unfortunately, heavy rain and high winds caused them to gather by mid-day. As conditions worsened, most moved into a concrete parking garage at and near the clubhouse. Suddenly, Sheriff Cooke received the call: A mile-wide tornado was headed straight toward the golf course. Fortunately for this gathering, the monster missed them, but only by about one-quarter of a mile. Unfortunately, 500 homes in Windsor were in its path. Although no major injuries were reported, one life was lost. And what did people do afterward? "From the very beginning volunteers were arriving on the scene, calling and e-mailing with offers of help ranging from shelter, food, money, labor, or animal care…. They were ready and willing to do what was needed in order to get Windsor back on its feet."[18] In short, postdisaster assistance of this informal type comes in every form imaginable. As the recovery continues, the forms of aid shift. More and more victims now turn to relatives or friends for short-term shelter. Of course, many have described to me their ambivalence about such arrangements. It seems that for many, relatives are like fish. Visits beyond a week can get rather smelly!

But the list goes on. Help is given in other ways like providing temporary shelter and meals, babysitting, or loaning a car. And, of course, the hardest thing of all—confronting the enormous and usually painful job of cleaning up.

UNVEILING THE MANY FORMS OF VOLUNTEERISM

After they reviewed the range of volunteer assistance described in hundreds of disaster studies, Dynes and Quarantelli invented a conceptual map that nicely summarizes the various examples I have discussed throughout this entire chapter.[19] They used two somewhat abstract notions that I have alluded to throughout this chapter and the previous one: relationships and norms. By these terms they are referring to a distinction between actual behaviors of individuals (relationships) and expectations or beliefs that are held that guide their behaviors (norms).

This distinction emphasizes that all of us are guided in our daily behaviors by certain beliefs. We don't behave randomly. At least, most of the time, most of us don't. As with all other principles, however, there are exceptions. Some people behave more "randomly" than others; you just never know what you'll get when you ask them a question or contact them on their cell. When was your last "random" episode? In general, however, we mostly do what we think others expect from us. As a police chief, we should not act like we are the hospital administrator. As a husband, we should not act like a high school junior out on the prowl.

But throughout this chapter, wherein we have focused on immediate responses to a massive explosion, tornado, or whatever, what expectations are relevant? Are there any at all? Based on numerous studies over the past four decades, we now have a pretty good fix on this question. The answer? An emphatic yes! And the illustrations I have described highlight several important themes. Many of these are implied in the formulation Dynes and Quarantelli devised.[20] You see, they divided relationships (behavior) into two categories. Either they existed before the disaster or they were new, or *emergent* to use their term. Similarly, many norms or expectations about what people ought to do persist over time. They are operative prior to a disaster and continue to guide the choices people make during the response and recovery. Hence, such norms, like a mother's love of her children, are *enduring*. In contrast, some norms actually emerge during disaster responses. These new norms are labeled *emergent*. These four categories or "cells" form a neat classification system. Dynes and Quarantelli referred to it as a *typology of disaster volunteering*. Many social scientists use the term *typology* to refer to a classification system like this that is formed logically by combining certain qualities in a structured manner. This typology gives us a very useful way to think about the many ways people volunteer.

The point is this. When disaster strikes, we don't find ourselves at a total loss. Even if we are carrying our injured grandson out of a coliseum after an explosion has just demolished the place, our behavior reflects key values. We are guided by enduring norms. We are a grandparent. So we act like one. We proceed to behave in established relationships.

Because situations like this are unusual, however, and time is of the essence, frequently a great amount of improvisation occurs. Both new expectations—that is, emergent norms—and new relationships are improvised. So we grab a taxi rather than wait for an ambulance attendant. We and the driver are transporting a disaster victim. Such behaviors fit the criteria that define one of the cells in the Dynes–Quarantelli typology. Both an emergent relationship (behavior) and an emergent norm (expectation) are present. Neither we nor the taxi driver expected to be racing to a nearby hospital.

Another cell also was illustrated several times in this chapter. This cell reflects responses by people who are working within established organizational relationships being guided by enduring norms. Recall that I emphasized the many services provided by volunteers like those associated with the Red Cross. They sprang into action immediately after the 1963 Indianapolis Coliseum explosion as they do following almost all disasters. Their actions, like those in other volunteer organizations, reflect established relationships and enduring norms. They know who they are, what they can do, and how to do it. As such they represent a most important community resource as do their many counterparts that focus on different tasks (e.g., SAR, home repair).

The Indianapolis community suddenly faced several huge jobs. One of these involved hundreds of telephone inquiries about victims.[21] Which hospital should they contact? Unless you have been through an event like this, it nearly is impossible to grasp the extent of this job. As the media alerts the nation, telephones from everywhere are dialed. And the Internet hums as relatives in Dumas, Texas, Walla Walla, Washington, Trenton, New Jersey, and everywhere else it seems all converge to the scene using these less visible roadways. Or at least they try to. Too often telephones ring busy, remain unanswered, or yield only the all too familiar computerized voices (e.g., "If you know your party's extension, press two").

There also was much improvisation by the Indianapolis Red Cross volunteers. Additional organizational capability was added through the rapid installation of several extra telephone lines. Today, many chapters have this arrangement preplanned. What was once improvised has become part of their enduring institutional memory. They simply will expect telephone company employees to be guided by these agreements. But at the time of the response in Indianapolis, the system had not yet been designed or ever implemented by Red Cross workers. So they used their established relationships to expand their capacity by adapting emergent norms. This adaptation was a great help to the local Red Cross organization and, in turn, people seeking information about relatives or friends.

Recall the flood breakers in East Grand Forks?[22] They illustrate another cell in the typology, that is, enduring norms being enacted by people within sets of emergent relationships. Members of CB clubs were contacted. The club's officers volunteered their organization, and this brought a whole cadre of helpers. A single contact with a minister, Boy Scout troop leader, or the like brings a vast reservoir of helpers. They don't individually volunteer, but they can be counted on to come running. Once on scene, they can form new relationships with representatives from other agencies. In this case they became involved with engineers, school bus drivers, city public works truck drivers, and many others. In short, their units were extended as members enacted these emergent relationships.

Frequently, volunteers find their roles expanded. This comprises the final cell. Such volunteers are guided by enduring norms for the most part, but the disaster situation requires much more from them. Relatives are supposed to help each other—an enduring norm. But typically, they are not supposed to move in with us. I mean, a visit is fine, but for how long? Yet a disaster may produce just this. Not that their stay will become permanent; there is a limit. But since they are disaster victims, we will expand our tolerance levels. At least we'll try!

Disasters require many volunteers to expand their roles. This is true too of more formal units, be they rescue teams or amateur radio clubs. But emergency managers who are assigning tasks should be careful. Too frequently I have seen reluctance to put such people to work, even if it means delaying some important actions.

As I'm writing this, the images and words I encountered in a town I'll not mention returned to me briefly. The situation unfolded something like this.

"Well, see, I just felt that these kids might run into a body if I turned them loose in that debris. So I waited until some personnel from this other sheriff's department got here. I mean—you know what something like that could do to a seventeen-year-old."

So the rescue team made coffee and waited! After two days of waiting they were sent home, unused. While this particular sheriff had a point, to me he failed. Underutilization of specialized groups of volunteers, especially in tasks new to them, is one of the most common mistakes made by those seeking to manage a disaster. From his vantage point, he viewed the task of debris search as a totally new one for such a team. More properly, it was an expanded one, at best. Some of these rescuers had been to small aircraft crash sites. They had carried victims' remains for miles through mountain terrain too rugged for a helicopter landing. They didn't need, and certainly didn't appreciate, the overly protective attitude of this sheriff. I would label it as *patronizing*. I won't identify the terms the team members used.

This is another reason why I find this little chart useful. It not only emphasizes the great variety in volunteer responses to disasters, but it also can help people think differently about use of resources. You see, just like other norms, those related to volunteer organizations are not always shared. Most commonly, those in authority tend to expect too little from volunteers. They may even view them as a problem source rather than a rich resource. Think about it.

Occasionally, circumstances will require totally new or emergent roles for volunteers. For school bus drivers in East Grand Forks to be transporting high school kids out to the dikes really isn't all that big of a deal. But filling and moving sandbags into place was a new type of experience for many of these young people. Daily patrol shifts—"dike walking," as they called it—gave their parents a new experience too.

Should we expect the high school football team to move sandbags? Certainly, the few days they spent time on these dikes took them away from math lectures and chemistry experiments. But do you really think that in the long run it hurt them much? I would argue just the opposite. It really helped them! How so? It gave them a chance to do something for their community, to make a personal contribution, to be a part of things. And that giving of self—what volunteering in all of its many faces is all about—permits individuals to feel the emotion of bondedness, to have a sense of being more than an isolated creature facing the dangers of life all alone.

By nurturing volunteering, be it directed toward kin or strangers, be it by cooking a meal or rescuing a trapped child, emergency managers are enriching the capacity of individuals to cope. And in so doing, they are strengthening this nation. Those failing to integrate and nurture these resources, in turn, are lessening our resiliency—weakening our capacity to cope and conquer.[23]

Failure to integrate volunteer groups of various types was among the many deficiencies in the response to Hurricane Katrina. Using words that softened a reality I suspect others would describe much more harshly, the White House staff noted, for example, that "...faith-based and non-governmental groups were not adequately integrated into the response effort."[24] More on point was their quotation from the testimony of the president of Catholic Charities USA: "In spite of Catholic Charities having available FEMA trained and certified disaster response staff, we were not always allowed admittance to FEMA operations and local EOCs. This significantly impaired a more coordinated response by all of us."[25] Others, like a high-ranking Salvation Army official, stressed parallel concerns. This organization, which commonly has staff on the ground immediately after most disasters, "...wasn't permitted to have a liaison officer in the State's Emergency Operations Center (EOC)."[26] Such treatment is just the opposite of the type of nurturing efforts I view as essential.

Numerous other researchers have published additional examples and conclusions that are consistent with my view. Tony Pipa is a case in point.[27] His years of experience in the nonprofit sector provided a unique set of lenses for reviewing the Katrina response, what I would call *balances*. Among his key observations were the following key insights for policy makers and executives across the broad contours of the postdisaster helping networks:

> ...No effective coordinating structure existed to integrate the multitude of charitable organizations that responded....[28]
>
> ...Personal and pre-existing relationships among local nonprofits, foundations, and religious leaders played a significant role in their ability ... to act flexibly to fill human service needs in the midst of chaos.[29]

Finally, three other researchers—Lauren Fernandez, Joseph A. Barbera, and Johan van Dorp—have systematically reviewed the literature pertaining to spontaneous volunteer involvement in a wide variety of disasters.[30]

Their results are consistent with the themes of this chapter. That is, volunteers will arrive at the scene regardless of whether officials call them or not. But they also addressed the risks and challenges associated with such actions—matters like disruption of organized responses and even the morbidity and mortality of the volunteer, disaster victims, and emergency responders. Of course, as they emphasized so well, risks are also associated with the failure to effectively use volunteers, such as "morbidity/mortality of disaster victims," "damage to property," and "poor public perception of emergency responders."[31] Upon examining existing policy at local, state, and federal levels, they concluded that important work needs to be done if this key resource is to be used for everyone's maximum benefit: "Systems that exist to date are largely organization-based, and many are not applicable to large-scale disasters. To date, disaster volunteer management is not a robust part of many local, state, and national plans."[32]

Sometimes, however, things do work out, at least better than the critical vein I have been emphasizing during the past couple of pages on Katrina. A case study by Susan Sterett and Jennifer Reich provides important balance.[33] While thousands of Katrina evacuees made their way to nearby communities in northern Louisiana, Texas, or elsewhere, many were flown to more remote locations. The State of Colorado, under the blessing of then governor Bill Owens, agreed to accept 1,000. But no one knew how many might be headed his way. Regardless, people who had been experiencing the horror and heat of the New Orleans Superdome suddenly were flying west. The same was true for many who had been dropped off at the Houston Astrodome.

Months earlier, Denver had initiated an aggressive new plan to better attack the general problem of homelessness in a multidisciplinary manner. One minor ingredient that had been considered involved use of a dormitory at the former Lowry Air Base. Unfortunately, the building was scheduled for demolition. A local black pastor requested that it be used by his church to provide shelter for some of the region's homeless. The governor turned down the request.

Then Katrina hit. Shortly after the governor announced that Colorado would join several other states in accepting evacuees, the bureaucratic machinery shifted gears. It was announced that at least many of the evacuees would be temporarily housed in the dormitory. So teams of volunteers, along with some state-paid contractors, transformed the place into a new home. While perceptions differed as to who actually "controlled" this emergent work force, local churches played a significant role. Most of these churches had predominately African American memberships.

Among these were the same ministers who had made the original request. Homeless people would be served, but they were not the original potential client base. And while personnel from FEMA and both the Red Cross and Salvation Army fostered expectations that they were "in charge," representatives from various local churches were powerful advocates for the Katrina evacuees.

Gradually, these churches, and the coalition they formed, gained increased legitimacy and acceptance by both governmental and nongovernmental agencies. And as families were moved into rental units, the Colorado Coalition of Faith continued to assist them as long-term recovery processes emerged. A year later, it was reported that 14,000 Katrina evacuees were still living in Colorado—no doubt some by choice and others because of the very slow recovery in New Orleans and other sectors of the Gulf Coast.[34] Such protracted evacuations, somewhat akin to war-related refugees, surely cause continuing stress and trauma. Sometimes, however, differing groups with alternative visions of a community challenge can be laced together into an integrated system that gets a job done. Here's the evidence!

But such impacts were not limited to Colorado. Katrina mobilized significant portions of the Black population throughout the entire U.S.A. The specifics were documented carefully by Bill Anderson.[35] He demonstrated how Katrina became a "focusing event" with all of the consequences predicted by social science theories. For example, there emerged a massive mobilization, like the one in Colorado, to provide a wide variety of assistance to Black Katrina victims. Black activists also pressed FEMA and other governmental agencies "...to take more decisive and fair actions..."[36]

Even more important, however, Black activists pressed officials to "... initiate major public policy changes that would alter conditions related to race, class, and poverty which were perceived as major underlying factors in the continuing vulnerability of disadvantaged groups in the society to future disasters."[37] Anderson's insights nicely illustrate the social problems perspective I will outline in Chapter 11.

THE INSIGHTS

- Volunteers can be integrated into emergent work teams for specialized disaster tasks. Multiple teams can be laced together to form very complex networks, as illustrated by the flood breakers.

- Improvised communication structures can permit the required coordination within such networks. CB radios did the trick for the flood breakers.
- Disciplined volunteer groups, such as search and rescue teams and amateur radio clubs, can augment the resources of the core emergency organizations.
- Too often, too little is expected from volunteer organizations. Too frequently, they are underutilized in disaster responses.
- In the minds of some, volunteers are like yachts, but they need not be. Emergency management has a unique opportunity to offer involvement, but incentives are required to offset social and economic trends. One of the many negative costs of expanding poverty is a dampening of the volunteer spirit.
- Most disaster victims are aided by volunteer actions offered by relatives, friends, and neighbors. These actions are overwhelming to many victims who don't realize that such outpouring of assistance—a utopian mood—is common after disaster.
- There are patterns of neglect. That is, not all victims are aided equally, regardless of loss or damage. Less likely to receive assistance from informal sources are the elderly, ethnic minorities, and the poor. Officials in communities with larger numbers of such citizens must be prepared to do more since there will be less volunteering behavior.
- It is useful to identify different categories of volunteers to recognize that much volunteer behavior is emergent and unplanned.
- Cross-tabulating norms (expectations) with relationships (behaviors) produces four types of volunteers. Usually, only those who reflect the criteria of Type A are recognized (Type A, organizational volunteers; Type B, volunteers in extending roles; Type C, volunteers in expanded roles; Type D, volunteers in new roles).
- Volunteer groups must be nurtured and integrated into the overall disaster response. If this is not done effectively, they may become a problem source rather than a resource.

8

Organized Disorganization

Few have the privilege of walking among the debris piles in central Texas, and two months later of driving into Cheyenne, Wyoming, to talk with those who confronted a smaller cousin of the monsters that cut a diagonal swath through Wichita Falls. Even fewer could juxtapose these scenes with those I recall from my interviews following Hurricanes Andrew and Iniki and the Northridge earthquake that rocked the Los Angeles area, Hurricanes like Fran and Floyd, and—well, you get the point.

Disciplined comparisons from such places—both my own field work and that described by many others—reveal a consistency in responses among emergency organizations that is alarming. Not always, of course, because some progress has been made. But too frequently the same problems keep being described over and over and over. The only thing that seems to change is the degree of gray in my hair!

I first encountered disaster reality in Indianapolis, Indiana. I was an Ohio State University graduate student at the time and was employed by the Disaster Research Center (DRC). I was one of a four-person interviewing team. We arrived the morning after the *Holiday on Ice Show* had been stopped by a violent explosion that injured nearly 400 spectators. Many of the eighty-one killed still lay on the ice; the rink served as a temporary morgue. I guess I never really recovered from that experience. Despite other research interests, I have remained a disaster observer.

After our interviews were done, I was assigned the job of reviewing them along with hours of recorded emergency telephone and radio exchanges and piles of after-action reports. With a great deal of help from the center's three codirectors—Russ Dynes, Henry Quarantelli, and Gene

Haas—I wrote a short book. *Disaster in Aisle 13*, the first of many monographs to emerge from the DRC, depicted a response pattern I have since come to label organized-disorganization.[1]

Since that initiation, I seen evidence of this same pattern many times, many places. I am now convinced that a core managerial problem, constituting a critical sector of emergency management in a nation like ours, revolves around this response pattern.

RAINING IN INDIANAPOLIS

Let's return to that rainy night in Indianapolis. I want to use two examples from the 1963 response to clarify this notion of organized-disorganization. In my view, this concept holds a key that will take us toward a theory of emergency management that reflects the behavioral and political realities of this nation.

Unfortunately, despite good intentions, most disaster planners are using concepts borrowed from military texts. While these ideas are useful in such organizations, they are inappropriate for civilian contexts. So they fail those using them and exacerbate tensions among those with whom they come in contact.[2]

Recall the scene I painted at the outset of Chapter 6. Here was a victim trying to decide what to do. A massive explosion occurred beneath the tiered seats. Some spectators were thrown out onto the ice. But others were tossed upward, only to drop down into a cavern. You see, a small room beneath the seats literally had exploded when a spark from an electric heater ignited propane vapors. Although their presence was illegal, several propane canisters were found amidst the rubble.[3] What once had been seats were ripped apart. Many victims now lay inside this shallow cavern. Minutes before, the aroma of freshly made popcorn had permeated it. Now, it was an awesome crater in appearance, and many victims lay trapped under large slabs of concrete.

Firefighters arrived almost instantly. They realized early on that a large crane would be required to free those trapped, so one was requested. But which agency should secure it? That question really was never asked. Several began trying to get one. How many were needed? One.

But things got much worse. Initially, a police officer at the scene radioed to headquarters. "We need wreckers, cranes, or something." "Okay, I'll send all available wreckers within the next half-hour."

Now picture yourself being at a filling station on a rainy night. The hour is late—ll:25 p.m. or so. You are monitoring the police radio waiting for a chance to race to a car wreck. I mean, who wants to stand around pumping gas all night? So you hear this interchange. What's your first thought?

Here's our volunteer again. A crane—only one—was needed. When one got there it was used. Slabs of concrete could not be dragged off people; they had to be lifted. All wreckers dispatched, plus those showing up voluntarily, simply added to the intense congestion.

Change the scene. You are a nurse in a hospital emergency room. A man approaches. He is carrying a child. Maybe he's a fellow like the one I created in Chapter 6, or maybe it was Sam Wilson, whom you met in Chapter 1. You are organized, however. So quickly, you direct him to a side cubical and alert other emergency room staff that you have a patient. Before work is begun on this child, another man enters. He is helping his wife. She is covered with blood.

Maybe your thoughts are identical to those of the nurse we interviewed: "God, that must have been some wreck." You see, none of the hospitals in Indianapolis were forewarned of the flood of casualties that descended on them. They were caught off guard and ran through the night trying to catch up. Daylight brought relief, but the darkness was a blur: "If only we could have had three or four minutes advance notice. We would have activated our disaster plan. We could have at least been rolling when they got here."

The hospital best equipped to cope with large numbers of emergency cases had a somewhat different problem. It admitted twenty-seven victims. It was prepared to accept many more, however. Much staff time was spent trying to ascertain where all of the victims had gone. And they had a flood of inquiry cases: "Well, if they are not there, where are they? Where did they take my grandkids?"

Radio and telephone recordings indicated that police dispatchers thought most victims were there. This was a logical inference since most emergency organizations took injured there routinely. In fact, police dispatchers advised some worried family members that this was the case. But there was one small matter that played havoc with their logic. Remember the taxi cabs I described in Chapter 6? Recall, too, that most disasters most victims do not get to hospitals via official emergency vehicles. I doubt that any of these police dispatchers knew that; most don't even today.[4]

Okay. We have two examples. What do they say about the principle? Where is the organization? Where is the disorganization?

Upon learning of the explosion, staff members from each emergency agency proceeded. Most agencies were reasonably organized. Of course, some were more organized than others. That is typical, although the better organized units vary from city to city. In some places the fire departments have an edge. In others, it's the law enforcement agencies or medical units. No single agency type has a corner on the market when it comes to disaster preparedness.

In the Coliseum case, the Indianapolis Fire Department was pretty well organized *internally*. In contrast, at one point, seventeen different Indianapolis police officers were making independent requests for equipment. Rarely did they provide dispatchers with information about activities or decisions made at the scene.[5]

That's the organization. Although variable, personnel within each agency responded in a reasonably orderly manner. So where's the disorganization? While some is experienced within, the thing that hits like a freight train is the marked disorganization among the agencies responding.

The specifics vary; they reflect the details of the event. But consistently, case study after case study has documented this behavioral reality.[6] Responses are quick, but highly fragmented. Some mobilize with handicap because they are not notified—like the hospitals in Indianapolis. Frequently, a specialized resource is required; recall the crane? Members of one agency do not know that personnel in three others are trying to secure it also. Multiagency fragmentation is reflected throughout the entire response, although typically it is greatest during the first few hours after impact.

Why? Well, there are numerous reasons. But *the single most important cause* is the failure to understand a fundamental essence of emergency management. Disaster responses are multiorganizational; so too must be the managerial theory used by any trying to shape them. Without an appropriate theory, responses will continue to be ad hoc and relatively ineffectual. The only thing worse—and this happens all too frequently—is to try using an inappropriate theory.

Most of the time then, disaster responses are less effective because of *system failure*. It is not the absence or competence of personnel per se but rather that they are not working in sync with their counterparts in other agencies. There are exceptions, of course. During the Katrina response some New Orleans police officers were absent. Such *role abandonment* is exceptional, however. It rarely occurs. Indeed, prior to the arrival of Hurricane Ike (2008), officers were given paid time off to get their families out of harm's way. Consequently, their response showed it. Such a procedure should be standard in any emergency organization.[7]

"BUT WE DEAL WITH EMERGENCIES DAILY"

You can't believe how often I encounter statements like this: "But we deal with emergencies daily." It is a managerial attitude set that neutralizes learning. Sure, law enforcement personnel, like fire and many medical staff, do confront emergencies daily. People get shot. Car wrecks can be horrible. Such events do tax their skills. They also prepare them for major disaster. But only partially, only to a limited degree.

Indeed, in some ways, especially for those operating at the managerial levels, these frequent responses create a type of trained incapacity. Successes with routine emergencies reduce the capacity to see the unique needs of situations that are qualitatively different. Why? Because a disaster brings demand loads, both in quantity and quality, far in excess of what one, two, or three local emergency services agencies can handle. A multiagency response is required. It is forthcoming, but typically it is fragmented and poorly coordinated.

The scope of demands produced by major disasters brings many agencies into action that normally are involved in other tasks. They are only peripherally linked with the core set that daily deal with car wrecks, domestic shootings, or what have you. Like who? Well, let's look at some specific cases. I've noted the 1963 Indianapolis disaster several times. The core organizations responding were these, although there were many others who contributed.[8]

Indianapolis Coliseum Explosion, October 31, 1963

1. Indianapolis Police Department
2. Indianapolis Fire Department
3. Indianapolis and Marion County Civil Defense
4. Indianapolis Area Red Cross
5. Indiana State Police
6. Marion County Coroner
7. Salvation Army
8. Indianapolis hospitals (5)

Turning to a couple of other cases but still focusing on the immediate rescue tasks, look at the array involved in Wichita Falls, Texas, following the 1979 tornado.[9] Unlike the Indianapolis case, no hospitals were included because of a more narrowly defined focus of study (i.e., search and rescue [SAR] activities).

Wichita Falls, Texas, Tornado, April 10, 1979

1. Wichita Falls Police Department
2. Texas Highway Patrol
3. Wichita Falls Risk Management Department
4. Wichita County Civil Defense
5. Wichita County Sheriff
6. Wichita Falls Fire Department
7. Texas National Guard
8. Wichita Falls Traffic
9. Wichita Falls Public Works
10. Sheppard Air Force Base
11. Gold Cross Ambulance
12. Texas State Parks and Wildlife
13. Volunteer fire departments (6)
14. Amateur Radio Emergency Service (ARES)
15. American Red Cross
16. Texas State Highway
17. American Rescue Dog Assn. (Dallas Unit)
18. Ft. Sill Helicopter Teams (MAST)

Perhaps unique because of its scope and physical location, which included much land area monitored by federal agencies, the prime search and rescue agencies responding to Mount St. Helens included the following.[10]

Mount St. Helens Eruption, May 18, 1980

1. Cowlitz County Sheriff
2. Lewis County Sheriff
3. Skamonia County Sheriff
4. U.S. Forest Service (Vancouver)
5. Washington State Division of Emergency Service
6. U.S. Air Force—304th Air Rescue and Recovery Service (ARRS) (Portland AFB Oregon)
7. Washington State Army National Guard
8. U.S. Air Force—303rd Air Rescue and Recovery Service (ARRS) (March AFB, California)
9. Lewis County Civil Defense
10. U.S. Forest Service (Packwood)
11. U.S. Army 3rd Squadron 5th Calvary
12. Washington State Aeronautics

13. U.S. Coast Guard Astoria Air Station
14. American Red Cross
15. Salvation Army
16. Salkum SAR Group
17. Cowlitz County Civil Defense
18. U.S. Forest Service (Randle)
19. U.S. Army—593rd Support Group
20. U.S. Army—54th Medical Detachment
21. U.S. Air Rescue— 6th Detachment, 602 Technical Air Control Wing (TACW)
22. Washington State Air National Guard
23. Civil Air Patrol
24. Lewis County ESAR
25. SAR Dog Association
26. Cowlitz County Coroner
27. Toledo Fire Department

These three examples illustrate what case after case documents. Disaster responses are not identical to routine emergencies. From the perspective of the tasks commonly performed by agency personnel, however, there are parallels. Medical personnel still will treat the injured once they get to them. Law enforcement personnel will assume responsibility for security. But personnel in both types of agencies may now find military, volunteer, and other resources participating too.

The task is too big for the cast that performs during daily emergencies. The effort must be expanded. Infusion of new participants requires new organizational strategies both within, to some degree, but especially among the agencies participating.

The management of what Allen Barton and others have labeled the *mass assault* is the core problem of that portion of emergency management best labeled emergency operations.[11] It is an awesome task. All too frequently, the individuals on whom it is dumped are simply overwhelmed. I still recall watching the late sheriff of Larimer County, Colorado, trying to cope during the 1976 Big Thompson Canyon tragedy. The stress he felt was painfully evident.

When I arrived in Lyndon, Kansas, two years later and talked with the sheriff of Osage County, the parallel was striking. He told me how surprised he was when the county civil defense director showed him a list of the seventy-eight different organizations that personnel involved. These were all assisting in the rescue and recovery of those four score Kansans who had planned an evening of relaxation at Lake Pomona. Who would have dreamed that a twister would capsize the showboat *Whippoorwill?*[12]

Seventy-eight different organizations! That is the management task I am talking about. It is one that remains invisible to most people because of its relative infrequency and short life span. While relatively infrequent for any given county—how many years will pass before Osage County, Kansas, has another disaster?—the job crops up daily somewhere within the United States. Case study comparisons now provide us with a series of insights that could aid in designing appropriate managerial strategies. No professional emergency manager needs to start from scratch. Much is known.

SORTING OUT ORGANIZATIONAL RESPONDERS

After reviewing response profiles from nearly 300 disasters, DRC researchers devised an exceedingly useful way to sort out organizational responders. Dynes, Quarantelli, and several individuals associated with the DRC have used this procedure in many analyses. Their device—known as a typology—emphasizes the quality of *emergence*. It is similar to the framework I discussed in Chapter 7. There we examined the many roles of volunteers.

Here a distinction is made between tasks and structure.[13] Organizational tasks can be classified as either "old" or "new." So too are structures. They either were in place prior to the disaster event, or they emerged afterward and would be regarded as "new." Four analytical cells or categories are created when these two dimensions are cross-classified. We can see examples of each of these in the cases I just described.

How so? Well, look again at the list of organizations involved in the search and rescue activities following the Wichita Falls tornado. *Existing systems* (i.e., those reflecting both "old" tasks and structures) are rather obvious. They formed the core of the response—agencies like the Wichita Falls Police and Fire. While stressed to the hilt, these agencies went forward doing many tasks they confronted daily.

But other individuals were placed into rather new situations—asked to confront tasks unlike those they performed regularly. Their relationships with other authorities remained, but new expectations (emergent norms) pushed them into new activities. Examples? Personnel from the Texas State Highway Department, like those from the Wichita Falls Public Works, were thrust into debris search. While they commonly are using heavy equipment to clear streets, even after floods or wind storms, the searching for trapped victims *extended* their organization into a domain most had not experienced. Similarly, but even more dramatically extended, was the City Traffic Department, which was designated as the primary search and rescue coordinating agency.

In the well-used DRC typology then, these represent systems wherein people were working within "old" or predisaster organizational structures but were doing new tasks. Commonly referred to as *extending systems*, they maintained their basic structure but took on new tasks.

Commonly, some organizations *expand* during disaster responses. This expansion occurs because someone must seek to establish new linkages among the numerous responders. That is, to tie all of the organized groups together—to reduce disorganization—some must establish new relationships. In many cases these are new relationships with divisions of organizations wherein some type of linkage existed before, but the quality is now different. *Expanding systems* like these are represented by a third cell in the typology: one that reflects people essentially doing the same tasks they typically completed but improvising new structures whereby to get the job done.

Probably the best example of this was the role assumed by the city civil defense office, which in Wichita Falls in 1979 used the moniker of the Risk Management Department. Organized-disorganization? I asked the director about it. He recounted his trauma. He tried to implement a disaster plan of which he was rightfully proud. It had been through a full-scale test just days before these vicious dancing monsters arrived. Yet all electrical power was gone. Radio communication was impaired greatly. And with no way to communicate from the disaster site—a forty-seven-mile long swath—to the various headquarter settings, the task was enormous.

A good example of a totally new relationship for his organization was the linkage to the American Rescue Dog unit. He had not known of the availability or potential of such an SAR weapon prior to this tragedy. When contacted by representatives from Dallas, a new linkage was added, a new resource used. And his organization was thereby *expanded* through it.

Finally, there were many short-lived emergent groups not listed previously. These groups are not listed in my analysis because we used an organizational perspective in this particular study. Hence, we did not seek to track down such units. These *emergent systems* are very common during disaster responses, however; they frequently perform important tasks. Probably the best documentation of such a group in the entire disaster literature was that written by the late Lou Zurcher.[14] A summary of his article detailing his participation on a clean-up crew after the Topeka tornado appears in the description he later prepared with Jim Taylor and Bill Key.[15] Too many emergency managers don't seem to grasp the presence of these groups, nor do they understand their contributions.[16]

Despite even the most careful planning, all disasters bring surprises. Improvisation will occur; it must be expected. And when catastrophic disasters like Hurricane Katrina happen, the evidence of this principle can be overwhelming. Sally Jenkins, a *Washington Post* staff writer, for example, wrote about the mayor of Gulfport, whose people badly needed a truck. So he ordered his police chief to "hot-wire" one. Her comment from the mayor was telling: "When you send your law enforcement out to steal things, that's when you know you're in a different situation."[17]

More reflective and comprehensive regarding lessons that could be learned from Katrina, Mannie Garza emphasized sixteen key observations. Relevant to my point here was number 14: "Large-scale disasters require first responders to be creative and willing to sometimes break the rules."[18] He provided medical evacuations as examples. When premature infants, for example, were removed from their hospital isoletts, (specialized cribs), half a dozen could be transported in padded, empty, water bottle boxes. And eighteen-wheeler trucks were used to move critical patients from Charity Hospital to the airport where they were airlifted out.

This is not to say that lawlessness prevails or that there is complete breakdown in the social fabric. Rather, reflecting core values of compassion and concern for others, within a context of urgency and scarce resources, improvisation is to be expected, and any trying to be "overly bureaucratic" will be remembered just that way. New conditions require and legitimate alternative ways of getting the job done.

Organized-disorganization? You bet. And why? Because this entire array of organizational actors are at the scene, all trying their best. And whose job is it to see to it that each stays out of the way of the others? Indeed, how can they even communicate, much less get organized? That is the essence of the challenge.

IS COMMUNICATION THE PROBLEM?

Yes, communication is a problem in disaster responses. Indeed, most emergency managers I have interviewed stress this as the main problem.

And to a degree they are right, especially when it comes to cross-agency communications. Therein lies the core of the problem. Why? Well, let's start with an example.

You know, most people don't really understand the basic mathematical concept of compounded growth rates. Maybe you too have fallen for the joke. Remember how it goes?

> "Which pay rate would you prefer? Under Plan A you will work for one month—eight hours per day, five days per week—at $100 dollars per hour." Sounds pretty good, doesn't it? "Plan B is quite different. Under it, you start very low—one penny for your first hour. But every hour you work, the next hour's rate is double the one before."

Okay. Remember confronting this as a kid? Which pay plan would you pick? The check at the end of the month under Plan A wouldn't be bad. At first glance this might sound like something a top rock star might get. Maybe, maybe not. Did you calculate it yet?

When I use this in a speech, I can always depend on some guy with fast fingers using his cell phone calculator. So when I spot him, I'll head over his way and ask him for the answer. Let's see, Plan A would go like this: $100 × 8 hours = $800; $800 × 5 days = $4,000; and $4,000 × 4 weeks = $16,000 for the month! Not bad, but hardly what many rock stars get these days. Regardless, it's not a bad salary—certainly more than my paychecks ever showed.

Now, what about Plan B? I mean, starting at one penny for that first hour sounds a bit ridiculous. But think about it: The rate doubles every hour. So, after one hour, you are at two cents. Hour three nets you another four cents. And hour four gets you up to eight pennies. And so it goes. Your cumulative total for day one is not too great: $5.03.

But you start day two at $2.56 per hour, right? Then things start to happen! Double that and you have $5.12, then $10.24, and so on. By the end of the day your rate has become $327.68 per hour. And your hourly rate at the end of day three? Would you believe $83,886.08? That means that your earnings for day three total $167,772.15.

Hard to believe at first glance; want to check my arithmetic? If you really want to have some fun, project this over a two-week period and see where you are. And to think that you started at one cent per hour—an embarrassment of riches, isn't it?

Cross-agency communication parallels this embarrassment but frequently brings few riches. The response to the *Whippoorwill* tragedy illustrates this point well. As I noted already, the sheriff informed me that the civil defense director had compiled a list of seventy-eight agencies that responded. Since our focus in that study was search and rescue activities, we narrowed in on the twenty that were most involved:[19]

Lake Pomona SAR Response, June 17, 1978

1. Osage County Sheriff's Department
2. Osage County Civil Defense Office
3. Osage County Coroner's Office
4. Osage County Attorney's Office
5. Kansas State Highway Patrol
6. Kansas State Parks and Resources Authority
7. Kansas State Game and Fish Commission
8. Kansas State Department of Transportation
9. U.S. Army Corps of Engineers
10. U.S. Army Reserve
11. Crable Ambulance
12. Franklin County Ambulance
13. Lee's Summit Underwater Rescue Team
14. Shawnee County CD Underwater Rescue Team
15. Burlingame Police Department
16. Lyndon Police Department
17. American Red Cross
18. Topeka Fire Department, Rescue #1
19. Carbondale Fire Department
20. Topeka Radiator and Body Works

These are the core set of agencies that responded. But remember, there were personnel from another fifty-eight that also contributed in some way. Using detailed interview data from officials in each of these twenty core agencies, we were able to construct a *social map* that displayed the communication structure that emerged. At first, we studied this quantitatively by examining the frequency of communication that agency personnel had with representatives from the other nineteen units. Was it "continuously," "about once per hour," or maybe "every few hours?" Some said that "about once a day" was more accurate for a few of the linkages. Often "no communication" was reported by a few organizational personnel whose agency had very specialized roles. For example, Topeka Radiator and Body Works communicated "continuously" with the Sheriff's Office, the Highway

Patrol, and American Red Cross but had minimal communications with the other agencies. The emergent network was composed of 148 linkages.

I had a draftsman who was accustomed to drawing complex electrical circuit diagrams to display these. His diagram was a sight—one skilled SAR type referred to it as "Charlotte's Web" when he used it in training seminars for many years. Of course, the linkages activated (148) represented only 39% of the total that would be possible theoretically (i.e., 20 × 20 = 400 − 20 = 380, since no organization has a link to itself). Still that is a lot of talking, and that does not include internal communications. To assess the relative centrality of each agency within the network, we examined the actual frequencies reported since these varied considerably. The results? Links coded as "no communication" accounted for 61% of the total. Those coded as "continuously" comprised 23% . Those reported as "about once per hour" made up 6%, as did those coded "every few hours." "About once per day" codes described 5%.

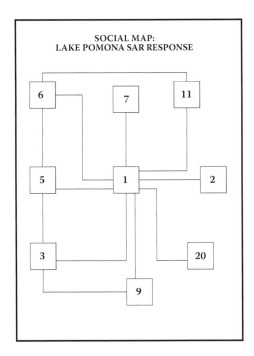

Figure 8.1   Social Map: Lake Pomona SAR Response

To give you a clearer idea of what one of these social maps looks like, I pulled out the most significant links. The social map diagram includes only the intense core of the larger web (i.e., the nine most central agencies). The numbers in the boxes correspond to the listing above (e.g., 1, Osage County Sheriff's Department; 2, Osage County Civil Defense Office).[20]

SOCIAL MAP: LAKE POMONA COMMUNICATION STRUCTURE

This map looks very simple. It is rather easy to see the centrality of the Sheriff's Department (1) and the key placement of the Coroner's Office (3), Kansas State Highway Patrol (5), and Kansas State Parks and Resources Authority (6). But to fully grasp the complexity of the emergent response network that actually performed the SAR mission after the *Whippoorwill* capsized, you must remember the context. The actual number of participating organizations was seventy-eight, not nine! And even among the twenty that were highly involved, we documented activation of 148 interagency linkages.

No one had even shown these managers social maps like these. When some—like the sheriff—saw these, his reaction was swift: "No wonder we had communication problems." And he's right.

The sheer volume of verbiage generated within a network of this complexity is mind boggling, and it has become even more complex with the addition of computer networks within and among agencies. It is overwhelming. The amount of resources required to receive and record this volume of information—much less disseminate it within each respective agency—is hard to comprehend. That is exactly what happens, though. Managers are simply overwhelmed by too much information from too many sources. There is no way it can be processed. Yet, like in the case of Indianapolis, the reverse can be true at times. The hospitals were not alerted initially. No linkage was activated, and staff learned of the explosion from victims coming through the front door or in the emergency room. By then, their ability to mobilize was impaired severely.

Voids or gaps in the response structure are just as problematic as excessive numbers of linkages and the overloads they create. I will remember forever the emotion shared with me by a Texas County Sheriff. There he stood on the banks of the Guadalupe River, and helicopters soared overhead. He could see a woman clinging to the tree branches, but she was hidden from their view.[21]

Around and around they flew, but he had no way to talk directly to the pilots. They were state—or in the case of military craft, federal—employees. It might have been possible for him to have radioed from his cruiser back to his own headquarters. Dispatchers there could have related his directions to the State Patrol, which in turn could have relayed the word to the pilot. "Not a very good way to run a railroad," he said to me. "Not a way to save lives," I replied. So to solve the problem he went out and purchased some CB radios. "At least this way I can talk to these guys, or whoever, next time we face a mess like this."

That exchange took place in August 1978. The north and south forks of the Guadalupe, the Medina, and their various tributaries flooded three counties in the Texas Hill Country. This is an area that lies to the northwest of San Antonio. Within three counties—Bandera, Kerr, and Kendall—residents along these waterways experienced extensive flooding. Some—twenty-five to be exact—did not live to tell of their experiences in the worst disaster within the United States that year.

Now fast-forward twenty-one years. I am listening to the emergency management director of Pitt County, North Carolina, describe incredible rescues. Hurricane Floyd had hit here and numerous other locales with a vengeance. But after surviving the wind, the rains came. These dumped on top of fully saturated soils, reflecting a recent visit by Hurricane Dennis.[22] Suddenly water was everywhere. Hundreds of people had to get out of their homes or risk drowning. Once again helicopters arrived on scene. But once again, a local government official was left without the communication equipment required to link the rescuers into the emergency management network.

When I interviewed the Pitt County sheriff, he described these problems in far more detail. He was the one tasked to coordinate the rescue effort, you see. As he continued describing his frustration, my mind back flashed for an instant. I was back in the Texas Hill Country twenty-one years earlier.

And then I read the report by the 9/11 Commission.[23] To be honest, sections of this report made me very sad. Throughout rescue efforts, communication failures were pronounced. Without getting off on a tangent, because that was a highly complex response, the following quotes from the commission report highlight the issues. They reveal why I felt sad:

> The FDNY's [Fire Department City of New York] radios performed poorly during the WTC [World Trade Center] bombing for two reasons. First, the radio signals often did not succeed in penetrating the numerous steel and concrete floors that separated companies attempting to communicate; and second, so many different companies were attempting to use the same point-to-point channel that communications became unintelligible.[24]

To solve this problem, at least in part, a repeater system was installed in 1994. This was funded by the Port Authority, which proposed that it should be turned on and left turned on at all times: "The FDNY requested, however, that the repeater be turned on only when it was actually needed because the channel could cause interference with other FDNY operations in Lower Manhattan."[25]

So what happened on September 11? The commission discovered the following:

> One button on the repeater system activation console in the North Tower was pressed at 8:54, though it is unclear by whom…. The activation of *transmission* on the master handset required, however, that a second button be pressed. That second button was never activated on the morning of September 11.
>
> Because the second button had not been activated, the chief on the master handset could not transmit. He was also apparently unable to hear another chief who was attempting to communicate with him from a portable radio, either because of a technical problem or because the volume was turned down on the console…. Because the repeater channel seemed inoperable—the master handset appeared unable to transmit or receive communication—the chiefs in the North Tower decided not to use it.[26]

Furthermore, did you realize that the Emergency Operations Center (EOC) for New York City had been located within the World Trade Center complex? Of course, it was destroyed. So once again people improvised. The EOC was reconstituted shortly thereafter "…at a cruise ship facility on the Hudson River."[27] That's the kind of "stepping up to the plate" that is a signature disaster response. It took precious hours, but interagency communications greatly improved once this key structure became fully operational.

As bad as the communications problems were during the 9/11 response, they were nothing compared with what occurred during the efforts to manage the impacts of Hurricane Katrina.[28] The first sentence in the Communications Chapter of the House Select Committee report pretty well summed it up: "Massive inoperability—failed, destroyed, or incompatible communications systems—was the biggest communications problem in the response to Katrina."[29]

Like the 9/11 response, analysis of these communications problems could comprise an entire book. But to nail the point down, consider these examples.

> After surviving Hurricane Katrina's initial blow, the radio communications system for the New Orleans police and fire departments dissolved as its radio towers lost their backup power generators in the ensuring flood.[30]

And in Mississippi?

> Most of its state and first responder communications capabilities were inoperable during and in the immediate aftermath of the storm, forcing the various responders to rely on satellite phones and radios (which experienced their own problems due to wind damage and interference).[31]

In today's world, many seem to require continual cell phone use, either by an ear plug, a unit held in their hand, or a wireless receiver affixed within the dashboard of their car. So why didn't this technology solve the problem? The answer was documented by those who testified before the committee:

> Verizon Wireless serves the Gulf coast with two major switching stations in Baton Rouge and Covington, Louisiana. These serve as the links between cell phones antennae scattered throughout the region and the rest of the global network. While the stations themselves remained operational during and after landfall, the Covington facility lost connectivity with the cell towers due to two breaks in the connecting fiber-optic ring run by BellSouth. Normally, a fiber-optic link provides redundancy: If one link is cut, information can still travel along the other route. Katrina, however, knocked out both sources because of physical damage to the fiber-optic cable.[32]

Yes, communication is a problem, and cross-agency communication is especially troublesome. But sadly, more radios or cell phones are not the sole answer.

What is needed is not more communication but rather properly controlled communication. Not every agency needs to communicate directly with all others. This especially is true when multiple governmental jurisdictions are represented—state, federal, and several local governments. The answer lies not in more communication but in the careful design of a communication *system.* The key word is *system.* And typically, the multiple groups responding do not have this view of the forest. They fail to grasp a system, for each manager sees only the tree bearing his or her particular uniform.

COOPERATION IS NOT ENOUGH

After being told that communications was the number one problem, another response pattern emerges among local emergency executives: "Boy, I couldn't get over how everybody pitched in. I mean we've had some tensions among city departments these past few years. Things are getting tough around here. No one likes to see their budget cut, I guess. Maybe that's added to it. But during this disaster. No, sir. Everybody cooperated. There wasn't a thing I couldn't ask these other directors to do. And their people did it too."

The words will vary. A sheriff in Washington State won't say it exactly the same way that it comes out in the Texas Hill Country or Pitt County, North Carolina. The messages are the same, however. Cooperation was at an all-time high.

You see, it's not just citizens at the scene who volunteer to help because the disaster has stirred them. The same goes for emergency personnel, at least to some degree. They too become caught up, at least temporarily, in the drama of the therapeutic community. But to exclusively focus on communication is wrong. The only thing worse is the common fallacy that more hardware will be the solution, which is another example of our propensity to invest in a quick fix. Problems in your disaster response? Communications? Okay, let's get better radio equipment. Ever heard it before? If not, you will if you become involved in some aspect of emergency management.

Communication needs are only the tip of the iceberg:

> Cooperation does not necessarily result in coordination, and improved communication does not necessarily result in better management.

Now we are getting to the core of the problem. You see, we get a fragmented response primarily because the units responding are in fact separate organizations; *each exhibits a high degree of autonomy.* Each has its legitimacy rooted in statutes or charters that vary. Hence, each has a sphere of authority that differs from the others—more or less. Daily, they pretty much go their separate ways. Of course, some are more interdependent with each other because their day-to-day tasks bring them together, but even city police and fire department personnel exhibit relatively high degrees of autonomy in relationship to each other.

Frankly, this high degree of autonomy is the real culprit, one typically not recognized.[33] But, as I argue in the final chapter of this book, this culprit is also a major source of strength of American society. So although organizational autonomy must be recognized head on as the culprit, the best solution does not lie in increased centralization at the federal level of the complex intergovernmental system.

Although relatively low degrees of task interdependence allow each organization to go its separate way on a daily basis, disasters are a new ballgame. The interdependence among the responding units is much greater, but the managerial strategies to transform these separate—rather autonomous—units into an integrated weapon are lacking. So researchers continue to document case after case of fragmented agency responses. Cooperation did not lead to coordination.

During my field work in the 1960s, 1970s, 1980s, and 1990s, very few officials I interviewed even grasped the composition of the total response network in all of its diversity and richness. There were exceptions; some local emergency managers had seen the light. But too often the efforts of various local government departments, community agencies of various types, and private sector organizations did not mesh very well. Furthermore, federal resources were not well integrated with those provided by state agencies. Many local executives found their field personnel at a loss when it came to absorbing National Guard units or specialized military units, like search and rescue teams, into their organizational framework. Few local managers have stood back to see the forest, much less have asked how it might be better managed.

It is the entire multiagency network that must be managed if emergency responses are to be effective. Communication flows cannot just be willy-nilly; they have to be designed and controlled just as they are within operating organizations on a daily basis. Within such diverse mixes of agencies, no single unit has the authority to take control and dictate policy to all others.

So the situation is handled. Ad hoc arrangements are agreed to for a few days. The disaster is conquered. And what remains in the memories of the core executives? For many there is a lingering residue focused on a few instances of severe conflicts. Typically these are over matters of who had authority to make certain kinds of decisions. Sometimes these are rather bizarre.

For example, I mentioned the Osage County sheriff who had the job of trying to coordinate personnel within seventy-eight different agencies. Recall the case of the *Whippoorwill?* What I didn't mention was that Lake Pomona is a federal reservoir. Army Corps of Engineers personnel had authority over many aspects of the facility. But Lake Pomona is located within a state park, and Kansas Game and Fish personnel routinely serve as the key law enforcement agency. It is their uniform you spot at the entry portals. Yet the county sheriff had search and rescue responsibilities, as do most other county sheriffs.

Who should take charge? In this case—after some discussion—the principals agreed that the sheriff should. So he did, although a few present required a bit of convincing.

In the case of the Coliseum explosion—recall Indianapolis—a different pattern emerged. Local city agencies were present in mass. Initial direction was provided by on-scene city fire officials. Later, a multiagency command center was headed by the city police. After the immediate rescue was completed, in a rather formal ceremony, the state police assumed overall command. Recall that the Coliseum was located within the State Fairgrounds.

My point is that responses to disasters in American society—from an organizational vantage point—are multiagency affairs. Resources, both equipment and personnel, are required from a diverse array of organizations. But who will try to assume responsibility for overall direction or management of these mass assaults remains ambiguous at times. Even those who try to impose some degree of order on the chaos they see around them are overwhelmed by the complexity of the managerial task. Communication flows are incomplete. A sheriff is left standing on a riverbank watching helicopters overhead, and a woman's arms grow tired, hopefully not before it is too late.

Finally, the job is over. Victims are gone; the rubble has been searched. The race of events is a blur, time referents inexact. But as each agency director retells his or her story, communication problems loom ever more important. Too often, however, this awareness is neutralized by a memory of accomplishment. "My people did one hell of a job." And they did. "And, God, did this community pull together—every agency pulled out all the stops." And they did.

But the managerial task—the structuring and control of the multiagency response system—drifts into the background like disappearing smoke. Disaster planning, typically ignored because of the priorities of the day, might receive a momentary notice. "Yeah, we've got to get to that next week—well, maybe next month."

As the moon returns to its fullness again, each separate agency has retreated back into its own niche. The view of the forest, something that a few glimpsed momentarily, is now lost. Next month's budget meetings will again absorb all attention. Community agencies have lost a unique opportunity, and if a few years go by without another flood or tornado or explosion, so what?

Of course, there always are a few who can't shake the memory, so they push ahead, sometimes with success. One year after the Coliseum explosion, for example, because of the efforts of the local Red Cross director, Indianapolis-area hospitals established a multihospital communication system.

When the former director of the Denver Office of Emergency Preparedness first read my accounting of the Indianapolis response in the early 1970s, he said to me, "The same thing could happen right here in Denver. We don't have any type of multihospital communication system, either." So he sat out to press for one. He was successful because he grasped the forest. He understood and had experienced the trauma of organized-disorganization. He realized the need for a *system* of communication.

Actually, he saw the need for multiple systems of communication that could be laced together into a coordinated whole. He had seen this need most vividly a few years earlier during the response to the 1965 flood that literally cut Denver into two pieces. You see, when the South Platte River flooded, debris piled up against bridge after bridge and eventually knocked them out, one by one.

Since that time I have had the privilege of meeting a whole lot of others who have the vision. These newer types of emergency managers reflect a rapidly transforming professionalization process that is one of the bright lights for our future as a nation. Many have not only the proper vision but also high levels of commitment and remarkable levels of tenacity.[34] I remain humbled by them. And I have been honored when some have explained to me how our research has assisted in their long-term struggle to make their community safer.

Not every community must experience disaster to become better prepared. Indeed, although experience can be the best teacher, too often it isn't; experience without reflection and subsequent adaptation is simply endurance.

What American communities need today are not more bureaucrats who can endure; rather, we need managers with a vision and commitment to it: managers who have the capacity to lead, who do grasp the forest, who understand the behavioral reality of organized-disorganization and are willing to tackle the managerial challenge it represents. But, as I elaborate in the final chapter of this book, America is not Japan. Our managerial strategies must reflect the American social structure as it is manifested at each layer of our social system, from family to community to nation. Strategies rooted in mythology are destined to fail—as they have to date with alarming frequency.[35]

I have had the privilege of reviewing a lot of postdisaster critiques. Frankly, some have been little more than "whitewashes." The focus seemed to be more on providing excuses for past failures rather than on hard, forward-looking assessments. Throughout this book, I use Hurricane Katrina as an example, so during one of my final editing sessions I felt the need to provide some additional balance for comments made prior and those in subsequent chapters.

As pointed out in an excellent critique booklet published by the Louisiana Office of Homeland Security and Emergency Preparedness (LOHSEP), a lot of people, both officials and volunteers, completed innumerable acts of accomplishment, even heroism.[36] This is not to deny the tragic reality of those who died—more than 1,300—or the trauma experienced by thousands. But we also must remember the following to keep balance in our perspective.

> ...1.3 million evacuated pre-landfall; 62,000 water, roof and attic rescues; 78,000 evacuated by bus and aircraft, including 12,000 hospital patients and their caregivers; 40,000 triaged at the [Louisiana State University] LSU Pete Maravich Assembly Center [Temporary Staging and Operations Area] TMOSA emergency room facility; another 2,000 triaged at Nicholls State TMOSA; no incidence of major secondary disease or health problems among evacuees; 40,000 housed at the Super Dome, all provided with food, water and shelter; 1,000 [Emergency Management Assistance Compact] EMAC deployments; located shelter for 25,000 within 24 hours; and the first use of the National Disaster Medical System in U.S. history.[37]

I don't know about you, but such statistics do not reflect the flashbacks I have when I hear the word *Katrina*. The following sentence from the LOHSEP report provides another layer of context. "Pre-Katrina modeling and predictions from the [Federal Emergency Management Agency] FEMA funded and directed Hurricane Pam planning workshop indicated that 60,000 would die from a Katrina-like storm. Instead, 60,000 were rescued."[38]

But this critique does much more than document fragments of information that help to provide balance to our interpretations of this tragic event. Also emphasized were the many failures that left thousands dead, injured, or emotionally traumatized. First a specific issue was identified. Each was followed by brief discussion and then a recommendation. The issues were organized into nine broad topics such as command and control, emergency communications, planning, and staffing. One of the issues within the public information section was very relevant to many of the points I have discussed, and it can provide you with important food for thought as you ponder the residual imagery that is called up when you hear the words *Hurricane Katrina.*

Issue: Focused Public Information Plan

Discussion: Public Information effort was not able to tell America about Louisiana's contributions to the Katrina support effort. As a result, numerous inaccurate reports and stories were generated and perpetuated by the national media, civic and governmental leaders without ascertaining the facts. Many of these inaccuracies became accepted as ground truth at the national level and have required significant effort to reverse. Additionally, public affairs issues and information sharing capabilities between state and local agencies were overwhelmed by the catastrophic nature of the event.

Recommendation: The state should give consideration to revising the current Emergency Operations Plan for Emergency Support Function 15. The ESF primary takes the lead in establishing a Joint Information Center (JIC). Key tasks for the JIC are: each ESF primary and support agency should have a knowledgeable, articulate representative in the JIC; JIC develops a focused and targeted media plan; JIC implements a proactive plan to engage the media in all aspects of the operation.[39]

If you ever read the other forty-three "lessons learned," you will have a much better understanding of why the response three years later was much better coordinated. That is not to say that the response to Hurricane Gustav was perfect, but certainly it surpassed the Katrina effort by miles. And part of the reason it did was because emergency managers at all levels of government had acted like professionals are expected to act. They reflected on their mistakes and implemented new approaches. These changes enabled them to be more capable when the next challenge arrived.

Such attitudes of professionalism were underscored in the final section of this critique, titled "A Closing Thought":

> Louisiana is not alone in its vulnerability to catastrophic events. There are lessons to be learned from Hurricane Katrina by all levels of government. The time to address these challenges and initiate change is now.[40]

THE INSIGHTS

- The initial response to community disaster is best described as *organized-disorganization.*
- Organized-disorganization reflects the high levels of autonomy exhibited by the responding organizations. Each is fairly well organized individually, although that varies. The disorganization reflects the multiorganizational nature of the response.
- Disasters are not routine emergencies. Interagency procedures that are appropriate for these situations do not fit the task environment created by disaster.
- Disasters evoke a rich array of diverse community organizations and agencies that have profoundly different operational procedures and cultures.
- Reflecting emergent tasks and relationships, established systems are complemented with systems best identified as extending, expanding, and emerging.
- Interagency communication often is identified as a key shortcoming in postdisaster critiques.
- Interagency cooperation often is identified as being high, but this does not necessarily produce coordination.
- Improved management of the emergent multiorganizational response network is required, not simply more radios or any other quick fix.
- Lessons can be learned by honest evaluation of failures and implementation of appropriate corrective actions. A lesson not implemented is a lesson not learned.

9

Life in a Fishbowl

I don't know whether you had goldfish as a kid. If you did or didn't doesn't really matter, I suppose, because you know what a little fishbowl looks like.

That imagery helps to communicate what many disaster victims have shared with me over the years. Following a flood, their house may be damaged structurally, or it may just have six inches of goop standing in the living room. If a tornado was the culprit, the roof may be off, or an entire side of the home may be gone—that is, of course, if it wasn't leveled. Regardless of the damage pattern, victim families report strong feelings about the side effects of convergence behavior. They get sick and tired of the endless stream of cars that pass by their home.

At times they will strike back. I've seen many a sign posted over a broken front window or out on a debris-covered yard: "Gawk, you bastards!" "Looters will be shot."

THE BITCH PHASE

Human emotions are a complex thing. Most people, of course, never experience being a tornado or hurricane victim. So when we read of someone's experience or talk with a friend or relative whose house was blown away, we may be puzzled. Why would they feel that way? Yet after years of careful documentation, a series of patterns have been discovered. Those associated with the immediate weeks after a disaster can be most puzzling. For emergency workers some of these responses can be extremely frustrating.

During the immediate postimpact period, most people are very active, although often frightened. Once family members are accounted for, even if some are hospitalized, there is a sense of gratitude: "Thank God we are okay."

Then the first wave of convergence begins. Friends and relatives, including some who may not have been around for years, begin contacting the family one way or another. Offers of help stream in from these sources. This includes disaster relief agencies like the Red Cross and even strangers. Yeah, that's right, even strangers. In fact, one of the things that many disaster victims have told me that they were the most surprised about has been actions by strangers. In some cases these may have been organized volunteers who were not wearing highly visible identification. They may have had an armband, badge, or patch on their shirt, but this was unnoticed. In other cases, these helpers may have been curious individuals who decided to tour the area. Once there, they became so overwhelmed with the clean-up needs that they offered to help. Disaster victims frequently report their surprise with the volume, type, and sources of help that arrive at their front door. "We never asked anybody for anything. These people just showed up."

For a brief period in their life they are in the news, maybe even with a picture of their kids or their home on TV. Offers of help are so profuse that many are turned down. "But, by God, they came by here and wanted to know what we needed. We hadn't even seen them during the past couple of years. But here they were, wanting to know what they could do." Sometimes just having a place for the kids to spend part of a day or two is the help given. To tired parents, however, such assistance comes at an important time.

Then things change. Just as fast as the media interest and kin contacts were started, they stop. Others, you see, are ready to go back to their daily routines of football games, golf dates, jobs, and the countless other activity cycles that occupied them before the disaster. This signals the onset of what seasoned disaster workers refer to as the *bitch phase*. Insurance adjusters, sales personnel of all sorts, and a cast of others being the second wave of convergence. The glamour is gone, but the mess remains. This prevents full resumption of previous living patterns. As the excitement subsides, others are less and less interested in hearing about their disaster experience. Suddenly, victims realize they are tired, very tired.

Yet there still is a lot to do. Often, the consequence of this transition is aggression. So victims begin to lash out at those around them. At times this even includes those who now arrive to help. They are tired of telling their story, tired of inquiries, and they want answers. "When will the water be safe to drink? When will we know the outcome of the flood rezoning proposal? Are they going to buy our house, or will we be given a building permit to go ahead and make repairs? When will we know?"[1]

The questions, of course, vary with the event. But the general pattern is clear. Victims enter into a bitch phase where they evidence impatience, at times hostility. They are ripe for organization. Increasingly, they are catered to by individuals who will seek to use the disaster as a political weapon. At times, of course, victim rights are the true issue. Other times, disaster victims are used by individuals to promote their own political ambitions or personal pocketbook.

LOOTING FEARS

Depending on the range of destruction, of course, entire neighborhoods may be unfit for people to live in for several days. When the destruction resembles what I saw in Wichita Falls, Texas, immediately after the 1979 tornado, the rebuilding of homes that were leveled at their foundations requires months, not days. Victims can move in with friends or relatives initially, but like fish, they too may begin to smell after three or four days!

Flash forward thirteen years, and the location is south Florida after Andrew's rampage. Add another seven, and I am standing near I-35 in Moore, Oklahoma. Same song, different place. But always there is pain. There are fears about the uncertainty of the future. And there is loss.

Even if victims remain in a home with temporary repairs, many express a fear of looters during this phase in the disaster life cycle: "Most people are out of here. Stuff is lying all around, and there's no way to seal off the sides of these houses. Anybody that wants to can simply come in here and go through these places tonight." The fear is real. Unfortunately, there are just enough rumors and actual looters to reinforce the myth—that's right, myth!

Very little looting actually takes place following most disasters. At least, that is the experience within the United States across hundreds of events that have been studied. Rumors? Yes, lots of them. Fears of looting? Yes, sometimes very intense. Actual cases of looting? No, they are very hard to find.

There are major exceptions, however. As more cross-national data have been collected, we have discovered some pattern variation. Within the United States, numerous instances of major looting have been associated with civil disorders. Dozens of cities experienced this during the late 1960s. Places in the headlines during those years included the Watts area of Los Angeles and Newark. More recently other rampages have been ignited when highly publicized actions by local authorities were defined by some as unjust.[2]

Henry Quarantelli and Russ Dynes reviewed interview data from several of these so-called ghetto riots and discovered some important differences in emergent perceptions.[3] This again underscores one of the principles of this book: Not all disasters are the same. These researchers concluded that, basically, people who are disenfranchised and alienated from the community are in a mild, albeit temporary, state of rebellion. They have harbored resentment against shopkeepers and landlords, for example, whom they feel have abused them for years.

If the truth were known, the frequency and extent of such abuse could be exposed and maybe defused. Unfortunately, what some of us would define as *excessive greed* is viewed by others as *good business*. Any time a small sector of a community skims off the cream and heightens the social constraints on others who flounder in poverty, rebellions can be expected. Tranquility may continue for years if those in power can maintain tight control and a stability in social arrangements that allow some to grow fat while others starve.[4]

Highly stratified communities are like powder kegs. Angry people are just waiting for an incident. Then a triggering event occurs. Recall police shooting a black youth who may have been an innocent bystander in a crowd or at a robbery scene. The crowd turns ugly really quickly. Maybe a few bottles or rocks are thrown. Warnings seem only to fuel the fire. Within an hour, a previously busy street is the scene of a rampage.

Prior to his passing, Fred Bates studied disaster recovery issues for decades. His early work was with the late Harry Moore in the late 1950s. He took this matter one more step. By looking at responses in places like Guatemala and other non-U.S. locations, Bates proposed that more post-disaster looting occurs elsewhere.[5] Why? Because many of these societies are more stratified. The gap between the richer and poorer is very wide. Bates concluded that governments and other sectors of these societies, including religious institutions, actively tried to maintain the status quo. In so doing, patterns of marked stratification continued year after year, decade after decade.

Hence, just like the boiling over that occurred in the mid-'60s within some American cities, when expectations for equal opportunity outran the pace of behavioral change, more stratified societies are potential hotbeds.

I suspect that where poverty is reinforced by customs, law, religion, and other institutionalized constraints, a particular event would not elicit the same degree of looting as it would in a place undergoing transition. When members of the underclass believe that things are about to change, their willingness to tolerate displays of wealth diminishes. Opportunities to loot those who are perceived as illegitimate and tyrannical are taken. Should we be surprised?

This interpretation parallels the conclusions reached by Bill Anderson and Russ Dynes following their assessment of the violence that rocked Curacao in the mid-'70s.[6] When members of the underclass begin to question the legitimacy of existing institutional arrangements that have kept them in poverty, looting behavior may be one form of political protest. Rather than being private acts by outsiders, the behavior is transformed. It becomes a symbol of protest used by families and small groups of friends who openly and defiantly engage in a rampage. Rather than experience any sanctions against their acts, people around them provide strong support for their courage to strike out at those identified as their oppressors.

As long as we stay within the confines of the United States and are referring to periods of recent history and typical local communities, the lesson is clear, however. Relatively little, if any, looting will occur after disasters. When we move to more stratified locations the probability of the impoverished seizing the opportunity presented by the disruption caused by a disaster increases dramatically.[7]

These patterns were observed in field work completed by Quarantelli following Hurricane Hugo in 1989. Shortly after his return from the island of St. Croix, where extensive looting was reported widely by the media, Quarantelli described his interpretations of this issue by emphasizing four key points to me. Years later he applied these interpretations to the Katrina response.[8]

First, although the media reports, especially TV coverage, could not be denied, his interviews with local authorities indicated that the extent of looting was less than implied in journalistic reporting. So there was extensive looting, but it was not as widespread as that depicted in the media imagery.

Second, St. Croix, like many other places in the world, is a highly stratified society. The wealthy are very wealthy and the poor live in marked poverty. While some are able to secure employment within the homes of the rich or lavish resorts, others wander about daily to sell their wares to trinket-seeking tourists. The plight of most reflects the stresses that peasants have endured throughout history. Tough—at times brutal—law

enforcement practices help keep the lid on. Such strained societies are rev-
olutions awaiting the next leader. While many hear the call, few succeed.
So these places persist over time as millions of peasants are born and die
long before they reach the life expectancy reflected in more just societies.

Third, there was a short period immediately after Hugo struck when
authorities lost it. A lapse in local law enforcement was followed by military reinforcement, but there were serious gaps. Some areas experienced
rampages while law enforcement personnel stood by and watched help-
lessly. In some cases they actually participated in "the payback party."

Fourth, petty theft was, and remains, a common occurrence in St.
Croix. So the hurricane presented a window of opportunity to expand a
preexisting pattern. Daily acts of thievery are symptoms of strained systems. The wealthier mitigate against these with a variety of strategies—
more bars on windows, more locks on doors, and more private security
personnel. But always, the thief in the night remains a real risk. Short-
term disruptions precipitated by disaster are akin to holes in the walls of
a dike. Until plugged, the rages produced by unjust systems are permitted
to spew forth.

Quarantelli's analysis helps us understand what many of us saw on
television shortly after Katrina made landfall. As I mentioned previously,
you too may have seen the invasion of stores in downtown New Orleans.
You may have seen some carrying several boxes of shoes or a dozen or so
pairs of slacks. If you were a shop owner who had evacuated prior to the
storm, would you fear looters? You bet!

Now let's juxtapose Quarantelli's four points with reports issued by
the Select Committee of the U.S. House of Representatives and the White
House.[9] Clearly, there were acts of looting. About that there is no argument. But what Quarantelli found in St. Croix was that the *extent* of looting was exaggerated. And Katrina? The White House report stated this:

> People began looting in some areas as soon as the storm relented....
> Exaggerated, unconfirmed claims of violent crimes and lawlessness took
> on a life of their own in the absence of effective public information to
> counter them.[10]

The conclusion reached by the Select House Committee was more pointed:

> If anyone rioted, it was the media. Many stories of rape, murder, and
> general lawlessness were at best unsubstantiated or worst simply false.
> And that's too bad, because this storm needed no exaggeration.[11]

Quarantelli's second point speaks to the earlier observations by Bates regarding social stratification. Like South Florida at the time of Hurricane Andrew, New Orleans reflected a comparatively high degree of social stratification.[12] Hence, as Walter Peacock and colleagues noted following Andrew, more instances of episodic looting and other forms of criminal behavior would be expected (see note 1). So compared with other American communities, places I have mentioned previously like Moore, Oklahoma, or Wichita, Kansas, more cases of looting would be expected within New Orleans.

What about a temporary lapse in police control? Again, both reports noted this feature. First, this from the House Committee, then the White House:

> In some areas, the collapse or absence of law enforcement exacerbated the level of lawlessness and violence.... The breakdown of law enforcement was particularly notable in New Orleans.[13]
>
> On August 31, most of the New Orleans police force was redirected from search and rescue missions to respond to the looting, detracting from the priority mission of saving lives.... Federal officials attempted to have law enforcement officers protect emergency responders against security threats. However, due to a lack of planning, arranging this support took several days, during which the situation grew worse.[14]

Finally, Quarantelli argued that to some degree the post-Hugo looting reflected continuity in a prestorm pattern of petty theft. Crime statistics for New Orleans and a few points of comparison put this matter into perspective.[15] For example, in 2003, Federal Bureau of Investigation (FBI) statistics indicate that the burglary rate for New Orleans was 1.21 times the national average (population 475,128; 4,879 burglaries). By contrast, both Atlanta, Georgia (population 431,043; 8,065 burglaries) and Cleveland, Ohio (population 468,446; 8,048 burglaries) had burglary rates that were 2.02 times the national average. Detroit ranked 1.78 (population 927,766; 14,100 burglaries). In short, statistics like these confirm Quarantelli's basic point. To some degree the post-Katrina looting behavior in New Orleans partially reflected continuity in a prior pattern of petty theft. Such patterns are found in most impoverished urban areas.

But the House Committee, like several social researchers, added an important extension to our understanding of such behavior: Not all looters are the same. Much of the activity that television cameras recorded reflected survival behavior, not greed or rebellion:[16]

In some cases, people looted stores for their survival and to diminish suffering, taking items such as food, water, clothing, flashlights, batteries, and camping supplies. At least some police departments were involved in breaking into stores and commandeering supplies needed for their departments, as well as those needed for feeding people in shelters before state and federal assistance arrived. One New Orleans physician said police helped him break into a pharmacy to get needed medications and supplies. In other cases, people looted for purely criminal purposes, apparently taking items for personal use or resale that would not be needed or were useless without electricity (e.g., televisions).[17]

BAD DREAMS

During the bitch phase, some adults, and a lot more children, report bad dreams. The content of these vary, but many may be related to the disaster that just occurred. Interviewers have noted parents who tell of their children awakening in the night: "She woke up two or three times last night. Every time it was the same thing. 'I want to get into your bed.'"

Psychologists know that such behavior is a common and normal response to crisis. Disasters are no different from any other types of fear-producing event, so bad dreams and other symptoms of *separation anxiety* should be anticipated. There are no easy solutions, but many mental health workers have now been brought into the disaster response team. If preplanned and worked out in a balanced manner, they can be an invaluable resource.[18]

Media messages can be directed to parents. They can be encouraged to watch for these symptoms. They need to be told that their children are normal. Your message to parents might go like this: "Your child is not sick but is responding in a normal way. You need to spend time with her. She wants to be held—to know you are there. If she wants to sleep with you, accept her. After a week or so, her anxiety will diminish, and so will her dreams. She'll soon be happy again in her own bed."

Following Hurricane Katrina, Lori Peek and Alice Fothergill traveled to numerous locations in Louisiana to gather detailed information on this disaster's impact on children.[19] Through more than three dozen interviews in shelters, schools, day care centers, churches, and the like, they carefully probed this heretofore unknown. They documented the enormous diversity in reality that this event presented. For example, some parents described how they evacuated to a relative's home—think kindly, nurturing grandma. These were the lucky ones. The event was more like a vacation.

For most, however, the temporary places of shelter were stressful for both child and adult. Even more protected places, like hospitals, morphed into "Freddy Kruger type" experiences for some. Case example? The researchers recount the experiences of a nurse named Debra, whose supervisors instructed her to bring family members to the hospital for safety. Debra had to care for patients who became increasingly problematic after the power was lost and supplies began to dwindle. Debra "...was panic-stricken several times when she could not find her nine-year-old daughter in the pitch black hospital halls."[20]

When many left, they assumed short-term departures. Special toys, like photo albums and other links to "home," were not taken. Hence, as the days passed by, establishing routines became more and more challenging. When your environment is in a state of flux and uncertainty levels are high, reaching the desired balance of flexibility and routines is most challenging. These conditions evoked a wide variety of coping responses. Knowledge of these could help future emergency managers, teachers, and parents. For example, older children were encouraged to maintain journals and draw pictures. Others devised collections of disaster jokes. All were needed as children confronted the challenges of establishing new relationships and friendships within whatever social context they proceeded to experience.

Like these victims—adults and children alike—emergency management officials must become more sensitive to and enact relief policies consistent with the diversity that define such populations: "A 'one size fits all' approach does not address the needs of the most vulnerable populations struck by disaster, and we must reconsider the distribution of disaster aid."[21]

While relatively rare, some children may benefit from professional counseling. It remains unclear, of course, if they may have needed such before the disaster. Whether such events actually produce severe mental pathology is debated less and less these days. They clearly do not. As with everything else, there are exceptions, however. Certainly, some children, and even some adults, are severely traumatized by what they experience during a tornado, hurricane, or earthquake. Generally, however, the natural healing process existent within most family and friendship networks is adequate to rebuild and restore. Disaster victims who demonstrate resourcefulness immediately before and after impact exhibit resilience in the weeks afterward.

That is why Valerie Swenson's mother was right. Remember her from my story in Chapter 1? If not, go back and reread "The Ceiling." That story will be relevant to the upcoming issues we explore in the next chapter, so a quick refresher will help both now and when you get there.

Data do indicate, however, that there is a temporary increase in the use of mood-altering substances such as alcohol, tobacco, sleeping pills, and tranquilizers. The spurt in the purchase pattern, however, is about the same as what communities evidence during the Christmas holiday period. After a short period of time, the consumption pattern pretty much returns to what it was before the disaster.[22]

In recent years, as more and more clinically oriented professionals have conducted research on disaster victims, the concept of *survivor guilt* has become popularized. It remains a controversial notion, although those who believe in it can be very convincing. Indeed, some advocates I have confronted firsthand have been so isolated in their own reading and range of professional contacts that they didn't even realize the idea was controversial.

In brief, the reasoning goes like this. Following the trauma of the emergency period, everyone experiences a sense of guilt: "Why not me?" Many people ask this when they learn of the deaths of other community members. Sounds reasonable? Certainly! But, so what? The clinical types, who undoubtedly have had some patients who reacted pathologically following a disaster, however, go on with the next step; that is, after a period of time, victims begin to evidence symptoms of various types that are manifestations of the guilt they feel for having survived when others didn't.

In a well-written book reflecting her long discussions with victims and clinical practitioners and her broad reading of the disaster literature, Beverley Raphael, an Australian professor of psychiatry, illustrates the type of orientation I am referring to here. The following is one of several examples she has provided:

> More generally, such conflicts, remorse, and regret may be felt by those who could not save their family or friends or who, to escape, had to ignore the pleas of others for help. For example, a man from the Norwegian oil rig suffered somatic and depressive complaints, which improved only when he was able to face and work through his guilt and shame at not being able to save his friend. Such a response may involve the sort of traumatic memory that is later vividly etched in the mind of the survivor, forever being reviewed, and perhaps forever a source of guilt; this is because the survivor may feel that his or her life was purchased at the cost of another's.[23]

While our understanding of this dynamic will improve as more rigorous research is completed, it is clear to me that we don't want to jump off the deep end. Nearly all disaster victims will think about those who were less fortunate; indeed, they may even feel some sense of guilt that buzzes them when they ponder a thought of gratitude. Many do the same thing when they drive by a poor section of town or see a war veteran in a wheelchair. This doesn't mean that they need therapy!

Unfortunately, therapy of various forms also has been popularized. Maybe, like lawyers, we have graduated too many clinical psychologists! Certainly, our society has entered a phase where therapy has become a bit of a panacea. My advice is to arm yourself by reading a good book like Raphael's so you can more adequately understand this point of view. If you are a local official, then try to build an outreach program to your local mental health community so that you can selectively involve those who reflect a balanced perspective. When disaster strikes, you can rely on them to help you provide resources to the tiny fraction of victims who might require this specialized type of assistance.[24] Then use this program as a barrier to keep the kooks out—and believe me, you can expect some to show up.

You may even encounter a few who will push you like one did me. After discussing the poor quality of many of the research studies in this area that reduce the credibility of the conclusions drawn, I stressed to this individual that the victims I had interviewed didn't seem to need therapy. Indeed, I said that some I had spoken to had revealed that therapy had been mentioned to them by a disaster relief worker and they were offended. The young mental health worker I was talking with responded with words that still send a chill up my spine:

> Well, Dr. Drabek, that's the very point. She may not know that she needs therapy. I can assure you, after I spend an hour or two with her, she'll realize it. All I need, really, is a chance to sit down and talk with her. Believe me, you would be surprised at how many people I have been able to help realize why they need to be in therapy.

Local elected officials and their emergency management personnel must protect disaster victims from being used by others regardless of the cause or ideology they represent. A few elected officials have approached me after one of my lectures to recount real horror stories: "My God, Doc, some of these mental health people that went in there were as disruptive as the disaster itself." Mental health counseling will be needed by some disaster victims, but the matter must be kept in proper perspective.

SHORT-TERM OSCILLATIONS

Recall the pattern exhibited by alcohol consumption documented first following the flash flood in Rapid City, South Dakota, back in 1972. Others documented it further and with greater precision after the incident involving the nuclear power plant on Three Mile Island.[25] People slightly increased their consumption of alcohol for a short time and then resumed their previous patterns.

This is but one example of a larger set of patterned variations. There are many others. Before discussing a few, note the possibility for confusion and even deception depending on one's cause. The records do indicate an increase. Some respond with alarm! Unless the trend lines are followed for several months into the future and carefully compared with those from years earlier, wrong conclusions can be drawn. Masked as scientific evidence, those with an ax to grind have some powerful ammunition.

One of the first efforts to date to pin down some of these short-term oscillations, as well as some longer-term changes I discuss in the next chapter, was a team put together by a political scientist at Northwestern University. By collecting information from four communities, Paul Friesema and his associates produced the best time-series analyses that ever had been done.[26] The four disasters and locations were (1) Yuba City, California (flood, 1955); (2) Galveston, Texas (hurricane, 1961); (3) Conway, Arkansas (tornado, 1965); and (4) Topeka, Kansas (tornado, 1966).

Examples? Well, would you believe divorce? Think about it. People are having troubles. They have been having frequent arguments—a lot of hostility and acting-out behavior rather than the kind of warmth and affection they may have known earlier. Suddenly, their house is leveled.

Now, for a week or two, lots of friends and relatives are asking how they can help. Lots of decisions have to be made. They were not killed and are grateful for that too. Thus, we really shouldn't be too surprised that the Northwestern team discovered that during the month after these events, the divorce applications decreased. Also, the number of marriages that would have been anticipated given a ten-year trend line decreased also. Then, during the next two or three months, a correction of sorts was made. Those who delayed their marriage joined others who were planning for those months anyway. Thus, a short-term increase was noted.

This too happened with divorces, although these data suggested an interesting surprise. While the volume of marriages projected caught up after six months, the divorces didn't. These disasters, and the delays they triggered, didn't stop people who were planning marriage from going ahead. But statistically, at least, a pattern appeared that indicated some who may have been considering divorce didn't follow through. The disaster caused a short-term deficiency in the number of divorces, a shortage that never was totally regained. Others have looked at various types of economic indicators, such as prices, housing starts, and newspaper circulation. In general, the patterned variability pretty much resembles that of marriages: There is a short-term decline, or increase, then a correction period, followed by continuity.

While some inconsistencies appeared in the data set, when Catherine Cohan and Steve Cole looked at trend patterns before and after Hurricane Hugo, the theme of continuity was validated.[27] They examined marriage, birth, and divorce rates for all years between 1975 to 1997. Since Hurricane Hugo hit in 1989, they wanted to see if marked variations occurred. They documented that there had been a declining rate in marriages until the year after Hugo. Then a net increase occurred in the seven most impacted counties. The next year, 1991, the former pattern of decline resumed. Birth rates were more stable except for a one-year increase the year after Hugo. And divorce rates, which had been very stable prior to Hugo, evidenced a one-year increase also. Thus, all three trend lines revealed short-term oscillation followed by continuity.

Continuity is the most important characteristic of the human side of disaster recovery. Sure there is disruption. There is hurt, and there are some tough nights. After five or six months, however, most people adapt and resume the living patterns they had known previously. That observation has a very important implication for anyone interested in improving the disaster management capacity and overall safety of his or her community.

These conclusions, of course, have to be adapted a bit when the event is one of catastrophic dimensions. To supplement field work I completed a few days after Hurricane Andrew, I returned to the Miami area about a year later. It was depressing to see block after block of houses covered in blue tarps and piles of ruined mattresses, furniture, and other trash still sitting curbside. How many months—maybe years—will it be before all families displaced by Katrina or Ike will be settled into permanent housing? Fortunately, our experience base with such events is too small to do much more than speculate. Let's hope it stays that way!

Six months into the Katrina response, hundreds of families were still unsettled, and places like Houston, Texas, where 150,000 survivors had been welcomed, were reflecting the strains of this sudden population influx. Some officials tried to put a positive face on the stresses by referring to "compassion fatigue," but others revealed fear that their community would be stuck with a large number of poor, some of whom might require long-term assistance. Some feared increased violence, both gang related and stress produced. Education and health-care facilities remained taxed. As Houston's Emergency Medical Services (EMS) medical director stated to *Newsweek* reporters, "Hospital CEOs [chief executive officers] are about to have coronaries."[28]

Despite the organized-disorganization found right after disaster events, various forms of antisocial behavior like looting or theft do not skyrocket. As I described previously, social conditions like those that depicted New Orleans after Katrina may lead some to requisition needed supplies like water or diapers. Who could blame? And, of course, reflecting a daily pattern of petty theft, a few will be caught on camera carrying out TV sets or boxes of shoes or pushing shopping carts loaded with new pants. Until the normal constraints provided by social and legal structures are restored, some will reach through the temporary cracks in the social fabric for personal gain. Despite increases in altruism, greed doesn't ever disappear totally in the postdisaster environment. And as the recovery period continues, old habits reemerge, both the good and the bad.

I suppose that whenever large amounts of money appear on the scene, some will seek to reach through any cracks they can find in the social control structures to run off with some crumbs. The fact that the hurricane victim family roof remains leaking and covered in blue tarps just doesn't matter. They got "theirs" and will move on to the next town. The U.S. Government Accountability Office (GAO) staff put it well: "The influx of federal financial assistance available to victims after a major disaster provides increased opportunities for fraud, waste, and abuse."[29]

Reviewing fraudulent activities after the 2005 Gulf Coast hurricanes and several other disasters, the GAO staff identified two key areas of concern: (1) contractor fraud; and (2) disaster victim assistance payments. They cited such evidence as the more than 7,000 formal complaints that were filed by Hurricane Andrew (1992) victims with the Miami-Dade County Construction Fraud Task Force from August 1993 through March 1995. These helped to return more than $2.6 million to homeowners following the successful convictions in more than 300 felony and 290 misdemeanor cases. Such information triggered some communities to establish credential programs for contractors. Homeowners were urged to hire only those who could present proper photo identifications signifying that they had passed all of the checks to obtain their credential.[30]

Following the 2005 Gulf Coast hurricanes—Wilma, Katrina, and Rita—the GAO staff "...estimated improper and potentially fraudulent payments related to the Individuals and Households Program application process to be approximately $1 billion of the first $6 billion provided."[31] In addition, nearly $20 million was made in duplicate payments to people who registered twice. This resulted in 890 indictments as of September 2008. Data like these resulted in strong recommendation "...for states to establish effective controls to minimize opportunities for individuals to defraud the government."[32]

The central conclusion of the GAO staff regarding upcoming responses to Hurricanes Ike and Gustav during the balance of 2008 and on into 2009 is sobering. But it adds another important element in expanding understanding of the human side of disaster.

> By creating such a fraud protection framework—especially the adoption of fraud prevention controls—government programs should not have to make a choice between the speedy delivery of disaster recovery assistance and effective fraud protection.[33]

WINDOWS OF OPPORTUNITY

Once the tornado has passed or the river has nearly returned to its banks, every community I have heard about exhibits a parallel pattern. Interest in the event is high. Heroes are being identified and, quite appropriately, being recognized. People are talking about how bad it could have been and why they were lucky this time around.

Following Hurricane Elena, the director of the emergency management program in Pinellas County, Florida, was able to press forward with his plans to move into a new Emergency Operations Center. When I interviewed him several months earlier, he told me of the plans. About a year after Elena's visit, I visited Pinellas County again. This time I interviewed his successor. Seems that the fellow I interviewed during my first visit had moved "upstairs." He now was in charge of a larger unit within county government. Emergency management was one of several programs he now had under his command.

Elena created a window of opportunity. If you were to visit the Pinellas County EOC, you would see the outcome. Now don't get me wrong: The EOC was in the pipeline. The quality and scope of computerization, however, was aided by the director's quick response to take advantage of this window of opportunity. He was ready. And the citizens of Pinellas County are safer today because he used this hurricane to press for needed improvements.

This point was stressed to me over and over again when I conducted a survey of a small, but nationally representative, sample of emergency managers.[34] The time to strike is within one month after the disaster. Community attitudes toward mitigation measures are softened then too. That is, this is the time to get approval on such things as construction of flood protection devices and warning systems. Resistance for any one of a variety of reasons is weakened, temporarily. If the leadership can be mobilized, and if planning has been done so that much of the usual wheel spinning can be short-circuited, important gains in disaster preparedness can be made. Failure to move quickly, however, can blow the opportunity.

This frequently happens too, simply because the folks charged with coordinating the cleanup are too overwhelmed by that task to devote any energies to going beyond. That is why those who are most effective will do their homework. They may not have the equipment purchase forms typed out, but they have a list. They have a set of rationales and an understanding of how quickly these windows of opportunity will be shut.

"WHEN CAN WE GO HOME?"

Anyone who ever has been to a community a few weeks after a disaster recognizes this question. People want to get on with their lives. What they don't want is indecision. During the bitch phase, officials are confronted with this question continually—as they should be. More so than any other thing that local governments can do to help the mental health of disaster victims is to speed up the decision-making process. Those who can rebuild at their old locations ought to be told of this quickly. They should be helped to get going. If there is to be some relocation, that too ought to be expedited.

Bob Bolin followed me into Wichita Falls in 1979. He focused his data collection on the recovery process. The following extract from his report is exceedingly revealing:

As the reconstruction process continues, community level decisions can affect the hierarchy of return.... One need only look at the Wichita Falls city council's indecisions on the placement of mobile homes. Victims didn't know from week to week whether the trailers they had placed on their house lots were legal or illegal, or for that matter whether [the Federal Emergency Management Agency] FEMA might confiscate them. That such uncertainty in the early stages of recovery was stressful was readily apparent from interviews with victims. The city council, however, had to consider both the early return to normalcy and the longer-term consequences of their decision. In their rush to take decisive action to help victims by permitting mobile homes on private lots, they acted so quickly that they then reversed themselves repeatedly until they returned to their original decision.[35]

Despite future vulnerability, most people want to rebuild at their home site. If local, state, and federal officials can put together an equitable package of "buy-outs" following a major disaster, many can be persuaded to get out of the area. Following the terrible flash flood (1976) in the Big Thompson Canyon, about seventy miles from Denver, Colorado, many homeowners were pressed to do just that. The federal coordinating officer appointed by President Jimmy Carter patched together a variety of federal funding sources to accomplish the largest flood relocation that ever had occurred up to that point in time. A survey conducted about three months after the flood indicated that despite the horror of knowing that 144 people had perished and the extensive damage, over "...one-half (53%) of the victims were unwilling to sell their land to the government."[36]

Similarly, Robert Geipel discovered that the earthquake victims who populated the northeastern edge of Italy, known as the Friuli region, exhibited a strong commitment to place.[37] Most had started to rebuild following massive destruction. That was in 1976. A few months later the area again shook. Much of the reconstruction effort was destroyed. How many now wanted to relocate? Geipel discovered that only 1.6% of the 6,568 surveyed were interested in leaving permanently or for a short time.

Because most social scientists within the United States are middle class and career oriented, they fail to grasp the sense of place that others within the society reflect. So they confront a southern farmer who has been flooded out several times and they cannot understand why his family would clean up, make repairs, and move back. His answer does not differ from the Friulians'—this is home!

Despite this, and because of an expanded mitigation priority within FEMA, record numbers of Americans living in flood-prone areas along the mighty Mississippi and its tributaries elected to move following the massive and prolonged flooding during 1993 and 1994. This type of mitigation will be seen again in the years ahead, but I doubt that it will do much to the overall vulnerability of the nation, because Americans are just too good at putting structures into hazardous places. And, so far at least, we have been unwilling to require existent building codes to be enforced properly, much less to approve more stringent regulations.[38] The costs of such freedoms are high. Most Americans still don't realize that if we don't pay up front, we may pay more later.

THE INSIGHTS

- The bitch phase of disaster recovery reflects high fatigue levels among victims. At first overwhelmed by the scope and volume of helpers, they now find the mess remains.
- Disaster victims are vulnerable during the bitch phase. Their hostility may be intensified when basic questions remain unanswered and others seek to mobilize them for political purposes.
- Fear of looters escalates as extended family and other trusted helpers return to their predisaster priorities and activities.
- While rare following most disasters, there are exceptions. Looting behavior occurs most commonly when the following social conditions prevail: (1) highly stratified community; (2) petty theft as preexisting pattern; and (3) temporary loss of legitimate law enforcement personnel. And always, we can expect exaggerated media reports to reinforce the myths about looting within the public psyche.
- Various short-term stress symptom patterns are common, including bad dreams and other forms of sleep disruption and survivor guilt. For most people these are transitory and disappear gradually without professional mental health counseling.
- Short-term oscillations in behavior patterns occur. Increased use of alcohol and other mood-altering drugs reflect rates akin to holiday periods or other short-term stress events. Similarly, divorce rates, like marriage rates, will fall off briefly. These and a wide variety of other patterns (e.g., housing starts, newspa-

per circulation) return to predisaster states within six months or less.

- Effective emergency managers recognize that disasters provide a short-term window of opportunity when funding for program enhancement will have greatest levels of support. Wise managers have the rationale and program needs identified in advance so they can strike while the iron is hot.

10

What about My Psyche?

Recall the lingering fears and tears experienced by Valerie Knudson? Val is the fictional character I introduced in Chapter 1. She was the victim of "The Ceiling." Val represents a lot of earthquake victims I have interviewed over the years who have described similar symptoms. Fortunately, most, like Val, also experience the healing power of family, friends, and other components of the postdisaster therapeutic community, so, over time, their symptoms gradually disappear.

But there are exceptions. Like other matters of disaster response, there is pattern variation. Some heal more quickly than others. And some events are far more destructive to the human psyche than others. Let us never romanticize these matters. All disasters are terrible human events. Some people do lose loved ones. Most disaster victims experience some degree of physical destruction. Houses are flooded or blown apart; cars and boats are tossed about. And often items of great sentimental importance are gone forever. The sense of loss can be acute.

I remember the listings I made from interviews that the late Bill Key had obtained from a firm we hired to interview victims of the 1966 tornado in Topeka, Kansas.[1] They had been asked to describe what they had lost that had sentimental value. What did they point out? Photo albums, dishes that belonged to a grandparent, and trees. One elderly man, for example, described at length how he had planted a tree when each of his grandchildren was born. Now, the trees were all gone. Another spoke similarly of a rose garden in which she had invested a great deal of money. More important than the money, however, were her time and the feelings of attachment. Such feelings reflect the human side of disaster.

AN ATYPICAL EXAMPLE

Okay. So disasters do hurt people and result in lingering feelings of loss. Do these persist forever? Do disaster victims really ever recover? This question is important. It also is very complex. I'm not going to pull a typical academic stunt and dodge it. But I don't want to distort or mislead either. So let's start with a case that has obtained a great deal of publicity, at least within certain circles. It has been used for years by some mental health advocates to justify intervention programs. It also has been used by some attorneys to pave the way for victim compensation following certain events.

In 1972, the tiny hamlet of Buffalo Creek, West Virginia, was damaged severely by a flash flood.[2] This catastrophe had many atypical qualities. The victims were Appalachians, many of whom had been laid off at nearby coal mines, which had provided jobs for years and thereby nurtured a way of life for the residents of Buffalo Creek that could be found in countless other rural communities throughout West Virginia, Kentucky, Tennessee, and elsewhere.

The event itself was unusually horrifying. It struck in the night and put virtually everyone close to death. All of the survivors lost relatives or friends. Furthermore, there was evidence of culpability. For several years the Buffalo Mining Company had been dumping debris in a canyon, which formed a small dam. As rainwater drained into this area, it was detained temporarily. Then suddenly, without warning, and in the dead of night, the tiny town was hit with a savage glut of mud-filled water.

A law firm brought some brilliant analysts to Buffalo Creek to assess the degree of psychic impairment.[3] This information played a critical role in the suit that was filed against the Pittston Company, the parent organization of the firm operating the mine. Two years later an out-of-court settlement was reached with the law firm—to the tune of $13.5 million! Some of this "...went to 650 survivors who were litigants in this case from among the more than 4,000 survivors of the disaster."[4]

Research has continued on the survivors of Buffalo Creek, some of whom may be interviewed again even after this book is published. Originally, survivor guilt and the collective sense that they had lost their community were used by analysts like Kai Erikson to explain the psychic impairment diagnosed by the visiting psychiatrists. In fact, despite its methodological weaknesses, Kai Erikson's book, *Everything In Its Path*, remains the best written and most penetrating disaster case study available.[5] Erickson reported that 93% of the 615 survivors who were examined

"...were found to be suffering from an identifiable emotional disturbance."[6] This was one and one-half years after that horrible night of death.

Another research team conducted follow-up studies that were published nearly a decade after this tragedy.[7] They came armed with more rigorous methodological tools than had been available to the initial investigative teams and included nonvictim control samples. These, of course, provided important comparison points, yet the results were shocking:

> ...Among those followed as long as 4–5 years post-disaster, over 30% continued to suffer debilitating symptoms.... 30% indicated increased alcohol consumption; 44% increased cigarette smoking, and 52% increased use of prescription drugs. As expected, these increases tended to occur in families in which the adults displayed the more severe symptoms, particularly with regard to anxiety and depression.[8]

This is powerful stuff. You can see why mental health advocate groups have incorporated this case into their literature and programs. But this case must be placed into context. Indeed, field work completed by T. P. Schwartz-Barcott over three decades later suggested a portrait of much greater self-healing and community resilence.[9] Sure, Buffalo Creek residents still remembered the flood. But just like you and I probably never will forget certain televised images of the World Trade Center attacks, many talked about going forward. Thus, Schwartz-Barcott suggests that even after disasters as horrifying as Buffalo Creek, long-term recovery can be more positive than might be expected. Given Erikson's brilliant write-up of the initial trauma experienced, these conclusions provide important context. See why you need to know more about the human side of disaster?

MODAL PATTERNS

In contrast to the findings from Buffalo Creek are a large number of other studies that present a different picture.[10] Let's be clear here, however. Disaster victims do experience a great deal of stress and varied degrees of subsequent anxiety, worry, and even mild depression as they seek to put their life back in order. But none of these responses reflect the extreme portrait from Buffalo Creek.

Prior to the 1966 tornado that cut a massive swath through Topeka, Kansas, my friend Bill Key was the director of the Social Science Division of the Menninger Foundation. They had conducted two large surveys of family and individual functioning about a year earlier. Key and I teamed up to conduct a follow-up study that remains unique in the literature.[11] Why? Because we had the luxury of having information from people before they were disaster victims. Then, three years afterward these *same individuals* were interviewed again. We also matched a family with each victim family and reinterviewed them. So we had both pre- and postevent data as well as victim and control samples. We augmented this data set with four other samples of 100 families each. That is, we *randomly* selected victim families with high incomes and low incomes along with corresponding sets of nonvictims. To date, this remains one of the most rigorously designed studies on this issue, although a few others have come close.[12]

What's the bottom line? No matter how we rearranged our data base, *there was no evidence of long-term debilitating impacts.* Some people expressed heightened storm anxiety, either for self or child. Hence, they reported being more quick to go to the cellar when tornado warnings were issued. A few indicated that their children still expressed fear whenever such warnings appeared on TV. But these residues are a sharp contrast to the portrait of pathology coming out of Buffalo Creek.

Indeed, when we examined victim expectations about their futures and compared these with those they had reported prior to the tornado, we made an astonishing discovery. Truthfully, when we first got the computer printouts, I was sure that we, or the computer, must have made a mistake. Even after cross-checking everything and having the data rerun, I still was not convinced. So one day I sat down with the original interview schedules and tallied each answer on this question by hand. The result? We had been right all along!

Over time, both groups—that is, victims and nonvictims—became somewhat more pessimistic about the future. Overall, their degree of change closely approximated that recorded for a national sample of U.S. citizens during the same time period. Now for the punch line: The victims declined in optimism ever so slightly. The nonvictims declined much more. It was as if being a tornado victim and experiencing the utopian mood of helpers afterward had isolated them somewhat from the overall decline in spirit that afflicted the rest of the nation during those years (i.e., 1966–1969). We pursued this issue and found that those victims who participated most fully in the utopian mood of the recovery period did not decline at all. They actually evidenced *increased optimism* about their futures, in contrast to the national trend.

Of course, this is only one study. And both it and the event were a long time ago. Since then there have been thousands of disaster events and hundreds of studies. Still, this modal pattern comes through.[13] After his exhaustive review of the literature, George Warheit drew a firm conclusion. Generally speaking, disasters that are community-wide do not cause increases in psychotic behavior.[14] Can't be much clearer than that! But what about Valerie? Is she just making up her stories of lingering fears? No, she's not. For her, and many like her, these types of stress symptoms are common, and for most they are transitory. According to Warheit, disasters "...may increase the prevalence of subclinical symptoms of anxiety, depression, psychoneuroticism, and/or other psychophysiologic complaints among some persons in the general population. However, the little longitudinal information available indicates that most of these symptoms persist for a relatively short period of time and are self-remitting...."[15]

PATTERNED VARIATIONS

There are three key pattern variations. First, disaster events differ in many ways. Some, like Hurricanes Andrew (1992), Katrina (2005), and Ike (2008), are true monsters. They affect thousands of households and dozens of communities. And some, like the Buffalo Creek flash flood or even the very deadly one that hit my state of Colorado, the Big Thompson Canyon Flood in 1976, are more horrifying for many. When lots of people die and surviving victims know them personally or actually see them perish, the impacts on the psyche are more pronounced.

Second, as Bob Bolin's follow-up study of the Wichita Falls, Texas (1979), tornado documented, much victim stress derives from "response generated demands" as opposed to those directly related to the disaster agent.[16] That is, sometimes local officials actually make things worse.[17] This can happen in many ways and sort of reflects the downside of the "utopian mood" I described in Chapter 7. Bolin documented one aspect of this in his follow-up interviews with tornado victims who described their life in a newly built trailer park. As they told him, the actual tornado, as frightening as it was, was nothing compared with the longer-term stress they confronted now. So although they felt grateful to have a place to live for a while that was more private than a community shelter, they encountered serious problems. The most common complaints reflected the cramped quarters, especially when several children were present. Others complained about unfamiliar or "troublesome" neighbors; wiring, plumbing, or heating; and lack of responsiveness by managers when told of these and other problems.[18]

193

After reviewing the work of others, Bolin came to realize that temporary housing was but one of four common sources of psychosocial stress that affects many disaster victims. Other areas that have been documented include the stresses related to evacuation and emergency shelter, relocation, and recovery and reconstruction issues.[19] As I watched television coverage of thousands of people trying to endure life at the Superdome or the New Orleans convention center, following Hurricane Katrina in September 2005, I was reminded of Bolin's conclusions. Undoubtedly, future researchers will document various stress impacts on many of these people that will reflect this evacuation or the subsequent relocation. Others will be highly stressed by things that happen during recovery and reconstruction following Katrina. Unfortunately, the same will be true for many Galvestonians or others who lived nearby in coastal areas of Texas or Louisiana prior to Hurricane Ike.

Third, as Katrina also demonstrated so well, existing social inequalities are exacerbated by disaster. In our study of the Topeka tornado, we documented several patterns of neglect.[20] The poor, ethnic minorities, and to a lesser degree the elderly suffered more than others. At the opposite end of the age curve are those most vulnerable of all: children. Both our interviewees and many of Bolin's reported recurring nightmares among kids. While I am doubtful of the estimate, the National Mental Health Association has claimed that 30% of child victims from Katrina are likely to develop posttraumatic stress disorder (PTSD).[21] Mental health experts pointed not to actual events experienced but rather to children hearing repeated rumors of violence. One father said, "You couldn't pay her to go to the bathroom." You see, his daughter kept hearing *unverified* stories of children being attacked in the Superdome's bathrooms.

As months passed, many Katrina victims, especially the poor, continued to suffer from all three of these pattern variations; that is, they were hit with a triple whammy. First, the storm was a monster with horrible impact. Second, so-called response-generated demands were extreme and lasting. And third, social inequity was pronounced. Various mental health surveys reflected these realities. For example, a widely reported analysis conducted by Ronald Kessler of Harvard Medical School documented a doubling of mental illness from prestorm levels. His team surveyed more than 800 Katrina victims in three states: Louisiana, Mississippi, and Alabama. Among these, 14% had severe symptoms; another 20% had mild to moderate symptoms. Normally, nightmares, inability to stop thinking about the hurricane, and similar symptoms that comprise PTSD would dissipate over a year. Kessler's team documented that 21% had such symptoms in 2007, which compared with 16% in 2006.[22]

PTSD is a symptom pattern that gained popularity following the return of Vietnam veterans during the late 1960s and early 1970s.[23] "Shell shock," or whatever it might be called, had been noted among some soldiers in prior wars. But the numbers following Vietnam caused many to take notice. In part, this may have reflected the divisiveness within the country at the time, increased acceptance of mental trauma as a legitimate and treatable condition, and a host of other factors. Two experts who examined the issue reached this conclusion, which strikes me as being balanced. You see, lots of Vietnam veterans were "…distrustful and suspicious of government institutions as a result of their painful war and homecoming experiences, quickly learned that even when they took the initiative to seek professional assistance for their stress-related symptoms, the treatment received was likely to be inadequate and frequently counterproductive."[24]

During the past three decades or so, many have explored the possible impacts of disaster on the human psyche. Some have focused on specific symptom patterns like PTSD, whereas others have examined a variety of behavioral indicants of stress. In Chapter 8, I summarized the work from a team at Northwestern University headed by Paul Friesema. They concluded that there were some short-term spikes in such matters as death and divorce rates.[25] Within six months, however, earlier trend patterns reappeared.

Following Hurricane Hugo, which smashed into Charleston, South Carolina, and other nearby coastal areas in 1989, Catherine Cohan and Steve Cole also looked long term[26] (see Chapter 8). When they reviewed marriage, birth, and divorce rates from 1975 to 1997 in numerous impacted counties, they validated the pattern discovered by the Northwestern University team. Marriage rates, for example, had been on a decline until the year after Hugo, when there was a net increase. Then in 1991, the earlier long-term trend continued. You see, in the midst of recovery, some people simply put off a pending marriage for several months.

So too with divorce rates. There had been a stable pattern until Hugo. Then there was one year with an increase. Having babies followed the same trend line. The authors' interpretation strikes me as being reasonable: "For some, natural disaster may have hastened a transition they were already moving toward, but at a slower pace. For others, natural disaster may have led to a transition that might not have occurred if not for the disaster."[27]

One of the questions I have been asked about frequently when reviewing this general topic pertains to suicide. Apparently, some media reports have planted this seed. And it's no wonder: It seems that any research that points to a negative impact gets a lot of visibility. A few years ago, the very prestigious *New England Journal of Medicine* published a scholarly report concluding that disasters cause increases in suicide rates.[28] Needless to say, the study set off a media feeding frenzy! And with such statistics in hand, everybody that was anybody got on the bandwagon. Talk shows had so-called experts coming out of the woodwork to explain the signs and signals. After any disaster, it was proposed by some, extensive mental health interventions were required to avoid seeing more and more people sink into the depths of despair that could result in death.

Unfortunately, the media coverage was most scant months later when a *retraction* appeared.[29] It turns out that the research team had made a mistake. When they reviewed their data sets, they discovered a computer error: "We regretfully report that we have discovered an error in computer programming and that our previous results are incorrect."[30] Unfortunately, such reports do not get the headlines.

So where does this leave us? Well, my general conclusion, using our Topeka study and dozens that have followed as grounding points, is that there are vulnerable populations within all communities who suffer the most after disaster. Psychic injury, including symptoms reflective of PTSD, does occur. So, for a while, some victims like Valerie do experience such stress symptoms as nightmares and feelings of panic, irritability, and depression.[31]

Often these same vulnerable populations, in part reflections of economic inequalities, are more neglected after disaster, just as they are before. In Topeka, for example, we documented that victims who participated more fully in the post-tornado therapeutic community reported fewer signs of lingering stress. Recently, this was validated in an exceptionally well-executed study focused on the 1993 Midwest floods.[32] Using statewide survey data collected in Iowa in 1992, Jim Stimpson compared results with a second survey done about sixty days after the peak of the flooding. This is one of the few studies completed to date to have preevent data and a control group like we had in Topeka. Of course, unlike our study, in which a follow-up three years after the tornado was used, Stimpson assessed possible short-term changes in PTSD.

Stimpson's study validated three conclusions that are consistent with our earlier work. First, for the short term at least, flood victims as an overall group evidenced a moderate increase in stress symptoms like those assessed by PTSD measures. Second, individuals who had higher levels of a sense of control before the flood were less likely to experience these symptoms. Third, people who had strong social support groups, which probably would remain activated in the months after Stimpson's second survey, reported few stress symptoms. Such are the psychic costs of social isolation, costs that are exacerbated by disaster.

Two final points about pattern variation need to be mentioned. Poor people, and others who suffer the human indignities of extreme social inequality, do make choices. Their capacity to perceive and implement choices, however, is very limited. Hence, their sense of control also is limited. Lack of hope limits one's ability to see a way out. And dire economic circumstance means that just getting through the day takes all the energy and stamina one can muster. Such are the psychic costs endured daily by vulnerable populations. And disaster only exacerbates such costs.

Second, recall the issue I raised toward the end of Chapter 6 regarding litigation fears. I suggested that such fears could hamper future helper behavior. A study of Katrina and Rita victims who suffered from pre-hurricane psychiatric disabilities documented frequent discrimination in emergency shelters and the receipt of relief services.[33] Furthermore, "mismanaged evacuations resulted in the loss, mistreatment, and inappropriate institutionalization of people with psychiatric disabilities."[34] In part, these actions occurred because staff lacked appropriate training or were unsure of their legal risks: "Some doctors, especially those from out of state, were hesitant to volunteer or provide treatment in shelters because of fears of liability associated with treating strangers without having access to medical records."[35] The report emphasized that there is great variation among the fifty states regarding Good Samaritan laws. When medical doctors and other health professionals arrive at a disaster scene after crossing a state boundary—sometimes several—the applicable law becomes very problematic.[36] Clearly, this issue goes far beyond the single population group composed of the psychiatrically disabled. But equally clear is that this group, like other vulnerable sectors, will suffer disproportionately until relevant policy changes are implemented.

But, like people, communities also differ. Some places reflect higher levels of cohesion, consensus, and helping networks, whereas others are more lacking. Topeka, at the time we studied the impacts of the 1966 tornado, had its poor, elderly, and ethnic minorities. But, overall, the place reflected the values and culture that nurtured a wide range of networks that provided social support to most in the community.

A contrast was documented by Kroll-Smith and Couch when they penetrated Centralia, a small town in Pennsylvania.[37] When a fire in a garbage dump ignited an outcropping of coal that eventually reached to underground deposits, a different type of response emerged:

...The community suffered from severe, debilitating conflict. Instead of aiding and cooperating with each other, neighbor struggled against neighbor, creating as much havoc above ground as the fire created below.[38]

In short, like disasters and people, not all communities are the same. The modal profile of the therapeutic community response and its impact on blunting the psychic harm caused by a tornado, flood, or earthquake is just that: the modal profile, not the exception. And there are exceptions. Sometimes it may be both the town and the event. For example, the fire in Centralia burned on for over two decades before the federal government finally authorized funds to buy out the residents and assist in their relocation in October 1983. And during those years, different groups tried to promote their particular view of the risk and what actions should be taken. As arguments intensified, each group accused others of seeking to destroy the town: "This process of reciprocal blame attribution escalates into a conflict that may, as in the case of Centralia, became more debilitating than the hazard agent itself."[39]

KINFOLK AND FRIENDS

Disasters change people. But social systems, like communities, sometimes reflect changes too. Several researchers have documented that existing trends are accelerated after disaster strikes. One of the first to document this idea was Bill Anderson, a member of the team at the Disaster Research Center at The Ohio State University that completed extensive fieldwork in Alaska following the 1964 earthquake.[40] Since his pioneering work, others have examined the patterns of change in a variety of places. The late Fred Bates and Walter Peacock analyzed this matter in Guatemala City following the 1976 earthquake; Betty Morrow and Peacock examined the changes brought about by Hurricane Andrew.[41] Joe Scanlon and John Handmer[42] focused on Port Arthur, Tasmania, where a lone gunman, without warning, killed thirty-five and injured nineteen others on Sunday afternoon, April 28, 1996. The massacre added fuel to a movement already underway in Australia regarding gun control. So consistent with Anderson's earlier observations, Scanlon and Handmer traced through numerous specific factors that help us understand why this massacre figured so importantly in the "nationwide Agreement on Firearms" that was implemented in all states and territories by May 1997.

Microsystems, like extended family and friendship groups, change too because of disaster. Key and I examined dozens of data patterns from the Topeka families impacted by the 1966 tornado.[43] The results were clear and many-sided. The overall conclusion was without ambiguity: The response to the 1966 tornado tightened relationships among kin groups. Three years afterward, many victims interacted more frequently with their parents. Compared with their rate prior to the tornado and the matched control groups, this increase in interaction frequency was but the first of several indications of change.

As we drilled down deeper, we discovered that this held true for their married children and siblings. They simply were interacting more frequently with these kinfolk. And when asked who they visited with more—relatives or friends—the tornado victims more often replied "relatives." This was a change over time as well as in comparison with the control group. We also asked how often they borrowed things from relatives and did favors of various types for them. Once again, victim families reported a higher frequency. The same pattern was revealed when we asked about problem solving, for example, "If you were in an emergency and needed money, would you prefer to ask: Relative, friend or other?"[44] Before the tornado, more nonvictims than victims picked relatives. After the tornado, victims shifted (44% prior picked relatives vs. 57% afterward) and far exceeded the proportion of nonvictims who stated they would seek out a relative.

The conclusion is that disasters caused these families to appreciate their relatives much more. They were now bonded to them much tighter. It was these social groups who also loomed high during the therapeutic community response. It was these people who showed up to help clean up the mess, to babysit, to offer the loan of a car, to help with extra bills that piled up, and so on.

While relatives reflected the greatest amount of increase in bonding, friends were noticed too. Such linkages existed before the tornado for about one-third who were victimized that June evening. Afterward, these linkages were strengthened. The frequency with which these victims got together with their friends increased over the years.

Since they were seeing relatives and friends more, someone had to lose out, and the losers in our study were neighbors. In part this was because of relocation, but that was not the full story. When we examined those who stayed in the same home, the pattern persisted. During the recovery, neighbors had their own problems. It was relatives and friends who helped the most in the immediate storm aftermath. Three years later, these bonds showed the greatest levels of change. These bonds were now stronger among the victim families than they had been previously.

When Bolin reviewed his data from the 1979 Wichita Falls, Texas, tornado, he validated two of these patterns.[45] Visitation with kin increased, just like in Topeka. What differed a bit was the friendship pattern. Both the victim and nonvictim samples in his study also reflected an increase in visits among friends. Thus, the tornado impact may not have been the key unless, as he argued, the event may have changed the perspectives of both groups a bit. Regardless, the lesson is clear: Disasters bring many family and friendship groups closer together. When the chips are down, these are the people that most often will be there for you. And surviving disaster is a powerful way to learn this.

"THIS IS MY MOTHER"

Like many daughters, Valerie turned first to her mother. And like many mothers—especially the good ones—Valerie's reflected the tough love that has sustained human communities over the centuries. Remember her advice? "Get over it!" It is exactly within such support networks that the nurturing can occur. Healing of psychic scars occurs naturally within these types of family groupings—mothers with daughters, fathers with sons, husbands with wives, and within other types of partnerships wherein intimacy, privacy, and love are nurtured and experienced.

During the past decade, several researchers, most of them female, have documented issues and conclusions that reflect these types of insights. Impacted personally by Hurricane Andrew, Morrow and Elaine Enarson have been at the forefront of this group.[46] When disaster is viewed through the eyes of such women, as we would expect, additional modal patterns are seen. Some of those parallel areas Key and I examined earlier. For example, we assessed the impacts of the Topeka tornado on husband–wife task sharing, marital happiness, and frequency with which spouses went out together without their children.[47] No matter how we arranged the data, the patterns remained subtle; that is, victims seemed to be about the same as nonvictims.

There were several subtle but consistent differences that collectively indicated some change, however. Though the difference was slight, our data suggested that three years after the tornado, victims rated their marriages a bit less satisfying but were going out without their children somewhat more frequently than they had previously. Women within victim families, however, were more frequently participating in the family decision-making process. This and several other task changes suggested that females had emerged from this disaster as being *more central and dominate* within the household.

Given our sample—remember this was Topeka, Kansas, in the late 1960s—we did not examine a whole series of issues that have surfaced in more recent research. For example, single mothers were not studied. Clearly, today, they represent an important group that is highly vulnerable in any disaster. And, as Morrow and Enarson documented after Hurricane Andrew, most people seeking help for their families were women.[48] As months drifted by, some women discovered that the post-Andrew recovery process was just too much for the men in their life. If they were lucky, the man just didn't return home one night. But others did return after some time of heavy drinking. This helped unleash pent-up frustration: "Informants described increasingly violent relationships as couples endured month after month in tents, cars, and half-repaired homes."[49]

Following the massive flooding and fires that struck Grand Forks, North Dakota, in April 1997, Alice Fothergill completed interviews with forty women, once shortly after the event and again about a year later. She spoke informally with some three or four times during this period,[50] and she learned a great deal about domestic violence, including instances of physical battering. The lingering psychic pains of such relationships of repeated abuse—both emotional and physical—is another of the costs of the disaster aftermath that also is part of the picture. This dark side must not be ignored. And, as I emphasized already, again it is the poor who suffer most. Validating past research, Morrow and Enarson put it this way: "Two years later the poorest areas are far from recovered, and thousands of families are still living in damaged, crowded, and/or substandard temporary housing."[51]

Recovery after Hurricane Katrina has gone fine for some. But Irwin Redlener's observations about more vulnerable populations validate the conclusions reached earlier by Morrow and Enarson. Clearly, the lessons from Andrew were not learned. So the pattern is repeated, and more people are hurt. Most among those are poor, and a significant proportion are nonwhite:

> Current recovery problems include prolonged stays for displaced persons in inadequate temporary shelters, exposure to formaldehyde in the trailers, poor or no access to health and mental health services, poor access to schools for children, and lack of employment opportunities for their parents.[52]

And with insights from the Gallop Red Cross database I discussed in Chapter 4, we glean another important bit of evidence that underscores the buffering effects stable social networks provide.[53] There we learned that significant proportions of the threatened population decided to "evacuate by division." That is, as Katrina approached, about one-third of the families decided to split up. Almost always, it was men who stayed behind. Most had jobs, and most were black and also attached to their church.

While the measures of both short- and long-term stress were crude at best, the patterns were clear-cut.[54] Those who split up prior to Katrina's arrival reported higher levels of both short- and long-term stress. Maybe it was because they feared losing their job if they left, or maybe other factors were operating—the exact reasons remain unknown—but the higher stress levels were a consistent pattern difference. Thus, the type of evacuation strategy Katrina victims adopted seems to have affected the levels of stress experienced. So once again the psychic costs of fractured, unstable, or incomplete social networks are documented. And for some, professional intervention may be what a humane society would provide.

For the most vulnerable victims—children—follow-up studies are very discouraging. For example, a study team from the Children's Health Fund at Columbia University reported that approximately 20,000 children remained displaced two and one-half years after Katrina. And because of their experiences during displacement, another 50,000 or so remain at high risk (estimated to be between 46,000 to 64,000 based on surveys completed) for, among the predictions, lowered academic achievement, loss of access to health care, or even the onset of such mental disorders as depression, anxiety, or other symptoms. In short, "Not only has their health not improved since the storm, over time it has declined to an alarming level."[55]

Following significant storms like Gustav and Ike that smacked our coastlines during fall 2008, such patterns are bound to be repeated within thousands of "families" of various compositions. Undoubtedly, communities impacted by these more catastrophic storms will be changed in ways that go far beyond that documented in any of the research I have summarized herein. And while some will suffer lingering psychic pain, others will grow more rapidly in positive directions. They will have better futures than they would have had without conquering these terrible storms.

For these and other disaster victims, two other adaptations we documented in Topeka also may be validated, at least in some form. Both are important aspects of the natural healing processes through which most victims deal with disaster-induced psychic injury. Since they are spending more time with relatives and friends in the postdisaster years, something has to go. We documented that for voluntary associations of all types, be it the Parent–Teacher Association (PTA), Veterans of Foreign Wars (VFW), Boy or Girl Scouts, or what have you, three years after the Topeka tornado, victim *participation levels had declined.*[56] This decline was in comparison with both previous rates and the nonvictim sample.

There was one exception, however. Church attendance and commitment increased among disaster victims.[57] This actually reflected a larger type of change: a view of life priorities. Of course, some focused on lingering fears, especially among children, especially during stormy weather:

> My oldest girl doesn't shake and cry like she used to, but is just getting over it. But we are all afraid of storms.[58]
> Some of the little kids are terribly scared of storms now. They're real skitsy about a storm coming on.[59]

But for most, their interpretations of how they had changed emphasized themes that reflected optimism and activism.[60] For many this meant better storm preparedness, like construction of basements and storm shelters. Others expressed closer community ties and appreciation for the help they received. Some even described how they had benefited by having house improvements completed that were needed prior to the tornado. The benefits others emphasized were more psychological and philosophical. They spoke of "being a stronger person" and realizing that "...the important things in life are not material things."[61] Such is the diverse nature of the human response. For some, psychic pains in various manifestations will linger,[62] but for most, the natural healing powers of informal social support groups will make them okay. And many will be more than okay. Through the process of conquering, they will set their sights higher and enjoy life more fully.

THE INSIGHTS

- Most disaster victims do not suffer long-term psychic injury.
- Disaster impacts vary depending on the severity and degree of horrification of the event and other qualities like community cohesiveness.
- Disasters bring families and friends closer together; this change persists for years.
- Vulnerable groups, especially children, may evidence higher levels of negative impacts including future storm anxiety.

- Disasters may intensify outbreaks of anger, including spousal abuse, especially within families already stressed.
- Years afterward, disaster victims participate less frequently in most voluntary associations and maintain less contact with neighbors.
- Disaster victims express more religious and antimaterialistic perspectives on life; many increase their participation in religious organizations.
- Having conquered a disaster event, years afterward most disaster victims view themselves as being stronger emotionally.

11

What Must Be Done?

What must be done?[1] Well, there's a lot—more than I can summarize in this single chapter. But the bottom line is that we must develop an expanded vision. A more *strategic* approach is required in our understanding of disaster and our efforts at coping.

Unfortunately, since the attacks on 9/11, several areas of emergency management policy have been going in the wrong direction. Sizeable portions of our infrastructure—dams, bridges, water and sewer systems, to name the most obvious—have been neglected. So not only have our vulnerabilities increased, but important policy changes also have weakened our capacity to respond. Excessive focus on potential attacks by terrorists, increased use of military type planning models, and decreased authority and flexibility for local and state governments are among many of the specifics. Even worse, these policy shifts have weakened national resiliency by disenfranchising our most important resource: citizen volunteers. Clearly, it is time to change, time to adopt a more strategic vision. The vision must be rooted in the knowledge base that has been built regarding the human side of disaster.

Disasters will happen. Communities, of course, will recover, at least eventually. And people? Yes, they will suffer. But then, isn't that just the way life is? Certainly, human suffering has been around forever. Right? No, not really—at least not to the degree that we experience today. The "we," of course, forces us to ask about our personal circumstances—and those of others who are more distant. Clearly, millions of humans are alive at this instant whose life expectancy and physical suffering do not differ much from that experienced by the typical citizens in France, Germany, or the United States about a century or two ago. Before that, if you want to read some history or anthropology that presents reality rather than romantic dreams, most people living in most places could not even imagine the limits on human suffering that we now take for granted. At no other time in history have there been people concerned about the number of minutes defining "acceptable response times" for paramedics to reach the home of a man having a heart attack. So what is the point? It really is a simple one. Our perceptions of risk, like our views on human suffering, have changed dramatically over the centuries—not totally or universally, of course, but there has been significant change.

Few American citizens will accept or tolerate the type of human pain and trauma that a century ago was still defined as resulting from "acts of God."[2] Most of us do not accept natural disasters as "God's will." When we watched hundreds wading through toxic soup in New Orleans after Katrina, most of us were horrified. This simply was not right. Not acceptable! So the first thing to be done is improve our understanding of risk and the social processes whereby the public and policy makers construct perceptions that define acceptable limits.

VARIABLE PERCEPTIONS OF RISK

Not everyone is willing to fly. Indeed, there is a small percentage of the population in every industrialized society who simply refuses. Some rejecters, of course, claim that the risks are too great, so they proceed to drive across country, and around town, failing to accept the clear implications of consistent statistical patterns. The average American is in much greater danger speeding along a metropolitan freeway than relaxing in a DC-10 or a "triple 7." Yet some who define the risk of driving an automobile as being well within their acceptable limits do mental somersaults when it comes to flying.[3]

When confronted with statistics that establish airline safety, those who are uncomfortable with flying offer revealing insights into the complexity of the human psyche.[4] Risk assessment processes have been explored by numerous researchers during the past four decades. Although there are still a lot of unanswered questions, we have come a long way in understanding the social factors that operate to establish alternative definitions of acceptable risk. Informed policy making requires clear understanding of these social constraints, for they are the stuff that molds community conflicts. When leaders cannot mobilize reasonable levels of consensus about the risks associated with natural and technological hazards, the policy-making process grinds to a halt. Too often, bad decisions get made or good ones fail to be implemented. The consequence is that everyone is a loser, often without ever knowing it.

Where should nuclear power plants be located? Should they be built at all? Why would any reasonable person argue for construction when other power sources are available? Why place any community at risk?[5] Such questions parallel those that can be asked about building in areas that are flood prone, can't they? And what about earthquakes, avalanches, or volcanoes? You see, the referent hazard can change, but questions about acceptable risk are the same. So what are some of the factors that shape risk perceptions? Obviously, the question, like its answer, is complex. But let's consider five basics.

The most important factor that splits people into accepting a particular risk or refusing to do so is experience. It is next to impossible to convince someone who has lived near a river for all of his life that he is at risk if flooding never has occurred. And if a flood has already come to that area? You would not believe the number of folks I have interviewed who explained to me that they wouldn't have a future flood because they had their 100-year flood a year or so prior. They fail to understand the most elementary principle of probability theory—the mathematics underlying the scientific basis for predictions about 100-year floods and other extreme events.

Such references are limited to the immediate. That is, flood predictions are referring only to the current time period. Just because a major one happened last year does not change the probability estimate for the months ahead. Ever talk to a casino patron who told you that her machine was "due" because it hadn't "hit" for a while? This is the same logic, except in reverse—and equally wrong![6] Of course, unlike events in nature, slot machines may be programmed to pay out in any desired pattern—all within "legal limits," that is. So, not all, maybe none, are programmed to function strictly in accordance with "pure" randomized probability curves. Ever meet a person who has a "favorite" machine?

Experience, then, has a curious effect on people's risk perceptions. If it hasn't flooded, that is taken as evidence that it won't. Even if it has, there are creative interpretations offered that lead many to conclude that they are safe. Ring familiar? If not, go back to Chapter 3 and reread the section on warning responses. You see, the social dynamics are very similar. Denial and evidence to support a sense of invulnerability are operative here too.

What if you decided to move to California? You might encounter relatives who would express certain fears: "Aren't you worried about earthquakes?" Their expressions, regardless of content or intensity, may exacerbate your concerns. And if they should, fear not. Once there, you will reduce your sense of risk by learning from the natives: "Oh, earthquakes? They just come with the territory. Nothing to worry about really. My family's been here for years. It's just something to learn to live with out here. Sure gives the comedians lots of material." So what's going on? The same social learning processes we have discussed previously are at work. People use humor to neutralize fears that may be building up about risks. So when Californians were surveyed at different points in time, researchers discovered that the longer they lived there, the less risky they perceived the earthquake hazard. Familiarity does breed acceptance. Familiarity of risk, usually, although not always, lessens fear levels.[7]

Research in Florida has added a corollary to this pattern. John Cross surveyed a group of people at three different points in time: 1976, 1982, and 1987.[8] His results did not support the familiarity hypothesis, at least not at first glance. People living in the Florida Keys were asked about the likelihood of a damaging hurricane during the next ten years. The percentages indicating a "strong likelihood," shifted upward across the years. That is, 61% expected one in 1983, whereas 64% did six years later. This is one of the first investigations into the stability of risk perceptions over time that documented this pattern.

To me, it says two things. First, through very effective emergency management programs, local governments are doing a better job in helping Florida citizens to realistically recognize the increased risk they confront because of the enormous growth cycle they have enjoyed for over three decades. Florida remains a hot spot, especially for Midwesterners wanting to escape the winter cold. Equally important is the fact that Cross was able to find the same people. Having arrived in Florida, they didn't leave. Hence, as I have emphasized repeatedly, more and more people are relocating into areas of high risk. The hazard varies, but the risk level has increased. And just like the millions who have moved into earthquake country, most new Floridians have little experience with hurricanes. Public information campaigns may be altering these risk perceptions; so, too, is the continuing stream of information regarding global warming and other longer-term environmental changes. Even more potent, I suspect, are destructive hurricanes like Hugo, Andrew, Katrina, and Ike. Tropical storm seasons like 2005 and 2008, which broke records for the number and intensity of major hurricanes, will impact this too. How and exactly why are questions meriting more research.

Both the age and gender structure of a community or family influence risk perceptions.[9] Like we saw with disaster warning responses, social learning processes vary. In general, females indicate higher fear levels although they sometimes know less about the technical details of most hazards. Similarly, as people mature, their knowledge base expands. Unfortunately, as evidenced by their responses to disaster warnings, their sense of skepticism does too. Although older people may know more specifics about the history of flooding or hurricanes in their community, their level of acceptable risk expands too. This is especially true when it comes to doing anything that might reduce their vulnerability. Mitigation actions of whatever type are less likely to be accepted by those whose risk perceptions have been blunted by years of indifference.

Of course, people who are poor have little time to worry about invisible risks. That is one reason disaster relief officials who have responded to some of the major catastrophes of our lifetime have experienced increased frustration. When well over 100,000 Bangladesh peasants perished during the spring 1991 tropical storms, the linkages between risk perceptions and development were revealed dramatically—at least they were to those who cared to look. Most Americans didn't, of course. Rather, it was easier to ignore the suffering and rationalize that it was someone else's job.

The same is true for places like Haiti. In fall 2008, Haiti was hit by four consecutive hurricanes: Fay, Gustav, Hanna, and Ike. Nationwide, 425 people were killed, and more than 60% of the food harvest was destroyed. Televised images of those impacted in the deadly Boxing Day tsunami (December 26, 2004), in which nearly 200,000 died, add an explanation point! Development along coastal areas, many of which like Puket, Thailand, have been transformed into tourist meccas, put people at risk. Some—namely, the tourists—were not poor, of course, but those there to service their needs reflect centuries-old inequalities, as do those working the fields.[10]

Within our communities, the poor evidence parallel attitudes of fatalism. Rooted in cultural traditions of passivity and acceptance of one's fate, they, like millions in other lands, are reluctant to entertain an alternative life perspective. Given their experiences this reluctance is understandable, although not necessarily morally acceptable. For if they assume more responsibility for their plight—evidence higher levels of what some psychologists call "fate control," others "self-efficacy"—they may become a challenge to those who currently benefit from their passivity and acquiescence.[11]

The distribution of risk, not unlike the distribution of wealth, reflects the contours of social power. There are many important stakeholders whose positions of privilege and power would be threatened if the poor—both within and outside our national boundaries—began to question their plight by beginning to adjust their notions of acceptable risk. Definitions of disaster that are rooted in fatalistic phrases like "acts of God" are only the tip of the iceberg that comprises this social constraint. Explicit recognition of this and expanded awareness of the social and political implications that follow are the real reasons we must understand the variability in perceptions of risk.[12] Do you think that some in positions of authority might attempt to manipulate your perceptions of risk to convince you that a new dam is necessary? What about a war? What about new limits on your civil liberties? Your degrees of privacy? I urge you to ponder these questions and think critically about how they relate to the human side of disaster.

All this discussion brings me to a fundamental conclusion. We must both enhance our capacities to respond and to reduce our vulnerabilities. Charles Perrow pointed out how decentralization of everything from coastal populations to chemical processing facilities was constrained by the lack of will among politicians who side with the corporate rich.[13] Consequently, without real campaign finance reform, the types of transitions required are not likely. Hence, we probably will see minimal change in reducing the size of the targets that may be attacked by our enemies or destroyed by the natural forces of nature—that is, unless a new vision of emergency management is adopted. Such a vision, it seems to me, is consistent with that espoused by the wisest within the emergency management community—men like the late Gilbert F. White and former Federal Emergency Management Agency (FEMA) director James Lee Witt. In his superb biography of White, Robert Hinshaw described White's bottom-up approach. He noted the consistency with that espoused by Witt.[14] Indeed, he illustrated the point with this quotation from Witt's 1993 presentation at the Natural Hazards Workshop: "Such an approach will put the focus back on our communities and establish a 'bottom-up' approach to emergency management and public safety that is responsive to the people's needs."[15]

DISASTERS ARE NONROUTINE SOCIAL PROBLEMS

When we begin exploring issues like these, we are taking an important step. It is one that *must* be taken to expand our understanding. Disasters and our responses to them do not occur in isolation from the everyday and more routine problems of living, yet disasters differ from problems like crime or divorce in many ways.[16] The most important of these differences is our relative absence of moral judgments about the victims—at least most of the time. Anyone's house can be demolished by a tornado or earthquake. Their vulnerability is not of their own choosing or because of misjudgment. Or is it? When we think of people choosing to build as close to the waterfront as local officials will permit, can we really say they had no choice in risk selection? Furthermore, pondering an example like this forces us to ask, "Who are these local officials, and what gives them the right to tell people where they can or cannot build their house?" Inquiries like this deepen our understanding of the human side of disaster if we push them further and really explore this implicit social problems context.[17]

Four key principles are particularly relevant. First, *there is an interdependence among social problems.* When we focus on crime, for example, we quickly become aware of the relevance of dysfunctional families, failing schools and poverty—so too the way we define disasters, our immediate responses to them, and our efforts to reduce future vulnerabilities. All of these matters are linked to core community values and other community resource needs. We can't allocate money for disaster preparedness or prevention without explicit recognition that we are impacting other community programs. The program might be disaster related, like a major mitigation effort, or it could be one designed to reduce poverty, such as job training or child-care assistance. We must sense such interdependencies, and, even then, the trade-offs may remain illusive.

Second, *the socially powerful have greater influence in defining what is and is not a social problem.* This too is true for disasters. At first glance that may seem untrue. But consider the social processes whereby the poor and elderly more frequently reside in areas more prone to flooding. Are the wealthy usually impacted when a tornado cuts through a mobile home park? The principle is complex, but the insights it can provide are most profound.

Third, *the definitions of what is and is not a social problem change over time.* Today, many are concerned about sexual predators who lurk within Internet chatrooms. This is quite a shift from years ago when a female teacher was not even allowed to marry and pregnant high school students

211

were required to drop out so their "condition" would remain unnoticed by their more "innocent" peers. So too it is with the changed perceptions of terrorism. Although many had used the tactic of terrorism previously, be it in Ireland or the Middle East, the attacks on September 11, 2001, have been used successfully by certain political leaders to promote a remarkable shift in the perception of risk among Americans. Indeed, since those attacks, both polls and textbooks clearly document that terrorism is perceived as a pressing social problem.[18] Other forms of disaster, be they flooding, wildfires, or earthquakes, have not attained comparable status. It is important to ask why this has happened. As with any other shift in risk perception, we must ask, "Who gains?"

The tactic of terrorism can be implemented in many ways. Use of explosives is most common. Remember, Timothy McVeigh and a few others loaded easily obtained materials into a van and blew out a side of the Alfred P. Murrah building in Oklahoma City on April 19, 1995. This action left 167 dead and 460 injured. In contrast to McVeigh, who left the scene, so-called suicide bombers elevate perceptions of fear even more. And it is such fears that in turn are being used by some to promote redirections in disaster policy. I comment further on this matter in an upcoming section, but let's first see the implications of our social problems perspective for suicide bombers.

While not studied as thoroughly as others who have resorted to violence, such as abusive parents, gang members, and spousal murderers, suicide bombers have been examined in recent years.[19] After reviewing large segments of this research literature, Robert Brym offered six key lessons:

1. "Suicide bombers are not crazy."
2. "It's mainly about politics, not religion."
3. "Sometimes it's strategic."
4. "Sometimes it's retaliatory."
5. "Repression is a boomerang."
6. "Empathize with your enemy."[20]

Hence, consistent with a social problems perspective on other matters, Brym advocated understanding of larger structural, cultural, and historical contexts for both moral and pragmatic reasons. Why? Because unless you kill nearly everyone, or assist warring groups to do so to each other, you can't eliminate the motivations that foster terrorism. The solution does not lie in further violence, unless of course you can accept what most people define as immoral—that is, genocide.[21] As with potential burglars, this does not mean that we never lock our doors, but the answer to burglary does not lie in a policy perspective focused solely on programs encouraging the purchase of additional locks. So too Brym pushed us to rethink. We must understand the concept of empathy if we want to design more effective counterterrorism strategies: "Seeing the enemy's point of view increases one's understanding of the minimum conditions that would allow the enemy to put down arms."[22]

Fourth, *sociological analyses of social problems preclude blaming the victims.* It is impossible for most of us to begin to understand the depth of the impact of poverty: the daily struggle to get by, an existence wherein hope and dreams for a better future are nonexistent. So when the levees broke after Hurricane Katrina moved past New Orleans, many of the poor and elderly surfaced. They had not heeded the evacuation advisories even when the label *mandatory* was attached. Surprise, surprise! So they suffered even more than they had in the months before the storm. Some—at least 1,300—died. Fortunately, as discussed in Chapter 4, the more proactive evacuation strategies implemented prior to the arrival of Gustav and Ike during fall 2008 resulted in significantly lower death tolls. Still, the deaths of nearly 100 (67 from Ike and 24 from Gustav) might have been prevented. As with other social problems, public policies related to disaster must go beyond blaming the victims. The implications of this perspective were reflected in a report issued by the Russell Sage Foundation after Hurricane Katrina.[23] Manuel Pastor, a professor of Latin American and Latino studies and codirector of the Center for Justice, Tolerance and Community, headed the six-person team that prepared this report. A couple of quotations make the point:

> It is said that the first step of a program to eliminate addiction is to admit you have a problem. In a society seemingly hooked on putting hazards in the backyards of those already burdened by poverty and racial discrimination, owning up to the reality would make a good starting place for policy making.[24]
> Katrina did open a window on the dark side of America—the economic and environment vulnerability of low-income people and minority communities. We can close that window, or we can use the new view to chart a better, healthier, and more equitable future for us all.[25]

While working on my first disaster case study—the explosion in the Indianapolis Coliseum (reread Sam Wilson's story about the taxi ride in Chapter 1) in 1963—I still recall my puzzlement. In the weeks that followed some of the people we had interviewed that worked in emergency organizations were charged as criminals. The charges came from a grand jury.

These charges were not related to the emergency response, however, but rather had to do with their failure to prevent. The inadequate inspection system, the real structural deficiency, could not be found guilty; only people could be prosecuted. Henry Quarantelli and I concluded that "...putting other persons into the same position could have made little difference."[26] Indeed, "not only does individual blame draw attention from more fundamental causes, but it might actually give the illusion that corrective action of some sort is being taken."[27] By recognizing that disasters are nonroutine social problems, our vision is expanded. And it is precisely this type of expanded vision, and recognition of the policy implications, that must be reflected among the new group of professionals focused on disaster.

PROFESSIONALISM IN EMERGENCY MANAGEMENT

It is hard for most of us to imagine a society without medical doctors. They, like lawyers and accountants, have gained a foothold of legitimacy that precludes much questioning. Their services are needed and obviously merit compensation at reasonable levels. As individuals, they enter our lives when we believe their technical knowledge will assist in problem solving. Few of us would dream of trying to build a fifty-story office complex unless we had the benefit of an architect, structural engineer, and several other types of professionals. The same principle applies to a courtroom experience, be we defendant or plaintiff.

When we think about people suffering following tornadoes, hurricanes, or earthquakes, a different collection of occupational identities come to mind. Let's see, who would they be? Police, fire, and medical uniforms come into view quickly, don't they? If we let the vision mature, especially if we have been at such sites, other uniforms appear. Ambulance drivers and paramedics are specialized aspects of the medical contingent, and utility workers from telephone, electric, or natural gas firms represent critical private-sector resources. The list could be expanded, but that isn't necessary for the point—one that often eludes even the most seasoned rescue personnel. Given all of these different specialists, each of whom reflects sophisticated skill and knowledge areas, who is going to put all the parts together? Who is the professional that provides this service?

As strange as it may seem, for decades this function—interagency coordination—was not recognized explicitly. Hence, fragmented responses, accurately dubbed organized-disorganization, characterized disaster scenes. Due to a variety of historical factors, local civil defense offices were at the fringe of the disaster response networks and were relatively impotent in performing this coordination function. Few understood it, and even fewer had much idea of how to go about doing it. Fortunately, things are changing. But the transformation is just beginning. Emergency management is an emergent profession—not one that has attained full legitimacy.[28] Poor responses to storms like Katrina, however, will push this profession backward a bit. Once lost, credibility is hard to repair. And it seems like everyone has loads of ideas about how the profession should proceed.

The process has evolved far enough, however, that we can see what needs to be done during the next several decades, at least within the United States. While parallel processes are operating in many other nations, our knowledge of these remains thin.[29] Cross-societal comparisons of the evolution of emergency management comprise a critical research agenda that awaits any who might accept the challenge. But let's focus on the United States and note seven long-term trends. Accelerating the scope and pace of these comprises a partial answer to the question posed by our chapter title: What must be done?

Before reviewing these seven trends, however, I want to clarify my focus. My view of emergency management reflects the *community perspective* that has informed my research experience. I've been looking at disasters from the bottom upward rather than from the top down. So in the next several sections of this chapter, when I refer to *emergency managers,* I really am referring to local emergency managers, not state or federal government employees. Given the composition of most postdisaster emergent organizational networks, this focus covers a lot, but certainly not all, of the critical issues of reform.

First, during the past forty years, the level of professionalism among emergency managers has increased. Rapidly expanded training opportunities by the Federal Emergency Management Agency's National Emergency Training Center in Emmitsburg, Maryland, is an obvious point of progress. Less visible, but far more expansive, are the hundreds of seminars provided by staff associated with the fifty-state emergency services agencies. Workshops, classes, and formal degree programs are becoming very popular within traditional academic institutions.[30] Collectively, these varied training opportunities represent an impressive array of settings and content specialties. But expanded training programs remain the first plank in an action agenda. Given current levels of turnover due to many forms of job mobility, emergency management education must be improved in both quality and quantity.

A requirement of all professions is a solid knowledge base. As reflected by this book and numerous others, a great deal has been learned within a variety of disciplines that can help local emergency managers do their jobs better. This second long-term trend of scientific research must be accelerated in the future so that the emergency management knowledge base can be improved.[31] It must be expanded in several ways. But this can occur only if more scholars are encouraged to join the existing community of disaster and hazard researchers. And the linkages must be tightened between this community and those out in the field practicing the art of emergency management. While this trend is most visible today, it must be accelerated in the future if the profession is to grow and have the tools required for the challenges it will confront.

With this expanded knowledge base has come a rise in the number and legitimacy of professional associations. Paralleling the American Medical Association and the American Bar Association are such organizations as the International Association of Emergency Managers (IAEM) and the National Emergency Management Association (NEMA).[32] Expansions of these specialized units reflect a third important development. All professions have evidenced the emergence of parallel associations that distribute new knowledge, establish membership criteria and performance standards, and award certification when earned. Both of these specialized associations are augmented by related groups like the International City/County Management Association, International Association of Fire Chiefs, and International Association of Chiefs of Police.

Fourth is the matter of professional domain or territory. Just what is the job of an emergency manager? As I explained toward the end of Chapter 8, highly fragmented community responders are being replaced with more coordinated networks. The unit that ties all of the pieces together is the emergency management office. Ideally, the emergency management team, including representatives from various departments and agencies who populate the Emergency Operations Center (EOC) during a crisis, performs the coordination function within the overall community response to any disaster. And by *response* in this context I mean throughout the *entire life cycle* of disaster (i.e., preparedness, response, recovery, and mitigation). Clarification and legitimacy of agency mission is the fourth long-term trend that must be nurtured.

Before IAEM became IAEM, it had other names reflecting other times when different philosophical premises and program concerns had priority. Its name used to be the National Coordinating Council on Emergency Management. Prior to that, many interested in disaster preparedness maintained membership in the U.S. Civil Defense Council—yes, civil defense. Attack preparedness, including the threats represented by chemical and biological agents, continues to be a part of emergency management, but during the 1980s a revolution occurred as this expanding group of professionals campaigned to identify the key function of community coordination following major disasters. Further elaboration and improved conceptualization of this function must occur in the years ahead. Since the attacks of 9/11, homeland security has increased in priority. Exactly how the broader issues of homeland security, like border, port, and airport protection, will be merged with emergency management concerns remains problematic. These issues and concerns must be addressed and integrated into the evolving professional frameworks.

Have you visited any countries with centralized governments? If not, you really can't appreciate the differences—and I believe the freedoms—that our decentralized system permits. As the emergency management function became more widely understood and clarified, local governments experimented with structure. Should the function be assigned to the fire department? Makes some sense, doesn't it? At least it does until you hear the case from a county sheriff or other law enforcement agency director.

Today, the structural nesting of local emergency management agencies varies widely, although more and more local programs are functioning as independent agencies.[33] This fifth trend must be extended in the years ahead. Regardless of where the function may be nested for day-to-day administration, all emergency managers must have frequent and direct access to the chief administrative executive or elected official.

The city manager, not the fire chief, is responsible ultimately for the emergency management function. So too is the county administrator, not the sheriff. Hence, the fifth thing that must be done is to close the gap between emergency management professionals and the chief executive officer. Variability in the structural nesting of the function will continue for the foreseeable future, but what must not continue are the weak links that exist in many communities. Unless the emergency manager is linked tightly to the key point of authority and power, the capacity to perform the interagency coordination function is neutralized.

Additionally, local emergency managers must nurture tighter linkages with state agencies and their federal partners. This is especially true for terrorism preparedness and other aspects of homeland security. These threats, which may only intensify in the foreseeable future, require improved coordination among myriad specialized state and federal agencies including law enforcement and public health.

Indeed, as the professionalization process continues, I suspect that the job title of *emergency management* may be replaced with a broader and more fitting designation for the professional services and competencies required. *Emergency government* will provide a more desired conceptual framework that will replace *top-down management* orientations. Equally important, an *emergency government* orientation will replace inappropriate bureaucratic concepts like *efficiency* and *effectiveness* of narrowly defined *programs* with newer emphases on shared governance and greater community participation. This paradigm shift is an important part of the expanded vision I believe is necessary. This is a sharp contrast to alternative policy orientations that emphasize increased centralization at the federal level.

The sixth need reflects significant technological innovation. Like other executives, many emergency managers began to implement microcomputer technologies into their programs during the early 1980s. Evidence gathered to date indicates that the adoption and implementation process has followed curves much like those of previous eras when farmers were introduced to new strains of corn or massive picking machines.[34] Some are quick to adopt; others think only of trying to retire before they are forced into accepting a new way of doing things.

During the late 1980s, as events like Hurricane Hugo and the Loma Prieta earthquake made headlines, the relevance of microcomputers for emergency management was demonstrated. Those attending emergency management meetings witnessed countless demonstrations as new software systems were created. While some complained that they didn't have the funding to initiate these new tools, others found monies from a wide variety of sources, often within the private sector, to forge ahead. After obtaining the components most were shocked at the staff time required for training and inputting the resource files that formerly had filled notebooks or note card boxes. Sometimes this reflected faulty logic or incomplete data sets, but usually it just reflected the massive amounts of information that are required to effectively perform the coordination function.

While exemplary initiatives can be identified in places like Pinellas County, Florida, or St. James Parish, Louisiana—to mention but two—the response capability of the entire nation remains reduced because of the failure of government to press information technology into action. The social barriers to the implementation process are complex but can be overcome with the proper incentives. Both here, and especially abroad, acceleration of this implementation process remains a number one priority.[35]

All disasters are local in nature. Yet there are times when the damages are so extensive that state and federal resources are required. These resources remain under the control of local and state officials, however. This reflects the wisdom of the constitutional framers who saw great dangers in an overly centralized governmental system. Intergovernmental partnerships pose challenging coordination issues, however. And that's where FEMA comes in. Since its creation in 1979, this agency has provided funding and training to enhance the capabilities of state and local governments. It also serves as the lead agency within the federal bureaucracy. In theory, at least, local government EOC staff members coordinate directly with their counterpart within the state EOC. State officials there, working directly with their governor, partner with designated FEMA representatives through the federal coordinating officer (FCO).

Under the terms specified in the Robert T. Stafford Disaster Relief and Emergency Relief Act (42 U.S.C. 5121 et seq.), when local government resources are exceeded, assistance can be requested from the state. When state resources are exceeded, federal assistance can be requested through FEMA. Under these circumstances, a Presidential Disaster Declaration can be made, and the president then appoints an FCO. Through the FCO, the enormous resources of dozens of federal agencies can selectively be tasked to assist local and state governments.

This basic structure was taxed, however, when Hurricane Andrew smashed into south Florida and portions of Louisiana in 1992. Response delays became symbolized by the words of one very frustrated local emergency manager—Kate Hale—who asked, "Where the hell is the cavalry on this one?" Staff and administrative changes made during the Bill Clinton presidency resulted in an enhanced FEMA and improved levels of preparedness within state and local jurisdictions. Effective responses to the major disasters of the 1990s—like the 1994 Northridge earthquake in California, extensive flooding in the Midwest in 1993, and Hurricanes Fran (1996) and Floyd (1999)—enhanced the visibility, legitimacy, and acceptance of the evolving profession of emergency management. James Lee Witt, who had served as Clinton's director of emergency management in Arkansas, had the president's ear, and everyone knew it.

Armed with a new professional identity, extensive information technology applications, and a clarified definition of agency mission, emergency managers who had experienced the transformations of the '80s and '90s had begun to sense an improved public image. This seventh, and final, long-term trend must be accelerated in the coming years. Gradually, those in other agencies have begun to see emergency managers as professional peers, not retired military officers who were wanting only water stored for "the big one." Older images of civil defense and philosophies limited to military tactics of command and control have begun to vanish. Women, and other minorities, increasingly have bought into the field.

Following the 9/11 attacks, there was widespread public concern. "Will other attacks be forthcoming?" "How safe are we?" "Whose job is it to protect us from potential terrorists?" President George W. Bush responded with the largest governmental reorganization in our nation's history, and the Department of Homeland Security (DHS) was birthed in 2002. Within the authorizing legislation was a requirement that DHS develop a comprehensive National Incident Management System (NIMS) and a comprehensive National Response Plan (NRP). In 2008, NRP was modified and renamed as the National Response Framework (NRF). NRF effectively replaced the Federal Response Plan (FRP) created earlier by FEMA. It is applicable, however, only to large-scale events—that is, events that would result in a Presidential Disaster Declaration.

But there is more to the DHS shift in nomenclature, direction, and priorities. The basic goal of the NIMS requirement is to provide *consistency*; that is, throughout all states and all local jurisdictions, a common management framework is to be implemented that would be operative for all disasters regardless of the precipitating agent. And this "all-hazards" framework is to be implemented with the Incident Command System (ICS). ICS grew out of successful applications within the fire services community. It establishes an incident management system through five functional areas: (1) command; (2) operations; (3) planning; (4) logistics; and (5) finance/administration. Presumably, all emergency management agencies will function within this standardized framework.[36]

As in the past, however, policy as written is not necessarily policy in action. Hence, future disaster researchers must critically examine the actual outcomes of this and other policy innovations. As the 9/11 Commission pointed out so clearly, a directive signed by New York City major Rudy Giuliani two months prior to the attacks did not produce the interagency coordination expected and needed, especially between the fire and police agencies.[37]

Today, most citizens do not understand or recognize the function of emergency management or its crucial role in disaster response. Media critiques have pointed fingers of blame in a simplistic fashion so as to disguise the real shortcoming in interagency responses. Failure of local government to legitimate an emergency management program whereby

the coordination function could be accomplished is hard for most reporters to conceptualize, much less communicate to an apathetic public.[38]

Following Hurricanes Katrina, Rita, and Wilma in fall 2005, a failed
emergency management system was criticized widely. Not since the introduction of the DHS color-coded terrorist warning scheme—the Homeland
Security Advisory System (HSAS)—had emergency management in general, and FEMA in particular, received the brunt of the late-night com-
ics' ridicule. While "lessons learned" were emphasized, the White House
review noted up front that "the President made clear that we must do
better in the future."[39] More to the point was this conclusion:

> Today there is a national consensus that we must be better prepared to
> respond to events like Hurricane Katrina. While we have constructed a
> system that effectively handles the demands of routine, limited natu-
> ral and man-made disasters, our system clearly has structural flaws for
> addressing catastrophic incidents.[40]

As might be expected, the House report was even more pointed:

> We are left scratching our heads at the range of inefficiency and ineffec-
> tiveness that characterized government behavior right before and after
> this storm. But passivity did the most damage. The failure of initiative
> cost lives, prolonged suffering, and left all Americans justifiably con-
> cerned our government is no better prepared to protect its people than it
> was before 9/11, even if we are.[41]

And also, as might be expected, proposed solutions varied widely.
The White House vision was rooted in a two-part solution: (1) "Define
and implement a comprehensive National Preparedness System"; and (2)
"Foster a new, robust culture of preparedness."[42] The proposed "model"
for NPS is the approach used for national security:

> This system is built on deliberate planning that assesses threats and
> risks, develops policies and strategies to manage them, identifies specific
> missions and supporting tasks, and matches the forces or capabilities to
> implement them. Operationally organized, it stresses the importance of
> unity of command from the President down to the commander in the
> field.[43]

This highly complex matter is summarized in several pages wherein
various organizational issues are discussed, such as the role of the regional
offices within DHS and the role of Congress. Throughout, however, the
theme of *unity of command* is emphasized:

One model for the command and control structure for the Federal response in the new National Preparedness System is our successful defense and national security statutory framework. In that framework, there is a clear line of authority that stretches from the President, through the Secretary of Defense, to the Combatant Commander in the field. When a contingency arises, the Combatant Commander in that region executes the missions assigned by the Secretary of Defense and the President. Although the Combatant Commander might not "own" or control forces on a day-to-day basis, during a military operation he controls all military forces in his theater; he exercises the command authority and has access to resources needed to affect outcomes on the ground.[44]

The second plank of the solution is *creating a culture of preparedness.* This requirement reflects risk perceptions that are revealed in such statements as these:

> Complacency of our citizens presents a real challenge.... But we are a Nation at war, and we have a responsibility to be prepared.... We know that our enemies plot further attacks against us. We must continue to prevent them and, if necessary, respond. Regrettably, lives will be lost, citizens displaced, and property destroyed.[45]

In this paragraph, the report states, "We cannot prevent natural disasters."[46] That is the only mention of natural disasters within the entire section labeled as "Future Challenges." But the next sentence reveals the perception of risk and resulting priority within the perspective: "And though we work tirelessly against them, we cannot anticipate nor prevent every type of terrorist attack against the homeland."[47] And what of the historic intergovernmental partnership arrangements among local, state, and federal agencies? The report states, "The new culture of preparedness must stress *partnership* among all levels of government."[48] One paragraph above this statement, however, the policy for catastrophic events is announced loudly and clearly:

> Today, we operate under two guiding principles: 1) that incident management should begin at the lowest jurisdictional level possible, and 2) that, for most incidents, the Federal government will generally play a supporting role to State and local efforts. While these principles suffice for the vast majority of incidents, they impede the Federal response to severe catastrophes. In a catastrophic scenario that overwhelms or incapacitates local and State incident command structures, the Federal government must be prepared to assume incident command and get

assistance directly to those in need until State and local authorities are reconstituted.[49]

This view of "the problem"—that is, respective roles within the intergovernmental system—is a sharp contrast to that of most local and state emergency managers with whom I have spoken. Their orientation was summed up, at least partially, by Bruce Gaughman, director of the Alabama State Emergency Management Agency.[50] In his role as president of NEMA, Gaughman emphasized the following:

> Our nation's emergency management officials feel like they are trapped without the tools to make the changes necessary to address immediate needs, similar to Bill Murray's character in "Groundhog Day." Except instead of waking up to the same song and dance every day, we are waking to the same findings and recommendations we heard after Hurricane Andrew.[51]

He went on to emphasize that various reports done after the Andrew response emphasized that there was a minimal "natural constituency" for emergency management until after a disaster occurred and that the federal government should not try to become a 911-type first responder. Alternatively, in his view, the role of the federal government should be focused on enhancing the capacity of emergency management efforts at the state and local levels. Furthermore, Gaughman argued that, "FEMA is and should be the agency of choice to coordinate the functions of the federal government in response to disasters, regardless of their cause."[52] He continued, "…I personally believe that true all-hazards grants related to preparing for, responding to, and recovering from disasters belong back within FEMA in order to ensure the programmatic mission of the organization and maintenance of relationships at the state and local levels."[53] And finally, Gaughman stated that, "NEMA does not support an increased role for the active duty military in disaster response."[54]

It seems to me that Gaughman has it about right, except I would go two more steps. First, the evidence on global warming is increasing every day, although some still seek to discredit the linkages between our pollution behaviors and climate changes. In his summary article for the *Encyclopaedia Britannica 2008 Book of the Year,* John Streicker emphasized that we are the lone holdout; that is, every other industrialized nation signed off on the Kyoto Protocol except the United States. This major treaty is designed to attack global warming head on by systematic reductions in greenhouse gas emissions:

At the United Nations Climate Change Conference held in December 2007 in Bali, Indon., delegates used the findings of the [International Panel on Climate Change] IPCC fourth assessment to discuss what would succeed the protocol. Although many issues remained, the delegates reached a consensus on the course that would be followed....[55]

So stay tuned! This is a topic that you will learn much more about in the coming decades. Hence, I would urge a major shift in federal priorities.[56] Reduce the myopic vision that guides much of the terrorism preparedness effort, and emphasize coping strategies for global warming impacts. Of course, far more should be done to reduce our collective carbon imprints. But despite the best mitigative efforts, creative approaches to future global warming impacts should be a top priority within the emergency management community.

Second, various federal policies, including the Patriot Act, must be revised to guarantee fundamental civil liberties to all Americans.[57] Heightened civilian protection cannot be accepted as an excuse for data mining and other invasions of privacy.[58] One example of where this excessive fear of terrorism has led is the rider attached to the John W. Warner Defense Authorization Act of 2006 (October 17, 2006; PL 109-34). According to one analyst, this rider added natural disaster to a list of conditions wherein the president would be permitted to take over local authority. By making it easier for the president to declare martial law, *posse comitatus* statues that restrict military personnel could be subverted.[59] Policy changes like this are a real threat to civil liberties and must be reversed.

Obviously, these matters are complex and will remain issues of debate in the coming decade as they have in the past. Indeed, thorough examination of the alternative roles among the various stakeholders groups within the intergovernmental system undoubtedly will be the focus of several future books. But these issues are the context within which my community orientation is nested. So, too, are my proposed solutions, which are not designed to address the federal level organizational system or even the intricacies of the overall intergovernmental system, of which it is one part. Rather, my focus is on the local or community emergency manager.

So what must be done at the local government level? Those committed to improving the safety of American citizens must identify ways of improving the public image of this new class of professionals, that is, the local emergency manager. But such improvement must be earned through performance excellence. Public relations bull will not work! As an improved public image evolves, all of the normal processes of recruitment and retention will follow in course. To the extent that it isn't done, the nation will continue to increase the proportion of the population at risk.

STRATEGIES FOR MAINTAINING
ORGANIZATIONAL INTEGRITY

What must local emergency managers do? In one sense the answer is simple: They must adopt a shift in vision. *They must break out of the strictures of operating as bureaucrats and become community change agents.* Some, of course, already have adopted this newer and more professionalized vision. Unfortunately, too many still define their job in narrower terms that reflect the procedures of their required paperwork but not the passion or ethics of a reformer.

As an outgrowth of several reports that gradually legitimated "comprehensive emergency management," local agency guidance documents reflected longer-term planning goals.[60] Years ago, Dave McLoughlin summarized a general planning framework that incorporated the full disaster life cycle: mitigation, preparedness, response, and recovery.[61] With these four phases as a starting point, he introduced the key notions of hazard analysis, capability assessment, and capability maintenance as planning tools. Once evaluations of these three topics have been made, a local manager can then identify important capability shortfalls. These in turn can be used to design a multiyear development plan with specific annual objectives.

By using this framework, agency objectives can then be linked to potential funding sources ranging from local government budgets to funds desired from state and federal programs and various private-sector organizations.[62] This "planning by objective" framework has been implemented successfully by many local emergency managers whose programs have helped reduce the vulnerability of their communities.

But much more is required. That is where a paradigm shift must occur. To enact the professional vision of emergency management I am proposing, this type of "training mentality" must be replaced with education rooted in problem-solving skills that enhance creativity and a sense of passion focused on reform rather that paper shuffling. Unfortunately, I suspect that more recent policy directives that emphasize *consistency* and *standardization*, like NIMS, also will prove inadequate.

I came to this insight as I interviewed large numbers of emergency managers and talked to others informally. Some, of course, were simply

225

incompetent or minimally interested in their job. Others meant well but lacked the capacity for this expanded vision. As a result, they were content to fill out forms and push a bit for some equipment upgrades, but they could not break out of the bureaucratic box within which they lived. Then there were the exceptions—men and women whose talk and actions revealed a *more strategic approach* to their job. They understood the bureaucratic planning frameworks of the type McLoughlin outlined. They understood NIMS and ICS, but they went beyond these modified models rooted in theories of bureaucracy. They understood that their true mission was one of "emergency government" in the broadest sense of that concept.

In an effort to capture some of the wisdom held by these emergency managers, I did a lot of listening. Some of it was in the hallways, cafeteria, and other settings at the National Emergency Training Center in Emmitsburg, Maryland, where I lectured many times during the past thirty years. Two major research projects, however, provided unique opportunities to uncover "the hidden curriculum" required for this new vision to be implemented.[63]

In part, broader exposure to intellectual tools of history, system analysis, critical thinking, and communication skills will push the movement. Thus, future graduates from recently designed emergency management and homeland security programs within institutions of higher education *may* evidence the knowledge and passion I see as essential. Let's hope so. But let's also remember that others have been exposed to higher education programs too. Unfortunately, such exposure offers no guarantees that high quality professional behavior will follow.

It is my opinion that there is much more to being a local emergency manager than NIMS and ICS reflect. While both of these address some of the technical management issues local emergency managers confront, they do not speak to the political and community resource issues that become most important during disaster responses.[64] The skills and knowledge base required is complex, multifaceted, and evolving. Through two research projects, however, I believe I gained at least a glimpse of some core knowledge that is imperative. I didn't create it; I just listened and tried to codify it a bit. The essence of what I learned is that effective emergency managers, either knowingly or just instinctively, implement a *series of strategies* whereby they nurture their programs through the creation of supportive interagency relationships. These reflect trust and cooperation, not orders or threats. Collectively, they enhance the *legitimacy* of the emergency manager as a local governmental employee and their agency as a required and desired function of government.

I discovered that being an effective emergency manager in small towns, like Durango, Colorado (home of the Durango-Silverton train), or Groton, Connecticut (submarine capital of the world), requires different *tactics* from those that fit bigger cities like Wichita, Kansas, or Peoria, Illinois. And what works in places like those will not fit well in metropolitan areas like Los Angeles or Dallas.[65]

Yet, at the strategic level, there is continuity; there is a sameness. As with the four key managerial functions that comprise emergency management—mitigation, preparedness, response, and recovery—there were *common strategies* that effective local emergency managers were using. As the place varied in population size, reflecting fundamental cultural differences, so, too, the *tactics* differed. But the strategies were the same. It is an understanding of these, and a commitment to their implementation, that the emergency managers of the future must aspire to. Certainly I don't believe that I have documented all that are being used, but I'm certain that the following are among the most important. These are illustrative, not exhaustive.

Mitigation Strategies

Among several that I discovered, *regulation* and *coalition building* are fundamental. In Wichita, Kansas, for example, an experienced emergency manager told me of his efforts to establish a new regulation in his tornado-prone community.[66] He said, "If we could get our local commissioners to adopt an ordinance that would require all mobile homes to be 'tied down' we could reduce wind damage." Hence, he quietly researched the issue and discovered people in the community who realized the worth of the idea. Gradually, he blended technical expertise with political activism so that a group of concerned citizens pressed for change. He was not out front on a white horse but worked quietly behind the scenes to enhance awareness and encourage action. While implementing this tactic, reflective of the more abstract *strategy of regulation*, he also illustrated the *strategy of coalition building*. You see, it was not he who took the issue to the commissioners; rather, it was a group of concerned citizens, whose fears had been focused on a specific policy change that they desired to reduce community vulnerability.

Others accomplished parallel results regarding mitigation through using tactics reflective of the *strategy of cooptation*. For example, by carefully selecting advisory committee members, they established pipelines into diverse sectors of the community. Two-way communication flows meant that key ideas could be circulated by people viewed as legitimate within that sector of the community. And too, these same individuals kept the local manager more aware of community sentiment and reaction to policies under formulation.

Preparedness Strategies

Previously I described the bind that some local managers told me about when I was interviewing during the 1980s. In Chapter 5, I noted the community conflicts that some confronted when they tried to implement crisis relocation planning (CRP). A wise official in Los Angeles told me of the importance of "agenda control." He used this strategy to squelch the emergent controversy. Instead of waiting for the polarization that might result from extremists on both sides of this policy initiative, he acted quickly. He presented the board of supervisors with a policy proposal, which they adopted. If read one way, it appeared that they rejected the federal plan. The "structured ambiguity" contained within the policy statement, however, was read by others, including those in the state and regional FEMA offices, to mean support. By keeping the issue off the public agenda, his program averted a potential torpedo.[67] Other managers described actions to me that reflected use of the *strategies of joint ventures* and *committees*. In contrast, some pointed to new technologies they had implemented that revealed their successes in use of the *strategy of entrepreneurial actions*.

Working within these types of bottom-up, community-oriented approaches, successful emergency managers reach out to the full range of organizational executives who control the bulk of resources within their locale, including businesses, nonprofits, and volunteer agencies of all types. They cannot "order" any of these people to get ready for disaster, but they can and must encourage and guide. Rather than using fear as their primary motivation, they can bring broader visions of corporate responsibility and protection. I discovered that customers of tourist businesses expected hotel and other staff to know what to do prior to a hurricane or after an earthquake, for example. Where they didn't, customers were disappointed.[68]

When I have lectured on this topic to both business executives and emergency managers, I emphasized customer satisfaction. Poor customer satisfaction costs money! People don't return to hotels, for example, where they feel they were put at risk or handled poorly. Hence, a small investment in staff training and development of a disaster plan is just good business. My surveys documented that such preparedness within a wide variety of tourist businesses (e.g., hotels, motels, restaurants, museums) was very spotty. Subsequent research, more broadly focused, validated my findings across the full range of business firms.[69] Later surveys, like one conducted by Office Depot, continued to document a mixed picture. For example, only 58% of business owners had a disaster plan in place. As I would expect based on my interviews, this survey also documented a key difference between those who had a plan and those who did not: experiencing disaster. That is, nearly three-fourths (74%) of businesses located in areas that had been impacted by disaster within the past five years did have a plan. Wise emergency managers use a variety of preparedness strategies to cultivate and nurture widespread participation by business executives in disaster planning. It's just good business.

This strategic view of management goes far beyond the visions of agency mission frequently described by paper-shuffling bureaucrats; the men and women who are operating within this broader and newer vision of emergency management recognize the complexity and turbulence of the environment within which their agency is nested. To nurture its integrity and well-being they have learned how to actively confront sectors of that environment. While their specific tactics vary with the cultural context within which they are working—rural area versus metropolitan, for example—all are using a series of strategies that others must learn.

Let me emphasize, however, that they are, almost without exception, ethically grounded. That is, their maneuvering and behind-the-scenes activities are not motivated by personal or agency embellishment. They are not after a buck, nor do they want public praise. Their personal mission, like that they promote for their agency, is to reduce community vulnerability and enhance the quality of life for all citizens, not just the financially secure. They display an understanding of and a commitment to *emergency government* in the broadest and best sense of the concept.

DISASTER RESPONSE COORDINATION STRATEGIES

But disasters still will happen. When they do, the local emergency manager must now implement another set of strategies to insure that a multiorganizational network will emerge rapidly so that a more coordinated response will be forthcoming. Thus, at least five types of *coordination strategies* must be implemented quickly. To the degree they are not, fragmentation will result. Heroes will still emerge, but hurt and death will be maximized because people, both officials and ordinary citizens, will experience structures that fail them.

It doesn't have to be that way. The chaos of organized-disorganization can be managed, at least somewhat. But it will be only if this new professional—the local emergency manager—has built high levels of agency legitimacy and rapidly implements at least five types of coordination strategies to guide the response and recovery phases.

Core Strategies

Core strategies help to define system purpose.[70] Many managers I talked to told me of how they had implemented the strategy of *domain clarification* during their disaster response. As various needs were identified, good preparedness planning usually identified which agency would do what. At times, however, unanticipated needs appeared. Then, domains had to be extended, or totally new mission boundaries had to be encouraged. Thus, through both domain clarification and at times *jurisdictional negotiation*, effective emergency managers guided community responses by implementing these and other core strategies.

Consequence Strategies

Disasters bring disruption of organizational environments that require quick responses.[71] Urgency means, however, that it is easy for people to trip over each other. So wise managers told me how they quickly implemented various tactics that reflected a strategy I called *display of decisions*. For example, many used the tactic of frequent multiagency briefing sessions wherein key actions completed were summarized quickly, new problems were identified, and various groups were tasked with finding solutions. While this was going on, other personnel used various *information technologies* to alert segments of the community that were at risk and to keep communications flowing among field units of various types and their incident commanders.

Most crucial in this regard was the activation of a community *emergency operations center*. Effective managers had nurtured the multiorganizational training experiences required for these structures to spring to life rapidly, and they knew how to nurture an EOC social climate wherein information and decisions reflected a sense of calmness rather than hysteria. Equally importantly, they knew that most personnel would tend to stay too long. So before bad decisions were made due to fatigue, schedules were implemented that ensured sleep, break time, and a continuous supply of good food.

Customer Strategies

Who are the customers of the local emergency manager during a disaster response or the longer-term recovery?[72] Obviously, those managers I met with who were the most effective had thought this matter through very carefully. They were ready to *facilitate media relations* quickly, and they mobilized teams to *document damage assessments* with efficiency and thoroughness. Of course, *citizen needs* were received, routed, and followed up to reduce further hurt, both physical and emotional.

Control Strategies

The "results"-oriented style that these strategically savvy managers reflected led them to implement a host of control strategies.[73] Some told me how they had made *reference to planning documents* when agency personnel evidenced conflict or confusion. Other told stories of how they had guided network members by *reference to prior experiences*. Sometimes this referred to a training exercise, but more often it was a prior disaster where an important lesson had been learned but temporarily forgotten.

As I noted in the previous section, the Bush Administration mandated the implementation of NIMS, including the tactical management model ICS.[74] Both are useful types of control strategies, but according to many of the local emergency managers I interviewed, they serve as only one tool among many. Even those who used and taught ICS, for example, placed this tool within a broader context of the more strategic perspective I propose that will point us toward improved theories of emergency management.

Thus, another control strategy is *decentralization of decision making*. One local emergency manager described it this way:

> At the tactical level of managing a disaster, within certain agencies like the fire or perhaps police departments, this kind of organizational model makes good sense [i.e., ICS]. But when you think of the level of the community emergency operations center, I personally don't think the ICS is workable. As the alternative model, what I see in our county is what might be called a "web concept." In the center of the wheel of this, the hub of the web is the emergency operations team captain. Maybe we

should call this a team concept. And from that central point going outward in a horizontal manner rather than a vertical dimension, are various spokes.

You have so many different community agencies that reflect very different organizational styles. That is why it requires a team concept to
pull together all of these agencies into an effective emergency operations center team. The ICS is a top-down management model. I thought
for awhile when I first got here that it was really the model that was
being used. But now I have a much different understanding because the
EOC that we use here really works as a web type of management style.
It is a loosely coupled management system. Each agency representative
working here frequently crosses their organizational boundaries to collectively work with the others to try to solve problems.[75]

Emergent collaborative planning examples seemed to crop up in nearly
every interview I conducted. For despite the best efforts at trying to come up
with every "what, if" imaginable, actual disasters always bring surprises.
Similarly, improvisation also occurred when managers implemented the
strategy of creating *emergent community–government partnerships*. Through
these and other strategic interventions, local managers coordinated the
rapid responses of those arriving on scene in the minutes and hours after
impact. And during the longer-term recovery, they used other tactics that
reflected these same control strategies.

Cultural Strategies

Finally, the wisest emergency managers were fully aware of the cultural
differences among the myriad agencies that were involved in picking up
the pieces.[76] Many told me how they worked to ensure that those in, for
example, law enforcement came to better understand the very different
perspectives reflected among personnel associated with the Red Cross or
other human service organizations. Thus, understanding and using the
strategy of *enhancing awareness of cultural differences among responding agencies* is another element in this newer strategic perspective. Other cultural
strategies included the promotion of interagency cross-talking, building a
shared vision, developing an in-house school house, and supporting cel-
ebrations of success.

All of these observations are consistent with a plea that Russ Dynes
made years ago:[77] Emergency managers must operate within a community
problem-solving managerial model. They must not fall prey to false prophets whose experience base has been limited to military or paramilitary

bureaucracies. Thus, the image and rhetoric of "command and control" must be replaced with a more strategic framework. Understanding of and respect for community diversity does not preclude unity of command. Rather, trust and legitimacy become the basis for compliance. As with parenting, shouting orders has limited utility. And just like parenting, building relationships of trust, especially when ethically difficult choices are required, is hard work. So is the implementation of other core principles of emergency management—principles like collaboration, flexibility, and professionalism.[78]

On March 28, 2007, just after a severe thunderstorm warning was canceled, a tornado struck the small southeastern community of Holly, Colorado. After describing the impacts, responses, and recovery actions, the Prowers County sheriff, Jim Faull, offered the following closing thought. I can't say it any better:

> I would say that everyone needs to be prepared for a natural disaster.... Most of the first responders here know each other and work well together ... don't underestimate the ability of the citizens of your town and county to step up to the plate to get things started![79]

Yet while I laud Sheriff Faull's emphasis on preparedness, personal relationships, and citizen volunteers, his term *natural disaster* is a problem. Even though I too used this term to introduce the "many faces" of disaster at the outset of this book, our broader perspective requires that we explicitly recognize the inherent limitations in this term. As Lee Clarke put it so well, the key lesson from Katrina "...is that there is *no such thing as a natural disaster.*"[80] Why? Because "...institutional failures put people in harm's way."[81] And by using the term—which can be helpful for certain purposes—we always must be mindful that this term "...deflects attention and responsibility from the institutions that actually put people at risk."[82] This awareness—echoing the wisdom of Chester Hartman, Gregory Squires, Charles Perrow, Steve Picou, and others—is at the heart of the social problems perspective that I introduced early in this chapter.[83] And it is this perspective that forms the core of the new paradigm required for emergency management. This perspective must replace the "trained incapacities" that flow from workshops and classes designed for paper shufflers.[84] The profession of emergency management demands more! The nation deserves more!

Disasters and emergency management must be balanced within the *range of social problems* that confront any community. It is too easy to focus on this single tree and fail to grasp the larger forest. To return to my example of blaming the victims of Katrina who failed to evacuate, balance is required. Recall that many of those who refused to leave reflected the constraints of poverty, limited mobility due to age, and the harshness of a life of discrimination because of their ethnicity. Hence, within the requirements of programs to assist the poor in climbing out of the trap of poverty and of provisions to help the elderly enjoy their last days with some sense of dignity, funding for emergency management must be placed in priority. Buying more radios to enhance the capacity of rescuers to pull impoverished disaster victims from their hurricane impacted homes is the short-term fix required. Attacking the roots of poverty, for example, is the broader context within which the profession of emergency management must view its goals and purposes, both domestically and internationally.[85]

After reviewing the key factors that have resulted in the collapse in many past societies, Jared Diamond offered a conclusion that reflects much wisdom. All emergency managers should remember his words as they seek balance within their program and within their community:

> When people are desperate, undernourished, and without hope, they blame their governments, which they see as responsible for or unable to solve their problems. They try to emigrate at any cost. They fight each other over land. They kill each other. They start civil wars. They figure that they have nothing to lose, so they become terrorists, or they support or tolerate terrorism.[86]

CONCLUDING PRINCIPLES

I have discussed a wide range of topics in the preceding pages. Hopefully, you have found lots of food for thought here as you have made this journey. Going back to each chapter and reviewing the basic insights will provide good refreshers, both now and in the months ahead. In contrast to those summary statements, which were designed to highlight key points made within a few pages, I want to end this book with a statement of basic principles. At one point in the writing process I considered putting these up front, right after the title page. Reconsideration led me to place them here. While I didn't have a fixed number in mind that had to limit the list, I revised it several times with an eye toward brevity and succinctness, balanced by comprehensiveness and depth. Unlike other portions of this book that were designed for quick reading, this list of basic principles merits considerable thought over extended periods of time. I firmly believe there are profound implications held within that will stimulate you to make connections to future disasters and will enrich your personal philosophy of emergency management. To the extent that it does, our labors have not been in vain. We are counting on you!

- All disasters are the consequences of human decisions. That is the first, and most profound principle.

- One star-filled night, high in the mountains, a young couple held each other momentarily and gazed upward in awe. Meanwhile, their young child crawled toward their campfire. She placed her hand on the hot rocks they carefully had arranged to reduce the risk of a forest fire. When human actions violate the laws of the universe, they suffer. The essence of all disasters is human suffering. That is the second principle.

- When a hurricane wanders in the ocean, there is no disaster. When it capsizes a ship or makes landfall and rips into built environment, people die. Death, destruction, and disruption of daily routines are varied forms of human suffering. That is the third principle.

- Flooding of some lands cannot be prevented, regardless of the number of dams that might be built. Always we are pressed to ask, "What is the appropriate use of flood-prone areas?" Elaborations of this fourth principle are obtained by substituting flood with earthquake, hurricane, tornado, volcano, or other hazard.

- Some people impose risk on others. The distribution of risk is socially governed. As with power, privilege, and prestige, the distribution of risk is subject to human manipulation and choice. Rarely is this process understood or recognized. That is the fifth principle.

- When humans are mobilized to take territory and material resources, or to impose religious or political systems on others, we have war. War remains, as it has been throughout human history, the form of disaster that has caused the most extensive amount of human suffering. That is the sixth principle.

235

- Human choices can be made to prevent war and other forms of disaster. We need not kill each other or place people in situations of high risk without their knowledge or consent. A risk-free environment is neither possible nor desirable, however. Nevertheless, disasters, including war, can be mitigated substantially. That is the seventh principle.

- Increasingly, modern governments recognize emergency management as a legitimate function of government. Within the United States, as between nation-states, there is considerable variability as to how this function is shared among numerous bureaus. The greater the level of dissensus about the way the function is shared, the greater the fragmentation in disaster responses and the more extensive the degree of human suffering. That is the eighth principle.

- The function of emergency management is to enhance the capacity of a community to (1) assess its risks (vulnerability analysis); (2) maintain a state of response readiness (preparedness); (3) coordinate the multiple and diverse units that spring into action when disasters occur (response); (4) pick up the pieces afterward in a manner that minimizes trauma and suffering (recovery); and (5) implement a balanced approach to use of its natural resources and technological interventions to achieve a level of community risk that is acceptable, equitable, and legitimate (mitigation). That is the ninth principle.

- A new profession is emerging on a worldwide scale in response to the broadened recognition, acceptance, and understanding of the community function of emergency management. Those who will be most successful in this new profession will evidence a high tolerance for conflict and uncertainty, a firm grasp of their own philosophy of emergency management, and a solid belief that they, as single human beings, can make a difference in the extent to which others of their species experience premature death, suffer trauma, or lose material possessions. That is the tenth, and final, principle.

NOTES

CHAPTER 1

1. Based on Thomas E. Drabek, *Disaster in Aisle 13: A Case Study of the Coliseum Explosion at the Indiana State Fairgrounds, October 31, 1963* (Columbus, Ohio: College of Administrative Science, The Ohio State University, 1968), pp. 1–11. This explosion was caused by LP gas, which was being used illegally within a concession area (i.e., a radiant heat device was being used to keep popcorn warm). A grand jury investigated the incident, and several individuals were charged with various crimes. For details, see Drabek, *Disaster in Aisle 13*, pp. 113–121, 183–187. More than 400 lawsuits were filed that exceeded $70 million. "The LP gas firm's insurance distributed $1.1 million among 379 victims and estates. An out-of-court settlement of $3.5 million resolved hundreds of other individual suits." Vickie J. West, "Coliseum Explosion," in *The Encyclopedia of Indianapolis*, Ed. David J. Bodenhamer, Robert G. Barrows, and David Gordon Vanderstel (Bloomington, Indiana: Indiana University Press, 1994), p. 459. About 2:00 a.m. on November 6, 2005, a deadly tornado cut across western Kentucky and southern Indiana. Miraculously, no deaths were reported in Kentucky, but 22 died in Indiana. More than 200 were injured throughout the 15- to 20-mile path. Most of the deaths occurred in a mobile home park. This was the deadliest tornado to hit Indiana since April 3, 1974, when 52 died. See *Rocky Mountain News*, November 7, 2005, p. 22A and *1975 Britannica Book of the Year* (Chicago: Encyclopaedia Britannica, Inc., 1975), p. 239.
2. Based on Drabek, Harriet L. Tamminga, Thomas S. Kilijanek, and Christopher R. Adams, *Managing Multiorganizational Emergency Responses: Emergent Search and Rescue Networks in Natural Disaster and Remote Area Settings* (Boulder: Institute of Behavioral Science, University of Colorado, 1981), pp. 31–55. A somewhat similar incident occurred October 2, 2005, when the *Ethan Allen* tipped over in Lake George, located in upstate New York in the Adirondacks. Some were pulled to safety by pleasure boaters, but others were trapped beneath the boat. Weather was calm and sunny, however, so the reasons for the capsizing remained unclear. The sheriff's officials concluded that despite the high death toll of 20 elderly passengers, "…neither the vessel's owner nor its captain committed a crime." *Rocky Mountain News*, February 4, 2006, p. 32A.

3. Based on Drabek, *Disaster Evacuation Behavior: Tourists and Other Transients* (Boulder: Institute of Behavioral Science, University of Colorado, 1996), pp. 51–55.
4. Ibid., pp. 55–58.

CHAPTER 2

1. American Association of Railroads, *Hazmat Transport by Rail* (Washington, DC: Policy and Economics Department, Association of American Railroads, 2008), p. 1. See also Office of Hazardous Materials Safety, *Hazardous Materials Shipments* (Washington, DC: Office of Hazardous Materials Safety, Research and Special Programs Administration, U.S. Department of Transportation, 1998), pp. 1–2.
2. Earlier estimates were $3.4 billion; for example, see National Science Foundation, *A Report on Flood Hazard Mitigation* (Washington, DC: National Science Foundation, 1981), pp. 27–29. Dennis Mileti estimates that for the twenty-year period between 1975 and 1994 flood losses ranged between $19.6 billion to $196 billion. Some years, like 1993, the range was between $3.4 billion and $34 billion. I selected $8.8 billion as a midpoint within this range. Mileti, *Disasters by Design: A Reassessment of Natural Hazards in the United States* (Washington, DC: Joseph Henry Press, 1999), p. 72.
3. The best analysis to date is Mileti's, whose estimate for losses resulting from natural disasters is $50 billion annually. Mileti, *Disasters by Design,* p. 66. For a brief but very readable survey of the range of hazards confronting the United States, see William L. Waugh, Jr., *Living with Hazards, Dealing with Disasters: An Introduction to Emergency Management* (Armonk, NY: M. E. Sharpe, Inc., 2000).
4. Mileti estimates that natural disasters resulted in the death of 24,000 victims between the years 1975 and 1994. This averages about twenty-four per week. Another 96,000 were injured during this same twenty-year period. Mileti, *Disasters by Design.* For summary articles on Hurricanes Katrina, Rita, and Wilma in 2005, see, for example, *Rocky Mountain News*, September 2, 2005, pp. 34A–44A (Katrina); *Rocky Mountain News*, September 23, 2005, pp. 30A, 32A–34A (Rita); *Rocky Mountain News*, October 24, 2005, pp. 25A, 30A (Wilma). For a summary of the impacts of the tornado in Evansville, Indiana, see *Rocky Mountain News*, November 7, 2005, p. 22A. For coverage of the April 2006 tornadoes, see Kristan M. Hall, "Tornadoes Devastate States; 27 Dead in Tennessee," *Rocky Mountain News*, April 4, 2006, p. 28A.

   For the Greensburg, Kansas, tornado see Roxana Hegeman, "Twisters Leave Trail of Wrath," *Denver Post*, May 6, 2007, pp. 1A, 23A. The Windsor tornado was written up by Shane Scofield, "Tornado Wallops Windsor," *Colorado Sheriff* 29, no. 1 (2008):5–6. For coverage of the Holly tornado, see Anthony Mestas, "Killer Twister Strikes without Warning," *Pueblo Chieftain*, March 20, 2007, pp. 1–2. For the central Florida tornadoes, see Jim Ellis, "Devastating

Tornadoes Drop out of the Sky before Sunrise," *Pueblo Chieftain*, February 3, 2007, p. 1, "2007 Central Florida Tornadoes," *Wikipedia* (accessed October 11, 2008, from http://en.wikipedia.org/wiki/2007_Central_Florida_tornadoes). For the 2008 tornadoes see Hegeman, "Tornadoes Kill at Least 22: Survivors Search through Rubble in Okla., Mo., Ga.," *Rocky Mountain News*, May 12, 2008, p. 19.

In later years the death toll for the Big Thompson Canyon flood was revised upward (i.e., from 139 to 144 killed). So too, the original cost of $35.5 million in property damages was estimated to be $115 million in 2006 dollars (included 418 homes destroyed; 52 businesses; 438 vehicles and numerous bridges, roads, and power and telephone lines). See Deborah Frazier, "Flood Recalled on 30th Anniversary," *Rocky Mountain News*, August 1, 2006, p. 18A, "Top 10 Deadliest Floods in Colorado," *Rocky Mountain News*, June 20, 2008, p. 5.

5. Mileti, "A Normative Causal Model Analysis of Disaster Response" (Doctoral dissertation, University of Colorado, Department of Sociology, 1974).

6. See National Science Foundation, *Report on Flood*, pp. 23–25.

7. Ibid. Jared Diamond has summarized extensive research on ice cores as a way to assess long-term climate change in several places, especially Greenland. See Diamond, *Collapse: How Societies Choose to Fail or Succeed* (New York: Viking Penguin, 2005). These assessments document variability in storminess, which is an important type of climate change (p. 218). This is but one of the five key factors that comprised an interpretative framework explaining why some societies persisted for centuries whereas others died. The other four factors are as follows: (1) environmental damage; (2) hostile neighbors; (3) friendly trade partners; and (4) societal response to problems originating within the other four areas.

8. Quoted by Aileo Weinmann, "Increasing Vulnerability to Hurricanes: Global Warming's Wake Up Call for the U.S. Gulf and Atlantic Coasts," *News & Views* (Reston, VA: National Wildlife Federation, 2008), p. 1. The literature on global warming is voluminous and sometimes highly technical. Fortunately, good summaries appear with regularity, for example, Maarten K. van Aalst, "The Impacts of Climate Change on the Risk of Natural Disasters," *Disasters: Journal of Disaster Studies, Policy and Management* 30, no. 1 (2006):5–18 (entire journal issue has articles on climate change); Juliet Eilperin, "Livelihoods Die as Arizona Gets Drier: Scientists Blame Global Warming, and Predict Worse," *Washington Post National Weekly Edition*, February 14–20, 2005, p. 31; Tim Flannery, *The Weather Makers: The History and Future Impact of Climate Change* (New York: Atlantic Monthly Press, 2006). For physical science aspects of natural disasters including global warming, plate tectonic shifts that cause earthquakes, and the like, see Patrick L. Abbott, *Natural Disasters* (4th ed.) (New York: McGraw-Hill Book Companies, 2004). See also Martin Parry, Osvaldo F. Canziani, Jean Palutikof, Paul van der Linden, and Clair Hanson (Eds.), *Climate Change 2007: Impacts, Adaptation, and Vulnerability* (New York: Cambridge University Press, 2007); William R. Cotton and Roger A. Pielke,

Human Impacts on Weather and Climate (New York: Cambridge University Press, 2007); Angus M. Gunn, *Encyclopedia of Disasters: Environmental Catastrophes and Human Tragedies* (2 volumes) (Westport, CT: Greenwood Press, Inc., 2008).

9. Amanda Staudt, Nancy Huddleston, and Ian Kraucunas, *Understanding and Responding to Climate Change: Highlights of National Academies Reports* (Washington, DC: National Research Council, National Academies of Sciences, 2008), p. 1.

10. Ian Burton, Robert Kates, and Gilbert F. White, *The Environment as Hazard* (New York: Guilford Publishers, Inc., 1993). Population concentration in massive urban areas increases vulnerability. Examples of "mega-cities" include Tokyo-Yokohama (27.2 million), Mexico City (20.9 million), and São Paulo (18.7 million). See James K. Mitchell, *Crucibles of Hazard: Mega-cities and Disasters in Transition* (New York: United Nations University Press, 1999), p. 29. For details on the Pakistan earthquake (October 8, 2005), see the American Red Cross, "International Services: South Asia Earthquake," January 5, 2006, pp. 1–5 (accessed February 15, 2006, from http://www.redcross.org/news/ds/profiles/disaster_profilei-sasiaearthquake.html).

11. *2005 Britannica Book of the Year* (Chicago: Encyclopaedia Britannica, Inc., 2005), p. 58. See also Tad S. Murty, U. Aswathanarayana, and Niru Nirupama (Eds.), *The Indian Ocean Tsunami* (New York: Taylor & Francis Group, 2007). Unfortunately rapid and widespread dissemination of amateur video sometimes resulted in distortion. For example, Gurtner assessed responses in southern Thailand, especially the Phuket tourist area. "While reality revealed that only a small proportion of the island of Phuket had been affected—rarely extending beyond three blocks from the beachfront—headlines around the world proclaimed that the tropical island paradise of Phuket had been completely devastated and/or destroyed (*Phuket Gazett*, 2005)." Yetta K. Gurtner, "Phuket: Tsunami and Tourism—A Preliminary Investigation," in *Crisis Management in Tourism*, Ed. Eric Laws, Bruce Prideaux, and Kaye Chon (Wallingford, Oxon, UK: CASB International, 2007), p. 222. Other major tsunamis have occurred on the Indian Ocean near Sumatra, including one in 1883 when Krakatoa erupted killing more than 40,000 along coastal areas. See Lee Walking, "Facts About the 1833 Indian Ocean Tsunami," *TsuInfoAlert* 7 (2005):16. Other significant earthquake-triggered tsunamis occurred in the area in 1797, 1843, and 1861. In February 2006, a massive landslide covered most of a village in Liloan, Philippines. Almost all of the 1,800 residents were killed despite a massive rescue effort, which is just another example of vulnerabilities facing people in poorer countries. See Carlos H. Conde, "Survivors Few after Landslide," *Denver Post*, February 19, 2006, p. 2A. The following year a cyclone struck coastal areas of Bangladesh (November 2007). More than 3,000 were known dead, and more than 1,000 remained missing. According to Red Crescent Society (the Islamic version of the Red Cross) offi-

cials, the final death toll could exceed 10,000 once nearby island communities were searched. Pavel Rahman, "Cyclone Survivors Tell of Horror, Hunt for Dead," *Rocky Mountain News*, November 20, 2007, p. 27.

For coverage of Cyclone Nargis in Myanmar, see *Rocky Mountain News*, May 6, 2008, p. 24; May 7, 2008, p. 26; May 8, 2008, p. 31; May 9, 2008, p. 32.

12. Jerd Smith, "Security Lacking at DAMS in West," *Rocky Mountain News*, August 20, 2008, p. 25.

13. Office of Homeland Security, "Homeland Security Presidential Directive—3" (Washington, DC: Office of Homeland Security, 2002). Following Hurricanes Katrina and Rita, Denver officials were questioned about disaster evacuation planning, "...including torrents of water roaring down Cherry Creek or the South Platte River" because of dam failures. While they would have only a few hours to move hundreds that now occupy areas that would be flooded if various dams failed, "...Denver's Office of Emergency Management and other major agencies have yet to develop a strategy for moving people quickly in the face of an onrushing wall of water...." J. Smith, "Preparing for the Unthinkable: The Chance of a Catastrophic Dam Failure in the Metro Area is Remote, but Experts Say Officials Should Be Ready. They Aren't." *Rocky Mountain News*, February 18, 2006, p. 25A.

14. For a general treatment of terrorism, see Philip Jenkins, *Images of Terror: What We Can and Can't Know about Terrorism* (New York: Aldine de Gruyter, 2003). Historical context has been summarized nicely by Daniel Benjamin and Steven Simon, *The Age of Sacred Terror* (New York: Random House Trade Paperbacks, 2003). See also Brian T. Bennett, *Understanding, Assessing, and Responding to Terrorism: Protecting Critical Infrastructure and Personnel* (Hoboken, NJ: John Wiley & Sons, 2007); Bruce Bongar, Lisa M. Brown, Larry E. Beutler, James N. Breckenridge, and Philip G. Zimbordo (Eds.), *Psychology of Terrorism* (New York: Oxford University Press, Inc., 2007); Russell D. Howard, James J. F. Forest, and Joanne Moore, *Homeland Security and Terrorism: Readings and Interpretations* (New York: McGraw-Hill, 2006); David L. Altheide, *Terrorism and the Politics of Fear* (Lanham, MD: AltaMira Press, 2006); Huseyin Durmaz, Bilal Sevinc, Ahmet Sait Yayla, and Siddik Ekici, *Understanding and Responding to Terrorism* (Fairfax, VA: IOS Press, 2007); Waugh, *Terrorism and Emergency Management: Instructor Guide* (Emmitsburg, MD: Emergency Management Institute, Federal Emergency Management Agency, 2000).

15. The detailed histories and actions by the 9/11 terror group is summarized in National Commission on Terrorist Attacks Upon the United States, *The 9/11 Commission Report* (New York: W.W. Norton & Company, 2004). See also Stuart A. Wright, *Patriots, Politics, and the Oklahoma City Bombing* (New York: Cambridge University Press, 2007).

16. For more detailed discussion of these terms, controversy about their definitions and the epistemological implications for researchers, see E. L. Quarantelli (Ed.), *What Is a Disaster?: Perspectives on the Question* (London: Routledge, 1998); Ronald W. Perry and Quarantelli (Eds.), *What Is a Disaster? New Answers to Old Questions* (Philadelphia, PA: Xlibris Corporation, 2005).

Throughout this chapter, I have included statistics regarding death tolls and damage estimates. My intent is to illustrate the range of disaster events. But such data should not be misinterpreted to mean that these are adequate indications of the "size" of a disaster event. Although many of us have found it useful to differentiate among disaster events using such analytic criteria as *magnitude, scope,* and *duration* of impact along with other matters like *length* or *uncertainty* of forewarning, it is clear that these concepts are inadequate for the type of theoretical work needed. Adding less easily quantifiable notions like *social worth of objects impacted* (including human, built, and natural objects) hints at the social factors that are important in understanding response variations. This is but one aspect of the more complex issue that addresses a most fundamental area of inquiry, that is, "What is a disaster?" Or more correctly, perhaps, "What social processes are operative that result in certain events, but not others, to become defined by a specified population group as being a disaster?"

17. For elaboration on the examples used in this section, see Drabek, *Social Dimensions of Disaster* (2nd ed.) (Emmitsburg, MD: Emergency Management Institute, Federal Emergency Management Agency, 2004). Disasters may be caused by many other "agents" such as fires, avalanches, drought, and even extreme heat or cold. Though few deaths occur, huge financial losses also may result through such hazards as hail, subsidence, and expansive soils. Lightning usually kills only one or two persons in particular strikes but, in the aggregate, results in more deaths each year than any other nondisaster weather condition; for example, from 1975 to 1994, National Climate Data Center reported 1,444 deaths. See Mileti, *Disasters by Design*, p. 80. Excellent case studies of these other disaster agents include Denise Gess and William Lutz, *Firestorm at Peshtigo: A Town, It's People, And the Deadliest Fire in American History* (New York: Henry Holt, 2002); John W. Jenkins, *Colorado Avalanche Disasters: An Untold Story of the Old West* (Ouray, CO: Western Reflections Publishing Company, 2001); Michael H. Glantz (Ed.), *Drought and Hunger in Africa* (New York: Cambridge University Press, 1987; Eric Klineberg, *Heatwave: A Social Autopsy of Disaster in Chicago* (Chicago: University of Chicago Press, 2002); Ethan Rarick, *Desperate Passage: The Donner Party's Perilous Journey West* (New York: Oxford University Press, 2008). For summaries of social science research on wildfires, see Terry C. Daniel, Matthew S. Carroll, Cassandra Mosely, and Carol Raish, *People, Fire and Forests: A Synthesis of Wildfire Social Science* (Corvallis: Oregon State University Press, 2007); Gregory Larson, Vita Wright, Coda Spaulding, Kelly Rossetto, Georgi Rausch, Andrea Richards, et al., *Using Social Science to Understand and Improve Wildland Fire Organizations* (Gen. Tech. Rep. RMRS-GTR-201) (Fort Collins, CO: Rocky Mountain Research Station, Forest Service, U.S. Department of Agriculture, 2007).

18. American Automobile Association, *Tourbook: Arizona and New Mexico* (Heathrow, FL: American Automobile Association Publishing, 2005), p. 146.

19. Joyce Robins, *The World's Greatest Disasters* (Secaucus, NJ: Chartwell Books, Inc., 1990), pp. 6–10.

20. Borgna Brunner, *Time Almanac 2002* (Boston: Information Please, 2001), p. 615. Death tolls and dates are China, May 22, 1927 (200,000 killed); Armenia, December 7, 1998 (25,000 killed); India, January 26, 2001 (20,000 killed). More recent flooding in India illustrates this point; for example, the Kosi River (in the state of Bihar) flooding killed at least 55 people and destroyed 250,000 homes plus 247,000 acres of crops. Rhys Blakely and Joanne Sugden, "Corrupt Officials Blamed for Kosi Flood that Leaves Millions Homeless in India," *Times-on-Line*, August 28, 2008, p. 1 (accessed August 29, 2008, from http://www.timesonline.co.uk/tol/news/world/asia/article4624947.ece?print-yes&randrum-1220004408). On May 12, 2008, the worst earthquake to hit western China in recent history left 69,227 dead and 17,926 missing (Sichuan, China). See "President Hu Raises 'Quake Relief Spirit' Banner for Nation," *China Digital Times*, October 11, 2008, p. 1 (accessed October 11, 2008, from http://chinadigitaltimes.net/2008/10/President-Hu-Raises-Quake-Relief-Spirit-Banner-For-Nation).

21. These and numerous other statistics are contained in the student handouts I prepared to supplement the chapter (Session 4) titled "Overview of Hazards and Disasters in the U.S.A." See Drabek, *Social Dimensions of Disaster*. Also, see case studies of specific events, such as Wallace Akin, *The Forgotten Storm: The Great Tri-State Tornado of 1925* (Gilford, CT: The Lyons Press, 2002); Erik Larson *Isaac's Storm* (New York: Vintage Books, 2000) (Galveston Hurricane of 1900); Philip L. Fradkin, *The Great Earthquake and Firestorms of 1906: How San Francisco Nearly Destroyed Itself* (Berkeley: University of California Press, 2006); Michael Punke, *Fire and Brimstone: The North Butte Mining Disaster of 1917* (New York: Hyperion, 2006).

22. Detailed summaries of this event and potential risk areas are contained in Drabek, Alvin H. Mushkatel, and Thomas S. Kilijanek, *Earthquake Mitigation Policy: The Experience of Two States* (Boulder: Institute of Behavioral Science, University of Colorado, 1983), pp. 61–74.

23. See Mileti, *Disasters by Design*, pp. 71–73. While statistical summaries like those of Mileti's help gain a broad perspective on flooding impacts, historical narratives like David McCullough's analysis of our most deadly flood add depth and intensity to our understanding of the human side. McCullough, *The Johnstown Flood* (New York: Simon and Schuster, 1987) (original publication 1967).

24. Hurricane death tolls and damage figures are from Drabek, *Social Dimensions of Disaster*. For listings of death tolls, damages, frequency, and many other hurricane facts, see Eric S. Blake, Edward N. Rappaport, and Christopher W. Landsea, *The Deadliest, Costliest, and Most Intense United States Tropical Cyclones from 1951 to 2006 (And Other Frequently Requested Hurricane Facts)* (Miami, FL: National Hurricane Center, National Weather Service, 2007). Gustav death toll (24) based on Ed Anderson, "Hurricane Gustav Death Toll at 24 Now," *Times-Picayune*, September 7, 2008, p. 1 (accessed September

30, 2008, from http://www.nola.com/hurricane/index.ssf/2008/09/ gustav_ death_toll_increases_to.html). Ike death toll (67) based on Monica Rhor, "Searchers Discover 3 More Bodies in Texas, Pushing Hurricane Ike's Death Toll to 67," *Courant.com*, (Associated Press), September 29, 2008, p. 1 (accessed September 30, 2008, from http://www.courant.com/news/ custom/latest/abs-bc-ike-deathsep29,6400012,print.story). For discussion of the impacts and lessons learned from Hurricanes Charley, Frances, Ivan, and Jeanne (2004), see Patricia J. Kershaw and Byron Mason (Eds.), *Lessons Learned between Hurricanes: From Hugo to Charley, Frances, Ivan, and Jeanne—Summary of the March 8, 2005 Workshop of the Disasters Roundtable* (Washington, DC: National Research Council, National Academies Press, 2005). Katrina sources included *Seattle Times*, "Katrina's Death Toll Remains a Mystery," February 11, 2006 (accessed February 11, 2006, from http://seattletimes.nwsource.com/cgi-bin/PrintStory.p1?document_id=2002798269@ zsection_id); "Economic Effects of Hurricane Katrina," *Wikipedia, The Free Encyclopedia* (accessed February 11, 2006, from http://en.wikipedia.org/ wiki/Economic_effects_of_Hurricane_Katrina). See also Select Bipartisan Committee to Investigate the Preparation for and Response to Hurricane Katrina, U.S. House of Representatives, A Failure of Initiative: *Final Report of the Select Bipartisian Committee to Investigate the Preparation for and Response to Hurricane Katrina* (Washington, DC: U.S. Government Printing Office, 2006). The House Committee report included the damage estimate in excess of $200 billion (ibid., p. 319). A report issued by the White House specified estimated damages of $96 billion, 1,330 deaths, and 2,096 missing (ibid., pp. 7–8); see U.S. White House, *The Federal Response to Hurricane Katrina: Lessons Learned* (Washington, DC: The White House, 2006). For a discussion of the 2005 hurricane season see *2006 Britannica Book of the Year* (Chicago: Encyclopaedia Britannica, Inc., 2006), pp. 169–170.

25. John M. Barry, *The Great Influenza: The Epic Story of the Deadliest Plague in History* (New York: Penguin Books, 2005).

26. Ibid., p. 460.

27. For details on the California fires, see Shaya Tayete Mohajer, "Calif. Fires Feed on Hundreds of Homes," *Denver Post*, November 16, 2008, pp. 1, 18; Amy Taxin, "Mobile Home Residents Return to Dwellings Destroyed by Fire," *Rocky Mountain News*, November 18, 2008, p. 27; "Bonfire's Flare-up Ignited Calif. Blaze," *Rocky Mountain News*, November 20, 2008, p. 40.

28. See "Hayman Fire," *Wikipedia, The Free Encyclopedia*, pp. 1–2 (accessed November 21, 2008, from http://en.wikipedia.org/wiki/Hayman_Fire). See also "Government Not Liable in Hayman Fire," *Rocky Mountain News*, November 26, 2008, p. 14.

29. Gillian Flaccus, "Rail Agency Says Engineer Failed to Stop: 25 Dead," *Sunday Denver Post & Rocky Mountain News*, September 14, 2008, p. 1. For more information of the two 747 jumbo jets that collided on the runway of the airport in Tenerife (Canary Islands), see Dan Crow and Chris Schmidt, "The Deadliest Plane Crash" (Boston, MA: WGBH Boston Video, 2006).

30. James Paton, "All Eyes on New Minn. Bridge: Amid Controversy, Longmont Company Builds 'Ultimate' Span," *Rocky Mountain News*, August 9, 2008. See also Hollis Stambaugh and Harold Cohen, *I-35 Bridge Collapse and Response: Minneapolis, Minnesota, August 1, 2007* (Emmitsburg, MD: U.S. Fire Administration, Federal Emergency Management Agency, 2008).

31. "Of the 6,774 HAZMAT events that occur on average each year, 5,517 are highway events, 991 are railroad events, and 206 are due to other causes." Federal Emergency Management Agency (hereafter FEMA), *MultiHazard Identification and Risk Assessment* (Washington, DC: Mitigation Directorate, FEMA, 1997), p. 274.

32. Robins, *World's Greatest Disasters.*, p. 120. For detailed analysis the Chernobyl disaster and its longer-term effects, see Boris Segerståhl (Ed.), *Chernobyl: A Policy Response Study* (New York: Springer-Verlag, 1991). See also Elena B. Burlakova and Valeria I. Naidich (Eds.), *20 Years after the Chernobyl Accident: Past, Present and Future* (New York: Nova Science Publishers, Inc., 2006).

33. Paul S. Gray, "Agriculture and Trade," in *Chernobyl: A Policy Response Study*, Ed. Segerståhl, (Berlin: Springer-Verlag, 1991), pp. 61–83.

34. For example, see Steven C. Spies, "Planning for WMD Terrorism Response: Factors to Consider," *Journal of the American Society of Professional Emergency Planners 7* (2000):1–15; John Mintz and Joby Warrick, "Are Our Biodefenses Up?" *Washington Post National Weekly Edition*, November 15–21, 2004, p. 6; Ramela Talwar Badam, "String of Train Bombs Kills 190 in Bombay," *Rocky Mountain News*, July 12, 2006, p. 23A; Glen Frankel, "London Subway Blasts Almost Simultaneous, Investigators Conclude Timing Devices, High Explosives Used," *Washington Post.com*, July 10, 2005, p. A19 (accessed February 15, 2006, from http://www.washingtonpost.com/wp-dyn/content/article/2005/07/09/AR2005070901248_pf.html). Badam, "Terror in India Kills Over 100," *Rocky Mountain News*, November 27, 2008, pp. 42–43; Ravi Nessman, "Bloody Wave of Terror Ends," *Rocky Mountain News*, November 29, 2008, p. 26.

35. John Leicester, "France Declares State of Emergency," *Pueblo Chieftain*, November 9, 2005, p. 10C; Keith Richburg, "Why Paris Is Burning: The Lack of Diversity Resembles Urban America Before the Riots," *Washington Post National Weekly Edition*, November 21–27, 2005, p. 22; Elaine Sciolino and Craig S. Smith, "Demonstrations Choke French Cities," *International Herald Tribune*, March 29, 2006 (accessed April 7, 2006, from http://www.igt.com/articles/2006/03/28/news/France.php). Ambika Ahuja and Grant Peck, "Protests Shut Thai Airport, Trapping Tourists," *Rocky Mountain News*, November 26, 2008, p. 30; Elena Becatoros, "Public Places Scrutiny on Greek Government," *Rocky Mountain News*, December 11, 2008, p. 30.

245

36. Evan Thomas with reporting from Arian Campo-Flores, Pat Wingert, Daren Brisco, Catharine Skipp, Lynn Waddell, and Jinkeol Park (*Korea Daily*) in Blacksburg; and Eve Conant, Holly Bailey, and Mark Hosenball, in Washington, DC, "Making Of a Massacre: Special Report," *Newsweek* 149, no. 18 (2007):22–31.

37. John N. Maclean, *Fire on the Mountain: The True Story of the South Canyon Fire* (New York: Washington Square Press, 1999). I also recommend the book that Maclean and his sister, Jean, tidied up after the death of their father, Norman Maclean. *A River Runs Through It* is a masterful accounting of family change, but *Young Men and Fire* is an equally well-written assessment of the Mann Gulch fire that left 13 firefighters dead in 1949 (Chicago: University of Chicago Press, 1972). See also Maclean's follow-up analyses of the "ghost" of the Storm King fire (i.e., the 1999 Sadler fire in Nevada) and others. His perceptive review of wildland fire policy is most informative and highly recommended reading (pp. 193–213). Maclean, *Fire and Ashes: On the Front Lines of American Wildfires* (New York: Henry Holt and Company, 2003). Even a beautifully written analysis like John Barry's story of the 1918 influenza pandemic and "the warriors" who fought it, gives us a different kind of understanding than a fictionalized account like that of Katherine Anne Porter, *Pale Horse, Pale Rider* (New York: Harcourt Brace & Company, 1936). She nearly died from this flu while working as a reporter for the *Rocky Mountain News* in Denver, Colorado. Fortunately, she survived to help us understand "the problem" through the eyes and words of her heroine, Miranda (also a newspaper reporter who also lost her lover). Miranda's suffering with the flu is eased momentarily when she shared words from an old spiritual with her lover Adam: "Pale horse, pale rider, done taken my lover away…" (ibid., p. 189). Respecting ripple effects like these are required of any who seek to gain real understanding of "the problem."

38. See Charles E. Fritz and Eli S. Marks, "The NORC Studies of Human Behavior in Disaster," *Journal of Social Issues* 10 (1954):26–41 and Fritz, "Disasters," in *Contemporary Social Problems*, Ed. Robert K. Merton and Robert A. Nisbet (New York: Harcourt, 1961), pp. 651–695.

39. T. Joseph Scanlon, "Disaster's Little Known Pioneer: Canada's Samuel Henry Prince," *International Journal of Mass Emergencies and Disasters* 6 (1988):213–232. See also Samuel Henry Prince, "Catastrophe and Social Change, Based Upon a Sociological Study of the Halifax Disaster" (Doctoral dissertation, Columbia University, Department of Political Science, 1920); Laura M. MacDonald, *Curse of the Narrows* (New York: Walker and Company, 2005 [a historical narrative by a Halifax native of the Halifax disaster]). Scanlon provides an informative discussion of his archival experiences regarding the 1917 Halifax disaster, and many fascinating details about the response and social impacts, in Scanlon, "Rewriting a Living Legend: Researching the 1917 Halifax Explosion," in *Methods of Disaster Research*, Ed. Robert A. Stallings (Philadelphia, PA: Xlibris Corporation, 2002), pp. 266–301.

40. For analysis of this issue, see Drabek, "Taxonomy and Disaster: Theoretical and Applied Issues," in *Social Structure and Disaster,* Ed. Gary A. Kreps (Newark: University of Delaware Press, 1989), pp. 317–345. Often, discussion of this issue has resulted from those like Quarantelli who have posed the question: "What Is a Disaster?" His view is that social factors, not geophysical qualities of an event, will prove to be most critical for comparative aggregation of results (i.e., generalization). More specifically, he proposes that we take a lead from the biological sciences using the concepts of genotype and phenotype. Thus, he suggests "that less obvious or visible characteristics are far more important than surface futures. Our prediction is that our eventual new paradigm will involve far more genotypical rather than the phenotypical features we now almost exclusively use." Quarantelli, "A Social Science Research Agenda for the Disasters of the 21st Century: Theoretical, Methodological and Empirical Issues and Their Professional Implementation," in *What Is a Disaster?,* Ed. Perry and Quarantelli (Philadelphia, PA: Xlibris Corporation, 2005), p. 341. See also Perry, "What Is a Disaster?" in *Handbook of Disaster Research,* Eds. Havidán Rodríguez, Enrico L. Quarantelli, and Russell R. Dynes (New York: Springer, 2006), pp. 1–15.

In his penetrating analysis of disaster events precipitated by toxic substances, Kai Erikson proposed that a "new species" had different social consequences from those induced by "natural" disasters. See Erikson, *A New Species of Trouble: Explorations in Disasters, Trauma, and Community* (New York: W. W. Norton, 1994). Analysis of the *Exxon Valdez* oil spill in Alaska validated Erickson's perspective according to Steve Picou and his associates; see Picou, Duane A. Gill, and Maurie J. Cohen (Eds.), *The Exxon Valdez Disaster: Readings on a Modern Social Problem* (Dubuque, IA: Kendal/Hunt Publishing Company, 1997). Upon researching Hurricane Katrina responses, Picou and his associates moved beyond arguing that technological disasters, maybe even those involving toxic materials, might not constitute a separate "type" of disaster. Rather, both therapeutic and corrosive processes might be present following all disasters. Hence, typologies based on any criteria—be they technological, toxic, or natural—impose limitations that may impede future theory construction. See Picou and Brent K. Marshall, "Introduction: Katrina as Paradigm Shift: Reflections on Disaster Research in the Twenty-First Century," in *The Sociology of Katrina: Perspectives on a Modern Catastrophe,* Ed. David L. Brunsma, David Overfelt, and Picou (Lanham, MD: Rowman Littlefield Publishers, 2007), pp. 1–20.

CHAPTER 3

1. Some of the ideas and examples first appeared in an article I published years ago; Drabek, "Shall We Leave? A Study of Family Reactions When Disaster Strikes," *Emergency Management Review* 1 (Fall 1983):25–29.

2. Drabek, *Disaster-Induced Employee Evacuation* (Boulder: Institute of Behavioral Science, University of Colorado, 1999), pp. 47–48.

3. Raymond W. Mack and George W. Baker, *The Occasion Instant*. National Academy of Science/National Research Council Disaster Study 15. (Washington, DC: National Academy of Science, 1961).

4. David Canter (Ed.), *Fires and Human Behavior* (Chichester: John Wiley & Sons, 1980).

5. Associated Press, "Probe Shows Fire Victims Fought Smoke," *Rocky Mountain News* (November 29, 1980), 48. By the way, if you've been to Vegas recently don't be confused. The current MGM is not the location where this fire occurred. You see, afterward, the MGM relocated to its current location directly across the street from New York, New York—diagonally across from the Excaliber. The 1980 fire occurred in the building currently occupied by Bally's. For a detailed case study of this disaster, see Leonard Ruchelman, "The MGM Grand Hotel Fire," in *Crisis Management: A Case Book*, Ed. Michael T. Charles and John Choon K. Kim (Springfield, IL: Charles C. Thomas Publisher, 1988), pp. 101–114.

6. Later, Quarantelli summarized his thesis findings in various publications; for example, "The Nature and Conditions of Panic," *American Journal of Sociology* 60 (1954):267–275; "The Behavior of Panic Participants," *Sociology and Social Research* 41 (1957):187–194. Years later he reviewed research by others that seemed to support—with slight modification—his original interpretations— "Panic Behavior in Fire Situations: Findings and a Model from the English Language Research Literature," paper presented at the Fourth Joint Panel Meeting of the United States–Japan Panel on Fire Research, Tokyo, Japan, February 1979. For a summary of current literature, see Anthony R. Mawson, *Mass Panic and Social Attachment: The Dynamics of Human Behavior* (Aldershot, UK: Ashgate, 2007). I found Dynes's critical review of Mawson's work very compelling—for example, "Mawson's long intellectual exercise is an interesting personal journey, but other than his typology, it adds little to our sociological understanding of panic." Dynes, "Review of *Mass Panic and Social Attachment: The Dynamics of Human Behavior*," *Contemporary Sociology* 37, no. 2 (2008):139.

7. Oral histories obtained from surviving miners clearly document this conclusion. See Robert P. Wolensky, Kenneth C. Wolensky, and Nicole H. Wolensky, *Voices of the Knox Mine Disaster: Stories, Remembrances, and Reflections of the Anthracite Coal Industry's Last Major Catastrophe, January 22, 1959* (Philadelphia: Commonwealth of Pennsylvania and Pennsylvania Historical and Museum Commission, 2005), pp. 21–99.

8. Norris R. Johnson, "Fire in a Crowded Theater: A Descriptive Investigation of the Emergence of Panic," *International Journal of Mass Emergencies and Disasters* 6 (1988):7–26.

9. Ibid., pp. 21–22.

10. Ibid., p. 24. More recent analysis of these data validated Johnson's original analysis. See William E. Fineberg and N. Johnson, "The Ties that Bind: A Macro-Level Approach to Panic," *International Journal of Mass Emergencies and Disasters* 19 (2001):269–295. Examples of more recent stampedes include (1) December 3, 1979 (Rock concert "The Who" in Cincinnati, Ohio, 11 killed); see Anne G. Hargreaves, "Coping with Disaster," *American Journal of Nursing* 80 (1980):683; (2) February 17, 2003 (E2 Nightclub, Chicago, Illinois, 21 killed; 57 injured); see Sharon Cohen, "Spray Used to Quell Fight Sparks Chaos at Chicago Nightspot," *Rocky Mountain News*, February 18, 2003, pp. 20A, 27A; (3) February 20, 2003 (fire during performance by Great White band at The Station, West Warwick, Rhode Island, 96 killed initially, 2 injured died within days plus nearly 200 other injuries); see Elizabeth Zuckerman, "Band Owners Dispute Whether Pyrotechnics Ok'd," *Rocky Mountain News*, February 22, 2003, pp. 25A–26A; (4) February 4, 2006 (people trying to enter a stadium for a popular game show, "Nowowee" in Manila, Philippines, at least 88 killed; 280 hospitalized); see *Rocky Mountain News*, February 4, 2006, p. 28A.

11. Peter H. Rossi, James D. Wright, and Eleanor Weber-Burdin with the assistance of Marianne Pietras and William F. Diggins, *Natural Hazards and Public Choice: The State and Local Politics of Hazard Mitigation* (New York: Academic Press, 1982).

12. From among several summaries, the one most helpful to me has been Harry B. Williams, "Human Factors in Warning-and-Response Systems," in *The Threat of Impending Disaster*, Ed. George H. Grosser, Henry Wechsler, and Milton Greenblatt (Cambridge, MA: MIT Press, 1964), pp. 79–104. I have summarized dozens of relevant studies on this and related aspects of warning systems for university professors teaching emergency management courses. See Drabek, *Social Dimensions of Disaster*.

13. Eve Gruntfest first documented where victims of this flood actually died. Later she led conferences on the lessons learned. See Gruntfest, *What People Did during the Big Thompson Flood*, Natural Hazards Working Paper #32 (Boulder: Natural Hazards Research and Applications Information Center, University of Colorado, 1977); Gruntfest (Ed.), *What We Have Learned since the Big Thompson Flood* (Boulder: Natural Hazards Research and Applications Information Center, University of Colorado, 1987); Gruntfest (Ed.), *Twenty Years Later: What Have We Learned since the Big Thompson Flood* (Boulder: Natural Hazards Research and Applications Information Center, University of Colorado, 1997).

14. Roger I. Glass, Robert B. Craven, Dennis J. Bregman, Barbara J. Stoll, Neil Horowitz, Peter Kerndt, and Joe Winkle, "Injuries from the Wichita Falls Tornado: Implications for Prevention," *Science* 207 (February 1980):734-738.

15. John E. Farley, "Call-to-Action Statements in Tornado Warnings: Do They Reflect Recent Development in Tornado-Safety Research?" *International Journal of Mass Emergencies and Disasters* 25 (March 2007):5.

16. Ibid.

17. Ibid.
18. Ibid., p. 30. In May 2008, 21 died when tornadoes hit various locations in Oklahoma and Missouri. Of these, about one half were in cars. Between 1985 and 2003, these are the locations where people died during tornado outbreaks: mobile homes (403); permanent homes (313); vehicles (96). Adapted from Alan Scher Zagler, "Lessons of Weekend Tornadoes: Don't Be Caught in Your Vehicle," *Rocky Mountain News*, May 13, 2008, p. 26.
19. Mileti, *A Normative Causal Model Analysis of Disaster Response*, Ph.D. Thesis (Boulder: Department of Sociology, University of Colorado, 1974).
20. Mileti, Janice R. Hutton, and John H. Sorensen, *Earthquake Prediction Response and Options for Public Policy* (Boulder: Institute of Behavioral Science, University of Colorado, 1981). Sorensen, Barbara M. Vogt, and Mileti, "Evacuation: An Assessment of Planning and Research" (Oak Ridge, TN: Oak Ridge National Laboratory, 1987).
21. Drabek, *Social Dimensions of Disaster*.
22. Drabek, "The Social Factors that Constrain Human Responses to Flood Warnings," in *Floods* (Vol. 1), Ed. Dennis J. Parker (London: Routledge, 2000), pp. 361–376; Michael K. Lindell, "Principles of Effective Warning Systems," *IAEM Bulletin* 20 (2003):1,6,8.
23. Perry and Marjorie R. Greene, *Citizen Response to Volcanic Eruptions: The Case of Mount St. Helens* (New York: Irvington Publishers, 1983).
24. Drabek, *Disaster Evacuation Behavior*.
25. Perry, *Comprehensive Emergency Management: Evacuating Threatened Populations* (Greenwich, CT: JAI Press, Inc., 1985).
26. Perry and Alvin H. Mushkatel, *Disaster Management: Warning Response and Community Relocation* (Westport, CT: Quorum Books, 1984). See also Perry and Lindell, "The Effects of Ethnicity on Evacuation Decision-Making," *International Journal of Mass Emergencies and Disasters* 9 (March 1991):47–68; Lindell and Perry, *Communicating Environmental Risk in Multiethnic Communities* (Thousand Oaks, CA: Sage Publications, 2004).
27. For detailed documentation and elaboration, see Drabek, *Human System Responses to Disaster* (New York: Springer-Verlag, 1986); Drabek, *Social Dimensions of Disaster*, 2004.
28. Timothy J. Haney, James R. Elliott, and Elizabeth Fussell, "Families and Hurricane Response: Evacuation, Separation, and the Emotional Toll of Hurricane Katrina," in Brunsma et al., *Sociology of Katrina* (ch. 2, note 40), p. 83.
29. Drabek, *Disaster-Induced Employee Evacuation*.
30. Elaine Enarson, Cheryl Childers, Betty Hearn Morrow, Deborah Thomas, and Ben Wisner, *A Social Vulnerability Approach to Disasters* (Emmitsburg, MD: Emergency Management Institute, Federal Emergency Management Agency, 2003).
31. Drabek, "Don't Blame the Victims," *Journal of Emergency Management* 3 (November–December 2005):22.

32. Legal implications of disaster warnings and other aspects of emergency management are discussed in Terry Margerum, *Will Local Governments Be Liable for Earthquake Losses?* (Berkeley, CA: Association of Bay Area Governments, 1979). See also John Pine, "Liability Issues," in *Emergency Management: Principles and Practice for Local Government*, Ed. Drabek and Gerard J. Hoetmer (Washington, DC: International City Management Association, 1991), pp. 289–307; Perry and Lindell, *Emergency Planning* (Hoboken, NJ: John Wiley & Sons, Inc., 2007).

33. Jerry T. Mitchell, Susan L. Cutter, and Andrew S. Edmonds, "Improving Shadow Evacuation Management: Case Study of the Graniteville, South Carolina, Chlorine Spill," *Journal of Emergency Management* 5, no. 1 (2007):28–34.

34. Ibid., p. 29.

35. Ibid., p. 31.

36. Ibid., p. 33.

CHAPTER 4

1. Many earlier hurricanes had even higher death tolls, for example, Galveston, Texas (1900), 6,000; Palm Beach, Okeechobee, Florida (1928), 1,836; New England area (1938), 600. See Mark S. Hoffman (Ed.), *The World Almanac and Book of Facts, 1993* (New York: World Almanac, 1993), p. 575.

2. Guy Daines, "Planning, Training, and Exercising," in Drabek and Hoetmer, *Emergency Management* (ch. 3, note 32).

3. Drabek, *Disaster Evacuation and the Tourist Industry* (Boulder: Institute of Behavioral Science, University of Colorado, 1994); Kirstin Dow and Cutter, "Crying Wolf: Repeat Responses to Hurricane Evacuation Orders," *Coastal Management* 26 (1998):237–252.

4. Drabek, *Implementation of Microcomputer Technology in Emergency Management Agencies* (Boulder: Institute of Behavioral Sciences, University of Colorado, 1991).

5. Post, Buckley, Suhuh, and Jernigan, Inc., "Hurricane Hugo Assessment: Review of Hurricane Evacuation Studies Utilization and Information Dissemination" (Washington, DC: U.S. Army Corps of Engineers and Federal Emergency Management Agency, 1990).

6. Harry Estill Moore, *Tornadoes over Texas* (Austin: University of Texas Press, 1958).

7. For a cross-societal perspective on conceptions of and adaptations to disaster, see Anthony Oliver-Smith and Susanna M. Hoffman (Eds.), *The Angry Earth: Disaster in Anthropological Perspective* (New York: Routledge, 1999).

8. Moore, Frederick L. Bates, Marvin V. Layman, and Vernon J. Parenton, *Before the Wind: A Study of Response to Hurricane Carla*, National Academy of Sciences/National Research Council Disaster Study #19 (Washington, DC: National Academy of Sciences, 1963).

9. Pinellas County Department of Civil Emergency Services, "Hurricane Elena Critique" (Clearwater, FL: Pinellas County Department of Civil Emergency Services, n.d.). A readable but detailed history and discussion of the technical workings of the coastal hurricane prediction and warning system has been prepared by Robert H. Simpson and Herbert Riehl, *The Hurricane and Its Impact* (Baton Rouge: Louisiana State University Press, 1981).

10. Stanley Pierson, *The Big Flood: California 1955* (Sacramento: California Disaster Office, 1956).

11. Scanlon and Massey Padgham, *The Peel Regional Police Force and the Mississauga Evacuation* (Ottawa, Ontario: Canadian Police College, 1980); see also Joseph M. Hans, Jr. and Thomas C. Sells, *Evacuation Risks—An Evaluation* (Washington, DC: U.S. Government Printing Office, 1974).

12. Quarantelli, "Evacuation Behavior and Problems: Findings and Implications from the Research Literature" (Columbus: Disaster Research Center, The Ohio State University, 1980), p. 110.

13. See National Transportation Safety Board, *Motorcoach Fire on Interstate 45 during Hurricane Rita Evacuation Near Wilmer, Texas, September 23, 2005* (Washington, DC: National Transportation Safety Board, 2007); "Hurricane Rita," *Houston Chronicle Special Report*, 2005, p. 1; "Most Say They Would Evacuate Again," *Houston Chronicle*, February 12, 2008 (accessed November 5, 2008 from http://www.chron.com/content/chronicle/special/05/rita/index.html).

14. Quarantelli, "Evacuation Behavior and Problems," p. 122.

15. John C. Brownson, "Snohomish County Emergency Management Briefing Paper: Evacuation" (Everett, WA: Snohomish County Department of Emergency Services, n.d.), p. 4.

16. Select Bipartisan Committee, *Failure of Initiative*, p. 2.

17. Ibid.

18. Ibid., p. 108.

19. Ibid., p. 109.

20. Ibid., p. 110.

21. Committee on Homeland Security and Governmental Affairs, *Hurricane Katrina: A Nation Still Unprepared* (Washington, DC: United States Senate, 2007), Chapter 16, p. 4.

22. Ibid.

23. I learned of Pine's class experience through Wayne Blanchard's Higher Education Project Report dated October 22, 2008 (Item #4). The referenced document is Harold C. Relyea, *Martial Law and National Emergency* (Washington, DC: Congressional Research Service, 2005).

24. Blanchard, Higher Education Project Report, November 10, 2008 (Item #3). Referenced document is Pat Grossmith, "Mandated Evacuation Lawful in Emergency," *New Hampshire Union Leader*, November 7, 2008.

25. Ron Perry has developed a typology of evacuations in which he cross-tabulates two dimensions: (1) duration of withdrawal (short term or long term); and (2) withdrawal relative to impact (preimpact or postimpact). This produces four combinations, each a different type of evacuation: (1) preventive (short term, preimpact); (2) rescue (short term, postimpact); (3) protective (long term, preimpact); and (4) reconstructive (long term, postimpact). The conditions producing each of these and their internal processes probably differ substantially, but to date careful comparison has not been made. See Perry, "A Classification Scheme for Evacuations," *Disasters* 2 (1979):169–170.

26. Charlie Melancon and William J. Jefferson. *Additional View Presented by the Select Committee on Behalf of Rep. Charlie Melancon and Rep. William J. Jefferson* (Washington, DC: U.S. Government Printing Office, 2006).

27. Ibid., p. 1. Emphasis (italics) of "how," "why," and "who" appear in original quotation. Melancon and Jefferson, like many others of us, believe that an independent commission modeled after the 9/11 Commission should have been established to investigate the Katrina response. "For these reasons, we conclude that only an independent commission with sufficient authority to obtain critical documents and other information from the Administration will be able to tell the full story of Hurricane Katrina. This endeavor is critical not only for historical and accountability purposes, but also to ensure that the nation will not falter again in the event of a future disaster." Melancon and Jefferson, *Additional View Presented by the Select Committee*, p. 54. See also Kathleen Tierney and Greg Gilbert, "Natural Hazards Center Recommends Independent Katrina Review," *Natural Hazards Observer* 30, no. 2 (2005):4.

28. Melancon and Jefferson, *Additional View Presented by the Select Committee*, p. 11.

29. Select Bipartisan Committee, *Failure of Initiative*, p. 112.

30. Ibid. Numerous books have been completed on Hurricane Katrina that dissect varied issues. For example, see Henry A. Giroux, *Stormy Weather: Katrina and the Politics of Disposability* (Boulder, CO: Paradigm Publishers, 2006); Jed Horne, *Breach of Faith: Hurricane Katrina and the Near Death of a Great American City* (New York: Random House, 2006); John McQuaid and Mark Schleifstein, *Path of Destruction: The Devastation of New Orleans and the Coming Age of Superstorms* (New York: Little, Brown and Company, 2006); Kirstin A. Bates and Richelle S. Swan, *Through the Eye of Katrina: Social Justice in the United States* (Durham, NC: Carolina Academic Press, 2007); Thomas Neff, *Holding Out and Hanging On: Surviving Hurricane Katrina* (Columbia: University of Missouri Press, 2007).

31. John Moreno Gonzales, "New Orleans Remembers Katrina Horror," *Rocky Mountain News*, August 30, 2008, p. 31.

32. Stacey Plaisance and Becky Bohrer, "1.9 Million Flee As Storm Zeros in on Gulf Coast," *Rocky Mountain News*, September 1, 2008, p. 28.

253

33. The NWS warning was reported very widely on television and in numerous print media. For example, see *Newsweek*, 152, no. 16 (2008):29. Coverage of the after-impact rescues also was widespread, for example, Christopher Sherman and Pauline Arrillaga, "Ike May Reveal Its Toll Slowly," *Sunday Denver Post*, September 14, 2008, pp. 1A, 23A.

34. Drabek, "Social Processes in Disaster: Family Evacuation," *Social Problems* 16, Winter (1964):336–349. See also Drabek, *Disaster Evacuation Behavior*.

35. Dow and Cutter, "South Carolina's Response to Hurricane Floyd" (Quick Response Report #128) (Boulder, CO: Natural Hazards Research and Applications Information Center, 2000), pp. 8–9. For a more general discussion of the impact of Internet usage on emergency management, see Gruntfest and Marc Weber, "Internet and Emergency Management: Prospects for the Future," *International Journal of Mass Emergencies and Disasters* 16 (March 1998):55–72.

36. Drabek and John S. Stephenson III, "When Disaster Strikes," *Journal of Applied Social Psychology* 1 (1971):187–203. You should realize that about one half of American families own some type of pet. For many, the "family" members will influence decisions about when to evacuate and where to go. For example, in my study of tourists, we documented that "...42% indicated that the site they selected for evacuation was influenced by the presence of their pet." Drabek, *Disaster Evacuation Behavior*, p. 102. See also Sebastian E. Heath, Philip H. Kass, Alan M. Beck, and Larry T. Glickman, "Human and Pet-Related Risk Factors for Household Evacuation Failure During a Natural Disaster," *American Journal of Epidemiology* 153 (2001):659–665; Heath, Susan K. Voeks, and Glickman, "Epidemiologic Features of Pet Evacuation Failure in a Rapid-onset Disaster," *Journal of the American Veterinary Medical Association* 218 (2001):1898–1904.

37. Perry, Lindell, and Greene, *Evacuation Planning in Emergency Management* (Lexington, MA: Lexington Books, 1981).

38. For example, Richard Titmus, *Problems of Social Policy* (London: Her Majesty's Stationery Officer, 1950); Fred C. Ikle and Harry V. Kincaid, *Social Aspects of Wartime Evacuation of American Cities*, Disaster Study Number 4 (Washington, DC: National Academy of Sciences/National Research Council, 1956).

39. Perry, Lindell, and Greene, *Evacuation Planning*, p. 67.

40. Haney et al., "Families and Hurricane Response," pp. 78–79.

41. Ibid., pp. 84–86.

42. David King, "How People Responded To the April 2007 Tsunami Warning in Cairns and Townsville," *Australian Journal of Emergency Management* 23, no. 1 (2008):10–20.

43. Ibid., p. 11. Additional statistics listed were adapted from tables appearing on pp. 11–15.

44. Ibid., p. 20.

45. Ibid.

CHAPTER 5

1. Moore et al., *Before the Wind.*
2. Perry et al., *Evacuation Planning*, p. 120.
3. Perry and Greene, *Citizen Response.*
4. Ibid., p. 94.
5. Moore et al., *Before the Wind.*
6. Drabek, *Disaster-Induced Employee Evacuation*, pp. 114–116.
7. Drabek, "Social Processes."
8. Quarantelli, "Evacuation Behavior and Problems," p. 91.
9. Communicated to me personally by Roy S. Popkin (former deputy director, Disaster Services, American Red Cross) following a workshop held at the Donaldson Brown Center for Continuing Education in Blacksburg, Virginia (February 1981). Later, Popkin summarized staff reactions to remarks offered by Quarantelli and Mike Carter (University of Minnesota Warning Study). See Roy S. Popkin, "Encounters of the Best Kind," *National Hazards Observer* 5, no. 4 (1981):9.
10. Moore et al., *Before the Wind.*
11. Perry, Lindell, and Greene, "The Implications of Natural Hazards Evacuation Warning Studies for Crisis Relocation Planning" (Seattle, WA: Battelle Human Affairs Research Centers, 1980), pp. 273–274.
12. Quarantelli,"Evacuation Behavior and Problems."
13. Perry et al., "Implications of Natural Hazards."
14. Ibid., p. 253.
15. See Donald Zeigler, Stanley D. Brunn, and James H. Johnson, Jr., "Evacuation from a Nuclear Technological Disaster," *Geographical Review* 71 (January 1981):1–16; Scanlon and Padgham, *The Peel Regional Police Force.*
16. James M. Kendra and Tricia Wachtendorf, "Community Innovation and Disasters," in Rodríguez et al., *Handbook of Disaster Research* (ch. 2, note 40), p. 324.
17. Drabek, *Disaster Evacuation Behavior,* p. 171.
18. Zeigler et al., "Evacuation from a Nuclear Technological Disaster."
19. The need for expanded research on vulnerable populations has been highlighted by several scholars. For excellent summaries of the research base, its limitations, and the agenda required for the future see Bob Bolin, "Race, Class, Ethnicity, and Disaster Vulnerability," in Rodríguez et al., *Handbook of Disaster Research* (ch. 2, note 40), pp. 113–129; Enarson, Alice Fothergill, and Lori Peek, "Gender and Disaster: Foundations and Directions," in Rodríguez et al., *Handbook of Disaster Research* (ch. 2, note 40), pp. 130–146. While children are mentioned as a type of vulnerable population in both of these chapters, the absence of the term *children* in the extensive index for the *Handbook* underscores the importance of this acute research need.
20. Summary based on Sarah Kliff and Catherine Skipp, "Recovery: Overlooked: The Littlest Evacuees," *Newsweek,* 152, no. 2 (2008):8; *Washingtonpost.com,* "What about the Children?" October 14, 2008, p. A16 (accessed October

24, 2008, from http://www.washingtonpost.com/wp-dyn/content/ article/2008/10/13/AR2008101302279_pf.html). See also "New National Commission on Children and Disasters Gets to Work," October 16, 2008, pp. 1–2 (accessed December 5, 2008, from http://www.savethechildren.org/ newsroom/2008/national-commission-children-disasters.html?print=t).

21. Drabek, *Disaster-Induced Employee Evacuation.*
22. Drabek, *Disaster Evacuation Behavior.*
23. Drabek, *Disaster-Induced Employee Evacuation*, pp 94-96.
24. Quoted from Michael Graczyk and Cain Burdeau, "Beached: Some Galveston Hurricane Victims May Not Be Allowed to Rebuild," *Pueblo Chieftain*, September 19, 2008, p. 12C. See also Jon Gambrell, "Evacuees Clog Road to Galveston, Then Are Kept Out," *Pueblo Chieftain,* September 18, 2008, p. 3A.
25. Graczyk and Burdeau, "Beached."
26. Drabek, *Disaster Evacuation Behavior.*
27. Perry and Greene, *Citizen Response.*
28. The January 4, 1982, *Emergency Management Newsletter* (Office of the Director, FEMA, Washington, DC) highlighted a parallel effort in Ohio. Shortly after pamphlets were distributed, Cardington, Ohio, was struck by a tornado. Lives were saved because of this public information effort; one that nearly was canceled in last-minute budget cuts.
29. Perry, Greene, and Lindell, *Human Response to Volcanic Eruption: Mount St. Helens, May 18, 1980* (Seattle, WA: Battelle Human Affairs Research Centers, 1980), p. 93.
30. Ibid.
31. Drabek, Donald Q. Brodie, Jessica Edgerton, and Paul Munson, *The Flood Breakers: Citizens Band Radio Use during the 1978 Flood in the Grand Forks Region* (Boulder: Institute of Behavioral Science, University of Colorado, 1979). For a somewhat opposing view of this recommendation, see an essay by Kelly Frailing, "The Myth of a Disaster Myth: Potential Looting Should Be Part of Disaster Plans," *Natural Hazards Observer* 31, no. 4 (2007):3–4. Frailing argues that we must not claim that looting never occurs during disaster responses. With that I obviously agree. And I am not proposing lawless vigilante groups. That too should be avoided. However, the tone and priority of recommendations—explicit and implicit—run counter to my emphasis on broadening the range of community participation. So I am concerned with statements like these: "…the police could concentrate their efforts on maintaining law and order and protecting property. There is nothing to be gained by private citizens taking the law into their own hands and endangering their lives in the process" (p. 4).
32. Perry et al., "Implications of Natural Hazards," p. 93.
33. Lindell and Perry, *Communicating Environmental Risk,* p. 115.
34. Although a military emphasis on civil emergency preparedness dates back at least to World War I when newly developed aircraft technology altered enemy attack possibilities, there have been numerous policy and administrative alterations since. Probably the most fundamental issue, however, was

that associated with a policy of Mutual Assured Destruction (MAD) adopted in the early 1960s by the Kennedy Administration. Today, the viability and relevance of this premise remain controversial. This controversy also was reflected in alternative public views regarding any civil emergency preparedness emphases that might be military related. The current policy of "all-hazards emergency management" implies an integration among managerial strategies. Hence, community evacuation plans, for example, those designed for hurricane threats, may have components that are somewhat applicable to several other types of events with totally different agents (e.g., flood, tornado, nuclear power plant accident, or terrorist attack). For a brief historical summary see Drabek, "The Evolution of Emergency Management," in Drabek and Hoetmer, *Emergency Management: Principles* (ch. 3, note 32), pp. 3–29. See also George D. Haddow and Jane A. Bullock, *Introduction to Emergency Management* (Burlington, MA: Elsevier Butterworth-Heinemann, 2008); David A. McEntire, *Introduction to Homeland Security: Understanding Terrorism with an Emergency Management Perspective* (New York: John Wiley & Sons, Inc., 2009).

35. For examples of such conflicts, see Drabek, *The Professional Emergency Manager: Structures and Strategies for Success* (Boulder, CO: Institute of Behavioral Science, 1987), pp. 43–49, 190–191; and Drabek, *Emergency Management: Strategies for Maintaining Organizational Integrity* (New York: Springer-Verlag, 1990), pp. 44–47, 127–138.

36. National Governors' Association, *Comprehensive Emergency Management: A Governor's Guide* (Washington, DC: U.S. Government Printing Office, 1979).

37. See Executive Orders 12127 of March 31, 1979 and 12148 of July 20, 1979.

38. There is a huge literature on all sides of the "Nuclear Winter hypothesis" that Carl Sagan and others popularized. A balanced summary for nonscientists is presented by Lydia Dotto, *Planet Earth in Jeopardy: Environmental Consequences of Nuclear War* (Chichester, UK: John Wiley and Sons, 1986). For analysis of the "Crisis Relocation Program" (CRP) initiative and its failure to be implemented, see Peter J. May and Walter Williams, *Disaster Policy Implementation: Managing Programs under Shared Governance* (New York: Plenum Press, 1986).

39. For examination of this controversy, both historically and politically, the following assessments are helpful. Perry, *The Social Psychology of Civil Defense* (Lexington, MA: Lexington Books, 1982); Thomas J. Kerr, *Civil Defense in the U.S.: Bandaid for a Holocaust?* (Boulder, CO: Westview Press, 1983); Lawrence J. Vale, *The Limits of Civil Defense in the U.S.A., Switzerland, Britain, and the Soviet Union: The Evolution of Policies Since 1945* (New York: St. Martin's Press, 1987).

40. Quarantelli, "The Origins and Impact of Disaster Research," in *The First 72 Hours: A Community Approach to Disaster Preparedness*, Ed. Margaret O'Leary (New York: iUniverse, Inc., 2004), p. 325.

41. Office of Technology Assessment, Congress of the United States, *The Effects of Nuclear War* (Washington, DC: Office of Technology Assessment, 1979) (available from The Superintendent of Documents, U.S. Government Printing Office, Washington, D.C. 20402, Library of Congress Catalog Card Number 79-600080).

42. Portions of behavioral research on disaster responses have been funded precisely on this assumption; that is, the disaster case is the best parallel existent to the nuclear war case. For elaboration of this point, including specific examples from both government funding sources and researchers, see "Comments" by Kerr (pp. 136–138) and discussion (pp. 139–142) provoked by his comments and those of Kreps (pp. 91–121) and Quarantelli (pp. 122–136) in *Social Science and Natural Hazards*, Ed. Wright and Rossi (Cambridge, MA: Abt Books, 1981). See also Quarantelli, "Disaster Studies: An Analysis of the Social Historical Factors Affecting the Development of Research in the Area," *International Journal of Mass Emergencies and Disasters* 5 (November 1987):285–310.

43. The preparations that occurred prior to the 9/11 attacks are most insightful. See National Commission on Terrorist Attacks, *9/11 Commission Report*.

44. Major reports that recommended new policies and organizational structures to combat terrorism prior to the 9/11 attacks include the following: 1995, *Report to the Attorney General and Director of Central Intelligence* (Joint Task Force on Intelligence and Law Enforcement) (Richards/Rindskopf Report); 2000, *Second Annual Report to the President and the Congress* (Advisory Panel to Assess Domestic Response Capabilities for Terrorism Involving Weapons of Mass Destruction) (Gilmore Commission); 2000, *Countering the Changing Threat of International Terrorism* (National Commission on Terrorism) (Bremer Commission); 2001, *Road Map for National Security: Imperative for Change* (U.S. Commission on National Security/21st Century) (Hart-Rudman Commission).

45. See Spies, "Planning for WMD Terrorism Response."

46. See Elizabeth B. Armstrong, "IAEM Members: Dept. of Homeland Security Org Chart" (Washington, DC: International Association of Emergency Managers, 2002); Office of Homeland Security, "Homeland Security Presidential Directive—3" (Washington, DC: Office of Homeland Security, 2002). For a sketch of a proposed "new vision" of a National Preparedness System, see U.S. White House, *Federal Response to Hurricane Katrina*, pp. 66–77. The 2006 "National Security Strategy" statement outlines the threats represented by potential proliferation of such weapons of mass destruction (WMD) as nuclear, chemical, and biological. Like the 2002 policy issued after the 9/11 attacks, this statement explicitly rejects the MAD doctrine mentioned in note 34 and repeatedly endorses a "first strike" action when required. This policy commonly is referred to as the Bush Doctrine. Not all Americans, however, are familiar with this phrase or this policy. See George W. Bush, *The National Security Strategy of the United States of America* (Washington, DC: The White House, 2006): "The United States can no longer simply rely on deterrence to

keep the terrorists at bay or defensive measures to thwart them at the last moment. The fight must be taken to the enemy, to keep them on the run" (p. 8). "The greater the threat, the greater is the risk of inaction—and the more compelling the case for taking anticipatory action to defend ourselves, even if uncertainty remains as to the time and place of the enemy's attack" (p. 18). "Our deterrence strategy no longer rests primarily on the grim premise of inflicting devastating consequences on potential foes. Both offenses and defenses are necessary to deter state and non-state actors, through denial of the objectives of their attacks and, if necessary, responding with overwhelming force" (p. 22). "If necessary, however, under long-standing principles of self-defense, we do not rule out the use of force before attacks occur, even if uncertainty remains as to the time and place of the enemy's attack" (p. 23).

47. Ann Marie Major and L. Erwin Atwood, "Assessing the Usefulness of the U.S. Department of Homeland Security's Terrorism Advisory System," *International Journal of Mass Emergencies and Disasters* 22, no. 2 (2004):77–101.
48. Ibid., p. 77.
49. Benigno E. Aguirre, "Homeland Security Warnings: Lessons Learned and Unlearned," *International Journal of Mass Emergencies and Disasters* 22, no. 2 (2004):103–115.
50. Ibid., p. 112.

CHAPTER 6

1. For description of this event, emergency responses, and adjustments made during the subsequent year, see Drabek, *Disaster in Aisle 13*.
2. James Taylor, Louis Zurcher, and William H. Key, *Tornado: A Community Responds to Disaster* (Seattle: University of Washington Press, 1970). Since this tornado there have been others with greater losses, for example, Lubbock, Texas (May 11, 1970, $135 million); Xenia, Ohio (April 3, 1974, $90 million); Omaha, Nebraska (May 6, 1975, $69.2 million); Wichita Falls, Texas (April 10, 1979, $300 million), and Oklahoma City area (including Moore, Choctaw, Midwest, and Del City), Oklahoma and Sedgwick County (including Wichita and Hayesville), Kansas (May 3, 1999, more than $1 billion). For more detailed discussion of tornado losses, see Mileti, *Disasters by Design*, pp. 82–83; Brunner, *Time Almanac 2002*, p. 618.
3. Taylor et al., *Tornado*, p. 16.
4. Ibid., p. 10.
5. Ibid., p. 11.
6. Drabek, *Strategies for Coordinating Disaster Responses* (Boulder: Institute of Behavioral Science, University of Colorado, 2003). For a brief summary of victim responses that somewhat parallels this assessment, but from the perspective of a clinical psychologist who began his disaster experiences

with the massive "Ash Wednesday" bushfires (1983) in Australia, see Rob Gordon, "Acute Responses to Emergencies: Findings and Observations of 20 Years in the Field," *Australian Journal of Emergency Management* 21, no. 1 (2006):17–23.

7. Anthony F. C. Wallace, *Tornado in Worcester,* National Academy of Science/National Research Council Disaster Study #3 (Washington, DC: National Academy of Sciences, 1956).

8. Stress research has much to offer emergency managers. Both individual and organizational coping responses are documented now, and adjustment mechanisms for increasing tolerance levels are being refined. See Hans Selye, *Stress without Disease* (New York: New American Library, 1975); Joseph E. McGrath (Ed.), *Social and Psychological Factors in Stress* (New York: Holt, Rinehart and Winston, Inc., 1970); Catalina M. Arata, Picou, G. David Johnson, and T. Scott McNally, "Coping with Technological Disaster: An Application of the Conservation of Resources Model to the Exxon Valdez Oil Spill," *Journal of Traumatic Stress* 13 (2000):23–39.

9. Taylor et al., *Tornado,* p. 36.

10. Ibid., p. 35.

11. I qualify this caricature here by the reference to Americans since our research base is limited. It has been suggested to me by Japanese disaster researchers that there may be some cross-national differences. Indeed, they suggested that more authoritarian societies may evidence less rapid initiation of action by individuals who may wait for direction from authorities. Such cross-national comparisons await future researchers. For elaboration, see Drabek, *Human System Responses,* p. 416; Walter Gillis Peacock, "Cross-National and Comparative Disaster Research," *International Journal of Mass Emergencies and Disasters* 15 (1987):117–133.

12. National Institute of Standards and Technology, *Final Report on the Collapse of the World Trade Center Towers* (Gaithersburg, MD: National Institute of Standards and Technology, Building and Fire Research Laboratory, 2005), p. 176.

13. Ibid., p. 160. Additional insights into evacuation behavior among World Trade Center (WTC) occupants will be available soon through survey results produced by a team headed by Robin Gershon, Department of Sociomedical Sciences, Columbia University Mailman School of Public Health.

14. For additional discussion of these two events and others wherein heroes are noted, see "Lenny Skutnik," *Wikipedia,* (accessed March 13, 2006, from en.wikipedia.org/wiki/Lenny_Skutnik); Drabek, "Managing the Emergency Response," *Public Administration Review* 45 (January 1985):85–92. The social processes that evoke more generalized attitudes of altruism are analyzed by Allen H. Barton, *Communities in Disaster: A Sociological Analysis of Collective Stress Situations* (Garden City, NY: Doubleday and Company, Inc., 1969). See also Joseph Cummins (Ed.), *The Greatest Search and Rescue Stories Ever Told* (Gilford, CT: The Lyons Press, 2002). Amanda Ripley examined the Air Florida 90 rescue in considerable depth and documented the

important role played by another bystander, Roger Olian, who like Skutnik received a Carnegie Hero Medal. Her analysis of the Hero Fund database and actions taken by these and other survivors are well worth a read. See especially Ripley, *The Unthinkable: Who Survives When Disaster Strikes—And Why* (New York: Crown Publishers, 2008), pp.179–202. For brief descriptions of other disaster events and heroic behavior see E. Lynne Wright, *Disasters and Heroic Rescues of Florida: True Stories of Tragedy and Survival* (Gilford, CT: Morris Book Publishing, 2006); Ray Jones and Joe Lubow, *Disasters and Heroic Rescues of California* (Guilford, CT: Morris Book Publishing, 2006).

15. For details of this crash and the emergency response, see *Rocky Mountain News*, December 22, 2008, pp. 1, 4–8.

16. See *Rocky Mountain News*, January 16, 2009, p. 1; David B. Caruso and Marcus Franklin, "'Miracle on Hudson': Airline Pilot 'Floats' Striken Plane into River; All 155 Saved," *Rocky Mountain News*, January 16, 2009, p. 25; Larry Neumeister and Caruso, "A Sudden Thud, Then 3 Minutes of Life-or-Death Decisions," *Denver Post*, January 18, 2009, p. 22A.

17. Erik Auf der Heide, "Common Misconceptions about Disasters: Panic, the 'Disaster Syndrome,' and Looting," in O'Leary, *The First 72 Hours* (ch. 5, note 40), pp. 353–354. See also Auf der Heide, *Disaster Response: Principles of Preparation and Coordination* (St. Louis, MO: The C.V. Mosby Company, 1989), pp. 167–175; Kathleen J. Tierney and Verta A. Taylor, "EMS Delivery in Mass Emergencies: Preliminary Research Findings," *Mass Emergencies* 2 (1977):151–157; Quarantelli, *Delivery of Emergency Medical Services in Disasters: Assumptions and Realities* (New York: Irvington Publishers, Inc., 1983).

18. For elaboration, see Drabek et al., *Managing Multiorganizational Emergency Response,* pp. 96–97.

19. Fritz and J. H. Mathewson, *Convergence Behavior in Disaster,* National Research Council Disaster Study #9 (Washington, DC: National Academy of Sciences, 1957).

20. McCullough, *Johnstown Flood,* p. 178.

21. Dynes and Quarantelli, "Helping Behavior in Large-Scale Disasters," in *Participation in Social and Political Activities,* Ed. David Horton Smith, Jacqueline Macaulay, and Associates (San Francisco, CA: Jossey-Bass Publishers, 1980), pp. 340–342.

22. Paul W. O'Brien and Mileti, "Citizen Participation in Emergency Response," in *The Loma Prieta California Earthquake of October 17, 1989—Public Response,* Ed. Patricia A. Bolton (Washington, DC: U.S. Government Printing Office, 1993), pp. B23–B30. Immediately after severe, unexpected, and especially life-threatening events, like earthquakes, nearly all people are stressed temporarily. Normal stress responses include mild anxiety and for some a quick throw-up, especially if they have just consumed a meal. Bladder and bowel functions often parallel feelings of urgency too. So after sitting through the show in the Indianapolis coliseum, my fictional grandfather, Sam Wilson, might have felt the need for a bathroom as the taxi cab headed to the hospital. Indeed, members of a Japanese disaster prevention panel underscored

this point recently when they simulated a 7.3 quake in Tokyo about noon-time. Their building occupancy data left them with a projection of 12 million people evacuating into the streets. Within hours they estimated that 810,000 would be searching for a toilet. "Toilet shortage not only makes [quake sur-vivors'] lives unpleasant, but causes hygiene and health problems." *Rocky Mountain News*, October 29, 2008, p. 30.

23. Committee on Homeland Security and Governmental Affairs, *Hurricane Katrina*, Chapter 21, p. 1.

24. Ibid., Chapter 21, p. 11.

25. Ibid., Chapter 1, p. 9.

26. Scanlon, "Strange Bed Partners: Thoughts on the London Bombings of July 2005 and the Link with the Indian Ocean Tsunami of December 26th 2004," *International Journal of Mass Emergencies and Disasters* 23, no. 2 (2005):153.

27. Ibid., p. 154. For additional details on this disaster, see Intelligence and Security Committee, Parliament, Great Britain, *Report into the London Terrorist Attacks on 7 July 2005* (London, UK: The Stationery Office, 2006).

28. Taylor et al., *Tornado*, p. 13.

29. See, for example, Drabek, "Sociology Research Needs," in *A Comprehensive Assessment of Research Needs on Floods and Their Mitigation*, Ed. Stanley A. Changnon, William C. Ackerman, Gilbert F. White, J. Loreena Ivens, Henry P. Caulfield, Jr., Thomas E. Drabek, et al. (Champaign: Illinois State Water Survey, 1983), pp. 107–133.

30. This theme is elaborated on in Drabek, *Some Emerging Issues in Emergency Management* (Emmitsburg, MD: National Emergency Training Center, Federal Emergency Management Agency, 1984). See also William C. Nicholson, *Emergency Response and Emergency Management Law: Cases and Materials* (Springfield, IL: Charles C. Thomas Publisher Ltd., 2003). Litigation issues regarding both volunteer first responders and issuance of hazard warnings also have surfaced in Australia. For example, see Elsie Hoh, "Legal Risks of Volunteer Firefighters—How Real Are They?" *Australian Journal of Emergency Management* 23, no. 2 (2008):46–60; Michael Eburn, "Litigation for Failure to Warn of Natural Hazards and Community Resilience," *Australian Journal of Emergency Management* 23, no. 2 (2008):9–13.

31. Ripley, *Unthinkable*, p. 211.

32. Ibid., p. 213.

33. Scanlon, "Strange Bed Partners," pp. 152–153.

34. Associated Press, "Feds to Restrict Volunteers at Disasters," September 1, 2007, pp. 1–2 (accessed September 3, 2007, from http://apnews.excite.com/article/20070901/D8RCQ1700.html).

35. Ibid., p. 2.

36. Among the many critiques of the use of bureaucratic management techniques in emergency management is Dynes, "Community Emergency Planning: False Assumptions and Inappropriate Analogies," *International Journal of Mass Emergencies and Disasters* 12 (1994):141–158. For an analysis of the nega-

tive consequences of the "classical bureaucratic" management model and an alternative, see David Osborne and Peter Plastrik, *Banishing Bureaucracy: The Five Strategies for Reinventing Government* (New York: Plume, 1998).

CHAPTER 7

1. For elaboration, see Drabek et al., *Flood Breakers,* pp. 25–26.
2. Ibid., pp. 44–53.
3. Ibid., p. 48.
4. This illustrates the concept of a disaster subculture; see Chapter 3. Another flood the following year (1979) was much worse and further formalized a civil defense committee and a "flood fight plan." Such subcultural development, including increased formalization of plans, parallels the hurricane warning system discussed in Chapter 4.
5. "Red River Flood, 1997." *Wikipedia, The Free Encyclopedia* (accessed March 13, 2006, from http://en.wikipedia.org/wiki/Red_River_Flood,_1997). See also Fothergill, *Heads above Water: Gender, Class and Family in the Grand Forks Flood* (Albany: State University of New York Press, 2004). In April 2006, the Red River threatened again, but the new levee system held. Also, once again students were filling sandbags in places like Fargo, where expectations paralleled those in Grand Forks, that is, 20 feet above flood stage. See *Rocky Mountain News,* April 4, 2006, p. 31A; *Denver Post,* April 6, 2006, p. 2A. As of this writing, the Red River once again threatens to overtop its levels and place thousands of homes and businesses at risk in Fargo, North Dakota and Moorehead, Minnesota. Volunteers have streamed in —many from out of the area—to pile millions of sandbags in an effort to reinforce temporary dikes. See *Denver Post,* March 29, 2009, p. 14A.
6. See Drabek et al., *Managing Multiorganizational Emergency Responses,* pp. 93–113.
7. "Katrina Lessons Learned," (accessed March 13, 2006, from http://www.midatlanticdogs.org/articles/katrinalessons).
8. Quoted in *NASAR Briefings* 4, August (1981):11.
9. Ibid., p. 3.
10. Wallace, *Tornado in Worcester.*
11. Dynes and Quarantelli, "Helping Behavior." Of course, in societies with more pervasive kin structures much higher levels of assistance are reported. For example, following an earthquake in Nicaragua, Ian Davis documented that 95% of the victims received assistance from extended family members. See Davis, "Disaster Housing: A Case Study of Managua," *Architectural Design* (1975):42–47. More recent analyses of such behavior have been completed by John J. Beggs, Valerie A. Haines, and Jeanne S. Hulbert, "The Effects of

Personal Network and Local Community Contexts on the Receipt of Formal Aid during Disaster Recovery," *International Journal of Mass Emergencies and Disasters* 14 (1996):57–78.

12. See Drabek and William H. Key, *Conquering Disaster: Family Recovery and Long-Term Consequences* (New York: Irvington Publishers, Inc., 1984), pp. 93–110.

13. Dynes and Quarantelli, "Helping Behavior," p. 345. Subsequent research has confirmed these conclusions. See Drabek, *Human System Responses,* pp. 152–153, 202–203. Distance from the impact scene, as would be expected, also affects the proportion of nonvictims that volunteer to help. See L. D. Nelson, "Proximity to Emergency and Helping Behavior—Data from the Lubbock-Tornado-Disaster," *Journal of Voluntary Action Research* 2 (1973):194–199.

14. Drabek et al., 1981, *Managing Multiorganizational Emergency Responses,* pp. 96–97.

15. O'Brien and Mileti, "Citizen Participation."

16. Ibid. These percentages total more than 100, because people were asked to identify any type of helping behavior they engaged in after the earthquake. Many completed multiple tasks. Each percent listed represents the proportion of the total sample who engaged in each specific; for example, 35% of the 918 people interviewed in Santa Cruz said they provided food and water to others.

17. Scofield, "Tornado Wallops Windsor," 5–6.

18. Ibid., p. 7.

19. Dynes and Quarantelli, "Helping Behavior."

20. Ibid., p. 348. Dynes and Quarantelli gave the following labels to each cell in this typology, which I omitted for the sake of simplicity. Their labels were as follows: Cell A, organizational volunteers; Cell B, volunteers in expanded roles; Cell C, group volunteers; Cell D, volunteers in new roles.

21. Drabek, *Disaster in Aisle 13,* pp. 71–79, 124–127.

22. Drabek et al., 1979, *The Flood Breakers,* pp. 45–53.

23. John Wilson and Marc Musick, "Who Cares" Toward an Integrated Theory of Volunteer Work," *American Sociological Review* 62 (1997): 694–713. This research provided empirical support for this and other themes in this chapter through analyses of a national study sample, that is, Americans' Changing Lives. These data documented that "...formal volunteering is positively related to human capital, number of children in the household, informal social interaction, and religiosity. Informal helping, such as helping a neighbor, is primarily determined by gender, age, and health." "Human capital" was measured by education, income, and functional health. They integrated their findings with those of others through a theory focused on both social and cultural capital. Social capital was assessed by number of children in the household and informal social interaction; cultural capital was measured by religiosity. p. 694. Although thousands of examples of volunteering could be documented from the 2005–2006 responses to Hurricanes Katrina, Rita, and Wilma, one of the more unusual was implemented in Pass Christian High

School. Students there received assistance from students at Pennsylvania's State College High School, who arrived to help them decorate for the annual prom. Others had fundraisers to help, and others collected 150 formal dresses that were donated for student use. Actions like these helped bring an increased sense of "normalcy" to this badly impacted community. See Kathy Hanrahan, "'Class of Katrina' Seniors Hold a Poignant Prom," *Rocky Mountain News*, March 27, 2006, p. 37A.

24. U.S. White House, *Federal Response to Hurricane Katrina*, p. 49. For detailed analysis of the ways church congregations in the Houston, Texas, area expanded and improvised their services to aid Katrina evacuees, see the case study published by Emily Holcombe, "Understanding Community-Based Disaster Response: Houston's Religious Congregations and Hurricane Katrina Relief Efforts." Pp. 107-119 in Brunsma et al., *Sociology of Katrina* (ch. 2, note 40), pp. 107–119.

25. Ibid.
26. Ibid.
27. Tony Pipa has held such positions as executive director of Warner Foundation, a private foundation in North Carolina that focused on bettering economic opportunity and race relations, and director of philanthropic services at Triangle Community Foundation in Research, also located in North Carolina. Material quoted is from a summary published by the Nonprofit Sector Research Fund, The Aspen Institute, in Washington, D.C. See *Snapshots* no. 42 (2006). Copies of the entire report are available at http://www.aspeninstitute.org. See Pipa, "Weathering the Storm: The Role of Local Nonprofits in the Hurricane Katrina Relief Effort" (Washington, DC: The Aspen Institute, 2006).

28. *Snapshots*, p. 2.
29. Ibid., p. 4.
30. Lauren S. Fernandez, Joseph A. Barbera, and Johan R. van Dorp, "Spontaneous Volunteer Response to Disasters: the Benefits and Consequences of Good Intentions," *Journal of Emergency Management* 4, no. 5 (2006):57–68.
31. Ibid., p. 61.
32. Ibid., p. 66. For additional research and strategies for integrating volunteers into disaster responses see Lauren E. Barsky, Joseph E. Trainer, Manuel R. Torres, and Aguirre, "Managing Volunteers: FEMA's Urban Search and Rescue Programme and Interactions with Unaffiliated Responders in Disaster Response," *Disasters: The Journal of Disaster Studies, Policy and Management* 31, no. 4 (2007):495–507.
33. Summary adapted from Susan M. Sterett and Jennifer A. Reich, "Prayer and Social Welfare in the Wake of Katrina: Race and Volunteerism in Disaster Response," in *Racing the Storm: Racial Implications and Lessons Learned from Hurricane Katrina*, Ed. Hillary Potter (Lanham, MD: Lexington Books, 2007), pp. 135–154.
34. Sterett, Reich, and Martha Wadsworth, "Katrina's Unsettled Aftermath: Colorado Still Host to 14,000," *Denver Post*, August 27, 2007, pp. 1E, 2E.

35. William A. Anderson, "Mobilization of the Black Community Following Hurricane Katrina: From Disaster Assistance to Advocacy of Social Change and Equity," *International Journal of Mass Emergencies and Disasters*, 26, No. 3 (2008):197-217.
36. *Ibid.*, p. 198.
37. *Ibid.*, p. 198.

CHAPTER 8

1. Drabek, *Disaster in Aisle 13*.
2. This point is detailed in Chapter 11. Relevant documentation includes Dynes, "Community Planning: False Assumptions and Inappropriate Analogies," *International Journal of Mass Emergencies and Disasters* 12 (1994):141–158.
3. See Drabek, *Disaster in Aisle 13*, pp. 113–121.
4. This pattern was documented again following the 1979 tornado in Cheyenne, Wyoming. See Drabek, *Taming the Frontierland Tornado: The Emergent Multiorganizational Search and Rescue Network in Cheyenne, Wyoming*. Technical Report No. 5, SAR Project (Denver, CO: Department of Sociology, 1979). Auf der Heide summarized additional research on this response. Auf der Heide, *Disaster Response*, pp. 172–175.
5. Drabek, *Disaster in Aisle 13*, pp. 42–45.
6. For examples, see Dynes, *Organized Behavior in Disasters* (Lexington, MA: Heath Lexington Books, 1970); Barton, *Communities in Disaster*; National Commission on Terrorist Attacks, *9/11 Commission Report*, pp. 278–323.
7. See Viki Smith and Allen G. Breed, "Cops Get Time to Help Kin Ahead of Storm," *Rocky Mountain News*, September 1, 2008, p. 31. For more detailed analysis of the role abandonment see Jane Kushma, "Role Abandonment in Disaster: Should We Leave This Myth Behind?" *Natural Hazards Observer* 31, no. 5 (2007):4–5.
8. Drabek, *Disaster in Aisle 13*, pp. 31–109.
9. Drabek et al., *Managing Multiorganizational Emergency Responses*, pp. 93–113.
10. Ibid., pp. 161–188.
11. See Barton, *Communities in Disaster*, pp. 171–184.
12. For prior discussion of the Whippoorwill disaster, see Chapter 6 and the fictional story in Chapter 1 in this volume. This research is summarized in Drabek et al., *Managing Multiorganizational Emergency Responses*, pp. 31–55.
13. Adapted from Dynes, *Organized Behavior*, pp. 136–146.
14. Zurcher, "Social-Psychological Functions of Ephemeral Roles: A Disaster Work Crew," *Human Organization* 27 (1968), pp. 281–297.
15. Taylor et al., *Tornado*, pp. 79–108.
16. For discussion and examples of the contributions of emergent groups in disaster responses, see Drabek and McEntire, "Emergent Phenomena and the Sociology of Disaster: Lessons, Trends and Opportunities from the Research

Literature," *Disaster Prevention and Management* 12 (2003):97–112; Drabek and McEntire, "Emergent Phenomena and Multiorganizational Coordination of Mass Emergencies and Disasters," *International Journal of Mass Emergencies and Disasters* 20 (2002):197–224; Quarantelli, "Emergent Behaviors and Groups in the Crisis Times of Disasters," in *Individuality and Social Control: Essays in Honor of Tamotsu Shibutani*, Ed. Kian M. Kwan (Greenwich, CT: JAI Press, 1996), pp. 47–68.

17. Sally Jenkins, "Surviving by Hook or by Crook: Mississippi Officials Used Ingenuity—and the Occasional Misdeed—after Katrina," *Washington Post National Weekly Edition*, September 26–October 2, 2005, p. 7.

18. Mannie Garza, "After Katrina: Mending Our Tattered Emergency Response Systems," *Homeland First Response* 3, no. 6 (2005):15.

19. Adapted from Drabek et al., *Managing Multiorganizational Emergency Responses*, p. 39.

20. This diagram and discussion were adapted from Drabek et al., *Managing Multiorganizational Emergency Responses*, pp. 40–42. For extended discussion of the process of creating a social map of organization communication, see Drabek, *Social Dimensions of Disaster*, Chapter 22, pp. 12–17.

21. Drabek et al., *Managing Multiorganizational Emergency Responses*, pp. 89–90.

22. See Drabek, *Strategies for Coordinating*.

23. National Commission on Terrorist Attacks, *9/11 Commission Report*.

24. Ibid., p. 283.

25. Ibid.

26. Ibid., p. 297.

27. Kendra and Wachtendorf, "Community Innovation and Disasters," p. 324.

28. Select Bipartisan Committee, *Failure of Initiative*.

29. Ibid., p. 164.

30. Ibid.

31. Ibid.

32. Ibid., p. 166.

33. The 9/11 Commission emphasized the high degree of autonomy that characterized the operational responses by the New York Police and Fire Departments. Hence, "...they were not prepared to comprehensively coordinate their efforts in responding to a major incident." National Commission on Terrorist Attacks, *9/11 Commission Report*, p. 285.

34. I have emphasized my respect for the emergency management profession and those who practice it with excellence in several publications. See, for example, Drabek, *Strategies for Coordinating Disaster Responses*; Drabek, *Emergency Management: Strategies*.

35. As is made clearer in the last chapter of this book, my view of emergency management reflects the experiential base of the research settings and questions wherein I have traveled both physically and intellectually. Though I have conversed with a good number of federal employees, whether they wear FEMA badges or serve in the National Park Service or what have you, most of my interviews have been with disaster victims or local government

officials. Thus, I reflect a community perspective rather than a federal orientation. My view of the emergency management "managerial problem" reflects that of one looking from the bottom upward rather than from the top down. But given the intergovernmental partnerships and emergent multi-agency networks that comprise the core of most disaster responses, I believe this vantage point is most instructive.

36. Louisiana Office of Homeland Security and Emergency Preparedness, "Lessons Learned: Hurricanes Katrina & Rita" (Baton Rouge: Louisiana Office of Homeland Security and Emergency Preparedness, n.d.).

37. Ibid., p. 7.

38. Ibid.

39. Ibid., p. 53.

40. Ibid., p. 55.

CHAPTER 9

1. Numerous examples are summarized by Peacock and the team that studied Hurricane Andrew. See Peacock, Morrow, and Hugh Gladwin (Eds.), *Hurricane Andrew: Ethnicity, Gender, and the Sociology of Disasters* (London: Routledge, 1997), pp. 107–112, 148–168.

2. The rampages following the acquittal of Los Angeles police officers accused of beating Rodney King (1992) is a frequently cited example. For a summary of this event and a comparison to a riot in Miami in 1980, see Michael Hooper, "The Value of Community Policing in Preventing Civil Disorder," *Network* 13 (1995):33–37. Diamond makes a parallel interpretation in his analyses of societal collapse by comparing the Rodney King riots to the conditions that probably existed during the last days of a Norwegian settlement in Greenland (Gardar). See Diamond, *Collapse,* pp. 272–273.

3. Quarantelli and Dynes, "Dissensus and Consensus in Community Emergencies: Patterns of Looting and Property Norms," *Il Politico* 34 (1969):276–291.

4. For elaboration on this point, see Gary T. Marx, "Issueless Riots," *Annuals of the American Academy of Political and Social Science* 391 (1970):21–33. See Auf der Heide, "Common Misconceptions about Disasters," pp. 362–364.

5. F. Bates (Ed.), *Recovery, Change and Development: A Longitudinal Study of the Guatemalan Earthquake* (Athens: Guatemalan Earthquake Study, University of Georgia, 1982). Following an earthquake in the late 1990s, McEntire and Sarah Mathis noted that Boris Porfiriev documented episodes of looting. Their survey of the "comparative disaster" literature, in which this single instance was highlighted, indirectly documents the great need for future cross-societal comparisons. See McEntire and Mathis, "Comparative Politics and Disasters: Assessing Substantive and Methodological Contributions," in *Disciplines, Disasters and Emergency Management: The Convergence and*

Divergence of Concepts, Issues and Trends from the Research Literature, Ed. McEntire (Springfield, IL: Charles C. Thomas Publisher, 2007), p. 185. Citation given is Porfiriev, "Social Aftermath and Organizational Response to a Major Disaster: The Case of the 1995 Sakhalin Earthquake in Russia," *Journal of Contingencies and Crisis Management* 4, no. 4 (1996):218–227.

6. William A. Anderson and Dynes, *Social Movements, Violence and Change: The May Movement in Curacao* (Columbus: The Ohio State University Press, 1975).

7. In this sense South Florida at the time of Hurricane Andrew (1992) represents the extreme end of community stratification pattern within the United States. Hence, as would be expected, there were documented cases of episodic looting and other forms of criminal behavior. See Enarson and Morrow, "A Gendered Perspective: The Voices of Women," in Peacock et al., *Hurricane Andrew* (ch. 9, note 1), pp. 130–131.

8. After his oral summary to me on the telephone, Quarantelli codified his ideas in a conference paper. See Quarantelli, "Disaster Associated Antisocial and Criminal Behavior: The Research Evidence." Paper presented at the Hazards 2002 Conference, Antalya, Turkey, October. Years later he elaborated his ideas through comparisons to the Katrina response. See Quarantelli, "The Myth and the Realities Keeping the 'Looting' Myth in Perspective," *Natural Hazard Observer* 31, no. 4 (2007):2–3.

9. Select Bipartisan Committee, *Failure of Initiative*; U.S. White House, *Federal Response to Hurricane Katrina*. (Note: Footnote numbers in original text have been deleted from passages quoted in this section.)

10. U.S. White House, *Federal Response to Hurricane Katrina*, p. 40.

11. Select Bipartisan Committee, *Failure of Initiative*, p. 360. Michelle Miles and Duke Austin completed an intensive analysis of the role of the media in propagating two specific rumors during the response to Hurricane Katrina: (1) marauding gangs; and (2) blown levees. Of course, as they point out, these were but two of dozens that existed for days. One of their conclusions is especially insightful: "Rumors rely on deep seated cultural narratives to survive, crises bring such raw narratives to the surface." Miles and Austin, "The Color(s) of Crises: How Race, Rumor, and Collective Memory Shape the Legacy of Katrina," in Potter, *Racing the Storm* (ch. 7, note 33), p. 46.

12. About 21% of the New Orleans population was below poverty level in 2003 compared with places like Miami (28%), Detroit (30%), or Cleveland (31%). These contrast sharply to such places as Denver (13%), Seattle (10%), or San Francisco (10%). U.S. Census Bureau, *American Community Survey Office* (Washington, DC: U.S. Census Bureau, 2004).

13. Select Bipartisan Committee, *Failure of Initiative*, p. 241.

14. U.S. White House, *Federal Response to Hurricane Katrina*, p. 40.

15. *2003 FBI Report of Offenses Known to Law Enforcement*, as listed by city (accessed September 15, 2005, from http://www.cityrating.com/citycrime. asp?city=new+orleans&state=LA). Same site for Denver, Atlanta, Cleveland, and Detroit.

16. See John Barnshaw, "The Continuing Significance of Race and Class among Houston Hurricane Katrina Evacuees," *Natural Hazard Observer* 30, no. 2 (2005):11–13. See also Barsky, Trainer, and Torres, "Disaster Realities in the Aftermath of Hurricane Katrina: Revisiting the Looting Myth," Quick Response Report #184 (Boulder, CO: Natural Hazards Research and Applications Information Center, 2006); Barnshaw and Trainor, "Race, Class, and Capital Amidst the Hurricane Katrina Diaspora," in Brunsma et al., *Sociology of Katrina* (ch. 2, note 40), pp. 91–105.

    Potter extended my understanding of the variations among looters and looting activities. She assessed how specific actions were perceived and both limits and justifications were constructed by victims and officials. Hence, to understand *looting* requires far greater specification of the multitude of behaviors and perceptions that comprise this complex mixture of actions. See Potter, "Reframing Crime in a Disaster: Perception, Reality, and Criminalization of Survival Tactics among African Americans in the Aftermath of Katrina," in Potter, *Racing the Storm* (ch. 7, note 33), pp. 57–59.

17. Select Bipartisan Committee, *Failure of Initiative*, p. 241.

18. For example, see Mary Lystad (Ed.), *Mental Health Response to Mass Emergencies: Theory and Practice* (New York: Brunner/Mazel Publishers, 1988).

19. Peek and Fothergill, "Reconstructing Childhood: An Exploratory Study of Children in Hurricane Katrina," Quick Response Report No. 186 (Boulder: Natural Hazards Center, University of Colorado, 2006).

20. Ibid., p. 3.

21. Ibid., p. 10.

22. One of the earliest studies to document this pattern was Mileti, Donald M. Hartsough, Patti Madson, and Rick Hufnagel, "The Three Mile Island Incident: A Study of Behavioral Indicators of Human Stress," *International Journal of Mass Emergencies and Disasters* 2 (1983):89–113.

23. Beverley Raphael, *When Disaster Strikes: How Individuals and Communities Cope with Catastrophe* (New York: Basic Books, Inc., Publishers, 1986), p. 67.

24. For a balanced review of this area see National Institute of Mental Health, *Mental Health and Mass Violence: Evidence-Based Early Psychological Intervention for Victims/Survivors of Mass Violence. A Workshop to Reach Consensus on Best Practices* (Washington, DC: U.S. Government Printing Office, 2002).

25. See Mileti et al., "Three Mile Island Incident;" Glen S. Bartlett, Peter S. Houts, Linda K. Byrnes, and Robert W. Miller, "The Near Disaster at Three Mile Island," *International Journal of Mass Emergencies and Disasters* 1 (1983):19–42.

26. H. Paul Friesema, James Caporaso, Gerald Goldstein, Robert Lineberry, and Richard McCleary, *Aftermath: Communities after Natural Disasters* (Beverly Hills, CA: Sage Publications, 1979).

27. Catherine L. Cohan and Steve W. Cole, "Life Course Transitions and Natural Disaster: Marriage, Birth, and Divorce Following Hurricane Hugo," *Journal of Family Psychology* 16 (2002):14–25.

28. Arian Campo-Flores, "Katrina's Latest Damage," *Newsweek* 147, no. 11 (2006):27.

29. U.S. Government Accountability Office, *Disaster Recovery: Past Experiences Offering Insights for Recovering from Hurricanes Ike and Gustav and Other Recent Natural Disasters* (Washington, DC: U.S. Government Accountability Office, 2008), p. 24.

30. Ibid., p. 25.

31. Ibid., p. 26. A footnote was deleted from the quotation that references U.S. Government Accountability Office, *Hurricanes Katrina and Rita Disaster Relief: Improper and Potentially Fraudulent Individual Assistance Payments Estimated to be Between $600 Million and $1.4 Billion*, GAO-06-044T (Washington, DC: U.S. Government Accountability Office, 2006).

32. Ibid., p. 27.

33. Ibid., p. 27.

34. Drabek, *Professional Emergency Manager*.

35. Bolin, *Long-Term Family Recovery from Disaster* (Boulder: Institute of Behavioral Science, University of Colorado, 1982), p. 62.

36. Harold C. Cochrane, Gruntfest, Marilyn Stokes, Heidi Burgess, Guy Burgess, and Lois Steinbeck, "Flash Flood on the Big Thompson: A Case Study" (Denver, CO: Western Governor's Policy Office, Institute for Policy Research, 1979), p. 21.

37. Robert Geipel, *Disaster and Reconstruction: The Friuli (Italy) Earthquakes of 1976* (London: George Allen & Unwin, 1982).

38. Thomas A. Birkland, *Lessons of Disaster: Policy Change after Catastrophic Events* (Washington, DC: Georgetown University Press, 2006).

CHAPTER 10

1. Drabek and Key, *Conquering Disaster*, pp. 70–88.

2. Erikson, *Everything In Its Path* (New York: Simon and Schuster, 1976). Forty-four years earlier (1928), the failure of the St. Francis dam in Saugus, California, flooded the Santa Clara River Valley in southern California. The official death toll was 450. Ray Jones and Joe Lubow. *Disasters and Heroic Rescues of California* (Gilford, CT: Morris Book Publishing, 2006). But this flash flood hit in the middle of the night, which left "…people caught in the embarrassing position of having been wakened as the flood swept them up, naked, and deposited them in a tree, to be found later by rescuers…" (ibid., p. 87). In the 1974 film *Chinatown*, we meet "Noah Cross," who brought water to Los Angeles by building a dam. As Jones and Lubow point out in their summary of the film and the 1928 dam collapse, "Men like Cross are

not satisfied to be wealthy; in fact, they can never be satisfied at all." Ibid, p. 83. In this case public anger was neutralized a bit by quick action from Los Angeles government officials: "The city council placed $1 million at the disposal of the Los Angeles Water and Power to settle claims, and it sent additional aid in the form of workers, materials, and equipment" (ibid., p. 87). No mental health surveys were conducted, however, among the disaster victims or other community members. For details, see ibid., pp. 81–88. As with other disasters, how human culpability, reflecting greed, incompetence, or other failings, affects long-term mental health impacts remains uncertain and requires further research.

3. See Robert Jay Lifton and Eric Olson, "The Human Meaning of Total Disaster: The Buffalo Creek Experience," *Psychiatry* 39 (February 1976):1–18.

4. "Corrections," *Footnotes* 30 (September–October 2002):1 (accessed December 20, 2008, from http:www.asanet.org/septoct02/departments.html). See also T. P. Schwartz-Barcott, "Recovering Community on the Anniversary of Buffalo Creek Disaster," *Footnotes* 30 (April 2002):1 (accessed December 19, 2008, from http://www.asanet.org/footnotes/apr02/fn7.html). For further details see, Gerald M. Stern, *The Buffalo Creek Disaster* (New York: Vintage Books, 1976); Erikson, *New Species of Trouble*.

5. Erikson, *Everything In Its Path*.

6. Ibid., p. 58.

7. Goldine C. Gleser, Bonnie L. Green, and Carolyn N. Winget, *Prolonged Psychosocial Effects of Disaster: A Study of Buffalo Creek* (New York: Academic Press, 1981).

8. Ibid., p. 141.

9. Schwartz-Barcott, *After the Disaster: Re-creating Community and Well-Being at Buffalo Creek since the Notorious Coal-Mining Disaster in 1972* (Amherst, MA: Cambria Press, 2008).

10. For a summary of these studies, see Bolin, "Response to Natural Disasters," in Lystad, *Mental Health Response* (ch. 9, note 18), pp. 36–37. For earlier summaries see Barbara Baisden, "Crisis Intervention in Smaller Communities," in *The Small City and Regional Community, Proceedings of the Second Conference,* Ed. E. J. Miller and R. P. Wolensky (Stevens Point: Foundation Press, Inc., University of Wisconsin, 1979), pp. 325–332. For a summary of more current research, see Drabek, *Social Dimensions of Disaster*, Session 29, pp. 1–37.

11. Drabek and Key, *Conquering Disaster*, pp. 31–69.

12. Bolin's study of the 1979 Wichita Falls, Texas, tornado is an excellent example, although he did not have pretornado data. Bolin, *Long-Term Family Recovery*. (Ch. 9, note 35) More recently, Jim Stimpson documented the psychological impacts of the 1993 Midwest floods using survey data collected in 1992 as a preevent measure, which he contrasted to a follow-up survey completed about two months after the worst impacts. Stimpson, "Flood and Psychological Well-Being: Direct, Mediating and Moderating Effects," *International Journal of Mass Emergencies and Disasters* 23, no. 1 (2005):27–48.

13. George J. Warheit, "Disasters and Their Mental Health Consequences: Issues, Findings, and Future Trends," in *Mental Health Response* (ch. 9, note 18), pp. 3–51.
14. Ibid., p. 14.
15. Ibid.
16. Bolin, "Response to Natural Disaster," pp. 36–37.
17. Warheit, "Disasters and Their Mental Health Consequences," p. 9.
18. Bolin, *Long-Term Family Recovery*, pp. 166–169.
19. Bolin, "Response to Natural Disasters," pp. 36–44.
20. Drabek and Key, *Conquering Disaster*, pp. 93–109.
21. Kevin Merida, "Katrina Rumors Could Scar Kids for Life," *Denver Post*, October 23, 2005, p. 11A.
22. Marilyn Elias, "Katrina Victims Struggle Mentally," *U.S.A. Today*, August 16, 2007, p. 1.
23. For example see Joe Gelsomino and David W. Mackey, "Clinical Interventions in Emergencies: War-Related Events," in Lystad, *Mental Health Responses* (ch. 9, note 18), pp. 211–238; Robert S. Laufer, "Human Response to War and War-Related Events in the Contemporary World," in ibid., pp. 96–129; Thomas A. Corales (Ed.), *Focus on Posttraumatic Stress Disorder Research* (Hauppauge, NY: Nova Science Publishers, Inc., 2005).
24. Gelsomino and Mackey, "Clinical Interventions," p. 213.
25. Friesema et al., *Aftermath*.
26. Cohan and Cole, "Life Course Transitions."
27. Ibid., p. 21.
28. Etienne G. Krug, Marcie-Jo Kresnow, John P. Peddicord, Lindal Dahlberg, Kenneth E. Powell, Alex E. Crosby, et al., "Suicide after Natural Disaster," *New England Journal of Medicine* 338 (1998):373–378.
29. Krug, Kresnow, Peddicord, Dahlberg, Powell, Crosby, et al., "Retraction: Suicide after Natural Disasters," *New England Journal of Medicine* 338 (1999):148–149.
30. Ibid., p. 148.
31. For a brief overview of posttraumatic stress disorder (PTSD) symptom patterns, see Danny Peterson, "Mitigation of Social Stress from Critical Incidents," *Journal of Emergency Management* 1 (Spring 2003):19–26. See also Robert J. Ursano, Carol S. Fullerton, Lars Weisaeth, and Raphael (Eds.), *Textbook of Disaster Psychiatry* (Cambridge, UK: Cambridge University Press, 2007).
32. Stimpson, "Flood and Psychological Well-Being," p. 27. See also Arata et al., "Coping with Technological Disaster."
33. Susan Stefan and Ann Marshall, *The Needs of People with Psychiatric Disabilities during and after Hurricanes Katrina and Rita: Position Paper and Recommendations* (Washington, DC: National Council on Disability, 2006).
34. Ibid., p. 15.
35. Ibid., p. 25.
36. Ibid., p. 25.

37. J. Stephen Kroll-Smith and Stephen Robert Couch, *The Real Disaster Is above Ground* (Lexington: The University of Kentucky Press, 1990).
38. Ibid., p. 6.
39. Ibid., p. 170. See also Robert E. Hartley and David Kenney, *Death Underground: The Centralia and West Frankfork Mine Disasters* (Carbondale: Southern Illinois University Press, 2006). Blame attribution is but one of the many responses that several researchers have documented following technologically induced disasters. Indeed, some have adopted the term *corrosive community* to characterize the range of social processes that may rip at the social fabric of a community. See Picou and B. Marshall, "Introduction: Katrina as Paradigm Shift," in *The Sociology of Katrina* (Ch. 2, note 40) pp. 12–13.
40. W. Anderson, "Disaster and Organizational Change in Anchorage," in *The Great Alaska Earthquake of 1964: Human Ecology,* Ed. Committee on the Great Alaska Earthquake of the National Research Council (Washington, DC: National Academy of Sciences, 1970), pp. 96–115.
41. F. Bates and Peacock, "Disaster and Social Change," in *Sociology of Disasters: Contributions of Sociology to Disaster Research,* Ed. Dynes, Brunna DeMarchi, and Carlo Pelanda (Milano, Italy: Franco Angeli, 1987), pp. 291–330; Morrow and Peacock, "Disasters and Social Change: Hurricane Andrew and the Reshaping of Miami?" in *Hurricane Andrew: Ethnicity* (ch. 9, note 1), pp. 226–242.
42. Scanlon and John Handmer, "The Halifax Explosion and the Port Arthur Massacre: Testing Samuel Henry Prince's Ideas," *International Journal of Mass Emergencies and Disasters* 19 (2001):181–208.
43. Drabek and Key, *Conquering Disaster,* pp. 292–309.
44. Ibid., p. 301.
45. Bolin, *Long-Term Family Recovery,* pp. 104–105.
46. See, for example, Morrow and Enarson, "Hurricane Andrew through Women's Eyes: Issues and Recommendations," *International Journal of Mass Emergencies and Disasters* 14 (1996):5–22. Another leader is Brenda Phillips, who was the spark behind the establishment of the "Gender and Disaster Network." See their website at http://www.fiv.edu/orgs/IHC/gender. See also Morrow and Phillips, "What's Gender Got To Do with It?", *International Journal of Mass Emergencies and Disasters* 17 (1999):5–11, and Phillips and Morrow, *Women and Disasters: From Theory to Practice* (Philadelphia, PA: Xlibris Corporation, 2008).
47. Drabek and Key, *Conquering Disaster,* pp. 192–292.
48. Morrow and Enarson, "Hurricane Andrew through Women's Eyes," p. 11.
49. Ibid., p. 14.
50. Fothergill. "An Exploratory Study of Woman Battering in the Grand Forks Flood Disaster: Implications for Community Responses and Policies," *International Journal of Mass Emergencies and Disasters* 17 (1999):79–98. For a more detailed analysis, see Fothergill, *Heads above Water.*
51. Morrow and Enarson, "Hurricane Andrew through Women's Eyes," p. 15.
52. Irwin Redlener, "Population Vulnerabilities, Preconditions, and the Consequences of Disasters," *Social Research* 75, no. 3 (2008):7.

53. Haney et al., "Families and Hurricane Response," pp. 86–89.
54. Current stress levels were assessed by responses to a question that asked about three specific symptoms: trouble sleeping, feelings of anxiety, and feelings of depression. Short-term stress was assessed by a question focused on how worried people were about the next few months. The long-term stress question was similar, but the time referent was changed to the next five years. Ibid., pp. 86–87.
55. Children's Health Fund, "Legacy of Shame: The On-Going Public Health Disaster of Children Struggling in Post-Katrina Louisiana" (New York: Children's Health Fund and National Center for Disaster Preparedness, Mailman School of Public Health, Columbia University, 2008), p. 14.
56. Drabek and Key, *Conquering Disaster*, pp. 343–346.
57. Ibid., pp. 346–358.
58. Ibid., p. 384.
59. Ibid., p. 384.
60. Ibid., pp. 385–386.
61. Ibid., p. 385.
62. Following the terrorist attacks of September 11, 2001, approximately $178 million in federal funding was appropriated for victim mental health assistance. As of spring 2006, about $211 million was expected to be appropriated for the estimated 500,000 victims who might be in need of some form of mental health service—"...which could include treatment for post-traumatic stress, substance above counseling, anti-anxiety medication, even art therapy for children too young to talk out their grief." Stephanie Smith, "Katrina Aid Slated for Mental Health," *Denver Post*, March 19, 2006, p. 16A.

CHAPTER 11

1. My initial title for this chapter was "What Can Be Done?" Upon completion and reflection I realized that the verb *must* was more appropriate. In making this change I was sensitized to the boundary that Robert Stallings discussed between the findings of a scientist using prescribed methods and those making value choices. Scientifically based knowledge can inform our choices and our views of available options and probable impacts. Hence, I consciously chose to cross this divide and offer "informed policy choices" that reflect my values stemming from the U.S. Constitution, including the Bill of Rights, and core beliefs like greater equity and fairness in social policy. See Stallings, "Methodological Issues," in Rodríguez et al., *Handbook of Disaster Research* (ch. 2, note 40), pp. 78–79.
2. Dynes advances a convincing argument that the Lisbon earthquake (1755) brought a paradigm shift, that is, the first "modern" disaster. Hence, this event was attributed to "natural" rather than "supernatural" causes, which in turn evoked a "...comprehensive plan for reconstruction which included

mitigation efforts to reduce future disaster effects." Dynes, "The Lisbon Earthquake in 1755: Contested Meanings in the First Modern Disaster," *TsuInfo Alert* 2 (August 2000):10. See also Dynes, "The Lisbon Earthquake of 1755: The First Modern Disaster," in *The Lisbon Earthquake of 1775: Representations and Reactions*, Ed. Theodore E. D. Braun and John B. Radner (Oxford, UK: Voltaire Foundation, 2005), pp. 34–49.

3. Charles Perrow's comparison of the risks associated with driving an automobile and being a passenger in an airplane is most informative. See Perrow, *Normal Accidents: Living with High-Risk Technologies* (New York: Basic Books, Inc., 1984), pp. 124–129. For a summary of the risk literature and its relevance to emergency management, see Michael Tarrant, "Risk and Emergency Management," *Australian Journal of Emergency Management* 21, no. 1 (2006):9–14.

4. George O. Rogers, "The Dynamics of Risk Perception: How Does Perceived Risk Respond to Risk Events," *Risk Analysis* 17 (1997):745–757.

5. Rogers, "Siting Potentially Hazardous Facilities: What Factors Impact Perceived and Acceptable Risk?" *Landscape and Urban Planning: An International Journal of Landscape Ecology, Landscape Planning and Landscape Design* 39 (1998):265–281.

6. Frequently labeled the *gambler's fallacy*, many incorrectly assume that if an event has occurred (like a jackpot on a slot machine), it is less likely to occur within the next several spins. See Burton et al., *Environment As Hazard*, pp. 109–110.

7. Fishermen, like those in other high-risk occupations, adapt to the risks they encounter and define them as expected features of their jobs; for example, Cynthia Lamson, "'I Think They're All Caught Up': An Inquiry of Hazard Perception among Newfoundland and Inshore Fishermen," *Environment and Behavior* 15 (1983):458–486. For detailed survey data on earthquake risk perceptions among Californians, see Ralph H. Turner, Joanne M. Nigg, and Denise Heller Paz, *Waiting for Disaster: Earthquake Watch in California* (Berkeley: University of California Press, 1986).

8. John A. Cross, "Longitudinal Changes in Hurricane Hazard Perception," *International Journal of Mass Emergencies and Disasters* 8 (1990):31–47.

9. See my summary of numerous studies on these social characteristics and others; Drabek, *Human System Responses*, pp. 327–331.

10. Linkages between disasters, risk, and development are complex issues. Among the analyses I have found helpful are Mary B. Anderson and Peter J. Woodrow, *Rising from the Ashes: Development Strategies in Times of Disaster* (Boulder, CO: Westview Press, 1989); Frederick C. Cuny, *Disasters and Development* (New York: Oxford University Press, 1983). See also Ariana Cubillos, "Haiti Appeals for Global Help as Storms Leave Muddy Misery," *Rocky Mountain News*, September 29, 2008, p. 29.

11. For research on the relationship between "fate control" and risk perceptions, see Duane D. Baumann and John H. Sims, "Flood Insurance: Some Determinants of Adoption," *Economic Geography* 54 (1978):189–196. "Self-efficacy" impacted

the risk perceptions and evacuation behavior of Coloradoans threatened by wildfires in 2002; for example, see Charles Benight, Gruntfest, and Kelly Sparks, "Colorado Wildfires 2002," Quick Response Research Report #167 (Boulder, CO: Natural Hazards Research and Applications Information Center, 2004).

12. For elaboration of this perspective, see Enarson et al., *Social Vulnerability Approach*; Wisner, "Capitalism and the Shifting Spatial and Social Disruption of Hazard and Vulnerability," *Australian Journal of Emergency Management* 16 (2001):44–50; Wisner, Piers Blaikie, Terry Cannon, and Davis, *At Risk: Natural Hazards, People's Vulnerability and Disasters*, 2nd Ed. (New York: Routledge, 2005).

13. Perrow, *The Next Catastrophe: Reducing Our Vulnerabilities to Natural, Industrial and Terrorist Disasters* (Princeton, NJ: Princeton University Press, 2007), pp. 314–325.

14. Robert E. Hinshaw, *Living with Nature's Extremes: The Life of Gilbert Fowler White* (Boulder, CO: Johnson Books, 2006).

15. Ibid., p. 185.

16. For elaboration of this "social problems perspective" on disasters, see Kreps and Drabek, "Disasters are Nonroutine Social Problems," *International Journal of Mass Emergencies and Disasters* 14 (1996):129–153; Kreps, "Disasters, Sociology Of," in *Encyclopedia of the Social and Behavioral Sciences*, Eds. Neil J. Smelser and Paul B. Baltes Vol. 6 (Oxford, UK: Elsevier Science, 2001), pp. 3718–3721.

17. Elaboration of this perspective was a central theme in my critical assessment of the directions in which emergency management policy drifted during the George W. Bush Administration. See Drabek, *Social Problems Perspectives, Disaster Research and Emergency Management: Intellectual Contexts, Theoretical Extensions, and Policy Implications* (Revision and expansion of the E. L. Quarantelli Award lecture) (Emmitsburg, MD: Emergency Management Institute, Federal Emergency Management Agency, 2008) (Higher Education Project website) (accessed March 28, 2008, from http://training.fema.gov/EMIWeb/edu/highpapers.asp).

18. Examples of such textbooks include J. John Palen, *Social Problems for the Twenty-First Century* (New York: McGraw-Hill, 2001); Robert H. Lauer and Jeanette C. Lauer, *Social Problems and the Quality of Life* (New York: McGraw-Hill, 2006); Frank J. McVeigh and Loreen Wolfer, *Brief History of Social Problems: A Critical Thinking Approach* (Lanham, MD: University Press of America, Inc. 2004); Kenneth J. Neubeck, Mary Alice Neubeck, and David Silfen Glasberg, *Social Problems: A Critical Approach* (New York: McGraw-Hill, 2007). Ian Lustick documented how the policy focus on terrorism has been used to deflect public policy in subtle and undesired ways. See Lustick, "The War on Terror: When the Response Is the Catastrophe," in *Emergency Management in Higher Education: Current Practices and Conversations*, Ed. Jessica A. Hubbard (Fairfax, VA: Public Entity Risk Institute, 2008), pp. 73–98.

19. Example studies include Robert A. Papes, *Dying to Win: The Strategic Logic of Suicide Terrorism* (New York: Random House, 2005); Ami Pedhazur (Ed.), *Root Causes of Suicide Terrorism: The Globalization of Martyrdom* (London:

Routledge, 2006); Christoph Reuter, *My Life Is a Weapon: A Modern History of Suicide Bombing* (trans. H. Ragg-Kirby; Princeton, NJ: Princeton University Press, 2004).

20. Robert J. Brym, "Six Lessons of Suicide Bombers," *Contexts* 6 (Fall 2007):40–45.

21. *Ibid.*, p. 45.

22. Ibid. A White House sanctioned report emphasized the complexities in defining *terrorism*. Furthermore, "…root causes of one terrorist action may have little in common with those of another." Subcommittee on Social, Behavioral and Economic Sciences and the Social, Behavioral and Economic Sciences Working Group, National Science and Technology Council, *Combating Terrorism: Research Priorities in the Social, Behavioral and Economic Sciences* (Washington, D.C.: National Science and Technology Council by Executive Office of the President, 2005), p. 7. Hence, "…the concepts 'pro-' and 'anti-social' depend on one's perspective and acts that one group regards as anti-social may be regarded as pro-social by another" (ibid., p. 8).

23. Manuel Pastor, Robert D. Bullard, James K. Boyce, Fothergill, Rachel Morello-Frosch, and Beverly Wright, *In the Wake of the Storm: Environment, Disaster, and Race after Katrina* (New York: Russell Sage Foundation, 2006).

24. Ibid., p. 15.

25. Ibid., p. 2 in "Executive Summary."

26. Drabek and Quarantelli. "Scapegoats, Villains, and Disasters." *Trans-Action* 4 (March 1967):12–17. Following Hurricane Katrina, I applied this framework to question those blaming the evacuees who required rescue. See Drabek, "Don't Blame the Victims," *Journal of Emergency Management* 3 (November–December 2005):19–23.

27. Drabek and Quarantelli, "Scapegoats," p. 16.

28. For historical analyses of the evolution of professionalism within emergency management, see Jennifer L. Wilson and Arthur Oyola-Yemaiel, "An Emergency Management Profession: Will We Make It?" *Journal of the American Society of Professional Emergency Managers* 9 (2002):74–81; Drabek, "Evolution of Emergency Management;" William J. Petak, "Natural Hazard Mitigation: Professionalization of the Policy Making Process," *International Journal of Mass Emergencies and Disasters* 2 (1984):285–302; Lucien G. Canton, *Emergency Management: Concepts and Strategies for Effective Programs* (Hoboken, NJ: John Wiley & Sons, Inc., 2007).

29. For analysis of the lessons learned and research needs regarding comparative (cross-national) emergency management and disaster research, see McEntire and Mathis, "Comparative Politics and Disasters." See also Peacock, "Cross-National and Comparative Disaster Research."

30. As of 2008, more than 125 academic programs existed at colleges and universities throughout the United States, and 111 more were in varied stages of development. Blanchard, "FEMA Emergency Management, Higher Education Project Update," Presentation at the Emergency Management Higher Education Conference (Emmitsburg, MD: Emergency Management

Institute, FEMA, Department of Homeland Security, June 2008). Federal investments in research also may yield new knowledge that will need to be integrated into these academic programs. In addition to traditional funding sources like the National Science Foundation, National Institutes of Mental Health, and U.S. Geological Survey, "Centers of Excellence" have been funded to form university partnerships that will focus on issues of homeland security, including preparedness for and response to large-scale disasters. As of 2006, five such centers had been funded. For example, one award went to Johns Hopkins University ($15 million over three years), whose staff will partner with several Florida universities, the University of Alabama, and others. See *Natural Hazards Observer* 30, no. 4 (2006):7 or visit http://www.dhs.gov/centersofexcellence/.

31. For discussion of a future research agenda see Committee on Disaster Research in the Social Sciences: Future Challenges and Opportunities, *Facing Hazards and Disasters: Understanding Human Dimensions* (Washington, DC: National Academies Press, 2006).

32. Although there is some overlap and diversity in the occupational identities of members, the International Association of Emergency Managers (IAEM) largely reflects local emergency managers, whereas the National Emergency Management Association (NEMA) is limited to state directors of emergency management in the 50 states, territories, and the District of Columbia.

33. As was noted in Chapter 5, the 9/11 attacks spurred the creation of the Department of Homeland Security (DHS). The Federal Emergency Management Agency (FEMA) was transferred into that department. Following the response to Hurricane Katrina, the structural placement, mission, and funding levels for FEMA elicited much debate. As David Walker (comptroller general of the United States) noted in his testimony before the Senate Homeland Security and Governmental Affairs Committee, the reorganization presented challenges. For example, "...when Congress created DHS, it separated FEMA's responsibilities for preparedness and response activities into two directorates. Responsibility for preparedness for terrorism disasters was placed in the department's Border and Transportation Security Directorate, which included FEMA's Office of National Preparedness. Other types of FEMA disaster preparedness and response efforts were transferred to the department's Emergency Preparedness and Response Directorate." Walker, "Hurricane Katrina: GAO's Preliminary Observations Regarding Preparedness, Response, and Recovery," Testimony before the Senate Homeland Security and Governmental Affairs Committee (March 8, 2006), p. 29. Walker noted that other organizational changes were being considered and that the White House report on Katrina stipulated that FEMA should remain within DHS: "If FEMA were to become independent of DHS, then a comprehensive approach to preparedness, response, and recovery may become even more difficult to maintain" (ibid.). In direct contrast, Senator Barbara Mikulski recommended, in no uncertain terms, that the key lesson from Katrina was the need to correct a mistake: "I voted for that change [i.e.,

to move FEMA into the DHS], but FEMA has lost its way.... FEMA must again become an independent agency...." Mikulski, "Hurricane Katrina Recommendations for Reform," Testimony before the Senate Homeland Security and Governmental Affairs Committee (March 8, 2006), p. 3. More recently (November 19, 2008), the IAEM's leadership formally adopted the policy position that FEMA should "...be restored to its former status as an independent agency reporting directly to the President." "IAEM—USA Calls for Restoring FEMA to Independent Agency Status," *IAEM Bulletin*, 25 (December 2008):5. The group further recommended that the head of FEMA should be a member of the President's Cabinet.

34. For a social history of the adoption and implementation of microcomputer into local and state emergency management offices, see Drabek, *Microcomputers in Emergency Management: Implementation of Computer Technology* (Boulder: Institute of Behavioral Science, University of Colorado, 1991).

35. Information technologies most relevant to emergency management have been summarized by Cutter, Christopher T. Emrich, Beverley J. Adams, Charles K. Huyck, and Ronald T. Eguchi, "New Information Technologies in Emergency Management," in *Emergency Management: Principles and Practice for Local Government*, 2nd ed., Ed. William L. Waugh Jr. and Kathleen Tierney (Washington, DC: International City/County Management Association, 2007), pp. 279–297. See also Nicole Dash, "The Use of Geographic Information Systems In Disaster Research," in Stallings, *Methods of Disaster Research* (ch. 2, note 39), pp. 320–333; Gruntfest and Weber, "Internet and Emergency Management;" Robin Stephenson and Peter S. Anderson, "Disasters and the Information Technology Revolution," *Disasters: The Journal of Disaster Studies and Management* 21 (1997):305–334.

36. Department of Homeland Security (DHS), "New On-Line Independent Study Course Announcement," (EMIGRAM #622) (Washington, DC: DHS, January 6, 2005). For detailed discussion of the "Incident Command System" (ICS) and its limitations, plus other concepts like the "National Incident Management System" (NIMS) see McEntire, *Disaster Response and Recovery* (New York: John Wiley, 2007), pp. 325–346. For detailed explanation, see DHS, *National Response Framework* (Washington, DC: DHS, 2008). See also Bullock, Haddow, Damon Coppola, Endem Ergin, Lissa Westerman, and Sarp Yeletaysi, *Introduction to Homeland Security* (Burlington, MA: Elsevier Butterworth-Heinemann, 2005); McEntire, *Introduction to Homeland Security*.

37. The directive was titled "Direction and Control of Emergencies in the City of New York:" "Its purpose was to eliminate 'potential conflict among responding agencies which may have areas of overlapping expertise and responsibility.'" National Commission on Terrorist Attacks, *9/11 Commission Report*, pp. 284–285. The behavioral reality following the WTC attacks, however, was that "...the [Fire Department of the City of New York] FDNY and [New York Police Department] NYPD each considered itself operationally

autonomous. As of September 11, they were not prepared to comprehensively coordinate their efforts in responding to a major incident" (ibid., p. 285).

38. Several sociologists have reviewed the 9/11 Commission Report and generally have commended the members and staff for their efforts; for example, "The staff was incredible, this is top notch research." Perrow, "Organizational or Executive Failures," *Contemporary Sociology: A Journal of Reviews* 34 (2005):99. Despite the accolades, various flaws were emphasized. Perrow, for example, accepted the conclusion of the commission that there were "massive organizational failures." He proposed, however, that remedies cannot be found through analyses limited to operational and managerial failures. Rather, executive failure must be acknowledged explicitly. A change at the executive level "...will only come about through the democratic process of either electing a new leader who brings in a new top management team and focus, or assigning blame so thoroughly that public pressure forces the executive behavior to change despite its mindset or ideology" (ibid., p. 107). Two other reviews that comprised *Contemporary Sociology*'s "Symposium on the 9/11 Commission Report" focused on other points of criticism. David M. Mednicoff, "Compromising Toward Confusion: *The 9/11 Commission Report and American Policy in the Middle East*," *Contemporary Sociology: A Journal of Reviews* 34 (2005):107–115; Tierney, "The 9/11 Commission and Disaster Management: Little Depth, Less Context, Not Much Guidance," *Contemporary Sociology: A Journal of* Reviews 34 (2005):115–121.

39. U.S. White House, *Federal Response to Hurricane Katrina*, p. 2.

40. Ibid., p. 66.

41. Select Bipartisan Committee, *Failure of Initiative*, p. 359.

42. U.S. White House, *Federal Response to Hurricane Katrina*, p. 66.

43. Ibid., pp. 66–67.

44. Ibid., p. 71.

45. Ibid., p. 79.

46. Ibid.

47. Ibid.

48. Ibid., p. 81.

49. Ibid.

50. Bruce Gaughman, "Hurricane Katrina: Recommendations for Reform," Testimony presented before the Senate Homeland Security and Governmental Affairs Committee (March 8, 2006).

51. Ibid., pp. 1–2.

52. Ibid., p. 3.

53. Ibid., p. 4. In 2008, FEMA officials introduced a new planning paradigm, the "Integrated Planning System" (IPS). This "scenario-based" system parallels the traditional military model rather than the risk-based approach reflected within comprehensive emergency management. For details see Larry J. Gispert, "Remain Vigilant Concerning New U.S. Integrated Planning System," *IAEM Bulletin* 25 (June 2008):2.

54. Gaughman, "Hurricane Katrina." The role of the military was among the many points of conflict during the response to Hurricane Katrina. After receiving a memo from the Bush Administration, Louisiana governor Kathleen Blanco refused to accept a proposed federalization of state law enforcement. Her refusal reflected the 1878 Posse Comitatus Act, which prohibits federal military personnel from performing civilian law enforcement unless approved for specific emergencies: "...the Posse Comitatus Act was passed specifically to address the frustrations of the South over the extended federal military presence after the Civil War.... Bush might have been risking not only the ire of Democrats...[but also]...some conservative Republicans who viewed themselves as patriotic Southerners." Vicki Bier, "Hurricane Katrina as a Bureaucratic Nightmare," in *On Risk and Disaster: Lessons From Hurricane Katrina*, Ed. Ronald J. Daniels, Donald F. Kettl, and Howard Kunreuther (Philadelphia: University of Pennsylvania Press, 2006), p. 251.

The Senate report (See Ch. 4, note 21) on Katrina also documented many of the tensions between Governor Blanco's office and officials within the Bush Administration. Review of several substantive footnotes reveals the details of the tensions based on documents and testimony obtained by committee. For example, see notes 154, 156, and 163 at the end of Chapter 25 and notes 488 through 577. Committee on Homeland Security, *Hurricane Katrina,* Chapter 25, pp. 31–32 and Chapter 26, pp. 93–98. The report also documented how "DOD culture" may have been a factor in delays in meeting assistance requests. See ibid., Chapter 26, pp. 19–20. Haley Barbour, governor of the State of Mississippi, also testified regarding this tension: "I made it very plain from day one that we didn't ...need the federal government to run our National Guard" (ibid., Chapter 26, p. 98).

55. John Streicker, "Climate Change—The Global Effects," *Encyclopaedia Britannica 2008 Book of the Year* (Chicago: Encyclopaedia Britannica, Inc., 2008), p. 173.

56. Popular media accounts may leave you wondering at times about climate change and its impacts. Much recent evidence now documents the politicalization of many research reports during recent years. For example, see Committee on Oversight and Government Reform, U.S. House of Representatives, *Political Interference with Climate Change Science under the Bush Administration* (Washington, DC: U.S. House of Representatives, December, 2007). Examples of "anti-global warming" statements include Arthur B. Robinson, Noah E. Robinson, and Willie Soon, "Environmental Effects of Increased Atmospheric Carbon Dioxide," *Journal of American Physicians and Surgeons* 12 (2007):79–90; Physicians for Civil Defense, "Is the Science Settled?" *Civil Defense Perspectives* 24, no. 4 (2008):1. For a balanced analysis of the implications of global warming for emergency managers, see George D. Haddow, Jane A. Bullock, and Kim Haddow, *Global Warming, Natural Hazards, and Emergency Management* (Boca Raton, FL: CRC Press, 2008).

57. Gary Hart's analysis of Homeland Security policy wherein he calls for major redirections is consistent with my view as is the position of Al Gore regarding erosion of civil liberties. See Hart, *The Shield and the Cloak: The Security of the Commons* (New York: Oxford University Press, 2006); Hart, *Under the Eagle's Wing: National Security Strategy of the United States for 2009* (Boulder, CO: Fulcrum Publishing, 2008); Al Gore, *The Assault as Reason* (New York: Penguin Press, 2007). See also Lustick, *Trapped in the War on Terror* (Philadelphia: University of Pennsylvania Press, 2006). A recent review of FEMA's progress since Katrina (2005) in handling a catastrophic disaster documented a mixed picture. Staff members of the Office of Inspector General identified nine areas critical to a successful response. In consultation with FEMA staff, two to five components were identified for each of these. The conclusion? "Moderate progress" had been made in five areas, "modest progress" in three, and "limited progress" in one. Various constraints ranging from budget shortfalls to reorganizations were noted by FEMA personnel regarding this mixed record of agency improvement since the failings in the Katrina response. For details, see Office of Inspector General, *FEMA's Preparedness for the Next Catastrophic Disaster* (Washington, DC: Office of Inspector General, DHS, 2008).

58. Robert Carl Schehr's criticism of the analysis of the U.S. Patriot Act by Amitai Etzioni is very helpful in pointing out the roles played by politically conservative organizations and individuals in the creation of this legislation. See Schehr, "The Marginalizing Rhetoric of Nationalism," *Contemporary Sociology* 34, no. 6 (2005):602–605; Etzioni, *How Patriotic Is the Patriot Act?: Freedom versus Security in the Age of Terrorism* (New York: Routledge, 2004).

59. Jeff Stein, "Fine Print in Defense Bill Opens Door to Martial Law," *CQ Homeland Security* (12/1/06) (accessed April 4, 2007, from http://public.cq.com/public/20061201_homeland.htm). In a review of the history and statutory authorities related to martial law, Relyea concluded: "Since the conclusion of World War II, martial law has not been presidentially directed or approved for any area of the United States. Federal troops have been dispatched to domestic locales experiencing unrest or riot, but in these situations the military has remained subordinate to federal civilian management." Relyea, *Martial Law*, p. 4.

60. National Governors' Association, *Comprehensive Emergency Management*. For a brief history of FEMA's "transitions" from the time of creation in 1979 to its merger into the DHS, see Richard Sylves and William R. Cumming, "FEMA's Path to Homeland Security: 1979–2003," *Journal of Homeland Security and Emergency Management* 1, no. 2 (2004):1–21 (Article 11). See also the testimony of Mikulski, "Hurricane Katrina Recommendations," regarding the congressional view of the role and mission of FEMA upon its creation in 1979 and following the response to Hurricane Andrew (see ch. 11, note 33).

61. David McLoughlin, "A Framework for Integrated Emergency Management," *Public Administration Review* 45 (1985):165–172. For elaborations on the implementation of community emergency planning (CEM) at the local level, see Lindell and Perry, *Behavioral Foundations of Community Emergency Planning*

(Washington, DC: Hemisphere Publishing Corporation, 1992), pp. 53–77. See also Lindell, Carla S. Prater, and Perry, *Introduction to Emergency Management* (Hoboken, NJ: John Wiley & Sons, 2007). For federal level emphasis, see Haddow and Bullock, *Introduction to Emergency Management*.

62. McLoughlin, "Framework for Integrated Emergency Management," p. 170.

63. Drabek, *Emergency Management: Strategies;* Drabek, *Strategies for Coordinating*.

64. Concerns about the implementation of ICS as "the model" for local emergency managers have been raised by several scholars dating back to an early article by Dennis E. Wenger, Quarantelli, and Dynes, "Is the Incident Command System a Plan for All Seasons and Emergency Situations?" *Hazard Monthly* 10 (1990):8–9,12. More recently, in their assessments of the failed Katrina response others have raised additional concerns. For example, Herman Leonard and Arnold Howitt proposed that technical aspects of a disaster response might be managed by the ICS but not the political. See Leonard and Howitt, "Katrina As Prelude: Preparing for and Responding to Future Katrina-Class Disturbances in the United States," Testimony before the U.S. Senate Homeland Security and Governmental Affairs Committee (March 8, 2006), p. 11. See also Hussein H. Soliman, "An Organizational and Culturally Sensitive Approach to Managing Air-Traffic Disaster: The Gulf Air Incident," *International Journal of Mass Emergencies and Disasters* 23, no. 2 (2005):75–95; Handmer, "American Exceptionalism or Universal Lesson? The Implications of Hurricane Katrina for Australia," *Australian Journal of Emergency Management* 21, no. 1 (2006):29–40; Neil Simon, "Part 1: Social Dimensions of Interagency Collaboration," *Journal of Emergency Management* 4, no. 1 (2006):13–16; David M. Neal and John Gaete, "The Use of Incident Command During Hurricane Katrina," *Natural Hazard Observer* 30, no. 1 (2006):8–9; Saundra K. Schneider, "The Disastrous Response to Hurricane Katrina: Blame It on the Bureaucracy?" in Hubbard, *Emergency Management in Higher Education* (ch. 11, note 18), pp. 113–132.

65. Drabek, *Professional Emergency Manager,* pp. 143–169. My emphasis on increased community resilience through more active citizen involvement is consistent with the views of others. For example, see Redlener, *Americans at Risk: Why We Are Not Prepared for Megadisasters and What We Can Do Now* (New York: Alfred A. Knopf/Random House, 2006); Stephen E. Flynn, *The Edge of Disaster: Rebuilding a Resilient Nation* (New York: Random House, 2007).

66. Drabek, *Emergency Management: Strategies,* pp. 69–70. For an extended discussion of frameworks, rationale, and specific mitigation strategies, see Pine, *Natural Hazards Analysis: Reducing the Impact of Disasters* (Boca Raton, FL: Auerbach/Taylor & Francis Group, 2008).

67. Ibid., pp. 133–135.

68. Drabek, *Disaster Evacuation*, pp. 71–100. Only 28% of the 185 tourist businesses I studied had a written disaster plan (see Table 4.1, p. 94).

69. "Disaster Preparedness Strategies for Small Business," Office Depot, Inc., 2008 (accessed July 18, 2008, from http://www.officedepot.com/a/promo/disaster/main/;jsessionid=000VJWaagV0CBREmZEV5z-5Wx1:...).

70. Drabek, *Strategies for Coordinating Emergency Responses*, pp. 69–78. As detailed in my book, I discovered that the typology of strategic choice developed by David Osborne and Peter Plastrik fit the emergency management function. See Osborne and Plastrik, *Banishing Bureaucracy: The Five Strategies for Reinventing Government* (New York: Plume, 1998).

71. Drabek, *Strategies for Coordinating Emergency Responses*, pp. 78–85.

72. Ibid., pp. 85–94.

73. Ibid., pp. 94–106.

74. See ch. 11, note 64 and the summaries presented in the U.S. White House, *Federal Response to Hurricane Katrina*. (ch. 11, note 44) and U.S. Comptroller General Walker's testimony, Walker, "Hurricane Katrina" (ch. 11, note 33).

75. Drabek, *Strategies for Coordinating Emergency Responses*, p. 101. I interpret Donald Moynihan's comparative analysis of the use of ICS in four disasters as validation of my conclusions: (1) Wild land-urban fires, Southern California, 1993 and 2003; (2) Oklahoma City bombing, 1995; (3) Pentagon attack, September 11, 2001; and (4) Hurricane Katrina, 2005. He noted, "In the thousands of pages of frequently scathing criticism that Senate, House, and White House reports directed toward the Katrina response, none of them questioned the basic wisdom of applying the ICS model." Moynihan, *From Forest Fires to Hurricane Katrina: Case Studies of Incident Command Systems* (Madison: IBM Center for the Business of Government, University of Wisconsin, 2007), p. 38. Since ICS will be used, he recommended awareness of these qualifications: "The first is that events may be moving so rapidly that a central command cannot keep up and therefore needs to be willing to allow independent action, as we saw in the wild land-urban fires. Another contingency is that if a network is not working or lacks capacity, incident commanders may seek to exert authority but find little response among subordinates. A final contingency is that incident commanders should be willing to opportunistically expand the network to include unanticipated members who offer resources that the existing network lacks" (ibid.). See also Moynihan, *Leveraging Collaborative Networks in Infrequent Emergency Situations* (Madison: IBM Center for the Business of Government, University of Wisconsin–Madison, 2005).

76. Drabek, *Strategies for Coordinating Emergency Responses*, pp. 106–121.

77. Dynes, "Community Emergency Planning." See also Neal and Phillips, "Effective Emergency Management: Reconsidering the Bureaucratic Approach," *Disasters: The Journal of Disaster Studies, Policy, and Management* 19 (1995):327–337.

78. A committee of knowledgeable experts identified eight core principles required for emergency management programs: (1) comprehensive; (2) progressive; (3) risk driven; (4) integrated; (5) collaborative; (6) coordinated; (7) flexible; and (8) professional. See Principles of Emergency Management

Working Group, "Emergency Management: Definition, Vision, Mission, Principles," in Hubbard, *Emergency Management in Higher Education* (ch. 11, note 18), p. 9.

79. Jim Faull, "Tornado Tests Town's Mettle," *Colorado Sheriff* 28, no. 1 (2007):9. Note that I would expand on Faull's analysis, however, by deleting the qualifier "natural" and explicitly recognizing that as the scope of the disaster increases outside aid may be delayed. For elaboration on this point see Lee Clarke, *Worst Cases: Terror and Catastrophe in the Popular Imagination* (Chicago, IL: University of Chicago Press, 2006).

80. Clarke, "Postscript: Considering Katrina," in Brunsma et al., *Sociology of Katrina* (ch. 2, note 40), p. 237.

81. Ibid.

82. Ibid.

83. Chester Hartman and Gregory D. Squires (Eds.), *There Is No Such Thing as a Natural Disaster: Race, Class, and Hurricane Katrina* (New York: Routledge, 2006). Additionally, see Perrow, *Next Catastrophe*, especially pp. 108–119; J. Steven Picou and B. Marshall, "Introduction: Katrina as Paradigm Shift."

84. For a more detailed and formal analysis of philosophical positions inherent in emergency management policy, see Timothy Beatley, "Towards a Moral Philosophy of Natural Disaster Mitigation," *International Journal of Mass Emergencies and Disasters* 7 (1989):5–32. See also Robert O. Schneider, "Principles of Ethics for Emergency Management," *Journal of Emergency Management* 4, no. 1 (2006):56–62.

85. Related to this issue is the matter of program and policy evaluation. That is, to what degree is a policy once implemented, at all cost-effective? I suspect that many criticisms of this type will be made regarding many homeland security initiatives. Veronique de Rugy concluded, for example, that "… economics suggests that if homeland security spending decisions are made on a political basis rather than on a sound cost benefit analysis, it will lead to the traditional public choice failures that plague government spending more generally. As a result, homeland security funding is likely to be misallocated….." de Rugy, "What Does Homeland Security Spending Buy?" AEI Working Paper #107 (Washington, DC: American Enterprise Institute for Public Policy Research, 2004), p. 1.

86. Diamond, *Collapse*, p. 516.

SUGGESTED READINGS

This short list of books is very selective. Serious readers are urged to review the Notes section for additional items. Extensive bibliographies appear in *Social Dimensions of Disaster* (Drabek, 2004) and the *Handbook of Disaster Research* (Rodríguez, Quarantelli, and Dynes, 2006). Three criteria guided selection: (1) current (i.e., published 2000 or later); (2) book length (i.e., no journal articles); and (3) general content (i.e., specialized or highly technical books were excluded).

Akin, Wallace. *The Forgotten Storm: The Great Tri-State Tornado of 1925*. Gilford, CT: The Lyons Press, 2002.

Altheide, David L. *Terrorism and the Politics of Fear*. Lanham, MD: AltaMira Press, 2006.

Anderson, Allen and Linda Anderson. *Rescued—Saving Animals from Disaster: Life-Changing Stories and Practical Suggestions*. Novato, CA: New World Library, 2006.

Barry, John M. *The Great Influenza: The Epic Story of the Deadliest Plague in History*. New York: Penguin Books, 2005.

Bates, Kristin A. and Richelle S. Swan (Eds.). *Through the Eye of Katrina: Social Justice in the United States*. Durham, NC: Carolina Academic Press, 2007.

Benjamin, Daniel and Steven Simmon. *The Age of Sacred Terror*. New York: Random House Trade Paperbacks, 2003.

Bennett, Brian T. *Understanding, Assessing, and Responding to Terrorism: Protecting Critical Infrastructure and Personnel*. Hoboken, NJ: John Wiley & Sons, Inc., 2007.

Birkland, Thomas A. *Lessons of Disaster: Policy Change after Catastrophic Events*. Washington, DC: Georgetown University Press, 2006.

Bongar, Bruce, Lisa M. Brown, Larry E. Beutler, James N. Breckenridge, and Philip G. Zimbardo (Eds.). *Psychology of Terrorism*. New York: Oxford University Press, Inc., 2007.

Brinkley, Douglas. *The Great Deluge: Hurricane Katrina, New Orleans, and the Mississippi Gulf Coast*. New York: Harper Collins Publishers (William Morrow), 2006.

Brunsma, David L., David Overfelt, and J. Steven Picou (Eds.). *The Sociology of Katrina: Perspectives on the Modern Catastrophe*. Lanham, MD: Rowman Littlefield Publishers, 2007.

Bullock, Jane, George D. Haddow, Damon Coppola, Endem Ergin, Lissa Westerman, and Sarp Yeletaysi. *Introduction to Homeland Security*. Burlington, MA: Elsevier Butterworth-Heinemann, 2005.

Burlakova, Elena B. and Valeria I. Naidich (Eds.). *20 Years After the Chernobyl Accident: Past, Present and Future.* New York: Nova Science Publishers, Inc., 2006.

Canton, Lucien G. *Emergency Management: Concepts and Strategies for Effective Programs.* Hoboken, NJ: John Wiley & Sons, Inc., 2007.

Carll, Elizabeth K. and Chris E. Stout. *Violence and Disaster.* Westport, CT: Praeger, 2007.

Clarke, Lee. *Worst Cases: Terror and Catastrophe in the Popular Imagination.* Chicago, IL: University of Chicago Press, 2006.

Committee on Disaster Research in the Social Sciences. *Facing Hazards and Disasters: Understanding Human Dimensions.* Washington, DC: National Academics Press, 2006.

Committee on Homeland Security and Governmental Affairs. *Hurricane Katrina: A Nation Still Unprepared.* Washington, DC: United States Senate, 2006.

Corales, Thomas A. (Ed.). *Focus on Posttraumatic Stress Disorder Research.* Hauppauge, New York: Nova Science Publishers, Inc., 2005.

Cotton, William R. and Roger A. Pielke. *Human Impacts on Weather and Climate.* New York: Cambridge University Press, 2007.

Cummins, Joseph (Ed.). *The Greatest Search and Rescue Stories Ever Told.* Gilford, CT: Lyons Press, 2002.

Daniel, Terry C., Matthew S. Carroll, Cassandra Moseley, and Carol Raish (Eds.). *People, Fire and Forests: A Synthesis of Wildfire Social Science.* Corvallis: Oregon State University Press, 2007.

Daniels, Ronald J., Donald F. Kettl, and Howard Kunreuther (Eds.). *On Risk and Disaster: Lessons from Hurricane Katrina.* Philadelphia: University of Pennsylvania Press, 2006.

Department of Homeland Security. *National Response Framework.* Washington, DC: Department of Homeland Security, 2008.

Diamond, Jared. *Collapse: How Societies Choose to Fail or Succeed.* New York: Viking, The Penguin Group, 2005.

Drabek, Thomas E. *Strategies for Coordinating Disaster Responses.* Boulder: Institute of Behavioral Science, University of Colorado, 2003.

Drabek, Thomas E. *Social Dimensions of Disaster* (2nd ed.). Emmitsburg, MD: Emergency Management Institute, Federal Emergency Management Agency, 2004.

Drabek, Thomas E. *Social Problems Perspectives, Disaster Research and Emergency Management: Intellectual Contexts, Theoretical Extensions, and Policy Implications.* (Revision and expansion of the E. L. Quarantelli Award lecture). Emmitsburg, MD: Emergency Management Institute, Federal Emergency Management Agency [Higher Education Project website], 2008. Accessed March 28, 2008, from http://training.fema.gov/EMIWeb/edu/highpapers.asp.

Durmaz, Huseyin, Bilal Sevinc, Ahmet Sait Yayla, and Siddik Ekici. *Understanding and Responding to Terrorism.* Fairfax, VA: IOS Press, 2007.

Enarson, Elaine, Cheryl Childers, Betty Hearn Morrow, Deborah Thomas, and Ben Wisner. *A Social Vulnerability Approach to Disasters.* Emmitsburg, MD: Emergency Management Institute, Federal Emergency Management Agency, 2003.

Etzioni, Amitai. *How Patriotic Is the Patriot Act?: Freedom Versus Security in the Age of Terrorism*. New York: Routledge, 2004.

Flannery, Tim. *The Weather Makers: The History and Future Impact of Climate Change*. New York: Atlantic Monthly Press, 2006.

Flynn, Stephen E. *The Edge of Disaster: Rebuilding a Resilient Nation*. New York: Random House, 2007.

Fothergill, Alice. *Heads above Water: Gender, Class, and Family in the Grand Forks Flood*. Albany: State University of New York Press, 2004.

Fradkin, Philip L. *The Great Earthquake and Firestorms of 1906: How San Francisco Nearly Destroyed Itself*. Berkeley: University of California Press, 2006.

Gess, Denise and William Lutz. *Firestorm at Peshtigo: A Town, Its People, and the Deadliest Fire in American History*. New York: Henry Holt and Company, 2002.

Giroux, Henry A. *Stormy Weather: Katrina and the Politics of Disposability*. Boulder, CO: Paradigm Publishers, 2006.

Gunn, Angus M. *Encyclopedia of Disasters: Environmental Catastrophes and Human Tragedies* (2 volumes). Westport, CT: Greenwood Press, Inc., 2008.

Haddow, George D. and Jane A. Bullock. *Introduction to Emergency Management*. Burlington, MA: Elsevier Butterworth-Heinemann, 2008.

Haddow, George D., Jane A. Bullock, and Kim Haddow. *Global Warming, Natural Hazards, and Emergency Management*. Boca Raton, FL: CRC Press, 2009.

Hart, Gary. *The Shield and the Cloak: The Security of the Commons*. New York: Oxford University Press, 2007.

Hartley, Robert E and David Kenney. *Death Underground: The Centralia and West Frankfort Mine Disasters*. Carbondale: Southern Illinois University Press, 2006.

Hartman, Chester and Gregory D. Squires (Eds.). *There Is No Such Thing As a Natural Disaster: Race, Class, and Hurricane Katrina*. New York: Routledge, 2006.

Horne, Jed. *Breach of Faith: Hurricane Katrina and the Near Death of a Great American City*. New York: Random House, 2006.

Howard, Russell D., James J. F. Forest, and Joanne Moore. *Homeland Security and Terrorism: Readings and Interpretations*. New York: McGraw-Hill, 2006.

Hubbard, Jessica A. *Emergency Management in Higher Education: Current Practices and Conversations*. Fairfax, VA: Public Entity Risk Institute, 2008.

Jenkins, John W. *Colorado Avalanche Disasters: An Untold Story of the Old West*. Ouray, CO: Western Reflections Publishing Company, 2001.

Jenkins, Philip. *Images of Terror: What We Can and Can't Know About Terrorism*. New York: Aldine deGruyter, 2003.

Jones, Ray and Joe Lubow. *Disasters and Heroic Rescues of California*. Guilford, CT: Morris Book Publishing, 2006.

Klineberg, Eric. *Heatwave: A Social Autopsy of Disaster in Chicago*. Chicago: University of Chicago Press, 2002.

Larson, Erik. *Isaac's Storm*. New York: Vintage Books, 2000.

289

Larson, Gregory, Vita Wright, Cade Spaulding, Kelly Rossetto, Georgi Rausch, Andree Richards, et al. *Using Social Science to Understand and Improve Wildland Fire Organizations: An Annotated Reading List.* (Gen. Tech. Rep. RMRS-GTR-201). Fort Collins, CO: Rocky Mountain Research Station, Forest Service, U.S. Department of Agriculture, 2007.

Laws, Eric, Bruce Prideaux, and Kaye Chon. *Crisis Management in Tourism.* Wellingford, Oxon, UK: CAB International, 2007.

Lindell, Michael K. and Ronald W. Perry. *Communicating Environmental Risk in Multiethnic Communities.* Thousand Oaks, CA: Sage Publications, 2004.

Lindell, Michael K., Carla S. Prater, and Ronald W. Perry. *Introduction to Emergency Management.* Hoboken, NJ: John Wiley & Sons, 2007.

Lustick, Ian S. *Trapped in the War on Terror.* Philadelphia: University of Pennsylvania Press, 2006.

MacDonald, Laura M. *Curse of the Narrows.* New York: Walker and Company, 2005.

Maclean, John N. *Fire and Ashes: On the Front Lines of American Wildfire.* New York: Henry Holt and Company, 2003.

Mawson, Anthony R. *Mass Panic and Social Attachment: The Dynamics of Human Behavior.* Aldershot, UK: Ashgate, 2007.

McEntire, David A. *Introduction to Homeland Security: Understanding Terrorism with an Emergency Management Perspective.* New York: John Wiley & Sons, Inc., 2009.

McEntire, David A. (Ed.). *Disciplines, Disasters and Emergency Management: The Convergence and Divergence of Concepts, Issues and Trends in the Research Literature.* Springfield, IL: Charles C. Thomas Publishers, 2008.

McEntire, David A. *Disaster Response and Recovery.* Hoboken, NJ: John Wiley & Sons, 2007.

McQuaid, John and Mark Schleifstein. *Path of Destruction: The Devastation of New Orleans and the Coming Age of Superstorms.* New York: Little, Brown and Company, 2006.

Moynihan, Donald P. *Leveraging Collaborative Networks in Infrequent Emergency Situations.* Madison: IBM Center for the Business of Government, University of Wisconsin–Madison, 2005.

Moynihan, Donald P. *From Forest Fires to Hurricane Katrina: Case Studies of Incident Command Systems.* Madison, WI: IBM Center for the Business of Government, 2007.

Murty, Tad S., U. Aswathanarayana, and Niru Nirupama (Eds.). *The Indian Ocean Tsunami.* New York: Taylor & Francis Group, 2007.

National Commission on Terrorist Attacks Upon the United States. *The 9/11 Commission Report.* New York: W.W. Norton, 2004.

Neal, David M. *Disaster Response: Principles and Practice.* Boca Raton, FL: CRC Press, forthcoming.

Neff, Thomas. *Holding Out and Hanging On: Surviving Hurricane Katrina.* Columbia: University of Missouri Press, 2007.

Nicholson, William C. *Emergency Response and Emergency Management Law: Cases and Materials.* Springfield, IL: Charles C. Thomas Publishers, 2003.

Noble, Dennis L. *The Rescue of the Gale Runner: Death, Heroism, and the U.S. Coast Guard.* Gainesville: University Press of Florida, 2008.

O'Leary, Margaret (Ed.). *The First 72 Hours: A Community Approach to Disaster Preparedness.* New York: iUniverse, Inc., 2004.

Papes, Robert A. *Dying To Win: The Strategic Logic of Suicide Terrorism.* New York: Random House, 2005.

Parry, Martin, Osvaldo G. Canziani, Jean Palutikof, Paul van der Linden, and Clair Hanson (Eds.). *Climate Change 2007: Impacts, Adaptation, and Vulnerability.* New York: Cambridge University Press, 2007.

Pastor, Manuel, Robert D. Bullard, James K. Boyce, Alice Fothergill, Rachel Morello-Frosch, and Beverly Wright. *In the Wake of the Storm: Environment, Disaster, and Race after Katrina.* New York: Russell Sage Foundation, 2006.

Perrow, Charles. *The Next Catastrophe: Reducing Our Vulnerabilities to Natural, Industrial and Terrorist Disasters.* Princeton, NJ: Princeton University Press, 2007.

Perry, Ronald W. and Michael K. Lindell. *Emergency Planning.* Hoboken, NJ: John Wiley & Sons, Inc., 2007.

Perry, Ronald W. and E. L. Quarantelli (Eds.). *What Is a Disaster? New Answers to Old Questions.* Philadelphia, PA: Xlibris Corporation, 2005.

Phillips, Brenda. *Disaster Recovery.* Boca Raton, FL: CRC Press, forthcoming.

Phillips, Brenda, Cheryl Childers, Ann Fothergill, and Deborah Thomas. *Social Vulnerability to Disasters.* Boca Raton, FL: CRC Press, forthcoming.

Phillips, Brenda D. and Betty Hearn Morrow. *Women and Disasters: From Theory to Practice.* Philadelphia, PA: Xlibris Corporation, 2008.

Pine, John. *Natural Hazards Analysis: Reducing the Impact of Disasters.* Boca Raton, FL: Auerbach/Taylor & Francis Group, 2008.

Potter, Hillary (Ed.). *Racing the Storm: Racial Implications and Lessons Learned from Hurricane Katrina.* Lanham, MD: Lexington Books, 2007.

Punke, Michael. *Fire and Brimstone: The North Butte Mining Disaster of 1917.* New York: Hyperion, 2006.

Rarick, Ethan. *Desperate Passage: The Donner Party's Perilous Journey West.* New York: Oxford University Press, 2008.

Redlener, Irwin. *Americans at Risk: Why We Are Not Prepared for Megadisasters and What We Can Do Now.* New York: Alfred A. Knopf/Random House, 2006.

Ripley, Amanda. *The Unthinkable: Who Survives When Disaster Strikes—and Why.* New York: Crown Publishers, 2008.

Rodríguez, Havidán, Enrico L. Quarantelli, and Russell R. Dynes (Eds.). *Handbook of Disaster Research.* New York: Springer, 2006.

Rubin, Claire B. (Ed.). *Emergency Management: The American Experience 1900–2005.* Washington, DC: Public Entity Risk Institute, 2007.

Schwartz-Barcott, T. P. *After the Disaster: Re-creating Community and Well-Being at Buffalo Creek since the Notorious Coal-Mining Disaster in 1972.* Amherst, MA: Cambria Press, 2008.

Scott, Cathy. *Pawprints of Katrina: Pets Saved and Lessons Learned.* Hoboken, NJ: John Wiley & Sons, Inc., 2008.

Select Bipartisan Committee to Investigate the Preparation for and Response to Hurricane Katrina, U.S. House of Representatives. *A Failure of Initiative: Final Report.* Washington, DC: U.S. Government Printing Office, 2006.

Stallings, Robert A. (Ed.). *Methods of Disaster Research*. Philadelphia, PA: Xlibris Corporation, 2002.

Staudt, Amanda, Nancy Huddleston, and Ian Kraucunas. *Understanding and Responding to Climate Change: Highlights of National Academies Reports*. Washington, DC: National Research Council, National Academies of Sciences, 2008.

Subcommittee on Social, Behavioral and Economic Sciences and the Social, Behavioral and Economic Sciences Working Group, National Science and Technology Council. *Combating Terrorism: Research Priorities in the Social, Behavioral and Economic Sciences*. Washington, DC: National Science and Technology Council, Executive Office of the President, 2005.

U.S. Government Accountability Office. *Disaster Recovery: Past Experiences Offer Insights for Recovering from Hurricanes Ike and Gustav and Other Recent Natural Disasters*. (Report to the Committee on Homeland Security and Governmental Affairs, U.S. Senate). Washington, DC: U.S. Government Accountability Office, 2008.

Ursano, Robert J., Carol S. Fullerton, Lars Weisaeth, and Beverley Raphael (Eds.). *Textbook of Disaster Psychiatry*. Cambridge, UK: Cambridge University Press, 2007.

Waugh, William L., Jr. *Living with Hazards, Dealing with Disasters: An Introduction to Emergency Management*. Armonk, NY: M.E. Sharpe, Inc., 2000.

Waugh, William L., Jr. *Terrorism and Emergency Management: Instructor Guide*. Emmitsburg, MD: Emergency Management Institute, Federal Emergency Management Agency, 2000.

Waugh, William L., Jr. *Terrorism and Weapons of Mass Destruction*. Boca Raton, FL: CRC Press, forthcoming.

Waugh, William L., Jr. and Kathleen Tierney (Eds.). *Emergency Management: Principles and Practice for Local Government* (2nd ed.). Washington, DC: International City Management Association Press, 2007.

White House, The. *The Federal Response to Hurricane Katrina: Lessons Learned*. Washington, DC: The White House, 2006.

Wisner, Ben, Piers Blaikie, Terry Cannon, and Ian Davis. *At Risk: Natural Hazards, People's Vulnerability, and Disasters* (2nd ed.). London: Routledge, 2005.

Wolensky, Robert P., Kenneth C. Wolensky, and Nicole H. Wolensky. *Voices of the Knox Mine Disaster: Stories, Remembrances and Reflections of the Anthracite Coal Industry's Last Major Catastrophe, January 2, 1959*. Philadelphia: Commonwealth of Pennsylvania and Pennsylvania Historical and Museum Commission, 2005.

Wright, E. Lynne. *Disasters and Heroic Rescues of Florida: True Stories of Tragedy and Survival*. Guilford, CT: Morris Book Publishing, 2006.

Wright, Stuart A. *Patriots, Politics, and the Oklahoma City Bombing*. New York: Cambridge University Press, 2007.

INDEX